The Medusa File

Secret Crimes and Coverups
of the U.S. Government

By

Craig Roberts

An Original Publication of *Consolidated Press International*

Copyright © by Craig Roberts

Cover art copyright © by Craig Roberts

Cover design by Craig Roberts (CPI) and Michael Steed (IdeaGraphics)

Cover design production by *IdeaGraphics*, 1615 South Denver Ave., Tulsa, OK 74119

ISBN: 0-9639062-4-0

First Consolidated Press printing: January 1997

10 9 8 7 6 5 4 3 2

Consolidated Press International (CPI), 3171-A South 129th East Ave, Suite 338, Tulsa, OK 74134.

Printed in U.S.A.

i

Books by Craig Roberts

Police Sniper (Pocket Books, 1993)

Combat Medic—Vietnam (Pocket Books, 1991)

Kill Zone: A Sniper Looks at Dealey Plaza (CPI, 1994)

The Medusa File (CPI, 1997)

The Walking Dead; A Marine's Story of Vietnam (Pocket Books, 1989
and Grafton Books, London, 1989)
(With Charles W. Sasser)

One Shot—One Kill; America's Combat Snipers (Pocket Books, 1990)
(With Charles W. Sasser)

Hellhound (Avon, 1994)
(With Allen Appel III and Allen Appel IV)

JFK: The Dead Witnesses (CPI, 1995)
(With John Armstrong)

We thought we ranked above the chance of ill.
Others might fall, not we, for we were wise—
Merchants in freedom. So, of our free-will
We let our servants drug our strength with lies.
The pleasure and the poison had its way
On us as on the meanest, till we learned
That he who lies will steal, who steals will slay.
Neither God's judgment nor man's heart was turned.

Rudyard Kipling
The Covenant
1914

The MEDUSA File

Contents

Introduction

I am a warrior. All of my life I have fought for what is right. In 1964 I joined the U.S. Marines to fight in Vietnam. A year later I found myself wading steaming rice paddies, slogging up rugged mountains, and hacking through dark jungles in the I Corps area of South Vietnam. After serving a year in combat as an infantryman and Marine sniper, I was medevaced out of country to spend the next six months in the U.S. Naval Hospital at Balboa, San Diego, recuperating from combat wounds and tropical diseases.

In 1969 I joined the Tulsa Police Department. For the next 26 years I would serve in assignments that included Patrol Division, Fugitive Warrants Squad, Bomb Squad, Tactical Squad (SWAT), plain clothes assignments, and for the last fourteen years, police helicopter pilot and maintenance officer for the Air Support Unit. I retired in April, 1996 to pursue a career in investigative journalism.

My discharge from the Marines in 1968 did not end my military career. In 1972 I enlisted in a reconnaissance platoon in the Army National Guard, was commissioned a second lieutenant in 1975, then served in the following capacities in a 27 year career in both the National Guard and the Army Reserve: rifle platoon leader, executive officer, tactical officer (Officer's Candidate School), detachment commander, infantry company commander, NCO school commandant, battalion staff officer, and finally, attachment to an F-16 fighter wing as Ground Liaison Officer (GLO) working in the Intelligence Section. I have served the past six years in this capacity and currently hold the rank of lieutenant colonel.

INTRODUCTION

Understanding my background will help the reader also understand the motivation behind this book.

In 1987 I had occasion to visit Dallas, Texas, for a law enforcement convention that lasted three days. During that time I made an afternoon trip to Dealey Plaza. There was no special reason other than it was close to my hotel and it was "the crime scene of the century." It was simply a case of curiosity.

Upon arrival I could not help but notice that the triangular-shaped street interchange known as Dealey Plaza was much smaller than I had imagined. Instead of an expansive park, it was simply a block square "green" crossed by three streets. After walking around I entered the Texas School Book Depository and rode the elevator to the infamous "Sixth Floor."

After wandering around the various exhibits on the floor I ended up at the window next to the "sniper's nest" window allegedly used by Lee Harvey Oswald to shoot President John F. Kennedy. I looked out to the street below.

At that precise moment I knew the government had lied to me concerning the death of JFK. I felt betrayed. I knew that neither Oswald, nor anyone else, could have accomplished the feat of marksmanship that the various displays on the floor attributed to him, and there was much more to this case than that exhibited in our official history book version. According to what the American people had been fed over the preceding quarter century, Oswald, the lone nut with a gun, shot JFK, then in turn was shot by Jack Ruby, who later died in jail before he could testify in any inquiry. Case closed.

But I knew then that this was not the case. The reason I knew is because I was a combat-experienced Marine sniper in Vietnam, and I could not have made the three shots with the ancient Mannlicher-Carcano carbine attributed to Oswald by the Warren Commission, at a moving target that was increasing in distance, around a bend, through trees, with the hardest shot being the farthest away, all in 5.6 seconds. I also discovered later that the top rated Marine sniper instructors at Quantico had attempted to recreate the shots attributed to Oswald and were unable to duplicate the feat.

I decided to investigate the homicide of Jack Kennedy. For the next six years I dug into the case, read everything I could find, interviewed scores of people, and made excellent connections with what would prove over the course of the investigation as outstanding sources of information about what really happens behind the scenes in national and international politics. I also discovered that to avoid the errors of other "Kennedy researchers" and to do a proper police-style investigation I would have to figuratively "leave Dealey Plaza" and explore many seemingly unrelated events that preceded the Kennedy assassination. This quest took me back over a century and I found myself uncovering not just a few previous government "coverups," but literally scores. I could not believe what I was uncovering. It was virtually a parallel version of history, but one in which no one would be proud of. Though as a police officer I knew first hand that the world was divided into two power structures: good and evil, I could not believe the amount of evil that had infiltrated into the highest levels of our government—the same government that sent me to Vietnam to fight those evil communists, and in the process was responsible for the death of over 58,000 of my colleagues.

Story after story came to light as I probed and dug. Many good people in the various levels of government assisted, most of them anonymously out of fear of retribution. As the word circulated that I was working on this project and that my motivation was to seek and expose the truth, plain brown envelopes and packages began to arrive. Faxes with no header issued forth from my fax machine, and occasionally I would receive very informative telephone calls at odd hours.

The end result of my investigation was a manuscript titled *Legacy of Dishonor*. It was divided into topic-sections, because in the end it was not just the story of my investigation into the assassination of JFK, it was a far greater reaching work. Though my journey began in Dealey Plaza, it did not end until I had traveled many roads, opened many doors, and explored a maze of conspiracies, crimes and coverups perpetrated by power structures that resided far above the levels of federal government. And I discovered that these same entities, which had established themselves in their lofty positions over the course of two centuries, were the actual puppet masters over their selected minions in all branches of our government. More importantly, I found that they have an agenda—and it is very sinister and evil.

INTRODUCTION

Though I had written or co-authored over a dozen books at the time, and my publishers in New York and Washington had published virtually everything I had written, not one publishing house in either city would accept *Legacy of Dishonor*. I was puzzled. I thought it my best work by far. Thousands of hours had gone into the research and writing and authenticating my material. I could not believe that it would not become an instant bestseller.

After the final rejection from the tenth publishing house, my agent called and said that he just couldn't do anything with it. Instead of wondering if the manuscript was simply a bad book, I felt as if a message was being sent that I must have struck some very high level "raw nerves" in New York and Washington. I just didn't know what to do next.

Then it happened. Two weeks after the final rejection I received a call from a trusted senior editor at a major publishing house. He said "I don't care what you have to do, you gotta get this book out to the American people."

"If you like, then why don't you publish it?" I asked.

"If I did, I'd lose my job. Besides, even if I wanted to, it would never see ink. The power structures and organizations you expose in your book just happen to own or control virtually every major house in town."

"Who do you think I should send it to?" I asked.

"I don't know. Maybe a small house out west. Just do whatever you have to. Get it published and out to the people. They have to know what you've stumbled onto and where this government is going...before it's too late."

I took his advice to heart and, after much soul-searching, decided to make a quantum leap and do something I had been considering for the previous two years. Since I was preparing to retire from the police department, I had decided to try to start my own publishing firm as a new line of work for my retirement years. What my friend had given me was my first project—a project I truly believed in. Even if it didn't make a dime in profit.

But I couldn't afford to "self publish" a manuscript as large as *Legacy of Dishonor* which weighed in at 650 type-set pages. The end result was that I had to extract the relevant JFK and historical-political sections to form a much smaller book which I could afford to publish with the limited budget that existed at the time. So was born *Kill Zone: A Sniper Looks at Dealey Plaza*, the first publication of my new company, Consolidated Press International.

Kill Zone was an immediate success, which, considering I had gambled my life savings on the project, was very gratifying. It was accepted for national distribution by a major distributor and became available in all book stores and mail order houses.

Then came the first of the problems that would plague the book for two years. I began receiving letters and calls from readers who wished to order the book, but could not find it anywhere. I explained that it was in the computers and microfiches of the bookstores and could be ordered locally. They replied that it was not listed.

Over the next two years the book "disappeared" from computer and microfiche listings on a regular basis. Not only would the power structures who control the publishing houses not allow it to be published through New York City or Washington, they would now interfere with its distribution after I did my end run around their "system."

It was war.

And I knew how to fight wars.

To this day I still battle monthly to make sure the listings for *Kill Zone* do not disappear from the bookstore computer data bases and microfiches. And that's not all....

The only way to counter an enemy attack is to go on the offensive by doing a flanking movement and striking at the enemy's rear. In the case of investigative journalism, this is done by exposing the enemy's weaknesses and exploiting them. *The Medusa File* does just that by bringing to the attention of the American people one thing the opposition cannot combat: The Truth.

What you are about to read is a chronological compendium of history, crimes, coverups at high levels, propaganda and lies that we have been exposed to for over fifty years. Not only will the reader be presented with the *Legacy of Dishonor* chapters and sections that were left out of *Kill Zone*, but new exposés of events that will take us on a long, dangerous journey into the maze of lies, deceit and disinformation that has been promulgated upon us by "The Power" for many years.

INTRODUCTION

If there is a central theme, it is to bring out into the light the truth behind many despicable crimes perpetrated upon us in the form of "case files" of events that are mere samples of the Big Picture. For this, I have investigated and collected files on such diverse, seemingly unrelated topics as: secret dealings with war criminals; government mind control projects; the POW/MIA affairs of World War II, Korea and Vietnam; use of unsuspecting servicemen and citizens as "guinea pigs" for insidious experiments in biological, nuclear and chemical weapons experiments; political use of children for scientific experimentation, extortion (and worse); secret manipulation and interfering in the internal affairs of Third World countries; international drug smuggling and money laundering; and the *real* issues, benefactors, and players behind "domestic" and international terrorism.

Those that have previewed this book have responded with two comments: "It's great! But aren't you afraid they'll kill you?"

My response to that is that I, like many of my brethren, went to war to fight enemies who threatened our country or our way of life. In the process I learned at an early age what it was like to face death on a daily basis. Death was no longer something I feared, and I would not let such a threat hold me back from what I considered a mission that had to be accomplished. For in "my war," many of my fellow warriors had fallen in the field of battle, and for some reason known only to God, I managed to survive the killing fields of Vietnam. Since then I have always felt that I was living on borrowed time, and I can only credit that with the feeling that God had other missions for me and more battles to fight. My years in the police force, my military career, and my writing efforts are merely extensions of a war that to me has never really ended. Like Don Quixote, I have continually found another windmill around the next bend, or over the next hill to joust. It is because I feel that my life has been dedicated to a higher calling, I know that I cannot shirk the call to battle.

For I am a warrior.

As the reader journeys through the pages of this book, it must be kept in mind that this is not an anti-government tome. Our government is the best government in the history of mankind. As long as it follows the Constitution and obeys the laws of the land and is accountable to We the People, it is strong and good. The good people in government far outnumber the bad, but those who corrupt the body politic when left unchecked and unexposed have a tendency to rise in rank and power and influence until their impact on the system far outweighs their numbers. It is only by being able to recognize the Machiavellian machinations behind the scenes, and by understanding the un-American and unconstitutional private agendas of certain people and organizations that we can take corrective action. Such actions can only be taken, however, by a citizenry that has been educated and awakened to the threat that looms over us today and is willing to take a stand and force those in political office to become personally accountable for their actions. The threat we face is now on a global scale, and we have been lulled into complacency by a system of lies, deceit and disinformation that inundates us through the controlled media, and certain politicos in government that are cells of a cancer that is malignant and growing.

As we approach the 21st Century—the Millennium—we can expect to see the power of evil increase. It is only by educating ourselves with the truth concerning political and historical events that we can understand the dangers we now face, and arm ourselves with the knowledge necessary to resist those who would corrupt our nation. The intent of *The Medusa File* is to provide the reader with a knowledge base of a multiple-headed beast that is growing and extremely dangerous—a veritable Medusa. Perhaps a "mirror" of truth will turn the beast to stone.

It is easier to perceive error than to find truth, for the former lies on the surface and is easily seen, while the latter lies in the depth, where few are willing to search for it.

Johann Wolfgang von Goethe

Reader's Note:

The Medusa File was originally written in third person, but in the final months of writing, I was personally involved with the investigations of the Oklahoma City bombing, the Amtrack derailment, and the downing of TWA 800. In these particular chapters I shift to first person, which breaks the standard rules of format. For this transgression I ask the reader's understanding.

I also ask the reader to not take anything written herein at face value. It is up to the reader to research these topics further and determine that what I have written is factual. It is the same test I would ask to be performed on everything one encounters in media.

Now, we must begin our story in World War II. It was during this great conflict that the powers of the modern world learned that they could do anything they wished, provided they knew how to cover up what they did, and then rewrite history to suit their private agendas.

And much more.

Part I

Into the Jaws of the Dragon,
Into the Mouth of Hell

"Muratas [prisoners] had their blood siphoned off and replaced with horse blood...they sweated to death under hot fans...were electrocuted, boiled alive, killed in giant centrifuges or died from prolonged exposure to x-rays. In all, some 3000 are said to have been murdered. Some were just killed off when there was an excess supply [of POWs.]"

> Unit 731
> Pete Williams
> and David Wallace

"I could not imagine that these things had happened without the Court in Tokyo being informed"

> Bert V. A. Roling
> Former Judge,
> International Military
> Tribunal for the Far
> East.

"The Committee also has been told 'there are no records.' There are records, and I hope that the enclosed de-classified documents will provide insight into the callous and culpable conspiracy between MacArthur and Ishii."

> Greg Rodriguez
> Former Mukden POW

Chapter 1

Devil Unit 731

On the morning of November 4th, 1941, a Japanese airplane circled low over the city of Changde in the Hunan Province of China. Within minutes, the pilot lined the nose up with a street that ran through a residential section of the city's East Gate District and leveled the wings. Throttling the engine back to reduce his airspeed, he slowed the plane until it was almost in a glide. Then he reached down and pulled the release lever.

But it was not a string of high-explosive bombs that fell on the unsuspecting civilians below. Instead, what issued forth from the aircraft were nothing more than grains of wheat and rice, bits of paper, and cotton wadding.

The load caught in the wind and dispersed in a pattern wide enough to assure a spread over several city blocks. This done, the pilot increased throttle, climbed away from the city, and banked for home base.

Within two weeks, symptoms of plague began to appear in the people of the East Gate District. By the end of the third week six people had died, and autopsies confirmed the disease. But bubonic plague was, by the 20th Century, a very rare disease. Where could it have come from? And why just in the East Gate District? It quickly became apparent that the outbreak of such a rare disease coincided with the reported flight of the solo Japanese plane over the district scattering "rice and grain." There had to be a connection.[1]

There was. The airplane, a Japanese Imperial Army Kawasaki Type-88 open cockpit biplane, belonged to a very special unit. It was one of seven custom-fitted aircraft assigned to a top secret Japanese experimentation center in Pingfan, Manchuria.[2] The Pingfan unit, code-named Unit 731 and disguised as a "water purification unit," conducted experiments that, if successful, might guarantee Japan's victory in the war. For the research being done concerned weapons of such horror and mass destruction that no country, including the United States and Great Britain could withstand them. Unit 731 experimented with bacteria.

And they used human beings as the guinea pigs.[3]

They had fought well, those intrepid American and Filipino soldiers on Bataan and Corregidor. They had fought long after the Japanese invaders had planned total victory. And they had continued to fight, even though they were desperately low on food, medical supplies and ammunition. Still they continued to resist the overwhelming forces of the Japanese 14th Army under General Homma. Even when General Douglas MacArthur abandoned them to their fates, eloquently promising "I shall return," as he boarded a PT boat for Australia, the Battling Bastards of Bataan fought on. But they could not resist forever.

Though the garrison on "the Rock"—the small island of Corregidor that guarded the entrance to Manila Bay—would continue to resist until May 6th, 1942, the troops under General Jonathan Wainwright on Bataan, out of supplies and suffering needless casualties, were forced to finally surrender on April 9th. Laying down their arms were almost 70,000 U.S. and Filipino troops. One of them was Master Sergeant Warren W. "Pappy" Whelchel, a member of the 200th Coast Artillery Anti-aircraft Regiment.

"This was the beginning of one of the most dehumanizing experiences ever perpetrated on humans," related Whelchel. "First was the famous Bataan Death March, where we, as human beings, were subjected to beatings, killings and forced marches during the heat of the day after being deprived of food, water and any medical attention whatsoever.

INTO THE JAWS OF THE DRAGON

"Upon arriving at Camp O'Donnell, Capas Tarlac, we were still deprived of adequate food, decent sanitary conditions, and medicine. As a result of these conditions, several thousand of us died from dehydration, dysentery, malaria and other tropical diseases.

"Around the 1st of July, we were put in narrow-gage train boxcars at Capas Tarlac to be sent to Camp No. 1 at Cabanatuan. One hundred Americans were crammed into each of these boxcars, and the doors were closed tightly...many died of suffocation during this trip.

"The conditions at Cabanatuan were not much better. During my short stay, I was on burial detail for thirty-three consecutive days. This camp was activated to separate the Filipinos from the Americans.

"Around the 1st of October, a group of us American soldiers numbering over 2000 were taken to Manila and put on the Japanese ship *Totori* Maru and shipped to Japan, and then to Manchuria. During the trip we were kept in the holds of the ship except for a period in the morning and a period in the afternoon of approximately twenty minutes for fresh air. We had no access to toilet facilities on the ship; we were given a few five-gallon water cans to use for our human wastes, and when the cans ran over, the Japanese made no effort whatsoever to have them replaced or removed from the holds in which we were forced to live. Men had to walk through this human excrement. Food was not adequate to sustain the human body, and there were no medical supplies for the Americans. Many of us died of exposure due to the inadequate clothing for the cold climate we entered, and others died due to unsanitary conditions—many from dehydration due to dysentery.

"[After] Landing at Pusan, Korea, approximately 150 of the Americans who were in the worst physical condition were sent to a building that was set up as a hospital. I was one of the 150...but it was too late for almost one-third of the men. They died at Pusan. The rest of the Americans were taken off the *Totori Maru* and sent to a camp in Mukden, Manchuria.

"After our stay at Pusan, we were put on trains and sent to Mukden ourselves."[4]

"Pappy" Whelchel was to spend the next three years of his life as one of 1,485 American and British prisoners of war that were herded into a very special prison camp in Manchuria—a camp run by a Japanese doctor.

5

General Shiro Ishii took his work very seriously. After all, was it not the Emperor's cousin, Prince Takeda, that held administrative responsibilities over Unit 731? And had not the Emperor's brother, Prince Mikasa, traveled all the way from Japan to visit the camp? It was obvious to all that the work being done at Mukden, Pingfan and Harbin was extremely important to the Imperial family—and to the Holy War.

And it was very secret work. Even Prince Takeda played his part by taking an alias, "Lieutenant Colonel Miyata," to protect both his identity and the importance of the project. It had always been so. That is why the camps were located in a remote part of Manchuria instead of Japan or Korea.

It had actually started in 1933, when then-Lt. Col. Ishii, a preventative disease specialist in the Epidemic Prevention Laboratory in Tokyo, was ordered to Manchuria to establish "medical facilities" for the Kwangtung Army. These facilities, however, were not intended to treat soldiers or prevent diseases. On the contrary, they were established to create weapons of war. Weapons of mass destruction.

Manchuria was an ideal proving ground for several reasons. Besides being remote, it was inhabited by several races. Chinese, Mongols, Russians, Koreans, and many other peoples of various tribes lived in primitive conditions that were conducive to the spread of biological contagions. A few more cases of disease would not be noticed by the outside world. And even if they were, who would care?

Ishii set up his first laboratory, codenamed *Togo*, in a reconditioned soy sauce factory outside of Harbin at Beiinho.[5] Over the next three years, the Togo unit grew to over 300 personnel, fifty of which were doctors. In charge on the military side of the house was a Lt. Col. Kanji Ishiwara, who was mandated by Army Headquarters to conduct bacteriological warfare experiments for offensive purposes. Experiments far too dangerous and politically sensitive to be conducted in Japan proper.[6]

In late 1935, the unit, then numbering over 1,000, had outgrown the small distillery. It moved into Harbin to a new two-story headquarters that was built in close proximity to the Harbin Military Hospital and was conveniently located near the Pinchiang railway station. Here, according to one of Ishii's doctors, Kajitsuka: "Detachment 731 was formed by command of the Emperor of Japan Hirohito, issued in 1936...Until 1941, the detachment had no number, but was called the Water Supply and Prophylaxis Administration of the Kwantung Army, and also the Ishii Detachment, because it was the custom in the Japanese Army to call Army units by the names of their commanders. The detachment was given the number 731 in 1941 by order of the Commander-in-Chief of the Kwantung Army, who gave definite numbers to all Army units and institutions."

The doctors who staffed the unit came both from within the army and from various civilian universities and hospitals in Japan. At a meeting in 1934, a list of promising names was drawn up at the 9th Japan Medical General Meeting at Kyoto University by professors Shozo Toda, Kenji Kiyono, Rinnosuke Shoji and Ren Kimura. The document, or *makimono,* was a scroll that listed research teams that should be formed and who would be responsible for forming them. Most were microbiologists and pathologists.

After three years in Harbin, Ishii, now promoted to Colonel, moved the unit to Pingfan. It had grown to 3,000 men, and being inside the city limits of Harbin was considered too unsecure for the security measures required to conduct such experiments. Pingfan, located in a secure area occupied by the Kwantung Army, proved ideal. No one was allowed to reside in or near the detachment's facility, and no unauthorized person was permitted to enter it. Even airplanes were forbidden to fly over the detachment's vast holdings. The unit's facilities were enclosed behind a triple set of fortifications. A high wall hid the facility from view; a moat lay beyond the wall to trap any intruder; and an electrified fence surrounded the inner perimeter to prevent escapes from within.

It had taken two years to construct the facility, which consisted of 150 buildings, a railway siding, a powerhouse, cooling towers, an incinerator/crematorium, an administrations building, an animal house and an insect-breeding lab. The entire complex covered over three square kilometers and could house thousands of people. One new recruit described his first impression of Pingfan: "...the central buildings towering skyward over other buildings, with all square-tiled facades, were larger than any of those I had observed on my trip over, including Osaka, Hsinking and Harbin...High earth walls were constructed with barbed wire fencing atop. It was obvious that this compound was isolated strictly from the outside world."

Unit 731 was divided into eight divisions that ranged from bacteriological research to water filtration. Of importance is the First Division, Bacteriological Research. This division was divided into more than twelve squads, each charged with investigating certain diseases for possible usage as offensive weapons of mass destruction. The main diseases studied in the early days included: anthrax, cholera, dysentery, plague, and typhoid.

Besides researching the diseases to ascertain which would prove to be the most ideal weapons under given circumstances, the unit also studied the means of mass producing them and distributing them. The distribution, they found, was the most difficult phase of employment. With the exception of certain respiratory infections, such as tuberculosis, pneumonia and influenza, germs could not simply travel from one person to another. They had to be carried by some means. This means is known as a "vector." Unit 731 constantly experimented with such vectors as fleas, rodents and airborne dispersal.

Of the diseases, pneumonic plague became the most studied. The bubonic form, which results from the bite of an infected flea, is relatively fast acting. The onset is abrupt, starting with chills, extreme weakness and high fever. The face becomes congested and the eyes grow red. Then the tongue swells, and finally delirium sets in. Death can result in as little as one day. As a weapon, Ishii felt plague would be ideal. The bacteria was relatively easy to reproduce and the vectors—rats with fleas—were cheap.

But the rats were slow to spread the disease in a tactical situation. If one wanted to infect an infantry battalion, then there had to be other means of doing so. For this, Unit 731 experimented with disease-carrying artillery shells and aerial bombs. These bombs, designated *Ha*, were made from a serrated clay housing and equipped with a Type 12 fuse and exploder. They weighed 25 kilograms each and carried hundreds of thousands of infected fleas in an airtight compartment filled with sand. The fuse was designed to shatter the bomb casing in an air burst over the heads of the enemy, scattering the fleas over a wide area. The artillery shells did not work as well and the idea was eventually discarded.

Tests for fragmentation and burst radius effectiveness for the various bombs and artillery shells were conducted at Anta Proving Ground, located five hours from Pingfan by truck. Here, prisoners were subjected to the direct blast of the various devices. Lt. Col. Toshihide Nishi observed one such experiment:

"The object of the experiment was to ascertain whether it was possible to infect people with gas gangrene at a temperature of 20 degrees centigrade below zero. This experiment was performed in the following way: ten Chinese prisoners of war were tied to stakes at a distance of 10 to 20 meters from a shrapnel bomb that was charged with gas gangrene. To prevent the men from being killed outright, their heads and backs were protected with special metal shields and thick quilted blankets. But their legs and buttocks were left unprotected. The bomb was exploded by means of an electric switch and the shrapnel, bearing gas gangrene germs, scattered all over the spot where the experimentees were bound. All the experimentees were wounded in the legs or buttocks, and seven days later they died in great torment."[7]

Between 500 and 600 prisoners were consigned to Unit 731 annually. According to Major General Kawashima, if a prisoner survived the inoculation of lethal bacteria initially, this fact did not save him from a repetition of experiments which continued until death from infection finally occurred. If a prisoner survived one experiment, he was nursed back to health in efforts to experiment with cures. This accomplished, the *murata* was injected with a different type of germ and the process repeated until the prisoner finally expired.

Perhaps the most diabolical means of vectoring the viruses was the *Fu*, or balloon bomb. Manufactured at 731's camp at Mukden, these large rice paper and rubberized silk balloons, each designed to carry cholera and typhus, were capable of being launched in Japan and flying across the Pacific in the Jet Stream to the United States. In actuality, several incendiary balloons of similar design were launched and managed to fly into the forests of the Pacific Northwest. Their purpose was to start forest fires. Though few ignited after completing the journey, six people were reported killed after tampering with downed balloons in an attempt to recover the incendiary mechanism. It is not known if biological bombs were indeed launched against the United States, however the wreckage of one balloon of the proper construction for such a device was reportedly found as far away as the southwestern desert and carried something "other than an incendiary."

The attitude of the U.S. military at the time was to cover up the fact that the Japanese had succeeded in reaching the U.S. with the balloons. Their fear was that if the Japanese found that their launches were successful, then they would intensify. The downside to this was that the American people were also left in the dark—hence people being killed when they tried to recover what they thought were "weather balloons."

To breed flea vectors, Ishii set up 4000 cultivators capable of producing up to 15 grams of fleas in each production cycle. Four special areas in Second Division were constructed to maintain a constant 30 degree centigrade temperature, and were stocked with metal jars containing rats to provide hosts for the fleas. His rat factories held tens of thousands of rodents, many bred on the installation, and others caught by special rat-catching teams sent to the local villages and towns.

But Ishii and his 731 technicians did not stop with germ warfare. Other horrendous experiments were conducted to ascertain what kind of reactions a human body would have to various conditions encountered in the field. One such experiment concerned frostbite.

The winters of Manchuria and Korea were harsh. So harsh that the chief concern of the Army staff for the troops in the field was frostbite. The doctors of Pingfan and Mukden knew that the hardest part of treating frostbite was in the thawing stage. Unless circulation could be restored in an expeditious and effective manner, the victim would suffer gangrene in the effected area and would then be forced to undergo amputation. To experiment with cures, reasoned Ishii, would require human subjects.

It was the job of the local *Kempeitai* (a cross between a Japanese version of the Gestapo and military police), and the *Tokumu Kikan* (Japanese Secret Service) to fulfill these needs. At first, local Chinese, Mongolians and White Russians were rounded up when needed. There was an adequate local supply of human fodder for the experiments, consisting of men, women and children. It was a simple matter of charging the victims with espionage or sedition against the Emperor, then trucking them off to one of the camps. These shipments, known as *Tokui-Atsukai*, were simply considered expendable consignments of "convicted criminals" that would disappear forever.

When there were not enough prisoners to send, the *Kenpeitai* enticed people to come to their headquarters for "jobs." In this way, men, women, children, and even pregnant women, were rounded up for experimentation. When a sufficient number had been gathered in the *Kenpeitai*'s Harbin holding post—the basement of the Japanese Embassy—Unit 731 was contacted to make a pickup.

After arrival at one of the 731's facilities at Pingfan or Mukden, the prisoners, known as *marutas* (logs of wood) were divided up by age, sex, and nationality. Each was herded into a separate holding block inside *Ro* block (*Ro* means square), the large prison inside the compound. At this stage, they became inventory for the various squads of the divisions.

For those who were used in the frostbite experiments, conducted under the guidance of Dr. Hisato Yoshimura, the ordeal was nothing short of torture. A medical orderly named Furuichi described how it was done:

"Experiments in freezing human beings were performed every year in the detachment, in the coldest months of the year: November, December, January and February. The technique of these experiments was as follows: the experimentees were taken out into the frost at night, at about 11 o'clock, and compelled to dip their hands into a barrel of cold water. Then they were compelled to take their hands out and stand with wet hands in the frost for a long time. Or else the following was done: the people were taken out dressed, but with bare feet and compelled to stand at night in the frost in the coldest period of the year. When these people had got frostbite, they were taken to a room and forced to put their feet in water of 5 degrees centigrade in temperature, and then the temperature was gradually increased. In this way means of healing frostbite were investigated."[8]

Another member of the Unit, Education Division Chief Nishi, recalled other experiments: "...with temperatures below -20 degrees centigrade, people were brought out from the detachment's prison into the open. Their arms were bared and made to freeze with the help of an artificial current of air. This was done until their frozen arms, when

11

struck with a short stick, emitted a sound resembling that which a board gives out when it is struck. "

Besides frost bite, the Japanese army was concerned with shortages of whole blood during battle. In an attempt to find a substitute for human blood, animal blood was considered. In one set of experiments, prisoners were tied down and drained of blood. As their blood was being extracted, it was replaced with horse blood. Every one of these prisoners died on the spot.

Various poisons were also tested. One favorite was the exotic toxin of the *fugu* or blowfish. Human subjects were injected with varying doses, then monitored to see how long it took them to die under each dosage. As in all experiments, the bodies of the human lab rats were incinerated in the electric furnace to leave no trace.

But of particular interest were the diseases. In the twelve years of the unit's existence, dozens of diseases were studied. They included: Botulism, brucellosis, cholera, dysentery, gangrene, glanders, influenza, meningococcus, salmonella, smallpox, tetanus, tick encephalitis, tuberculosis, tularemia, typhoid, typhus and epidemic hemorrhagic fever.

The disease experiments were costly to the *muratas*. Two and three died each day and were incinerated. No one could resist the experiments, for there was no way to escape and no way to fight back. Diseases were forcibly injected or administered through a special stick-shaped bacteria assassination weapon. They were also sprayed directly into the victim's face or concealed in food and drink. The prisoner had no choice but to succumb to the wishes of the experimenters.

In little more than a decade, General Ishii had managed to make drastic inroads into an area of research that would give Japan an arsenal of weapons that might rival America's atomic bomb.[9] But there was one question Ishii had yet to answer: would the diseases that worked on Asians also work on Caucasians?

What he now needed were Anglo prisoners. Australians, British and Americans.

Ishii chose the camp at Mukden for the experiments to be conducted on the new *muratas* that were to arrive from the Philippines, Singapore, Malaysia and other places that had fallen under the advance of the

Japanese Imperial Army. It was into this hell that Pappy Whelchel and 1,484 other Allied POWs were to be sent.

"Upon our arrival," recalled Whelchel, "we were taken to a barracks that was isolated from the other prisoners that had preceded us. After a period of time, a group of five or six Japanese medical personnel entered our barracks and called out various prisoner-of-war numbers that we had been assigned. The medical personnel gave the Americans various shots discriminately; not all the prisoners were given the same type of shots. This caused a considerable amount of anxiety among our group, as we felt that we were being tested for bacteriological immunity for their possible use of bacterial warfare against the Allied troops in the Far East."

"As a group, we did not receive the same shots. Some persons were checked for oral and rectal temperatures, some for the welts the shots caused, rectal tissues from some, rectal smears from others. All personnel were sprayed in the face by some kind of spray from a spray instrument similar to our Flit spray guns. After we were allowed to associate with other prisoners, we ascertained that we were the only ones that had received this treatment. The Japanese medical personnel were keeping accurate records of each and every one of us in this one barracks."[10]

Many other experiments were conducted on the Allied POWs, but most concerned the Americans and British. Other selected groups of Anglo-Saxon prisoners were not experimented upon. Instead, they became the control groups. It would do little good to find that some disease had been found to be effective, then later discover that it had come from outside the camp and had not been induced as part of a segregated experiment. To preclude this, the control groups were needed to monitor the invasion of outside germs, and at the same time, give a definitive separation between those that died from the diseases, and those who died because of general camp conditions.

In one experiment conducted on Americans, Japanese medical technicians came into the barracks when there were men too sick to leave and induced other germs into their systems. Greg Rodriguez, one of the Americans captured on Bataan, related that "A Japanese came in and looked me over and then placed a mirror in front of my nostrils. At the time, I thought: 'Well, he's just checking to see if I'm still breathing.' But, after a little bit, he came back again with a feather. He ran that feather up and down under my nostrils—and, later on, I discovered this was one of the methods used to get prisoners to ingest bacteria."

Many Americans were removed from the camp's population and transferred out to disappear forever. Dr. B.J. Brennan, an Australian, reported that one day the camp guards came into the camp, singled out around 150 Americans, then lined them up and marched them out of the camp. "They never came back and I never heard of any of them again."

Of those that stayed and died, dissections were performed on a routine basis to discover the progress of various diseases and what organs were effected. One prisoner named Frank James was assigned to the autopsy detail. Though extremely sick himself, he refused to go to the hospital because, "nobody that went in ever came out."

He described one particular day in June, 1943: "I went round to the hut and there must have been 340 bodies stacked there. Each body had a tag attached to his toe...Another fellow and I were told to lift the bodies up and put them on autopsy tables. Then, they [Japanese technicians in white smocks, their faces covered with cotton masks] began to cut them open."

James went on to describe carrying body after body to the building where the men in white coats were performing their grisly tasks. The doctors took certain organs and placed them in jars of liquid, then carefully labeled each jar with the identification number of a POW. At the end of the day, the specimens were loaded on trucks and taken from the camp.

The most horrible autopsies performed were done while prisoners were still alive. Live vivisections, though not commonplace, did occur. In these, the prisoner was placed on a table, sometimes anesthetized and sometimes not, then cut open to observe the progress of various diseases within the abdominal cavity. Under Dr. Kozo Okamoto and Dr. Tachiomaru Ishikawa, squads performed various anatomical studies on prisoners in which pathology squad assistant Kurumizawa understated, "to do this work, our sentiments were suppressed."

By 1944, Unit 731 was ready to begin offensive operations. Ishii, eager to "join his brothers in battle," laid plans to provide biological weapons for an attack upon American forces in Saipan. Japan had already lost over 24,000 troops in the battle, and the situation was looking grim for the Imperial Army. If Saipan fell, American bombers could be based well within striking distance of the home islands.

Ishii chose seventeen officers to lead an assault team that would sprinkle the Saipan airstrip with plague-infected fleas. The team and the containers of insects were put aboard ship, but before they could reach the battle zone, the ship was discovered by an American submarine and sunk.

Shortly afterward, Saipan fell. And in short order, American B-29s began to bomb cities in the Japanese main islands. It was not difficult to see that the war would soon be over, and Japan would not be the victor. Ishii had to prepare his unit for such an eventuality. He had to make plans to destroy all evidence of his crimes, remove all traces of the three facilities, get rid of the prisoners, then evacuate his personnel back to Japan before they could be taken prisoner by Allied forces.

As these plans were being made, Russian forces, under the Yalta Agreement, began to swell on the Soviet side of the Manchurian border. Then on August 9th, just after Hiroshima had been devastated by the Atomic Bomb, the Russians crossed the border in force and swept into Manchuria and Korea. Almost two million men, 5,500 tanks and 5000 aircraft swarmed into the Kwantung Army's operational area and began racing south—toward Ishii's camps. Ishii gave the orders to begin the destruction of evidence.

At Pingfan, the prisoners were the first to be destroyed. Troops of the 516 Chemical Warfare Unit gassed many of the POWs in their cells, and gave cyanide to still more in their food. Other witnesses—the 600 local Manchurian and Chinese laborers who worked for the Japanese and knew of the projects—were simply machine gunned.

The bodies were taken at first to the incinerators, but there were so many that the huge ovens could not handle the load. To expedite the affair, they were stacked inside *Ro* block's courtyard, coated with diesel fuel, and set afire. Still, this was not sufficient, so the Japanese began taking the bodies to the Sungari River where they, along with hundreds of sets of manacles, were thrown in.

For three days the local engineer brigade labored to rig the buildings for demolition. Thousands of pounds of dynamite and other explosives were used on the structures, but some were constructed so

15

well that they resisted the explosions. In a desperate effort to destroy what remained of the facility, eighty trucks were loaded with 50kg bombs and detonated. This last effort succeeded in destroying, or at least making unrecognizable, the majority of buildings and equipment.

On August 14th, the personnel of Unit 731 gathered up their families and possessions and boarded trains for Korea. Over 2,000 soldiers and dependents began making good their escape.

The next day the Emperor announced the surrender of Japan. As he was doing so, Ishii was making his own address. In it he swore each and every man to a life of total secrecy, a "life in the shadows." He ordered them to never reveal their military past, never to take government jobs in the future, and lastly, *never* gather or make an effort to see each other again.

But some, including himself, would not be able to keep this promise. For unknown to Ishii at the time, the U.S. Government knew of him and his activities. And they wanted him very badly.

But not for war crimes.

The existence of Unit 731 and its activities were no secret to the American government. As early as 1943, the Military Intelligence Service began picking up bits and pieces of information from various sources that began to build a picture of a top secret Japanese bacterial warfare experimentation center in Manchuria. In that year four Japanese soldiers captured in China told of the existence of a *Saikin Kenkyu sho*, or Bacteriological Experimental Center, at Harbin. They confirmed that it was controlled by the army, and that Imperial Army biologists were carrying out experiments of some unknown—and super secret—nature. They also stated that the commander of the unit conducting these experiments was a Major General of the medical service named Shiro Ishii.

Under further interrogation, they stated that a *Boekikyusui Bu*, or water purification unit, was also located in Harbin, and that this unit was responsible for collecting and evaluating the results of all biological experiments conducted by field units. Intelligence felt that this unit and Ishii's unit were either connected or were one in the same.[11]

Military Intelligence noted in their reports to Washington that these areas of Manchuria were so remote that gaining information about the

Japanese BW activities was extremely difficult. Still, information trickled out. In 1944, the U.S. Army Chemical Warfare division discovered that the Japanese were dropping what they termed to be "Christmas Balls," glass balls filled with what was suspected to be bacteria, along the China-Burma border in areas occupied by Allied troops. This information was passed along to all intelligence agencies for dissemination to field intelligence gathering units with the request that if any of these "bombs" were found intact, they should be handled with extreme care and turned in for analysis. It is unknown outside of military circles if any of these devices were recovered.

As these investigations were being conducted overseas, the U.S. Army Chemical Corps at Camp Detrick, Maryland, became concerned with defensive measures against bacteriological attack. With the Germans working on the V-1 "buzz bombs" and V-2 rockets at their research center at Peenemunde, and the Japanese developing BW weapons, the possibility of long range weapons of mass destruction being perfected by the Axis powers became a very real concern.

But instead of rockets delivering supersonic warheads filled with bacteria, the U.S. was assaulted instead by the oldest flying machine in history—the balloon. In December of 1944, Camp Detrick was notified that a huge balloon made of rice paper had just come down in Butte, Montana. But before technicians could respond to investigate the device, which they believed might carry some type of plague or other contagion, another report came in that a large rubberized silk balloon had landed in Washington state. Then, almost overnight, reports of landings of ten other balloons, ranging from Alaska to San Diego, came in. Colonel Murray Sanders, a Camp Detrick bacteriologist, caught a plane for Washington state, the central location chosen to examine the balloons that were recovered. He reported that: "The balloons were brought in and we all stood around them in a circle. All the scientific and military experts, all of us with our own thought. We examined them...[They] had obviously come from Japan. I told them that the prevailing winds would carry most of the Japanese balloons, comfortably, to the mainland of the United States. I told them that if we found Japanese B-encephalitis on any of the balloons, we were in real trouble."

But they didn't find any traces of bacteria or any devices that appeared to be designed to distribute germs or insect vectors. Still, the number of balloons that managed to cross the Pacific was frightening. Balloons launched in Japan into the Jet Stream could travel across the Pacific in thirty to sixty hours, then, depending on the weather on that particular day, follow air currents to different parts of North America until they finally dropped from the sky. Balloons were found at such distant locations as White Horse, Alaska; Hawaii; Vancouver Island; Grand Rapids, Michigan; ranches in Montana, and other places. During the month of March, 1945, alone, over 100 balloons were reported to have successfully crossed the ocean.[12]

The threat was very real, but of more concern to the Detrick officers and the government was the thought of civilian panic should this information get out. A tight lid was clamped on the investigation and strict censorship of the press and radio was instituted. Any balloons found by the civilian population were quickly rounded up and the finders sworn to secrecy as a matter of national security.

Because of the censorship, few civilian warnings were given of the danger involved should a balloon bomb be found. In Oregon, a party of fishermen came across one of the balloons and began to examine the incendiary device it had carried. It exploded and killed all six fishermen. In another report that leaked to the press before government censors could intervene, a woman in Helena, Montana, found a balloon and it too exploded, killing her. Still, the government maintained silence to the danger as far as public knowledge was concerned.

The implications of what could happen should the Japanese succeed in sending across deadly viruses and bacteria became of paramount importance to the military. Two meetings were held in March of 1945, one at the headquarters of the 7th Service Command in Omaha, and one at the headquarters of the Western Defense Command in San Francisco. In these meetings, the officers in charge of home defense listened for four days to Colonel Sanders and other representatives from Camp Detrick and Washington. The end result was that probable targets within the U.S. were identified and that there was little the military or civilian authorities could do should the enemy begin a balloon onslaught of biological warfare bombs.

The representatives of the various military branches also agreed that not only could such weapons change the direction of the war, but a huge armada of balloons would not be required to do so. If only one balloon got through, carrying the proper BW agent, a deadly epidemic might ravage the American population completely out of proportion to the effort expended in the attack. Hundreds of thousands of Americans—men, women and children—might die before such a disease could be brought into check.

According to recently declassified records, it was the fear of such a biological attack that spawned a super secret experiment jointly conducted by the Army and Navy. The task was to test the effectiveness of airborne viruses in an actual environment—one populated by American citizens.

Within weeks of the meeting, on a day selected because of ideal weather conditions, a task force of U.S. Navy warships steamed just off the coastline of Southern California. The residents of the sleepy beach communities dotting the shoreline were just beginning to awaken.

A gray mist from a low-lying marine layer partially cloaked the ships as they turned into the onshore breeze and rang for "all ahead, slow." When the ships were in the position noted in their sailing orders, sailors aboard one of the vessels cranked open a valve on a large pressure tank that rested on the stern. Within seconds a hissing stream of air, contaminated with influenza virus, rose into the atmosphere and began to drift ashore. When the tank was empty, the ships turned back toward San Diego, their mission complete. For the next few weeks the outbreak of flu was monitored at various surveillance stations set up along the coast and up to 250 miles inland.

Other tests were run in a similar manner. However, unlike the influenza tests conducted "as a defensive measure" against the expected BW balloon attacks, these were concerned with chemical warfare. Stimulants and other chemical compounds were released, then as before, the civilian population was monitored for the effects and the range of coverage by checking medical records at local hospitals. It is apparent that at this late period in the war the U.S. government was becoming more concerned over the future offensive effectiveness of such weapons than it was with protecting the civilian population against some last-ditch effort by the Japanese high command.

It was codenamed Operation *Olympia*. It was the planned invasion of the Japanese home islands, and was expected to cost over a million American lives. The assault was to occur on the island of Honshu with a combined naval, air and land strike of a magnitude never before seen in history. But just as the Allied forces stood poised on the doorstep of the Emperor's islands, an even larger force intervened. The Atomic bomb.

First Hiroshima, then Nagasaki were reduced to smoldering rubble. In Hiroshima, over 60,000 buildings were destroyed within a 9.5 mile radius of ground zero, and more than 71,000 people were killed. Nagasaki fared better, with only 35,000 dead. Within days Japan surrendered. The war was over.

It was now time for the world to pick up the pieces and begin reconstruction. It was also time to punish those responsible for the crimes committed during the war. Only by punishing those guilty of atrocities—crimes against mankind and violations of the laws of warfare—could their victims be avenged and future despots and tyrants be deterred.

In accordance with the Potsdam agreements, every enemy soldier accused of committing war crimes would be brought to trial before a war crimes tribunal.

Almost every soldier.

Chapter 2

The Naito Document And The Hunt For Ishii

The war against Germany and Japan was over. But a new war was just beginning. The Cold War. Already the Western powers and the Soviets were beginning to encounter growing tensions and were jockeying for political and geographic position in the new world alignment. Entire countries were forced to chose sides, most often with the power that happened to occupy them in the closing days of the war. In Europe, those countries under Soviet control found that instead of being liberated, they were merely occupied by a different army. In the western European countries, the threat of Communist expansionism became a very real concern. And in Asia, where the Red Army invaded Manchuria and China at the closing days of the war, there was little question what would happen within the territory they occupied.

As the war crimes tribunals began their investigations, bringing to trial Nazi and Japanese officers who, if convicted, faced long prison terms or the hangman's noose, the covert intelligence communities scrambled in a different direction. Both sides realized that scientific discoveries had been made by the opposing side that would enhance their own scientific efforts. But to reap the benefits of the spoils of war, they first had to locate the scientists and technicians involved and remove them from harm's way.

In the following months, while men such as Yamashita and von Ribbentrop were going to the gallows, other men, just as guilty of atrocities, were being spirited away from justice by the intelligence

21

services of virtually every victorious power. The United States was no exception.

For Ishii, salvation came in the form of Colonel Murray Sanders and the Camp Detrick chemical warfare staff. Sanders arrived in Japan aboard the S.S. *Sturgis*, a merchant marine ship loaded with technical specialists that had been dispatched to Japan under the express orders of General Douglas MacArthur. Their mission was to ferret out certain Japanese scientists and interrogate them for scientific data that might prove useful to the United States. As usual, it was a matter of national security.

Sanders' specific mission was to find out everything he could about the Japanese biological warfare machine, and if possible locate Ishii and any other members of his unit for debriefing. No decision had yet been made concerning their disposition. That would have to come later.

When the *Sturgis* docked at Yokohama, an amazing thing happened. As Sanders stepped down the gangplank to the dock, a middle-aged Japanese approached him and called him by name. Holding a photograph of Sanders, the Japanese, identifying himself in English as Dr. Naito, welcomed "Dr. Sanders" to Japan. In quick order he explained that he was to serve as the colonel's interpreter. Sanders was a bit puzzled at the encounter. Particularly since he recognized the photo as one taken at Camp Detrick. The only explanation would be that G-2 had somehow obtained the picture and had brought it to Japan and given it to the interpreter to help him in identifying Sanders.

What Sanders did not know at that time is the fact that Naito was one of the members of Unit 731—and he knew where others were.

In the following weeks, Sanders set up an office in the Dai Ichi building in Tokyo, the location of Supreme Allied Headquarters, and with the aid of Naito, began making discrete inquiries concerning the whereabouts of Japanese doctors and biologists that had served in Manchuria and had been involved with biological weapons experiments.

Very little useful information was produced. It was as if such things had never happened and Unit 731 had never existed. Naito, while appearing to work hard in his attempts to locate former 731 officers, skillfully guided Sanders' investigation down one blind alley after another. But Sanders was determined to press on until he had something useful to send back to Camp Detrick, and as the days turned into weeks, he began to suspect that Naito knew more than he let on.

Sanders changed tactics. He threatened to turn the investigation over to the Russians. This was more than a subtle threat to Naito. He knew that if the Russians began to investigate Unit 731, they would not stop at simply questioning people—and they would demand that all members of the unit be found and brought before the tribunal for prosecution. Sanders began to see results. Naito had maintained contact with certain senior officials of Ishii's staff and continued to meet with them on a regular basis in secret locations in the suburbs of the city. In the beginning, his main purpose was to act as an insulator between the former 731 officers and the U.S. investigation. But when Sanders threatened to turn the affair over to the Russians, Naito knew that a different ploy would have to be undertaken if they were to save themselves.

He produced what became known as the Naito Document.

The twelve pages of the handwritten paper gave the entire structure of Unit 731 including the chain of command and the command relationships with the Kwantung Army. And there was more.

"I felt it is my duty to tell you about BW all I know to help your sincere effort of investigation as a scientist," began Naito in his scrawling hand. "The purpose of this information is only to rescue our poor, defeated nation, and to avoid the damage, according to your words, that if we offer the truce [truth] as a science, you may help this poor nation with every your [sic] effort, but if we keep the matters secret which will be disclosed afterwards, every damages will be added to us...."

Naito went on to state: "There occurred a big consternation in the circle of higher officers of Japanese Head Quarter[s] when your inquire about BW began...A long disputation was done, whether they should answer to you with the true or not...the vice chief of general staffs and the chief of Bureau of War-Affairs (Army Ministry), have the fear that the fact that Japan had some laboratories for active BW will bring a big misfortune to the Emperor."

With the preliminaries out of the way, Naito described in minute detail the various chains of command, the financing and logistical structure, the general administration, and even the plans that had been made to use the weapons in an offensive capacity. It was apparent in the document that Naito feared retribution from the former Japanese General Staff for divulging even the existence of Unit 731. He ended the paper with the statements: "I have a large fear, that my [sic] this act (information) be against our General-staff. So I beg you to fire these papers immediately after you read this. I beg you, by the inquiry to the other officers, not to gustate this information in such a way as 'Information of Liet Col Naito says...' [or] 'It is evident, according to Dr. Naito's information...' I beg you to keep this information secret...."

Naito feared for his life.

Sanders then knew that Naito was a member of the unit in question and he knew where other members were. But he was at an empasse. The Japanese were afraid to come forward with information that would surely get them convicted of war crimes unless something could be done to ensure their safety.[13]

It was now a matter for the highest levels of command—and very possibly Washington itself. Just how important was it to get the information from the former members of 731? Enough to keep them from going to trial? Maybe even protecting them from discovery both now and in the future?

Washington said it was.

It then became a matter of speed. The Russians, who had captured the Harbin, Pingfan and Mukden camps—and liberated what few Americans and British that remained alive—were also looking for Ishii and his men. They already held some of the Unit's members, those that did not escape Manchuria soon enough or who had been left behind to finish destruction of the facilities, and were taking them to task at a trial in Khabarovsk. Each in turn, in order to save their own skins, eventually started pointing fingers at the staff officers. Specifically Ishii and his various subordinates who had fled to Japan.

Sanders met with MacArthur and a representative from Military Intelligence. After an hour of debate, MacArthur decided that the information that could be gleaned from the Japanese far outweighed any crimes they had committed.

"My recommendation," said Sanders, "is that we promise Naito that no one involved in BW will be prosecuted as a war criminal."

"Well, you're the man in charge of the scientific aspects of this," replied MacArthur. "If you feel you cannot get all the information, we're not given to torture, so offer him that promise as coming from General MacArthur. And get the data."[14]

Within three weeks any belief on Sanders' part that no human guinea pigs had been used disappeared. He was visited in his hotel room one night by a small Japanese who shinnied down a drain pipe to his window and crawled in to hand him a set of blueprints. The plans were diagrams of the *Uji* BW bomb. The man then said that 100 such bombs had been constructed, and several had been tested by detonating them in the center of a range where prisoners had been tied to stakes at varying distances. After mentioning that some of the prisoners had been killed due to the experiment, the little man left. Sanders was stunned.

Sanders returned to MacArthur, but was told to keep investigating. The statement provided by one unknown person was not enough to stop the deal.

Over the next three months Sanders located and interrogated several former Japanese officers mentioned in the Naito Document and from other leads. At the same time, the relations between the U.S. and Russia began to rapidly deteriorate. Past horrors of a war now won became footnotes to history. The main concern for both the military and the government was the possibility of war with the USSR. If that were to happen, considering the Japanese BW engineers that remained in Russian hands, it was conceivable that the inventory of weapons employed by the Soviets would include chemical and bacteriological devices of a horrendous nature. With this being the case, it was paramount that the U.S. had weapon parity—or superiority.

Lt. Col. Sanders was ordered home in 1946 to report the results of his investigation to Camp Detrick. After producing the Naito Document and explaining his findings, he began to grow ill. He had contacted tuberculosis and would not be sent back to Japan. The Unit 731 matter was turned over to another officer to follow up on, and for reasons unknown to Sanders, no one at Detrick seemed to be concerned about the reports of human experiments. Instead, it was decided to forget about the negative part of that particular situation and go on with matters more relevant to the Detrick scientists: finding exactly how

25

certain bacteria and viruses effect the human body when used in the form of a weapon.

And the Japanese from Unit 731, *because* of their human experimentation, knew.

The war trials taking place in Tokyo and other places across the war zone were drawing world attention. Class "A" trials, those of the most serious cases, were tried by the International Military Tribunal for the Far East. Others of lessor significance were tried by various commissions appointed by the Army and Navy. As each case came to trial and was disposed of, headlines announced the sentences. From varying prison terms to hangings, each war criminal that came before the tribunal was handed their verdict and sentenced.

Except the members of Unit 731.

After receiving their marching orders from both Washington and MacArthur, the personnel involved in dealing with the Japanese BW experts in Japan found themselves faced with a very tricky situation. They had to somehow get the information required by higher headquarters from their former enemies, make sure the details were kept secret from virtually everyone outside the Camp Detrick circle, ensure that it would not surface in any manner that would make it available as evidence in war crimes trials, and do all of this without drawing attention to their project. If what they were attempting was discovered, it would prove most embarrassing to the U.S. government.

In one top secret message sent to CINCFE (Commander-in-Chief, Far East—Douglas MacArthur), the problem was discussed:

1. To formulate a reply to CINCFE's radio [message] date 2 May 1947, recommending the retention of Japanese BW Information in Intelligence channels and that such material not be employed as "war crimes" evidence.

2. Part 2 of cable cited in paragraph 1 above states that General Ishii and associates would supply technical BW information if guaranteed immunity from 'war crimes' in documentary form. Ishii and associates have to date, voluntarily supplied and are continuing to supply such information without a documentary guarantee of immunity.

26

3. Nineteen Japanese BW experts have written a 60 page report concerning BW research using human subjects. A twenty page report covering 9 years of research on crop destruction has been prepared. A report by 10 Japanese scientists on research in the veterinary field is being written. A Japanese pathologist is engaged in recovering and making photographs of selected examples of 8,000 slides of tissues from autopsies of humans and animals subjected to BW experiments. General Ishii is writing a treatise embracing his 20 years experience in all phases of BW."

Over a year after the war had ended the intelligence services were still referring to Ishii as "general." And in this message alone, it is shown that there were no doubts concerning human experimentation. The message continued with a sub-part concerning the value of the information Ishii and his cohorts were providing:

a. Data already obtained from Ishii and his colleagues have proven to be of great value in confirming, supplementing and complementing several phases of U.S. research in BW, and may suggest new fields for future research.

b. This Japanese information is the only known source of data from scientifically controlled experiments showing the direct effect of BW agents on man. In the past it has been necessary to evaluate the effects of BW agents on man from data obtained through animal experimentation. Such evaluation is inconclusive and far less complete than results obtained from certain types of human experimentation.

c. In addition to the results of human experimentation much valuable data is available from the Japanese experiments on animals and food crops. The voluntary imparting of this BW information may serve as a forerunner for obtaining much additional information in other fields of research.

d. Desirability of avoiding "war crimes" involvement.

A. Since it is believed that the USSR possesses only a small portion of this technical information, and since any 'war crimes' trial would completely reveal much data to all nations, it is felt that such publicity must be avoided in interests of defense and security of the U.S. It is believed also that 'war crimes' prosecution of Ishii and his associates would serve to stop the flow of much additional information of technical and scientific nature.

B. It is felt that the use of this information as a basis for 'war crimes' evidence would be a grave detriment to Japanese cooperation with the United States occupation forces in Japan.

7. It is concluded that:

a. Information of Japanese BW experiments will be of great value to the U.S. BW research program.

b. In the interests of national security it would not be advisable to make this information available to other nations as would be the case in the event of "war crimes" trial of Jap BW experts.

c. The value to U.S. of Japanese data is of such importance to national security as to far outweigh the value resulting from 'war crimes' prosecution.

d. The BW information obtained from Japanese sources should be retained in intelligence channels and should not be employed in "war crimes" evidence.

RECOMMENDATION

8. It is recommended that:

a. SWNCC approve the above conclusions.[15]

b. After approval by SWNCC, the JCS be requested to transmit the message in Appendix "B" to CINCFE providing they have no objection from the military point of view.

c. All subsequent communications dealing with this phase of the subject be classified 'top secret.'"

The concern for secrecy in this message is readily apparent. What else can be seen is the references to the SWNCC (State, War, Navy Coordinating Committee), and the JCS—the Joint Chiefs of Staff. What the members of the SWNCC and the Joint Chiefs know, the President knows.

The Deal and the Cover Up...
Despite precautions taken to keep these dealings and decisions secret, the word leaked outside of military circles. Before a written guarantee of non-prosecution could be provided to Ishii and his cohorts by MacArthur, the bureaucrats at the Department of State became involved. Such moves on the part of the military would not normally

have involved the State Department unless plans were being made to bring the Japanese into the United States—or unless their opinion was solicited by the White House. There is also the possibility that the State Department became involved in response to Russian protests concerning the prosecution of certain war criminals that had not yet been located or brought before the tribunal. The Soviets, who were at that moment interrogating their own Japanese prisoners that had been involved with Ishii, were becoming increasingly adamant about finding out what Ishii and the rest of his staff knew about bacteriological warfare—and might be giving the Americans.

In an undated top secret message sent by the Department of State, who at that time was feeling the heat from the Soviets concerning the Ishii affair, a fence-straddling non-committal attitude was vested by the bureaucrats:

INTERROGATION OF CERTAIN JAPANESE
BY RUSSIAN PROSECUTOR

The Department of State cannot approve the proposal in SFE 188/2 that Colonel Ishii and his associates should be promised that BW information given by them will be retained in intelligence channels and will not be employed as 'war crimes' evidence. It is believed on the basis of facts brought out in the subject paper that it is possible that the desired information can be obtained from Colonel Ishii and his assistants without these assurances, and that it might later be a source of serious embarrassment to the United States if the assurances were given. At the same time, every practicable precaution should be taken to prevent the BW information possessed by Colonel Ishii from being made generally known in a public trial. It is therefore recommended that (1) that CINCFE, without making any commitment to Ishii and the other Japanese involved, continue to obtain all possible information in the manner heretofore followed; (2) that information thus obtained be retained in fact in intelligence channels unless evidence developed at the International Military Trial presents overwhelming reasons why this procedure can no longer be followed: and (3) that, even though no commitment is made, the United States authorities

29

for security reasons not prosecute war crimes charges against Ishii and his associates.[16]

In typical political double-speak, the Department of State gave the military their blessing to cover up the activities of Unit 731 without committing themselves to a pardon or written guarantee that 731 personnel will not be prosecuted after providing the much-sought after information. In reading between the lines of this message, dual meanings and escape clauses can readily be seen. After stating that the Department of State cannot approve the proposal granting the 731 people immunity to prosecution, they go on to state that "every practicable precaution should be taken to prevent the BW information possessed by Colonel Ishii from being made generally known in a public trial." The only way to do this would be to make sure a trial never occurred. The Soviet prosecutors would have milked Ishii *et al* until nothing secret remained should they be brought in front of the Tribunal.

Then, in typical bureaucratic fashion, the message tosses the ball into the military's court by recommending that "...CINCFE, without making any commitment to Ishii and the other Japanese involved, continue to obtain all possible information in the manner heretofore followed." And in the very next sentence, the State Department officials left themselves a back door. "...that the information thus obtained be retained in fact in intelligence channels *unless evidence developed at the International Military Trial presents overwhelming reasons why this procedure can no longer be followed."* [Author's emphasis]

This last statement plainly demonstrates the State Department's concern that the Soviets—and maybe the British, Dutch, Australian and other Allied prosecutors—might develop information that would force the U.S. to cough up Ishii for trial. This, as the message plainly states, would be very embarrassing to the U.S.

Finally, the last sentence, purposely vague in meaning concerning just what "security" is involved, ends the message with: "...that, even though no commitment is made, the United States authorizes for security reasons not prosecute war crimes charges against Ishii and his associates."

30

In Appendix "B" attached to the above message, the Department of State transmitted its concern over discovery that American POWs were used as guinea pigs:

> "...it should be kept in mind that there is a remote possibility that independent investigation conducted by the Soviets in the Mukden Area *may have disclosed evidence that American prisoners of war were used for experimental purposes of a BW nature and that they lost their lives as a result of these experiments,* and further, that such evidence may be introduced by the Soviet prosecutors in the source of cross-examination of certain of the major Japanese war criminals now on trial at Tokyo, particularly during the cross examination of Umezu, Commander of the Kwantung Army from 1939 to 1944 of which army the Ishii BW group was a part. In addition, there is a strong possibility that the Soviet prosecutors will, in the course of cross-examination of Umezu, introduce evidence of experiments conducted on human beings by the Ishii BW group, which experiments *do not differ greatly from those for which this Government is now prosecuting German scientists and medical doctors at Nuremburg.*" [Author's emphasis]

The State Department was doing its best to tiptoe around the issue and keep it in the hands of the military, away from the Soviets, and all without "embarrassing" the government. The final recommendation was to give the "Ishii group" vocal immunity, backed up with a vague written document only if necessary—signed by MacArthur.

Ishii and his officers found themselves between the veritable rock and the hard place. They had to trust the Americans to honor an oral agreement. These former enemies of the Emperor were members of the same force that provided the *muratas* that had been used in the most painful and deadly of experiments, of which most had died or later been murdered. How could they now be trusted to honor their commitment *not* to seek revenge and prosecute them? It was very hard for the Japanese to understand such a people, but Ishii had little choice. He agreed.

In secret meetings that occurred in 1946 in Kamakura, Ishii and his senior officers revealed all they knew about bacteriological warfare and experimentation on human beings. In return, a secret contract was made between the American representatives of Camp Detrick, Military Intelligence, and Ishii. Little did Ishii know that a message existed that *did* guarantee him and his subordinates immunity from prosecution and protection by the United States Government. Titled simply "Message to CINCFE," and probably sent by SWNCC, it came in two parts:

Part 1. Re URAD C-52423 of 6 May 1947. Recommendation in part 3B is approved. Information obtained from Ishii and associates on BW will be retained in Intelligence channels and will not be employed as war crimes evidence.

Part 2. All communications above subject will be classified Top Secret.

Meanwhile the War Crimes trials continued both in Tokyo and Nuremburg. Operating under a charter drawn up by the Big Four in London in 1945, the trials in Germany operated under a new set of rules that defined war crimes. In the past, the term "war criminal" referred to men found guilty of conventional war crimes—violations of the Laws of Land Warfare. But with information that had been developed by intelligence sources inside Nazi-occupied Europe concerning human experimentation in concentration camps, mass killings of civilians as "examples," genocide and other atrocities being committed by the Nazis, a new definition of war criminal was coined.

The new, wider jurisdictions of military tribunals now included crimes against "peace and humanity." It was now even against the law to even "wage war."

Crimes against peace included: "...planning, preparation, initiation or waging a war of aggression, or war in violation of international treaties, agreements or assurances, or participation in a common plan or conspiracy for the accomplishment of any of the foregoing."

Crimes against humanity were defined as: "...inhumane acts committed against any civilian population, before or during the war."[17]

Ishii's group fell into both categories. He had bombed civilian cities with disease-carrying bombs and other vectors, spread plague with flea-infested rats, injected civilian prisoners with various bacteria and poisons, and used civilians-men, women, children and babies—in a myriad of other horrifying experiments. But because the government was now gripped with Cold War paranoia, and the military found that it was able to hide almost anything under the guise of "national security," Ishii and his troops, without due legal process, were protected *by* the United States government. Or at least by a newly emerging inner circle of life-long bureaucrats, intelligence officials, and military officers that were rapidly discovering that they could operate above the law.

Under the secret protection of this covert clique of intelligence officials, not one senior officer of Unit 731 was ever prosecuted. In fact, they were not only protected, but prospered in the years after the war. Many, ignoring Ishii's orders not to seek public jobs or teaching positions, entered academia and became respected citizens of Japan. Others made fortunes in private industry and in medical research. For example: Dr. Kozo Okamoto, the pathology squad leader at Pingfan who conducted live vivisections on prisoners, became a professor at Kyoto University and director of the medical department. He later became professor emeritus of the university and medical director of the Kinki University at Osaka.

Dr. Kazu Tabei, who fed typhoid germs in milk to human prisoners to increase the germs' effectiveness by human cultivation, and who was responsible for testing one type of germ bomb on prisoners, joined the staff of Kyoto University and became a professor of bacteriology.

Dr. Hisato Yoshimura, the frostbite expert who froze people to death, joined the faculty of Kyoto Prefectural Medical College and later became its president.

Jun'ichi Kaneko, Unit 731's bomb expert, joined the Japanese National Institute of Health and continued bacteriological research.

Colonel Sanders' "interpreter," Naito, fared even better. He opened a blood bank, then speculated it into one of the biggest and most successful multinational medical suppy and pharmaceutical companies in the world. The company, known as the Green Cross Corporation, produces plasma, artificial blood and cancer-fighting interferon—all at

33

great profit. Subsidiaries include the British-based Alpha Therapeutic Ltd. located in Norfolk, England, and the Alpha Therapeutic Corporation with laboratories located in Los Angeles.

As for Shiro Ishii, he faded from public view into retirement in the village of Wakamatsu-cho where he lived on a comfortable pension—provided by the U.S. government—until his death in 1959 at the age of sixty-nine.[18]

In the months that followed the end of the war the American intelligence community, along with certain career bureaucrats, discovered that they could operate outside both the law and human morality. In the name of national security they could form their own private agendas, count on each other for secret favors, and conspire without fear of discovery or retribution. In fact, they could become a government within themselves. All they had to do was feed the politicians what they wanted or needed to hear, and at the same time keep their actual activities secret—both from unsympathetic elected officials, and from the American people.

The effort to hide the existance of Unit 731 from the public and the branches of government mandated to care for veterans was successful for forty years. As the few surviving former POWs that were held in Mukden and Pingfan came forward to the Veterans Administration claiming war-related disabilities that were cropping up with age, they were denied benefits by the government because the claims could not be substantiated. "There are no records of such an incident taking place," claimed the VA. Without written documentation that completely reported the incident at the time and the names of the people involved, the government would not honor any claim. It was because of this that the veterans such as Pappy Whelchel and Greg Rodriguez banded together and organized a coordinated effort to bring the matter before Congress. It took a Congressional investigation to declassify the records. If it had not been for these men coming forward, the existence of Unit 731, its crimes and the government coverup would never have been disclosed.

The former human guinea pigs of Mukden, shunned by the very government that sent them to war, were ironically forced by that same government to open a window to a hidden kingdom seldom glimpsed by the outside world. And it was only one window of a very large castle.

Part II

More Human Guinea Pigs

"They had been starved to death. Their arms were just little sticks, their legs had practically no flesh on them at all."

> Col. James L. Collins
> Infantry officer in relief
> of Nordhausen
> concentration camp.

"We worked in the center of the mountain with no air, and just had one small piece of bread and margarine to eat all day. It was horrible."

> Yves Beon, member of
> French Resistance held
> as slave laborer in V-2
> factory.

"If any specialists who are brought to this country are subsequently found to be listed as alleged war criminals, they should be returned to Europe for trial"

> JCS directive in
> reference to
> Operation *Paperclip*.

Chapter 3

Weapons Of Terror

Reaching the top of its parabolic trajectory of over sixty miles above the earth, the terrible missile nosed over slightly and began to arc toward its target. Its mighty 600,000 horsepower rocket motor was silent now, having cut off just a few minutes after launch. As it fell, the thirteen ton missile began picking up speed. Within seconds it was traveling at over 3,500 miles per hour—five times the speed of sound—and did so with virtually no noise signature discernable below. For the people who went about their daily business in the Chiswick area in West London, there would be no warning of what was to come.

From the ground, it first appeared as a dot in the sky. Then, if anyone had noticed, it quickly grew into a tiny needle-shaped object that fell almost straight down. Within seconds of first appearing, the tail fins would have been recognizable just before it disappeared below the city's skyline and impacted with a tremendous explosion.

Amid the scream of air raid and fire brigade sirens, panicked Londoners grabbed their children and elderly and raced for air raid shelters. No one knew what had happened, but all were sure whatever it was, it had been brought about by the Germans. Why had there been no warning? Where was the RAF? Why was there no sound of falling bombs or the distinctive putt-putt of the Doodle Bugs?

It was September 8th, 1944. Londoners had almost become accustomed to the constant bombardment of the little V-1s, the stubby-winged buzz-bombs that initiated Hitler's *Vergeltungswaffen*—weapons of vengeance—program, but this was something new.[19]

When the smoke had cleared and the wounded and dead removed from the scene, the RAF experts came in and examined the area. What they saw was incredible. The warhead, carrying over a ton of high explosive, had reduced buildings in the immediate area to rubble, shattered others at the farthest radius of the blast, started fires, and had created a gigantic crater at the point of impact. What they were witnessing was the results of the first V-2 ballistic rocket fired against Britain.

By war's end, almost 1,000 V-2s had been launched on England. Over 500 were targeted for—and reached—London, causing nearly 10,000 casualties. And when the V-1 and V-2 launching sites in France and the Low Countries were overrun by Allied troops, the Germans moved their installations beyond Allied reach and began launching rockets at Liege and Antwerp. These attacks killed 8,000 Belgians and injured more than 23,000. There was no question that this new long-range missile would influence not only the conduct of this war, but the next.[20]

By late June of 1944, Hitler's Fortress Europe began to crumble. A three sided vise had begun to squeeze the Nazi empire with men, weapons and material. On the south, the American 5th Army had taken Anzio, Salerno, advanced to the Rapido river, fought through Cassino and had taken Rome. The British Eighth Army, having by-passed Rome, drove the German Tenth Army ever northward.

In the west, the Allies had landed in France at Normandy and were pushing eastward, toward Germany. At the same time, the Red Army was engaged in a monstrous offensive that was to take it to Berlin. The *Wehrmacht*, *Luftwaffe*, and *Waffen SS* were involved in a massive fighting withdrawal, trading ground for blood. If the situation continued to deteriorate, Germany had little hope of survival.

It was from this chaos and ruin that Hitler decided upon the last-ditch efforts that he felt would turn the tide of battle in the Reich's favor. His plans included his most terrible secret weapons—weapons that by their shear destructive power would in modern terminology be known as "force multipliers." But the inventory was not as great as he had been led to believe. Many weapons, such as Germany's atomic bomb, were still under development. Other projects, such as jet aircraft and extra-long range artillery, were in their infancy but were slowly, though sporadically, becoming operational.

Leading the pack were the German rocket programs that had completed their initial development stages and had gone into the production phase. Unlike the nuclear physicists on the atomic bomb project, who had labored under such secrecy that they had been compartmentalized into fragmented cells that often wasted valuable research time in duplicated effort, the rocket scientists had been centralized under the firm leadership of one man: SS General Walter Dornberger.

Dornberger, an experienced artillery officer and professional engineer, had been assigned to head the rocket research project at Peenemunde, on the coast of the Baltic Sea. His SS connections proved advantageous in cutting red tape, and his personal influence with Hitler had been invaluable when seeking favorable attention in matters of importance—such as machinery, parts, fuel and labor.

Under Dornberger, Peenemunde had grown into an impressive rocket research center and factory. But in 1943, the facility was discovered by the Allies who promptly planned and executed a large-scale bombing raid that wreaked havoc on the facility. This attack not only demonstrated to the German staff the vulnerability of the location, but the possibility that a similar raid could cost them their dearest commodities—their scientists.

Dornberger realized that to protect both the personnel and the manufacturing facilities, rocket production had to be moved. He selected a secluded location in the Harz mountains of central Germany, near Nordhausen. Using slave labor provided by the nearby concentration camp at Dora, a huge underground network of tunnels were hewn out of solid rock. The tunnels were then filled with machine tools, assembly lines, rooms for laboratories and offices, and railroad tracks to move parts and completed rockets from one section to another. The new factory, named *Mittelwerke*, was a marvel of human engineering.

And a spectacle of human tragedy.

After the construction was completed, a labor force was required on the assembly lines to mass-produce the V-2s. To provide this force, the Germans once again turned to the SS at Dora who happily provided more prisoners. This was not a new technique for Dornberger. He had used the same method of providing a work force for Peenemunde when he utilized 10,000 prisoners from the concentration camp at Karlhagen to construct that facility. But the conditions and the work at Nordhausen were far more harsh than those encountered at the above-ground base at Peenemunde. Besides the cold, the brutal treatment and the lack of medical attention, the prisoners were required to work exhaustingly long hours on a starvation diet. One prisoner who managed to survive the hell of Mittelwerke stated that the normal diet was one piece of moldy black bread a day and if lucky, a bit of margarine. Those that did not die of disease or exposure starved to death. And when they died, they were simply dragged outside to the crematories and replaced by other inmates. In the two years of Mittelwerke's existence, over 20,000 prisoners lost their lives at the Dora/Nordhausen project.

In the winter of 1945, U.S. Army Colonel James L. Collins, who was leading an infantry unit in its advance through that sector, received an odd radio message from his forward units. "Colonel, you'd better get up here and see what we've got. It's terrible."

Collins rode up to the head of the column, bouncing over the rutted, pockmarked dirt road until he reached the designated location. He was horrified at the sight that greeted him. Near the cave-like entrance to a large hill, over 6,000 bodies covered the ground. He stopped and stared. Row after row of stick-like human forms lay stacked in rows like so much cord wood. Collins dismounted his Jeep and walked among the dead. It was obvious that all had been starved, but it was also apparent that many had been sadistically beaten—and several shot.

Besides the pungent odor of rotting bodies, a strange thick smell of burnt flesh hung in the air, drifting low over the valley from the chimneys of the crematoriums at Dora. The Americans stood frozen in shock. In all of the scenes of war they had witnessed in their advance across Europe, they had never encountered such a spectacle. They felt as if they had blundered into the lowest level of Dante's *Inferno*.

As the soldiers' shock turned to rage, they began to investigate further. First they found the crematorium furnaces with their doors still hanging open with partially burned bodies still stacked inside. Other skeletal forms lay stacked nearby waiting their turn. The coals were still hot. It appeared that the SS personnel who had been busily shoving the evidence of their crimes into the ovens had barely escaped the American advance—and they couldn't have gone far.

Armed search parties were sent out into the surrounding mountains and forests to track down the criminals while other soldiers cautiously entered the "cave." Inside they found Middelwerke—and the V-2s.

Chapter 4

Operation Paperclip: Grabbing The Nazi Scientists

The War Crimes units arrived at the same time as another group of American officers—a secret ordnance technical intelligence team under Major James Hamill. As the War Crimes unit, led by Major Herschel Auerbach, searched the surrounding hills and villages for those responsible for the deaths of the Dora prisoners, Hamill and his crew began to strip the facility of documents, V-2 rockets, technical drawings and anything else of scientific value—including the scientists responsible for the project.

But as Hamill and his men searched Mittelwerke, interviewing former prisoners, guards and technicians, it became apparent that he and Auerbach were searching for the same people. Auerbach's military police had located Mittelwerke's Technical Director, Albin Sawatzki, who the prisoners had fingered as one of the chief antagonists, and had imprisoned him in a make-shift pen in the camp yard. Under questioning, Sawatzki identified both SS personnel and members of the various scientific teams. He named the director of production, Arthur Rudolph, and the general manager, Georg Rickhey, and told the American officers where they could likely be found. He further admitted that Rudolph in particular was responsible for the prisoners work schedules and treatment.

Rickhey was quickly located and arrested. But before he could be brought before a war crimes tribunal, he was released. It seemed that the technical and scientific recovery teams wielded more power than the justice teams. Rickhey, as were his soon-to-follow cohorts, was considered a valuable commodity that now fell into the category of Spoils of War.

And as with the Japanese medical officers involved in the Manchuria experiments, the crimes committed by certain Germans who held expertise that might prove of future value to the American government would be overlooked.

It was called Operation *Paperclip*. In actuality it was a treasure hunt. It was a secret program devised by the U.S. military to track down and recruit Nazi scientists, recover technical booty, and spirit both out of Europe for service in the United States. It was the American answer to the Russian efforts to the same end. There were no delusions on either side concerning an emerging geo-political realignment between capitalism and communism that would form the post-war world. It was a matter of forgetting recent events, ignoring past crimes, and forging ahead with a new arms race. The only problem was that it was illegal.[21]

At first, Paperclip's mission was to locate the scientists and the technology, bring both back to the U.S., debrief them, then return them to Germany to answer any accusations brought up by the Nuremberg investigators. But it did not take long for the upper level players in the Joint Intelligence Committee (JIC), the Exploitation Branch under Army Intelligence (G-2), the Joint Intelligence Objectives Agency (JIOA), and the OSS (Office of Strategic Services) to determine that returning the Nazis to Germany was not advantageous to the intelligence community. To do so would not only make them available to trial, but to the Russians who, since the war in Europe ended in May of 1945, had also been busily rounding up every scrap of German technology they could find.

Endorsed by President Harry Truman, Paperclip went into high gear just as the Nuremburg trials were in full swing. As Nazi warlords were being given death sentences for war crimes and atrocities that included the massive deaths attributed to the concentration camps, the very people who were directly involved with thousands of those very same deaths were being protected by the covert community within the U.S. government.

It was a matter of national security. Just as it was when General Shiro Ishii was tracked down and offered a deal in Japan, the Nazi technical people were similarly approached. They could save themselves by agreeing to move to the United States where they could not only be protected from prosecution—but continue to work on their various projects. Or, they could answer for their misdeeds at Nuremburg. For the Germans, there was little choice. For the military-industrial conglomerate, it was a bonanza. The Allies were astounded at the incredible advances the German scientists had made in the realms of weapons development, physiological experiments, communications, aircraft development, chemical and biological warfare and other very specialized sciences.

For example, the German aviation industry had made drastic advances in jet propulsion and aircraft design. When Nazi Germany fell, models of strange new streamlined aircraft with swept wings of various configurations were found that were far in advance of anything the Allies had ever seen. New designs of turbojet engines were discovered that produced more power at a lighter weight than any in the Allied inventory. Rocket planes stood ready for flight that could out-climb and outrun any aircraft then available to the U.S., Great Britain or Russia. And there was more.

Besides the V-1 and V-2, the Peenemunde team had developed a very capable small liquid fueled missile known as the *Wasserfall* that could reach an altitude of 55,000 feet. Another design, the *Schmetterling* anti-aircraft missile, incorporated the features of the Hs 293 glider bomb,[22] had a 52 pound warhead, two solid-fuel booster rockets and a liquid-fuel engine which could drive it to a height of 45,000 feet—far higher than any conventional aircraft of the time.

The Messerschmidt Me-262 twin-jet fighter proved devastating in air combat, and had it not been misused by Hitler who demanded that it be used for attack/bombing missions, might have delayed the outcome of the war. In just one aerial engagement, the Me-262s attacked a flight of B-17s and destroyed fourteen within twenty minutes. The capabilities of German jets and the advances made in this area were not lost on the American aerospace industry.

44

Other weapons were equally amazing. The multi-barrel rocket launcher known as the *Nebelwerfer*, capable of launching chemical weapons, had participated in the invasion of Poland and terrorized the Russian army on the Eastern Front. A Brigade of these launchers could fire 108 rounds in ten seconds, and 648 rounds in 90 seconds.

As for artillery, the spectrum of weapons was amazing. The inventory included a super long-range multi-chambered cannon that sent a projectile down a barrel which automatically added an additional explosive charge behind the round as it passed each successive chamber, and a 80 centimeter (32" bore) railway gun known as *Gustav*.

But of more importance to the scientific search teams were the weapons of greatest range and greatest effect. The missiles, the germs, and the chemicals.

Of common knowledge is the death gas, Zyklon B. Zyklon B, the nerve agent manufactured by the German industrial giant I.G. Farben in Gendorf, was used in the concentration camps to murder millions of Jews, Gypsy's, Slavs, Poles and other "sub-humans." But lessor known to those outside the military and covert communities is the existence of three other deadly nerve gasses: Tabun, Sarin and Soman. These gases were so much more effective than the mustard agents stockpiled by the Allies that they quickly became the new super-secret chemical agents for the Cold War—for both sides. American picked Sarin, while the Soviet Union chose Tabun as their new chemical weapons. The reason for the choice was simple. A joint team of American, British and Canadian experts, headed by Commander A.K. Mills of the British Ministry of Aircraft Production, utilizing intelligence gathered during the war, discovered a chemical warfare experimental station used by the Luftwaffe, which led them to several other similar sites. In the end, the group was able to determine that Tabun, at one factory alone, was being produced at a rate of 1,000 tons a month. This particular factory, located at Dyhernfurth, was captured by the Russians—intact.

At the Wehrmacht's experimental gas station at Raubkammer, Mills' teams discovered evidence of massive human experimentation involving chemical agents. In one instance, over 4,000 photographs were discovered depicting mustard gas experiments on the skin of what appeared to be either political or concentration camp prisoners. Records showed that several of the prisoners had died because of the injuries that had been inflicted by the chemicals.

Further searching produced the people responsible. SS Brigadier General Walter Schieber, who had been in charge of the chemical industry under Albert Speer, was located in a detention camp. General Walter Hirsch, head of the Wehrmacht's chemical warfare section and thirteen cohorts were captured within weeks after the fall of Berlin. Interrogation of these people and others led the searchers to virtually every chemical warfare expert in the Third Reich. At least those not captured by the Russians.

In the search for the Nazi nuclear physicists responsible for Germany's efforts to develop an atomic bomb, a team headed by Lieutenant Colonel Boris Pash, former security officer over the U.S.'s Manhattan Project, stumbled onto something else of interest. The team, code-named "Alsos," discovered that a major biological warfare research base was located at the University of Strasbourg. Here, they found evidence that the University's head of biological warfare research, Eugen von Haagen, had deliberately infected Natzweiler concentration camp prisoners with spotted fever—killing several. Other professors at the university performed similar chemical and biological experiments on human subjects, chief among them the official SS representative, Professor August Hirt. Hirt, who provided the human guinea pigs for the experiments from various concentration camps, was known for his huge collection of human skulls which were gleaned from bodies sent to Strasbourg by Adolf Eichmann.

Hitler's chief of biological warfare was Kurt Blome, who had constructed the first biological warfare laboratory at the personal request of SS Reichsfuhrer Heinrich Himmler. Himmler, along with Blome, had decided on their own that biological agents would be deployed against Allied troops on both fronts as soon as the bacteria and viral agents could be identified, mass produced, and a suitable vector chosen. But like Unit 731, the Germans were having developmental and research problems in the BW field. Nevertheless, advances were made. But before any BW agents could be deployed, the laboratory was captured by the Russians.

German medical experimentation on concentration camp prisoners has been well-documented. Bizarre cases of experiments on various races, involving susceptibility to diseases, climates, diet and pain, abound. Attempts to transplant organs, change eye color, and even blood type—most all resulting in death—have been noted to have occurred in several camps. But some of the most incredible experiments involved "research" aimed at survival of Luftwaffe aircrews.

In a secret project that parallels that of Ishii's Unit 731, the Germans experimented with cold. The chief concern over pilots shot down over the North Atlantic was water temperature. Hypothermia could set in within minutes, often seconds, and if not checked, would result in death. Even if a flyer could be rescued quickly, there was still a question of survival if his body temperature had already dropped significantly. To understand more about possibilities of hypothermic survival and revival, the German doctors undertook a series of human experiments. The location chosen was Dachau.

Under the guidance of Professor E. Holzlohner of Kiel University, several doctors, including one Dr. Sigmund Rascher, conducted freezing experiments. This was done by immersing prisoners in freezing water and waiting until various limbs were almost frozen. They then pulled the victims from the vats and attempted to revive the various body parts. They also timed the freezing process to see how long it took a man to freeze to death in water. The success of such experiments can be summed up by the reactions of the members of the U.S. Army's 363rd Medical Battalion, 42nd Infantry Division, when they entered Experimental Block 5 at Dachau. Besides an overwhelming stench, the young soldiers found heads, arms, legs, torsos, and organs of every description lying about like so much human refuse. As Colonel Walter J. Fellenz, commander of the liberators stated, "We had opened the gates of hell."

As soon as the scientific investigation teams found out about Dachau, they swarmed in like flies. Thousands of documents bore mute testimony to what had gone on inside the electrified fences and wooden buildings. To the average soldier, Dachau was a house of horrors. But to the scientific discovery teams, it was a gold mine. Of interest to the aerospace specialists were the same subjects that concerned the Luftwaffe doctors. Besides the freezing experiments, tests wherein sea water was forced down the throats of prisoners to see how long they could live if stranded on a life raft at sea, and other experiments that tested the human body's ability to withstand high altitudes without oxygen were of supreme interest to the technology scouts. All of these

47

gruesome programs subjected the victims to excruciating pain, and in most instances, resulted in death.[23]

Most of these aeromedicine experiments came under the auspices of Colonel Hubertus Strughold, head of the Luftwaffe's Institute for Aviation Medicine in Berlin. Though investigators later determined that most of the information gleaned from the Nazis regarding the freezing, altitude and pressure tests was of little value in the long run—the Allies had already progressed beyond these "scientific achievements"—Strughold was saved from prosecution at Nuremburg by U.S. intelligence.

And there were others. But the best known examples of the fruits of Paperclip in the months following World War II, and into the 1950s and 60s, were the German rocket scientists and aeronautical engineers.

By the spring of 1946, the policy makers in the State-War-Navy Coordinating Committee (SWNCC) were in a quandary. Besides having to deal with Ishii and the former Unit 731 personnel, they were now faced with handling the proceeds of Paperclip. President Truman, after giving permission to import German scientists, made it clear—at least to the American public—that no war criminals were to be brought into the country. But the SWNCC, by way of its various intelligence organs, was quickly discovering that finding suitable German scientists who were not Nazis and were not suspected of war crimes or atrocities were few and far between. Almost every scientist and engineer was a member of the Nazi party, and many held memberships in three or four other Nazi organizations. Most of the higher ranking scientists and technicians were members of either the SS or SA. Almost all had either performed experiments on prisoners or had participated in the development and deployment of weapons of terror specifically used to attack the civilian population. It was becoming increasingly apparent to the various entities within the covert intelligence community that something would have to be done outside of the presidential directive to get these people into the U.S. while at the same time appearing to follow the rules.

In August of 1946, Acting Secretary of State Dean Acheson sent a copy of SWNCC 257/22, the revised Paperclip policy, to President Truman. According to the policy, the selected German scientists would be under military custody and control. They would be entering the country without visas, and after the War Department screened their backgrounds, and the State Department approved them, they would be offered contracts with either the military or private employment. Of interest is the section regarding political background:

"No member found by the Commanding General, USFET, to have been a member of the Nazi party *and* more than a nominal participant in its activities, or an active supporter of Nazism or militarism shall be brought to the U.S. hereunder." [Author's emphasis]

According to the revised 257/22, it was now acceptable to have been a Nazi, provided that one did not participate in too many of the party's activities.

On September 3rd, Truman, under the recommendation of Acheson, signed the document.[24] Now it was a matter of making sure that no overtly ardent Nazis, especially those with obvious backgrounds that would fall under the category of war crimes, were on the recruiting lists or were already in the country.

At this point, the Paperclip staff went totally out of bounds. Among those recruited and brought to the U.S. were such men as:

* SS General Walter Dornberger, former director of the V-2 operation at Peenemunde who used 10,000 slave laborers from the Karlshagen concentration camp in the construction and operation of the rocket site. Dornberger was first assigned to Wright Field, then later went to work for Bell-Textron and became the chief lobbyist for Bell Helicopter before and during the Johnson administration—and the Vietnam War.

* SS Major Werner von Braun, who headed the rocket program at Peenemunde and joined the SS at the personal request of Heinrich Himmler. Von Braun, along with 100 other top Nazi rocket technicians, was sent to Fort Bliss, Texas, near the White Sands Missile Range in New Mexico where he worked for Army Ordnance and General Electric in developing the Hermes II missile. He was later assigned to Redstone Arsenal at Huntsville, Alabama, and was also directly responsible for the army's Redstone battlefield rocket and the Jupiter IRBM. By July of 1960, NASA acquired von Braun's team to form the nucleus of the Marshall Space Flight Center at Huntsville. There, he and his team developed the larger Saturn I rocket, and the follow-on Saturn IB that carried the first astronauts to the moon. In

1970, von Braun became NASA's deputy associate administrator for planning, then in 1972, he left NASA to become vice-president of engineering and development at Fairchild Industries in Germantown, Maryland.

* Kurt Debus, former member of the SS and SA who joined the SS in 1939 and was assigned SS# 426559. Debus was responsible for using concentration camp prisoners from Dora as slave laborers at the V-2 factory at Mittelwerke. He later became the first deputy director of the Kennedy Space Center at Cape Canaveral for NASA.

* Kurt Blome, who established the BW research center for Himmler and who exposed concentration camp prisoners to plague by inoculation, was acquitted of war crimes at Nuremburg in 1947, brought to Camp David, Maryland, and quickly hired by the U.S. Army Chemical Corps to work on biological warfare.

* Major General Walter Schreiber, who assigned doctors to experiment on prisoners and funded the projects, was brought into the country and put to work at the Air Force School of Medicine at Randolph Field, Texas.

* Arthur Rudolph, director of operations at Mittelwerke where 20,000 workers died from starvation, beatings, and executions, and who had been a member of the Nazi party since 1931, was hired by NASA and assigned to work on the Saturn rocket program.

* Luftwaffe Colonel Hubertus Strughold, who as wartime head of the Luftwaffe's Institute for Aviation Medicine in Berlin oversaw the freezing experiments, was brought to the United States to head the new Air Force School of Aviation Medicine at Randolph Field. Two years later he was placed in charge of the new Department of Space Medicine.

* Hans Trurnit, who worked with Professor Holzlohner of the University of Kiel in conducting the freezing experiments at Dachau, and who was a member of the Nazi party and four other Nazi organizations, was brought to the U.S. Army's chemical warfare arsenal at Edgewood, Maryland, to work in the toxicology laboratory.

* Friedrich Hoffmann, who as a chemist had synthesized poison gases and toxins for the Luftwaffe's Technical Research Institute and the University of Wuerzburg's Chemical Warfare Laboratory, was sent to Edgewood to work on poison gasses.

* Konrad Schaefer, the German desalinization expert who experimented with means of converting sea water into a drinking water that resulted in two experimental programs involving force-feeding the treated sea water to inmates at Dachau, killing several. He was brought to the United States to work under Strughold at the School of Aviation Medicine.

And there were hundreds more. In all, over 1,800 former Nazis and 1,700 dependents were spirited out of Europe, away from prosecution at Nuremburg, and illegally smuggled into the United States to work for the U.S. government and private industry.

And it was easy to do. The covert community had discovered that only three things had to be done: "cleanse" each man's file of incriminating information, classify his case at a security level high enough to keep anyone outside of the intelligence community from gaining access to the individual or his records, and finally, label it all a matter of National Security.

Konrad Schaefer, for example, had been a defendant at Nuremburg. But the JIOA Director, Colonel Daniel Ellis, recommended his immigration to the State Department and told them that the JIOA had investigated Schaefer's background and had found nothing in his past that indicated that he was a Nazi or had committed any crimes.

Werner von Braun, originally evaluated as a dedicated Nazi and his file noted: "Subject is regarded as a potential security threat by the Military Governor," received a new security evaluation that stated: "No derogatory information is available on the subject...It is the opinion of the Military Governor that he may not constitute a security threat to the United States."

Arthur Rudolph's file was even worse. He was described at first evaluation as being "100% Nazi, dangerous type, security threat. Suggest internment." But JIOA created a new dossier that stated there was "...nothing in his records indicating that he was a war criminal, an ardent Nazi or otherwise objectionable."

As for Major General Walter Schreiber, whose file noted that he had assigned doctors to experiment on concentration camp prisoners and had handled the funding for the projects, was presented to the State Department as having a clean bill of health. No mention was made of the evidence presented against him at Nuremburg. It would not be until

1952, when newspaper reporter Drew Pearson publicized the Nuremberg evidence, that the true story behind Schreiber's war record came to light. He was quickly provided a visa and hustled off to Argentina.

Another Nazi, Siegfried Ruff, was even less fortunate. The former expert on high altitude experiments, who had participated in the Dachau high and low pressure chamber experiments that resulted in the deaths of 80 prisoners, failed to reach America. Even though sponsored by Colonel Robert Benford, the Army Air Force's Aero Medical Center's commander, and promised a job in America by the Air Force, his chances for clandestine entry were squelched when his wartime atrocities were exposed by reporter Pearson. In Benford's view, "the Air Force lost a great man." But these cases were exceptions. In the majority of instances, the conspiracy to protect and import the former Nazis was incredibly successful. In the opinion of 1947 JIOA director Bosquet Wev, there was no reason to "beat a dead Nazi horse."

World War II was over. The Cold War had just begun. For the soldiers, sailors and airmen coming home, it was time to take off the uniform and get back to living. It was time to forget the horrors of war that they had witnessed.

For the intelligence community, it was business as usual. With a new twist. The men who had participated in the various technical recovery operations had discovered a new-found power. They had found the means of going around the law, past the wishes (and orders) of the elected officials in government, and under the red tape of bureaucracy. They had come to the realization that they could do anything they wanted, provided it was classified above Top Secret, compartmentalized on a need-to-know basis, and done so for reasons of National Security.

They had found that they could be, when necessary, a government within themselves. They had found that they could operate above the law.

Chapter 5

The Gehlen Org: From OSS to CIA

During World War II, the OSS had infiltrated nearly two hundred agents into the Third Reich—almost three times as many as had been sent by Britain. Its operatives were inserted into almost every militarily significant city from Vienna to Berlin, Munich to Bremen. In all, over 70 cities had been salted with OSS spy teams by war's end.

The casualties had been heavy, but not exorbitant. Of the total number of agents that worked behind German lines, only thirty-six had been killed or captured. And of these, the majority were lost in the waning days of the war in the vicinity of the Last Redoubt of Bavaria. It was at this time that almost every civilian found on the road by the Gestapo was detained and questioned as to why they were not in uniform for the Fatherland, or at least under arms in a home defense unit. Even the best cover stories provided to the young OSS agents might fail such a test. Many did.

Still, the organization as a whole was remarkable in its conception, implementation and execution. The bravery of the field teams was beyond question. They were a necessary entity, brought about by drastic circumstances. But after Germany surrendered, the need for specially trained spy-commandos was considered by the White House to be nil. In fact, Truman considered the OSS a peacetime liability.

In a letter to General Donovan, he wrote: "I want to take this occasion to thank you for the capable leadership you have brought to a vital wartime activity in your capacity as Director of Strategic

Services. You may well find satisfaction in the achievements of the Office and take pride in your own contribution to them." He then promptly took steps to abolish the service, dividing the few necessary peacetime functions between the State Department and the War Department.

But from the ashes rose a new organization. One much more powerful—and sinister. And it would be an organization that would grow much faster than anyone could ever dream. For a very good reason.

On April 1, 1945, a convoy of eleven trucks wound its way through Bavaria, traveling south from Berlin, away from the advancing Red Army who was at that moment conducting their own *blitzkrieg* through eastern Germany. Aboard the trucks were hand-picked German intelligence officers who guarded a very special cargo. Inside crates that had been carefully stacked and hidden under the canvas tops of the trucks were the most valued prizes of the head of German military intelligence: the files on Russia.

The purpose of the convoy was not to transport the documents to the Last Redoubt, but to remove them from harm's way altogether for use as future bargaining chips with the advancing Allies. For the files, which were the fruit of five years of intensive intelligence gathering on Russia, were now the personal property of a youthful 40 year-old general named Reinhard Gehlen. And with them, he planned on bargaining his way to a very special arrangement—with the Americans.

Reinhard Gehlen, known as Hitler's spy master, had overseen a huge organization of more than 3500 spies scattered throughout both Eastern Europe and the Soviet Union. His top officers, Nazi zealots who had committed some of the most atrocious crimes of the war, had proven very effective in their efforts to extract information from prisoners and insert agents into Russia. The spies that were sent into the Soviet Union infiltrated not only the Red Army, but even the Soviet General Staff. The records Gehlen had amassed over the previous four years would be invaluable to the Allies—especially a select group of very interested Americans. Now it was only a question of saving the files and making the proper contacts on the American side. Gehlen was confident a suitable arrangement could be made for not only himself, but his organization.

Gehlen had been planning this move for months. He noted in his memoirs that, "Early in 1944 I told my more intimate colleagues that I considered the war lost and we must begin thinking of the future...and plan for the approaching catastrophe."[25]

And prepare they did. Within the crates were documents that detailed roads, bridges, factories, military installations, airfields, water supplies, communications sites and virtually every item of interest inside Russia and the satellite countries to a military planner. But of more interest were the hundreds of files he had amassed on the personnel at the top of the Soviet military machine including the Soviet High Command. Much of this information was derived by interrogation, torture and starvation of selected officers and soldiers of some four million prisoners taken on the Eastern Front. Those who did not cooperate were summarily executed. Those that did were often executed afterwards when they were deemed of no further value. It was for these reasons that Gehlen and his officers were adamant about being captured by American forces. If they were taken by the Russians, they knew what would happen to them.

Two months before Germany surrendered, Gehlen made his move. Along with a group of his most trusted senior officers, he microfilmed the vast horde of documents and had them sealed in water-tight metal drums. These drums were covertly removed from army headquarters in Berlin and transported to secret cache sites throughout the Austrian Alps. It was well for Gehlen that this effort was made. For when the convoy of trucks transporting the hard copies of the files reached central Germany, the convoy was spotted by Soviet planes and bombed. Five of the eleven trucks were destroyed, and with them, the files they carried.

Gehlen and his officers, after abandoning Berlin to make their way toward Switzerland and the Americans, were—according to official history—indeed fortunate. When they finally found an American unit to surrender to, instead of running into a by-the-book American officer who might have offered them up to the Russians in accordance with the Yalta agreements, they encountered Captain John Bokor. Bokor, who was described as a pragmatist who regarded the Soviets as the next potential enemy, impressed Gehlen as a person who, "...had no illusions about the way political events were turning. We became close friends."

Bokor, according to Gehlen's memoirs, ignored official policy. When he found out about the secret caches of records, he allegedly decided on his own to keep the matter confidential and quietly work to hand Gehlen, the records and the men of Gehlen's spy network over intact to the OSS. Then, according to Gehlen, Bokor quietly went around removing the names of Gehlen's men from the rosters of war criminals. Once this was accomplished, Gehlen turned part of his records over to Bokor who promptly spirited them away from the interrogation center without even Military Intelligence knowing of their existence. Within ninety days Bokor had direct liaison—and the personal support of—General Walter Bedell Smith, Chief of Staff of the Allied Supreme Command (who later headed the CIA), and General Edwin Sibert, the highest ranking military intelligence officer in Europe. Quite a feat for a mere captain.

At the same time, Gehlen's existence in Allied hands quite coincidentally became known to General "Wild Bill" Donovan, head of the OSS, and his station chief in Europe, Allen Dulles. In August, Gehlen and three assistants were covertly flown to Washington and secreted away at Camp David for interviews with both Military Intelligence and the OSS. Apparently the OSS offered the best deal, for within eighteen months the *Gehlen Org*, resurrected from the original Nazi spy network, had been installed in West Germany to act as the eyes and ears of the newly-created CIA.

The story that Captain Bokor, using great foresight and planning, managed all of these feats of clandestine operations on his own is too incredible to be true. It is not probable that a company-grade officer would risk his career to protect a Nazi war criminal, or put himself personally in jeopardy by wantonly violating international agreements. In any normal case, such activity would earn him a courts martial. It is even more improbable that Gehlen would stumble into the one American in a thousand that would quickly see the value in what Gehlen purported to offer and immediately begin work to protect not only Gehlen, but his officers.

What is more believable is that Gehlen had made these arrangements far in advance. By using certain trusted contacts within the German High Command who had both pre-war and current business dealings across national boundaries, Gehlen had coordinated a deal with a specified contact within the American intelligence community. Namely Allen Dulles.

Dulles knew Gehlen was coming. In April, one month before the war ended, and forty-five days before Gehlen surrendered to Bokor, Dulles ordered an aide to begin talks with the German general through intermediaries in Berlin.

While the Paperclip scientists were setting up shop in the U.S., Reinhard Gehlen began reestablishing his presence in West Germany. His organization, the *Gehlen Org*, quickly regained control of the majority of his former agents inside the Iron Curtain, and with the help of many of his former staff, put them back to work. Though he agreed not to hire any former Gestapo, SS or SD members, he sought them out and put them on the payroll—the *CIA*'s payroll—regardless of his promise. And the CIA did not stop him.

Among his recruits were Dr. Franz Six and Emil Augsburg. Six and Augsburg had been members of an SS mobile Death's Head killing squad that hunted down and killed Soviet Jews, intellectuals and partisans wherever they could be found. Six was known as a *Streber*, or Eager Beaver, for the enthusiastic manner in which he pursued his job. Gehlen also recruited the former Gestapo chiefs of Paris, France, and Kiel, Germany. Then, that not being enough, he hired Willi Krichbaum, the former senior Gestapo leader for southeastern Europe.

Gehlen was pleasantly surprised by what happened next. His new employer, the OSS, not only encouraged but financed an escape mechanism set up by Gehlen for former Nazis. The Gehlen Org established, with OSS help, "rat lines" to provide an underground escape network to be used by former war criminals to escape prosecution by German war crimes tribunals. By way of this organization, over 5,000 Nazis secretly made their way out of Europe to relocate around the globe.

Most went to South and Central America. The countries of choice were Argentina, Chile, Nicaragua and El Salvador. Within a few years after their arrival in these particular countries, the infamous right-wing government "death squads" made their first appearances. Of note in the expatriate community were such characters as Dr. Joseph Mengele, who specialized in crude genetic experiments on Jewish concentration camp inmates, and mass murderer Klaus Barbie, the infamous "Butcher of Lyons."

According to some sources, former OSS officer James Jesus Angleton, who later became CIA Chief of Intelligence, was the man responsible for providing the Nazis with new identities before their departure from the detainment camps. Angleton worked directly for Dulles.[26]

To satisfy his new employers, Gehlen realized that he had to produce information that was of value to Washington. He also realized that for an intelligence organization to be of value, and to justify a large budget, it had to have an entity that was considered a deadly threat to spy on. He knew that the Americans had little knowledge concerning both the Russians as a military machine, and what activities were transpiring behind the Iron Curtain. The Red Menace would fit the requirement of the ominous threat nicely. All Gehlen had to do was paint as bleak a picture of the situation as he could, and continue creating reports that indicated that the scenario was continually deteriorating. The more bad news he gave Washington, the more money he would have to work with. He knew that in peacetime, the only way to justify a large intelligence organization was to make sure there was always "an enemy at the gates."

He began by feeding information to Dulles—and consequently to Truman—that appeared to show that the Russians were poised to attack the West. He reported that the Soviet forces in eastern Europe were comprised of 208 crack assault divisions, most of which were high-speed capable motorized rifle and tank divisions. Such figures showed that the Communists outnumbered the Western forces by a ratio of ten-to-one.

Then, in early 1947, he reported to the fledgling CIA that his agents had noted subtle changes in Soviet billeting and leave policies, and that troops were being recalled for some unspecified reason. He alluded that this could be the beginning of a preparation phase for the suspected invasion.

This was followed by Gehlen's prediction that the Russians would move quickly once all troops and equipment had been activated and put into position for attack. It wouldn't be long until there was a Soviet *blitzkrieg*.

In actual fact, Gehlen's information could not have been further from the truth. By 1946, the Red Army was an over-extended, under-equipped, and exhausted force of combat-riddled units. Many of the battalions that had reached Berlin had done so on foot. There was not even sufficient motor transport to move one entire division without depriving another of its motorized assets. Almost half of the Red Army's transport was *horse drawn*. In addition to this, U.S. Army Intelligence had established that the majority of Soviet forces in Eastern Europe was bogged down in rebuilding the eastern zones, reorganizing security structures, and performing governmental administrative functions. According to the intelligence estimate, the Soviet ground and air forces would not be combat effective against the Western powers for at least the next decade.

The 10:1 Russian superiority figure that Gehlen referred to was unrealistic from the beginning. Gehlen well knew, as did Dulles and the other veteran OSS agents, that the Soviet divisional structure was far less in numerical manpower than its U.S. equivalent. A Soviet division was typically one third as strong as an American division. And its leadership was far less effective. Instead of being able to function in combat with flexibility by making on-the-spot field expedient decisions, the Soviet officers had to wait for orders from upper echelon before reacting to a change in the flow of battle. This fact in itself often caused the Soviets grievous losses, and even defeats, during land battles. The U.S. forces, on the other hand, encouraged battlefield decisions during the heat of conflict to be made at the lowest levels.

Still, the OSS—and the follow-on CIG (Central Intelligence Group which replaced the OSS)—chose to conveniently believe Gehlen. Over 70% of the reports submitted to Washington on CIA stationary were simply Gehlen's words. According to a former CIA officer, "Gehlen's reports and analyses were sometimes simply retyped onto CIA stationary and presented to President Truman without further comment."[27]

The results of such activities were exactly what the intelligence community—and the military—wanted. Truman ceased cutting the military budget; increased spending for weapons research, military equipment, aircraft and the space program; ordered an increase in the development and construction of nuclear weapons; and most importantly to the young CIA, began pumping millions of dollars into the "black" budget for covert operations. In the ten years that followed the war, the CIA consumed over $200 million dollars of funds that did not have to be accounted for.

According to Victor Marchetti, former chief analyst on Soviet military capabilities and author of *The CIA and the Cult of Intelligence*, "The agency loved Gehlen because he fed us what we wanted to hear. We used his stuff constantly, and we fed it to everybody else: the Pentagon; the White House; the newspapers. They loved it." Marchetti further explained, "Gehlen had to make his money by creating a threat that we were afraid of, so we would give him more money to tell us about it. In my opinion, the Gehlen organization provided nothing worthwhile for understanding or estimating Soviet military or political capabilities in Eastern Europe or anywhere else."

The final result of all these cloak-and-dagger exercises was a reputed Cold War that lasted for almost half a century, and cost American taxpayers alone over $8 *trillion dollars*.

Peacetime intelligence gathering had become big business—profitable to not only the growing intelligence organizations, but to the defense industry and the investors who financed both it and the government.

Chapter 6

Edgewood Arsenal

While the American public was focusing on the space race and the feats of the NASA scientists, other experiments were underway that were hidden from all but those within a very select group. At two locations in Maryland, Edgewood Arsenal and Camp Detrick, clandestine research teams had been formed to explore the data coming back from Japan and Germany concerning chemical and biological warfare. Material provided by Ishii's Unit 731 personnel, who were busily compiling documents detailing their human experiments with BW, was arriving at Detrick. Data and chemicals found in Germany, along with the Paperclip scientists and technicians involved with the original experiments, were now in place at Edgewood Arsenal. At both locations, programs were quickly implemented to continue development of both biological and chemical weapons using this newly acquired knowledge and the talents of the Germans.

Edgewood Arsenal was the most secret military base in the continental United States. It is located in a secluded area of the Maryland woods, twenty miles northeast of Baltimore. Unlike the open military bases that are accessible to the public, Edgewood is surrounded by security fences, sensors and armed guards. What goes on behind the fences and walls is classified at the highest levels.

Edgewood is the Army's center for developing and testing chemical warfare agents. Everything from poison gasses to deadly liquids are developed there. The experiments began in 1922 when the Medical

Research Division was created by the Chemical Warfare Service. The mission at that time was to work on defenses against chemical agents, especially the poison gasses developed by Germany in World War I. But defenses cannot be created until one understands the weapons. Edgewood quickly moved into the research and development of its own chemical weapons. In the early days, most of the experimentation concerned mustard gas, phosgene gas, and several other derivatives and combinations of poison gasses. But by the 1950s, Edgewood had progressed beyond poison gasses. The German Sarin and Tabun provided excellent nerve agents, and the earlier blister agents developed around mustard gas, and the choking agents, developed around phosgene and other chemicals, created a sufficient weapons inventory for any future war. Though more experiments would be conducted concerning riot control (choking) agents and various dioxons, Edgewood, in 1950, began exploring new horizons.

With the two German nerve gasses satisfactorily filling the requirement for future chemical weapons, both the military and the CIA shifted Edgewood's doctors and chemists attention to a new area of interest. Mind control.

To understand the mentality at the time, one must realize that the old wartime intelligence agencies had undergone massive transformations and reorganizations. The Office of Strategic Services, or OSS, which was originally created by Franklin Roosevelt, had grown into a huge paramilitary organization that employed both spies and soldiers. The OSS was active in all theaters of the war and utilized people of both American and local nationality in the makeup of operational teams. By the end of the war, OSS head William J. "Wild Bill" Donovan had convinced Harry Truman of the need of a peace time counterpart to the OSS. Truman agreed, and in an effort to organize the myriad of intelligence organizations into a manageable entity, and create a central organization that would be responsible for collecting the intelligence from the various military service intelligence organizations, created the Central Intelligence Group (CIG).

When the OSS was disbanded in 1946, many of its duties and personnel were transferred to the State and War Departments. Other offices within the OSS simply ceased to exist. And some organizations, left intact for the time being but unassigned, seemed to drift in the backwaters of Washington like forgotten step-children. It was at this time that Navy Secretary James Forrestal decided that this state of affairs was counterproductive to the national defense. He retained New York lawyer Ferdinand Eberstadt to study the situation, compile a report that would define U.S. requirements in the field of intelligence, and submit it for review. Eberstadt concluded that the country needed an organization that could operate both in war and peace, able to wage either as required.

The CIG, created by Presidential order in 1946, came under the watchful eye of a four-man council made up of the secretaries of War, Navy and State and one representative of the President. The group, known as the National Intelligence Agency, became the link between the cloak-and-dagger set and the President.

The first director of the CIG was Admiral Sidney Souers. But Souers was not enthusiastic about the job and resigned within six months. He was replaced by the flamboyant Lieutenant General Hoyt Vandenberg, nephew of Senator Arthur Vandenberg and a war hero in his own right. Under Vandenberg, the CIG quickly grew in strength to over 300 men and women. Then in August, 1946, Vandenberg succeeded in gaining control of the former OSS Strategic Services Unit, the espionage and secret intelligence organization that had provided both commandos and spies. With this acquisition, the CIG grew to over 1300 personnel—600 of which were overseas.

Vandenberg went for more assets. He succeeded in pulling in the Office of Operations, which was responsible for collecting information from American volunteers overseas; the Foreign Broadcast Information Service, which provided an excellent means of disseminating ideology overseas; and had managed to establish a liaison with the State Department's code breaking office which later became the National Security Agency. By then, the CIG had grown to 2,000.

On September 18th, 1947, in an effort to further consolidate the fragmented intelligence machine, Truman signed the National Security Act of 1947. NSA 1947 gave birth to a new organization, built chiefly from the CIG, known as the Central Intelligence Agency. The act also established a governing body to replace the NIA known as the National Security Council (NSC). The NSC, chaired by the President, would be the direct line of communication between the White House and the CIA. To head the new CIA, Truman appointed Admiral Roscoe

Hillenkoetter as its first director. Hillenkoetter, who had worked for Naval Intelligence in the Pacific, knew the value of both intelligence and secrecy and quickly set about creating an organization divided by departments, offices and compartments. As the Agency grew, so did its power. And the personnel who had served in the OSS and Military Intelligence during the war knew exactly how to use that power.

Truman, ever mindful of how power can corrupt, warned "this country wants no Gestapo under any guise." At the same time, he realized that unless the United States had an effective intelligence gathering network, the country might take back seat during the Cold War—and if the war turned hot, he didn't want another Pearl Harbor. The President could only hope that the CIA would do its job well—and not go beyond control. He had no idea what had transpired behind the scenes in the intelligence offices in the two years following World War II.

The Cold War led to an expansion of intelligence and asset gathering. Operation Paperclip, unknown to the White House, was still underway. It had supposedly been deactivated in 1948, but instead had merely gone underground. It would continue until 1973 before finally being discovered and disbanded.

In addition to Paperclip, a new JIOA project, which removed many of the restraints on Paperclip, was instituted. This new operation, codenamed National Interest, was designed to bring individuals into the U.S. that ranged from convicted Nazi war criminals to East Europeans of dubious backgrounds that the CIA considered of value. The only requirement to be met was that the acquisition was in the national interest.

There were two classes of acquisitions. The first and most visible were the Germans and Austrians who were of value to defense contractors, universities and private companies. The second, extremely secret, class concerned intelligence resources. Former spies, saboteurs and certain people having specific expertise in areas of value to the CIA were given safe haven in exchange for their services. These individuals were generally assigned to the super-secret Office of Policy and Coordination, otherwise known as the Office of Dirty Tricks.

In 1949, an act was passed to legally permit the CIA to import as many as 100 people per year "without regard to their inadmissibility under the immigration or any other laws." The only requirement was that the JIOA Governing Committee approve of the selections. Indeed a very convenient arrangement.

While the United States was reorganizing its intelligence capabilities, the Soviet Union was doing the same. In 1946, Moscow renamed all commissariats "ministries." The NKVD *(Narodnyi Komissariat Vnutrennikh Del*—People's Commisariat of Internal Affairs) became the Ministry of Internal Affairs *(Ministerstvo Vnutrennikh Del)*, and the NKGB *(Narodnyi Kommissariat Gosudarstvennoi Besonasnosti*—People's Commissariat of State Security) became the Ministry of State Security (MGB). Each had grown extremely strong, and despite power struggles, had become a threat to American interests both at home and abroad.

In an operation quite similar to Paperclip, the MVD managed to locate and round up over 6,000 German scientists and technicians from the Russian-occupied zone in Germany and forcibly move both them and their families to the Soviet Union. It was these scientists that brought the USSR into the space age, developed the MiG fighter planes, and designed the modern Russian tanks and artillery pieces.

And some of the scientists—medical doctors and psychologists—gave the Soviets another weapon: mind control.

By the time the United States became embroiled in the Korean War, the Russians and Chinese had developed various methods of psychological influence which became popularly dubbed "brainwashing." American prisoners of war returned from Asia describing various methods of brain twisting and thought control attempted by the communists. Running the gamut from mandatory classes in "proper thinking" to physical torture, and from sleep deprivation to chemical injection, the North Koreans, Communist Chinese and Russian advisors attempted to gain the ability to dictate not only the mental thought processes, but the physical actions of the subjects. The fear of such attempts was capitalized upon in the novel *The Manchurian Candidate*. In that story, an American POW had been turned into a time bomb—an assassin waiting unwittingly for a special mental trigger to be pressed by a pre-programmed stimuli. In this instance, it was a particular playing card. Upon seeing the card, the man went into a zombie-like state and followed orders without question. Including the command to commit murder.

The Soviets were not the only government interested in mind control. A CIA memo from the chief of medical staff dated January 1952 stated:

"...there is ample evidence in the reports of innumerable interrogations that the communists were utilizing drugs, physical duress, electric shock and possibly hypnosis against their enemies. We are forced by mounting evidence to assume a more aggressive role in the development of these techniques, but must be cautious to maintain strict inviolable control because of the havoc that could be wrought by such techniques in unscrupulous hands."

The author of this report was absolutely correct in his final warning. For as Colin Blakemore said, "The dream of every leader, whether a tyrannical despot or a benign prophet, is to regulate the behavior of his people."

Chapter 7

In Search Of The Manchurian Kandidate

It was codenamed MK/ULTRA. Its purpose was to determine what methods could be used to control personality behavior in human beings. It was the largest program of its kind ever attempted by an American intelligence agency. It may have been the only program.

In 1953, the Central Intelligence Agency, in coordination with Edgewood Arsenal and its German scientists, initiated experiments on human test subjects that included hypnosis, electroshock stimulus, extrasensory perception, sensory deprivation, subliminal suggestion, lobotomies, and various drugs. Of the drugs, those that came under the greatest scrutiny were the same hallucinogens and stimulants that found their way onto the streets of America during late 1950s and early '60s. They included marijuana, heroin, cocaine, amylnitrate, barbiturates, psilocybin mushrooms, mescaline, amphetamines, PCP, and most of all, lysergic acid diethylamide—LSD.

Within the barred windowed rooms and isolation wards at Edgewood, American servicemen and civilian "volunteers" underwent terrifying experiments. And in most cases, the test subjects did not know what kind of a chamber of horrors they had entered.

Master Sergeant James Stanley, a Fort Knox soldier who had volunteered to participate in an experimental program to test chemical warfare suits, found himself assigned to a room in which the furniture was bolted to the floor. Shortly after arrival, a doctor wearing a white coat handed Stanley a glass of clear liquid and ordered him to drink. "It's nothing more than water," he said.

Stanley, suspecting nothing, drank the liquid. Minutes later he lost his wits. Colors on the wall began to drift and run together, his body felt as if it was spinning and tumbling through the air, and he quickly lost all control of his reasoning. Then he became wild. In a fit of rage he began tearing at the door, trying to escape. With superhuman strength, he managed to break through the door and run down the hall screaming. When the drug finally wore off and he returned to the real world, he found himself physically restrained to his bed. The glass of water had been laced with a potent, mind altering dose of LSD-25.

Air Force Sergeant Lloyd Gamble, who also unwittingly participated in LSD experimentation at Edgewood, suffered recurring "trips" and flashbacks for two years afterwards. He became the victim of acute depression and even attempted suicide. In trying to find out later what had happened to him, he discovered that there was no information about the project available. It was not until 1975 that he became aware that he had taken LSD when the testing program became public after Congress convened hearings on the issue.[28]

To further test LSD, the CIA set up clandestine operations and fronts in both the U.S. and Canada. One such front was the Society for the Investigation of Human Ecology, which was established at Cornell University medical school. This organization was empowered to give grants to institutions both in the U.S. and in Canada to experiment with LSD. The project itself was administered by the CIA's Technical Services staff. From 1953 to 1958, the various test centers under control of Technical Services administered LSD to over 1,000 servicemen and civilians. Though records regarding civilian tests no longer exist, having been deliberately destroyed by the CIA in 1975, evidence has surfaced which indicates more than 7,000 servicemen had become guinea pigs for LSD, PCP and mescaline. The majority of this number were tested at Edgewood, but the Army permitted other tests to be conducted at Fort Bragg, North Carolina; Fort McClellan, Alabama; Fort Benning, Georgia; and Dugway Proving Ground, Utah.

To entice soldiers and airmen to volunteer, they were told that they would be serving their country by helping with harmless experiments, and for their participation, they would receive an extra $1.50 per day in pay, a three day pass every weekend, and a letter of commendation. The actual cost to the government for the MK/ULTRA program and its various follow-on projects would top $110 million.

This money was doled out to such institutions as the University of Maryland, Johns Hopkins University, Louisiana State University, Indiana University, Baylor, New York University, Tulane, University of Colorado, University of Utah, University of Pennsylvania and the University of Washington. All of these academic institutions became contract researchers under the drug experimentation programs.

Dr. Ewen Cameron, the first president of the World Psychiatric Association, was an early experimenter on the program. Cameron, in his efforts to see if he could "wipe clean" the memories and minds of people by the use of drugs, experimented with Thorazine, Seconal, Nembutal, Veronal and Pheneregan. His subjects, under the influence of some of these drugs, sometimes slept for 30 day periods, during which time a recording would be played continually to see if a mind could be reprogrammed or influenced by subliminal suggestion.

For those experimenting with LSD, what becomes even more bizarre is the fact that the test subjects were given dosages that were sometimes more than 100 times what was required for one "trip." In an investigation by the U.S. Army's Inspector General, it was discovered that the subjects were given doses of 150 to 200 micrograms, with the largest dose reported as 5,250 micrograms!

Even more frightening is the discovery that the CIA, in an operation codenamed Midnight Climax, gave LSD to the civilian population. According to a book titled *Acid Dreams: The CIA, LSD and the Sixties Rebellion*, the CIA set up bordellos in CIA safehouses in San Francisco, then spiked the drinks of customers with the hallucinogen. Then, by means of hidden cameras, the customer's actions were recorded.

It appears the CIA took the civilian tests a step further. On November 16, 1953, the CIA ordered ten kilos of LSD from the Swiss manufacturer, Sandoz Laboratories. This amount would provide *30 million doses!* Fearing skullduggery, Sandoz refused to take the order. The CIA then approached the Eli Lilly Company and asked the research department to attempt to crack the formula for LSD. A short time later, the scientists reported back that they had the formula and assured the Agency that "LSD would be available in tonnage quantities." One ton of LSD would yield over *2.5 billion doses.*

The National Mental Health's Addiction Research Center in Lexington, Kentucky, also became involved in the CIA's LSD research. Under the direction of Dr. Harris Isabell, the staff tested not only LSD, but scopolamine, rivea seed and bufonteine. In one LSD test, Isabell reported that seven subjects were administered the drug and all encountered a trip that lasted 77 days. Isabell was convinced that LSD held the secret to mind control and convinced the CIA that further experiments should be carried out at the University of Illinois Medical School, the University of Oklahoma, Mount Sinai Hospital, and Columbia University.

Meanwhile, back at Fort Detrick (upgraded from Camp status), an incident occurred that almost blew the cover of MK/ULTRA. Someone put seventy micrograms of LSD into a glass of Cointreau liquor and gave it to an unsuspecting civilian researcher—Dr. Frank Olsen. After the drug took effect, Olsen became very lively and animated. But the euphoric state did not last long and he soon entered a state of extreme depression. Olsen requested to see a psychiatrist, but was forbidden to do so by the Agency representatives. Instead, he was sent to Dr. Harold Abramson, a Mount Sinai immunologist—not even a psychologist. Four days later Olsen, in a frantic state of despair, dove through the window of his Washington Satler Hotel room and crashed onto the pavement below. He died instantly.

Though the police were summoned, agents forbade any type of investigation or autopsy. Olsen's family did not discover what had really happened until 1975 when the Rockefeller Committee revealed the actual circumstances surrounding Olsen's death.

Though ancillary and follow-on projects continued until 1975, MK/ULTRA ended officially in 1963. But during the MK/ULTRA years, according to a former CIA contract employee, the Agency set up a lab for underground chemists in the San Francisco Bay area in the early 1960s, and in 1967, released the formula for STP to the scientific community. STP, a chemical compound more powerful than LSD, became available on the streets of American within weeks of its release.

Linda Hunt, author of *Secret Agenda*, summed up MK/ULTRA and its Edgewood headquarters in these words: "In short, experiments on our own soldiers at Edgewood mirrored the horror stories that had unfolded in the dock of Nuremberg...Thousands of American soldiers, seven thousand of them between 1955 and 1975 alone, were used as unwitting guinea pigs in the tests. They were gassed, maced, and drugged in the search for the ultimate mind-control weapon."

The question that must be asked is: Did they find it?

According to some researchers, they did. Some theorists believe that selected field operatives and contract agents were programmed by the CIA to accomplish certain dangerous, possibly suicidal, objectives. The bizarre behavior of Lee Harvey Oswald, the assassination attempt on President Gerald Ford by Charles Manson family member Lynette "Squeaky" Fromme, the attempt on President Ronald Reagan by John Hinckley, the Jonestown, Guyana, mass suicide, and even David Koresh's control over his flock at Mount Carmel have been blamed on CIA mind control. Whether there is any substance to any of these claims is unknown. What is known, however, is the ability to control people by the combined use of drugs and psychological persuasion. An example of just this is the Sharon Tate and the LaBianca murders conducted by Charles Manson's "family."

Manson, a dedicated fan of the Beatles and amateur Acid Rock musician, saw hidden meanings in what many say are concealed messages in music. One example is a John Lennon song, wherein the title is said to be a coded reference to the drug—Lucy in the Sky with Diamonds. Lennon later wrote: "We must always remember to thank the CIA and the army for LSD. That's what people forget...They invented LSD to control people and what they did give us was freedom." Sixties acid guru Timothy Leary added: "The LSD movement was started by the CIA. I wouldn't be here now without the foresight of the CIA scientists." And finally, Allen Ginsberg questioned: "Am I the product of one of the CIA's lamentable, ill advised, or triumphantly successful experiments in mind control? [Has the CIA] by conscious plan or inadvertent Pandora's Box, let loose the whole LSD fad on the U.S. and the world?" By the evidence that is slowly surfacing through the efforts of former servicemen-experimentees and veterans groups, it appears that is exactly what happened.

Chapter 8

Operation Monarch and the Finders Case

On October 7th, 1995, I received a strange telephone call. The caller, a source with deep connections inside certain government agencies, asked only one question: Was I near the fax machine?

Three minutes later a series of pages began to arrive that would add a new chapter to my MK/ULTRA mind control research. A chapter that would expose an operation so bizarre that without the documentation that arrived, would be impossible to believe.

The cover sheet contained this lead-in:

"RE: The FINDERS File

Attached are a series of reports that have been leaked from a known and confirmed source inside Treasury. These documents are extremely disturbing—and explain a lot. Read every page starting at page one. Do NOT skip ahead, but study and remember every paragraph. The reason will become clear in the end. These documents are copies of the actual reports, complete with names, phone numbers, and letterhead. It has been checked out and is confirmed to be genuine. We believe this case is part of MK/SEARCH and MK/MONARCH. Both projects are follow-on sub-projects to the original MK/ULTRA. These reports will provide another piece of the international child kidnapping, pornography and satanic ritual abuse cases reported in Europe, Nebraska, and California. Use extreme caution who you show these reports to."

As I read each page of the reports, the significance of these documents began to come to light. What appeared to be a routine local child abuse case ended up being much, much more.

The case began in Tallahassee, Florida, on Thursday, February 5th, 1987, when the Tallahassee police department was notified by a concerned citizen that there appeared to be a case of child neglect or abuse occurring in a park in Tallahassee. The police responded to investigate, and what they found during their enquiry led them to call in a special unit of U.S. Customs which dealt with tracking and exposing international child pornography and white slavery cases.

The U.S. Customs reports are reproduced here in their entirety. Notations in brackets [ ] denote comments/explanations by interpreter/transcriber and are not part of the original report.

The Reports:

DEPARTMENT OF THE TREASURY
UNITED STATES CUSTOMS SERVICE
REPORT OF INVESTIGATION

Subject: "FINDERS"
Date of Report: 021287

This office was contacted by the Tallahassee Police Department (TPD) on February 5, 1987, who requested assistance in attempting to identify two adult males and six minor children, all taken into custody the previous day. The men, arrested and charged with multiple counts of child abuse, were being very evasive with police in the questions being asked of them pursuant the children and their condition.

This agent contacted SS/A Bob Harrold, RAC/Reston, Virginia, and requested telephone numbers and names of police persons in area police departments in an attempt to follow-up on two leads which were a Virginia license number and that the children had commented about living in a Washington D.C. commune.

Subsequently, this office received a telephone call from the Washington D.C. Metropolitan Police Department (MPD) inquiring about the men and children. This office put the MPD and the TPD in contact with each other.

RAC/JX: SAC/TA: RAC/DC

[Signature]
Walter F. Kreitlow II
Special Agent

Fredric D. Maiduk
Resident Agent in Charge

Office of Enforcement
227 N. Bronough St.
Tallahassee, FL 32301

Details of Investigation

On Thursday, February 5, 1987, this office was contacted via telephone by Sergeant JoAnn VanMETER of the Tallahassee Police Department, Juvenile Division. Sgt. VanMETER requested assistance in identifying two adult males and six minor children ages 7 years to 2 years.

The adult males were tentatively identified by TPD as Michael HOULIHAN and Douglas AMMERMAN, both of Washington D.C., who were arrested the previous day on charges of child abuse.

The police had received an anonymous telephone call relative two well-dressed white men wearing suits and ties in Myers Park, (Tallahassee), apparently watching six dirty and unkempt children in the playground area. HOULIHAN and AMMERMAN were near a 1980 blue Dodge van bearing Virginia license number XHW-557, the inside of which was later described as foul-smelling, filled with maps, books, letters, with a mattress situated to the rear of the van which appeared as if it were used as a bed, and the overall appearance of the van gave the impression that all eight persons were living in it.

The children were covered with insect bites, were very dirty, most of the children were not wearing underwear and all the children had not been bathed in many days.

The men were arrested and charged with multiple counts of child abuse and lodged in the Leon County Jail. Once in custody, the men were somewhat evasive in their answers to the police regarding the children and stated only that they both were the children's teachers and that all were enroute to Mexico to establish a school for brilliant children.

The children tentatively were identified as Mary HOULIHAN, white female age 7; Max LIVINGSTON, white male, age 6; Benjamin FRANKLIN, white male age 4; HoneyBee EVANS, white female, age 3; B.B. [Transcribers notes: possibly "BB" initials only, or "baby boy—name unknown"] white male, age 2; and John Paul HOULIHAN, white male, age 2. The children initially indicated that they lived in tents in a commune in the Washington D.C. area, and were going to Mexico to go to a school for smart kids.

This office contacted the Office of the RAC/DC and spoke with SS/A Bob Harrold. This agent requested telephone numbers and names of police persons in the area department that might be aware of said activities described by the children and to follow-up on the leads which were the Virginia license number and the check on the men's names with local law enforcement.

A short time later this office was contacted by Detective Jim Bradley of the Washington D.C. Metropolitan Police Department. Bradley indicated that the case here in Tallahassee appeared to be strongly related to a case he was currently working in the Washington, D.C. area.

He stated that the actions of the two men in custody in Tallahassee relative the children just might give his case enough probable cause to obtain search warrants to search the premises occupied by a cult group called FINDERS.

This agent directed Bradley to telephone TPD and discuss with police directly any activities forthcoming relative the instant case. At this time it was determined that there was no Customs violations found to exist and therefore this case is being closed pending receipt of additional information.

[This report ends with an NCIC (National Crime Information Center) report on the two adult male suspects. All enquiries came back "negative." The two individuals were not known, or at least had no criminal record in the national system]. The next report followed:

NEED TO FILE

To: Resident Agent in Charge   [whited out]   Date: 02/07/87

From: Special Agent [whited out—but signed Martinez]
Subject: Customs cooperation/interest in Tallahassee/Washington
MPD child abuse investigation.

On Thursday, 2/5/87, the duty agent, SS/A Bob Harrold, received a call from SS/A Walter Krietlow, USCS [United States Customs Service], Tallahassee, Florida. SS/A Krietlow was seeking assistance in contacting an appropriate local police agency to coordinate a child abuse investigation with the Tallahassee Police Department. SS/A Krietlow further requested assistance in checking some names, addresses and a vehicle through the Customs Child Pornography Unit data base, and stated there was some suspicion of the subjects being involved in supplying children for the production of child pornography. Further, he was informed by the Tallahassee Police Department that the children may have been enroute to Mexico from the Washington, D.C. area. The possibility of Customs interest in the investigation due to possible violations of the Child Protection Act of 1964 [1984?], and the alleged nexus with the U.S./Mexican Border were discussed and agreed upon. SS/A Krietlow related the following background information. SA/A Krietlow was contacted by the Tallahassee Police Department for assistance in identifying six children and two adults taken into custody in the Tallahassee area. U.S. Customs was contacted because the police officers involved suspected the adults of being involved in child pornography and knew the Customs Service to have a network of child pornography investigators, and of the existence of the Child Pornography and Protection Unit. SS/A Krietlow stated the two adults were well dressed white males. They had custody of six white children (boys and girls), ages three to six years. The children were observed to be poorly dressed, bruised, dirty, and behaving like animals in a public park in Tallahassee. The police were notified by a concerned citizen and all eight persons were taken into custody. The subjects were living out of a white 1979 Dodge van, Virginia license no. XHW-557. Upon being taken into custody, the adult white males refused to cooperate, one of whom produced a "business" card with a name on one side and a statement on the other. The statement indicated that the bearer knew his constitutional rights to remain silent and that he intended to do so. Upon interviewing the children, the police officers found that they could not adequately identify themselves or their custodians. Further, they stated they were enroute to Mexico to attend a school for "smart kids." SS/A Krietlow was further advised the children were unaware of the function and purpose of telephones, televisions and toilets, and that the children had stated they were not allowed to live indoors and were only given food as a reward.

After receiving the request from Tallahassee, SS/A Harrold contacted me while I was on official business at Customs Headquarters. He requested that I conduct computer checks on the Customs Child Pornography Unit data base. The checks were to be conducted on the names, addresses, and a vehicle provided by SS/A Krietlow. After conducting the computer checks, I made direct contact with SS/A Krietlow to inform him that all the checks were negative. At that time I was informed by SS/A Krietlow that the Tallahassee police had discovered large quantities of records, to include computer discs and a U.S. passport in the van. From some of these records the police had obtained tentative identification of the two adults, and partial identification of the children. furthermore, the two Washington, D.C. addresses had been discovered through these documents, one of which was verified through the vehicle registration. I advised SS/A Krietlow I was leaving Headquarters and he would be receiving a response to the remainder of his request from SS/A Harrold. I then left as stated and proceeded to conduct other business in the district.

A short time later, as approximately 11:30 a.m., SS/A Harrold contacted me by radio and advised me that a Detective Jim Bradley of the Washington, D.C. Metropolitan Police Department (MPD) was interested in the information provided by SS/A Krietlow, was in contact with Tallahassee, and would very probably be conducting search warrants in the area later in the day. He also informed me that U.S. Customs was invited to participate due to the continuing possibility of violations of law enforced by the Customs Service. As I was already in Washington, I terminated my other business and proceeded to make contact with Detective Bradley, Intelligence Division, MPD.

Upon contacting Detective Bradley, I learned that he had initiated an investigation on the two addresses provided by the Tallahassee

Police Department during December of 1986. An informant had given him information regarding a cult, known as the "FINDERS" operating various businesses out of a warehouse located at 1307 4th St., N.E. [Note: poss. 1507], and were supposed to be housing children at 3918/3920 W. St., N.W. The information was specific in describing "blood rituals" and sexual orgies involving children, and as yet unsolved murder in which the Finders may be involved. With the information provided by the informant, Detective Bradley was able to match some of the children in Tallahassee with the names of children known or alleged to be in the custody of the Finders. Furthermore, Bradley was able to match the tentative ID of the adults with known members of the Finders. I stood by while Bradley consulted with AUSA [Assistant U.S. Attorney] Harry Benner and obtained search warrants for the two premises. I advised acting RAC SS/A Tim Halloran of my intention to accompany MPD on the execution of the warrants, received his permission, and was joined by SS/A Harrold. SS/A Harrold accompanied the team which went to 1307 4th St., and I went to 3918/20 W. St.

During the execution of the warrant at 3918/20 W. St., I was able to observe and access the entire building. I saw large quantities of children's clothing and toys. The clothing consisting of diapers and clothes in the toddler to pre-school range. No children were found on the premises. There were several subjects on the premises. Only one was deemed to be connected with the Finders. The rest were renting living space from this individual. He was identified as Stuart Miles SILVERSTONE, DOB/061941, U.S. Passport No. 010958991(?) [number on original report questionable due to copy blurring]. SILVERSTONE was located in a room equipped with several computers, printers, and numerous documents. Cursory examination of the documents revealed detailed instruction for obtaining children for unspecified purposes. The instructions included the impregnation of female members of the community known as Finders, purchasing children, trading, and kidnapping. There were telex messages using MCI account numbers between a computer terminal believed to be located in the same room, and others located across the country and in foreign locations. One such telex specifically ordered the purchase of two children in Hong Kong to be arranged through a contact in the Chinese Embassy there. Another telex expressed an interest in "bank

78

secrecy" situations. Other documents identified interests in high-tech transfers to the United Kingdom, numerous properties under the control of the Finders, a keen interest in terrorism, explosives, and the evasion of law enforcement. Also found in the "computer room" was a detailed summary of the events surrounding the arrest and taking into custody of the two adults and six children in Tallahassee, Florida, on the previous night. There were also a set of instructions which appeared to be broadcast via a computer network which advised participants to move "the children" and keep them moving through different jurisdictions, and instructions on how to avoid police attention.

One of the residents was identified as a Chinese National. Due to the telex discovered referencing the Chinese Embassy in Hong Kong, he was fully identified for future reference: WANG/Gengzin, DOB/091747, POB/Tianjin, People's Republic of China, passport No. 224993 [?], entered the U.S. on January 22, 1987, admitted until December 31, 1987. He is in the U.S. as a graduate student in the Anatomy Department of Georgetown University. His Visa was issued on November 10, 1986, in London, England, number 00143.

During the course of the evening, I contacted Sector 4 to initiate a TECS check on SILVERSTONE, and initiate an archives check on him for the last four years. I also contacted SS/A Halloran to keep him advised of the proceedings and asked for and received permission to contact SS/A John Sullivan of the CPPU to query some names through the CPPU data base. SS/A Halloran told me he would call Southeast Region Headquarters to keep them posted on the proceedings as well. I later contacted SS/A Sullivan for the stated purpose, and in the discussion that followed, I gave him some background on the purpose of the request. I advised him that the information was not for dissemination at Headquarters, that Region was being notified, and that Region would probably contact Headquarters later if deemed necessary. SS/A Sullivan assured me that the information would go no further until official notification was made by Region. No positive matches were obtained from the CPPU data base. I was later joined at the W Street address by SS/A Harrold. SS/A Harrold advised me that there were extremely large quantities of documents and computer equipment at the warehouse, and that MPD was posting officers inside the building there and sealing the building until morning, in which a second warrant for that premises would be obtained and executed. SS/A

Harrold also advised me that the news media had been notified and had been waiting for the execution of the warrant at the 4th Street address. Detective Bradley later stated that the MPD Public Information Officer had been contacted by a Tallahassee reporter. When it became apparent the PIO had no information on the search warrants, the reporter contacted local media representatives and a check of public records containing the affidavits for the search warrants. Detective Bradley surmised that someone on the Tallahassee Police Department was the original source of the information for the press. I advised SS/A Halloran of the involvement of the press, and he stated that he would, in turn, relay the information to Region. SS/A Harrold and I assisted in the transport of the evidence seized pursuant to the warrant and cleared MPD after the press left the area.

On Friday, 2/6/87, I met Detective Bradley at the warehouse on 4th Street., N.E. I duly advised my acting group supervisor, SS/A Don Bludworth. I was again granted unlimited access to the premises. I was able to observe numerous documents which described explicit sexual conduct between the members of the community known as Finders. I also saw a large collection of photographs of unidentified persons. Some of the photographs were nudes, believed to be of members of Finders. *There were numerous photos of children, some nude, at least one of which was a photo of a child "on display" and appearing to accent the child's genitals.* I was only able to examine a very small amount of the photos at this time. However, one of the officers presented me with a photo album for my review. *The album contained a series of photos of adults and children dressed in white sheets participating in a "blood ritual." The ritual centered around the execution of at least two goats. The photos portrayed the execution, disembowelment, skinning and dismemberment of the goats at the hands of the children. This included the removal of the testes of a male goat, the discovery of a female goat's "womb" and the "baby goats" inside the womb, and the presentation of a goats head to one of the children.*

Further inspection at the premises disclosed numerous files relating to activities of the organization in different parts of the world. Locations I observed are as follows: London, Germany, the Bahamas, Japan, Hong Kong, Malaysia, Africa, Costa Rica [other countries—unintelligible]…'Palestinian.' Other files were identified by member name or "project" name. The projects appearing to be operated for commercial purposes under front names for the Finders. [Note: typical covert tradecraft] *There was one file entitled "Pentagon Break-In"* and others which inferred to members operating in foreign countries. Not observed by me but related by an MPD officer, were intelligence files on private families not related to the Finders. The process undertaken appears to have been a systematic response to local newspaper advertisements for babysitters, tutors, etc. A member of the Finders would respond and gather as much information as possible about the habits, identity, occupation, etc., of the family. The use to which this information was to be put is still unknown. There is also a large amount of data collected on various child care organizations. [note: obvious intelligence gathered prior to child-stealing/kidnapping operations]

The warehouse contained a large library, two kitchens, a sauna, hot-tub, and a "video room." *The video room seemed to be set up as an Indoctrination Center. It also appeared that the organization had the capability to produce its own videos. There were what appeared to be training areas for children and what appeared to be an altar set up in a residential area of the warehouse. Many jars of urine and feces were located in this area.*

I should also mention that both premises were equipped with satellite dish antennas. [note: note described whether these antennas were for satellite TV reception or for directional communications]

I discussed the course of action to be taken by MPD with Detective Bradley. He stated he was only interested in making the child abuse case(s). I was assured that all of the evidence would be available to U.S. Customs in furtherance of any investigative/criminal action pursued. MPD personnel were to begin around the clock review and sorting of the evidence until completed. Customs will have access after this is accomplished. This will include several U.S. Passports discovered during the search.

Upon leaving the 4th Street premises, I encountered a news media representative and was asked the reason behind U.S. Customs involvement in the investigation. I advised the reporter that I could not discuss anything and referred her to the PAO/DC. I left immediately thereafter.

There is no further information available at this time. It should take three to five days for all the information to be sorted, reviewed, logged by the MPD. I will maintain contact with Detective Bradley until the evidence is again accessible.

Respectfully submitted,
[Signature]
Ramon J. Martinez
Special Agent, USCS

[END of Martinez Report]

[Follow-up report—Martinez/Roundtree]

DEPARTMENT OF THE TREASURY
UNITED STATES CUSTOMS SERVICE
REPORT OF INVESTIGATION

Sub: FINDERS
Report Date: 04/13/87   Date of Offense: 02/05/87

On Thursday, February 5, 1987, Senior Special Agent Harrold and I assisted the Washington, D.C. Metropolitan Police Department (MPD) with two search warrants involving the possible sexual exploitation of children. During the course of the search warrants, numerous documents were discovered which appeared to be concerned with international trafficking in children, high tech transfer to the United Kingdom, and international transfer of currency.

DETAILS OF INVESTIGATION

On March 31, 1987, I contacted Detective James Bradley of the Washington, D.C. Metropolitan Police Department (MPD). I was to meet with Detective Bradley to review the documents seized pursuant to two search warrants executed in February 1987. The meeting was to take place on April 2 or 3, 1987.

On April 2, 1987, I arrived at MPD at approximately 9:00 a.m. Detective Bradley was not available. I spoke to the third party who was willing to discuss the case with me on a strictly "off the record" basis.

I was advised that all the passport data had been turned over to the State Department for their investigation. The State Department in turn, advised MPD that all travel and use of the passports by the holders of the passports was within the law and no action would be taken. This included travel to Moscow [USSR], North Korea, and North Vietnam from the late 1950's to the mid 1970's. [Such travel was illegal in those years, and these dates would include the Korean and Vietnam wars, wherein hundreds of orphans were produced]

The individual further advised me of circumstances which indicated that *the investigation into the activity of the FINDERS had become a CIA internal matter.* The MPD report has been classified SECRET and was not available for review. I was advised that the FBI had withdrawn from the investigation several weeks prior and that the *FBI Foreign Counter Intelligence Division had directed MPD not to advise the FBI Washington Field Office of anything that had transpired.*

No further information will be available. Nor further action will be taken.

ACTION TO BE TAKEN BY LESD/TECS:
No action to be taken on the basis of this report.

End of report

A CIA internal matter? What could this mean? Was the CIA mixed up in some type of international satanic child abuse, pornography and extortion ring? It would appear so. But were there other connections aside from this particular group?

Further investigation began to produce answers. The Washington D.C. group had much in common with other groups located across the country. Two such groups, known to be only part of a massive network, can be examined as examples.

In 1992, attorney John DeCamp published a shocking book titled *The Franklin Cover-Up.* In it he details a massive case of child abuse,

Satanic ritual murder, drug trafficking, pedophilic extortion and international intrigue. The case centers around certain high-ranking personnel in the Franklin Community Credit Union in Omaha, Nebraska. According to DeCamp, federal investigators closed the credit union in 1988 for investigation after a Nebraska Senate investigating committee discovered over 100 children had been used in an "international child abuse ring" being run in part by Franklin's chief executive officer, Larry King (no relation to the TV talk show personality).

As the investigation began to expose involvement of several high-powered government agencies and figures, the media began an attack on the investigation and those conducting it. According to investigative journalist Anton Chaitkin, "The FBI, Nebraska officials, and news media attacked the legislative committee and its witnesses in an atmosphere of rising violence and intimidation. In the course of this terror, the committee's chief investigator, Gary Caradori, was killed when his airplane unexplainably disintegrated. Troy Boner's brother [one of the child-victims that agreed to testify] was found shot to death at Offut Air Force Base. Alisha Owen's brother [another victim/witness] was found hanged in jail."

One of the former child victims, now an adult witness, courted death when he came forward to explain to Mr. DeCamp and others what he had been forced to do. Paul Bonacci, in an affidavit dated October 28, 1993, stated: "The real activity I and Alisha [Owens] and on occasion Troy Boner...were engaged in was functioning as drug couriers and recruiters [of children] for Alan Baer and Larry King [adult group members]...They were buying and selling large quantities of cocaine into the mid-west and using us as 'mules' to obtain the goods from the various airports and get the drugs delivered back to Omaha. Other prominent and wealthy Omaha citizens were also involved in this...the sex activities we did...were just tools to blackmail or compromise or pay off some judge or businessman or policeman or politicians generally, here in Omaha...in Washington, or other places."

DeCamp's book placed the main players in the middle of "a national and international organized crime syndicate, engaged in pedophilia, pornography, satanism, drugs, and money-laundering." Because of the number of politicians and bureaucrats involved on the national level, one can only imagine the impact on national security.

Anton Chaitkin, in an article titled "Franklin Witnesses Implicate FBI and U.S. Elites in Torture and Murder of Children," wrote "[Certain figures linked to the Omaha case] and their associates in the intelligence community [in Washington] are said to have managed homosexual compromising operations to keep congressmen, judges, military officers, diplomats, and foreign leaders 'in line'."[29]

This operation sounds very like the Finders case. Could it be that the Finder's warehouse was the headquarters for several international cult-rings and that the Omaha Credit Union was simply a 'branch office'? Chaitkin reveals more:

"The Franklin Credit Union is widely suspected of being among the savings institutions used for money-laundering by the CIA and others for Iran-Contra adventures. This precisely defines where Omaha's Larry King showed up in Washington, D.C.—in the bizarre homosexual wing of the Republican Party, which managed financing and public relations for the Iran-Contra guns-for-drugs trading games."

Bonacci and the other children were eventually diagnosed as suffering from Multiple Personality Disorder (MPD), which is the result of mental programming from a very young age. According to psychiatrists, people with MPD often have been forced to participate in acts of sexual degradation, sleep deprivation, torture, and other mind control programming methods to "crack" the mind. According to Bonacci, he was plunged into what he describes as a Satanic worship cult that has close ties with the intelligence services and certain deep-cover factions of the military. Bonacci told investigators that the cult-ring was centered at Offutt Air Force Base outside Omaha, the headquarters for the Strategic Air Command before its dismantlement and closure by the Clinton Administration. There, he was sexually victimized from the age of three years old on. The ring "trained" him by "tortures, heavy drugging, and sexual degradation, while instructing him in military arts including assassination."[30]

Chaitkin provides more damning information regarding CIA and military involvement in a covert action operation—and the codename for the operation—in his article. "Psychiatrists who have treated a growing number of MPD cases, victims of Satanic ritual abuse," writes Chaitkin, "report an alarming pattern of findings in many of their child patients. There is a structure to the personalities, conforming to what is evidently a deliberate breaking and reshaping of the mind. This phenomenon was identified to Paul Bonacci by his tormenters, and to other victims and witnesses, as the 'Monarch' project. At Offutt Airbase, Paul was told that what he and other children were being subjected to was an aid of national security."

Again, a criminal enterprise is cloaked in secrecy by the old tried and true cover story of "national security."

As we have seen in previous chapters, drugs, sensory deprivation, hypnosis, torture, and other brainwashing techniques on unsuspecting U.S. citizens are an admitted practice of not only the CIA, but of certain military and private institutions as well. Beginning in the 1950s, this unholy triumvirate worked together in operations carrying such innocent sounding names as MK/ULTRA, MK/SEARCH, Artichoke, Bluebird, and Monarch. In the Monarch project, the victims were small children that were re-programmed to lie, steal, spy, sabotage, kill and even commit suicide.

Chaitkin continues: "Professionals probing the child victims of MONARCH say there are clearly two responsible elements at work: the government/military, and cooperating Satanic (or more exactly pagan) cults. *These are multi-generation groups, where parents donate their own children, who are proudly called 'bloodline' or simply 'blood' cultists, to be smashed with drugs and electric shock, and shaped. Other children are kidnapped and sold into this hell, or are brought in gradually through day care situations."*

Bonacci told investigators of one trip to California, allegedly to a secret campground meeting place of the elite known as "Bohemian Grove." There he witnessed a Satanic ritual killing. "Paul was taken...to a wooded area in California, identified...as the Bohemian Grove. There Paul and another boy were forced to do sex acts with men, and to consume parts of a child whom they watched being murdered by the cultists. The body was to be disposed of by 'the men with the hoods.' A snuff pornography film was made of these events; it was directed by a man the party had picked up in Las Vegas whom Paul identified as 'Hunter Thompson'—the same name as a well-known sleaze culture figure."

During the investigation of the Omaha case, several events using the "Monarch children" were uncovered:

* Picking up cash in exchange for drugs in various Tennessee locations often involving country music personalities.

* Trips on behalf of NAMBLA, the North American Man-Boy Love Association, a pedophile group now given semi-official status by the United Nations. It is believed that NAMBLA has direct contact with European countries via computers that were tied in with the Finders group headquarters in Washington, D.C.

* Travel to Hawaii, New York, and Washington D.C. to compromise public figures by performing homosexual pedophile sex with them.[31]

* Travel to Bohemian Grove where a Satanic ritual murder was witnessed by Bonacci and fellow child-victim Mark Johnson of Denver, Colorado.

* Travel to Mexico for the transportation of drugs, guns and children.

* Survival skills training under a Captain "Foster" at Fort Riley, Kansas, and intelligence training under a Lieutenant "Bannister" at Fort Bragg, North Carolina. A Colonel "Livik" at Fort Defiance, Virginia, is said to have run a "military school" for Monarch inductees.

* Travel to Dresden, East Germany, where weapons were inspected for future use. There, the Monarch personnel were frequently neo-Nazis. It has been reported that this compartmentalized operation is closely tied to the Aryan Nation and other White Supremicist cults. (This fact begs an answer to the question "was Timothy McVeigh, the alleged Oklahoma City bomber, a Monarch operative?")

One name that keeps surfacing as one researches the Monarch project and ancillary operations is that of Lieutenant Colonel Michael Aquino. Lt.Col. Aquino, an Army intelligence officer, is also the high priest of the Temple of Set, a Satanic cult network that claims members from coast to coast. The Temple of Set was established by Aquino in San Francisco after he and his wife broke off from Anton LaVey's Church of Satan in 1975. Aquino's god Set is an ancient Egyptian destroyer-god, who is recognized as a historical form of Satan.

Aquino, who has written extensively on such topics as mind control, and the use of extra low frequency (ELF) electromagnetic force beam weapons in what he calls "MindWar," has been investigated for child molestation and the alleged use of children in Satanic rituals. Investigators in the Omaha case have written that Aquino was at one time a West European adviser to the U.S. Joint Chiefs of Staff, and is tied in with the Monarch project. According to the researchers, he has made trips to Germany where he once obtained use of a medieval castle which was once used by Heinrich Himmler, Hitler's concentration camp master, where Aquino allegedly conducted a black mass.

Paul Bonacci and other child victims have given evidence that Aquino played a central role in Monarch, and "was long time leader of an Army psychological warfare section which drew on his 'expertise' and personal practices in brainwashing from Satanism, nazism, homosexual pedophilia and murder."[32] Aquino vehemently denies this.

It should be mentioned at this point that there is another series of circumstances that appear to connect government mind control programs. First, the CIA based much of its MK/ULTRA program in the metropolis of San Francisco during the late 1950s and 60s. It was in San Francisco that the CIA set up a bordello to experiment on unsuspecting "Johns" with LSD-laced drinks. It was also in San Francisco that Dr. Timothy Leary, allegedly a CIA contract agent, pioneered the LSD-influenced drug revolution. And it was in San Francisco that Jim Jones organized his "People's Temple," prior to its move to Jonestown, Guyana. The People's Temple now appears to have been a massive government mind control experiment in which followers were turned into obedient slaves by means of drugs, mass hypnosis and a charismatic leader. When Congressman Leo Ryan attempted to investigate the allegations by family members, he was ambushed and killed at the Jonestown air strip by Jones' armed security guards.[33]

Finally, it was in San Francisco that Anton LaVey founded the Church of Satan and Michael Aquino started his Temple of Set. The evidence tends to point to more than simple coincidence. In fact, military sources have leaked that many of these mind control projects were directed out of the Presidio army base in San Francisco. The base has now been closed and turned over to the Gorbachev Foundation, wherein plans are made and initiated for further U.S. base closings, U.S. military scale downs, and conversion to global government. It appears that if Satan had a branch office, it would be in San Francisco.

But the mind control projects were not initiated in the United States or Russia or China. When one follows the players and projects back through history it can be traced directly to experiments conducted by Nazi scientists in World War II concentration camps. Certain projects conducted by German mind control engineers migrated to both the U.S. and Russia after World War II. The experiments conducted in the camps went beyond simple torture-for-compliance. The Germans brainwashed people, mostly adolescents, for military and covert purposes. The objectives were to see if a scientific environment with rigid parameters could produce such controllable personalities as fearless soldiers, robot factory workers, manual labor slaves, and programmed assassins.

At the end of the war many of these "scientists" were illegally brought into the United States under Projects Paperclip and National Interest. One such case involved a teenaged concentration camp inmate named Greenbaum, who went beyond being programmed as a subservient personality and actually progressed to the point of being himself a programmer. When he came to the United States he changed his name to "Dr. Green," and continued experimentation on others under U.S. government sponsorship. Interestingly, he found that he was most successful when he incorporated basic mind control methods with belief systems such as Theosophy and Cabalism. By removing fears of individual accountability to a higher power (such as God's eventual judgement of the individual), barriers were broken down that would permit programming of subjects to become killers who killed on command and showed no emotion or remorse. This type of programming might explain such bizarre recent events as the Texas Tower sniper, the Stockton Schoolyard Massacre, and the Luby's Cafeteria mass murder.[34]

America is not alone in its strange proliferation of insane lone gunmen. In Great Britain, several incidents have occured since World War II that have convinced the British population that guns are dangerous, evil and should not be left in the hands of the people. Among these were the Dunblane, Scotland, attack on an elementary school by a deranged gunman which resulted in the most massive anti-gun drive in the history of the British government.

Along this vein, one must consider the fact that the Tavistock Institute in England has been linked to post-war propaganda and continuing psychological warfare activities, and reportedly reaped its share of former Nazi mind control scientists from the fallen Reich. This might explain such events as Dunblane and a similar event in an English village several years before, both of which created a "gun ban" furor in the British press whenever gun-ban sentiments appeared to lag. Were the perpetrators something more than simply insane gunmen? It cannot be ruled out that instead they were actually British versions of the Manchurian Candidate.

Where is all of this going? What other purposes could government control of the population serve? Further research along this line provides us with clues that are very unsettling.

First, it takes little imagination to realize the advantages a corrupt government would have if it could disarm its population, then control its will. But to do so, especially in America, would require a massive effort to convince the masses to give up their weapons for "their own good." The only way this can happen is to repeatedly, using the media, demonstrate that "guns are bad. Guns cause crime. Guns and drugs are related. Guns are dangerous to children. Psychos get guns and kill large numbers of people/children," etc. Such ideas are projected repeatedly by means of a sympathetic controlled media, and by rigged government "studies" conducted by panels, commissions and off-shoot agencies such as the Center for Disease Control and private-agenda groups. Such has been the case since 1968 when the first "gun control" measures were put in place.

Second, certain segments of the population must be programmed to be robotic drones, incapable or unwilling to think on their own. In this scenario, the "individual" is the enemy of the state. Individual thinking and choice are not conducive to "peace and progress" and not permitted. Only by being part of "The Team," can the individual (follower) accomplish objectives or "outcomes." Of course, these "objectives and outcomes" are directed by the bureaucracy. This phase of population training is currently being accomplished by the public school system with such programs as "outcomes based education," and the introduction of New Ageism into the classroom. One has to remember that Adolf Hitler pioneered a similar tactic with his *Hitlerjugend* and state-sponsored school system. To quote the *Fuhrer*, "When an opponent declares: 'I will not come over to your side,' I calmly say 'your child belongs to me already. Who are you? You will pass on. Your descendants, however, now stand in the new camp. In a short time they will know nothing else but this new community.'"

Third, populations must be convinced to "trust the government out of fear." This is accomplished by media programming the masses to believe that government has their best interest at heart, would never do anything to harm the country, and at the same time fear what would happen to them as individuals should they criticize or protest government activities. Many Americans refuse to believe that anyone within the U.S. government would participate in such illegal activities as international drug running, money laundering, murder, kidnapping, human experimentation on unwitting subjects, corrupting the court system, or any number of other crimes that have already been documented—including mind control. No matter the evidence, the majority of people have been programmed to turn a blind eye to something they do not want to see or believe. This is called the "Three Monkeys Syndrome"—hear no evil, see no evil, speak [of] no evil. To ignore it is to make it go away.

To a great degree, Operations Artichoke, Bluebird, MK/ULTRA, MK/SEARCH and Monarch appear to be working.

Chapter 9

From Auschwitz To Edgewood

While the MK/ULTRA scientists at Edgewood were just beginning to explore the possibilities of the psychochemicals and other facets of mind control, their former I.G. Farben colleagues were putting the finishing touches on a much deadlier project. Poison gas.

One of the first discoveries made in the smoking rubble of Germany by the Paperclip scouting teams was the fact that the chemists of the German chemical conglomerate had discovered a new strain of deadly nerve gases against which the Allies had no defense. In their secret laboratories, located at such places as the University of Wuerzburg's Chemical Warfare Laboratory, the Luftwaffe's Technical Research Institute at Berlin, and the I.G. Farben factory at Dyhernfurth, in Breslau, the Nazi chemists developed two gases that would set the military standard for the next half century.

The two agents, Tabun and Sarin, were the most deadly nerve gases ever encountered by both the U.S. military and the Soviet forces. The standard issue gas masks of both nations were ineffective in filtering the agents and neither country had antidotes to counter the lethal effects. The discovery of this invincible weapon, which the high command feared would be put into the warheads of V-2 rockets, became one of the most sensitive and important issues encountered by the Allied high command. According to information received from intelligence sources, just one V-2 warhead could carry enough Tabun or Sarin to wipe out the entire population of London. This information, according to official history, was kept secret for two reasons: to avert public panic, and to keep the Russians from discovering that such a powerful weapon existed. In reality, it was kept hidden until American intelligence officers could seal secret deals with the I.G. Farben chemists.

Tabun had been invented in 1936 by Dr. Gerhard Schrader. It was so deadly that even a few drops could kill within minutes. Sarin, a derivative of Tabun, was almost five times as powerful. Both gases were commissioned by the Wehrmacht, and Otto Ambros, the senior director of I.G. Farben, had ordered a secret laboratory and massive manufacturing facility constructed at Dyhernfurth. Here, both gasses were developed and tested. Many of the tests were conducted on concentration camp prisoners, resulting in an unknown quantity of fatalities.

The tests confirmed the gases fatal efficacy, and within weeks of the conclusion of the test phase of Tabun, it was ordered into production under the codename "Trilon," the name of a common washing detergent.

It was at about this same time that the German army had suffered a horrendous defeat at Stalingrad. The German High Command, staggering from the reversal of events on the Eastern Front, was asked by Hitler if there was a sufficient amount of Tabun or Sarin to be used effectively on the Red Army. Ambros, who was summoned to the Reichstag to respond to the question, explained that he suspected that the Allies might also possess Tabun or a similar compound. The chemical structures of the gases had been discussed before the war in several international scientific journals, and he would be amazed if the Allied defense industry had not noted the information. And if they did, the combined Allied production capability could easily outstrip the strained German industry.

Hitler, who was deathly afraid of chemical warfare ever since his service in the First World War, agreed. If the Germans used the gas against the Russians, then it was only reasonable to assume the Allies might counter with their own versions. It was best to leave the dragon in its cave.

What Hitler did not know was that both American and British intelligence had underestimated the German chemical warfare resources and neither had the stockpiles of chemical weapons or the production capability the Germans feared. British MI-10, in a 1941 assessment of the Nazi chemical threat, reported that "It appears that the Germans have no new gas of surprising effect." And the Americans, relying on what information trickled out of occupied Europe (and what little British SOE provided), estimated that the Germans only possessed the same type of blister-agent mustard gas they had used in the First World War.

It was not until 1943 that Allied intelligence discovered anything new in Nazi interest in chemical warfare. The hint, a coded message regarding the issue of a new type of gas mask to the Wehrmacht, alerted the message intercept officers and the OSS that something was afoot. This was followed by information received from captured prisoners concerning a new gas that was supposed to be odorless, colorless, and quite deadly. But other than these few reports, little else trickled back to London regarding chemical warfare. Without more evidence, concern subsided. The Allied high command felt that the likelihood of an all-out chemical assault would not occur, even if the Germans had sufficient quantities.

They were wrong. By January of 1945, when Hitler began to feel the jaws of the Allied vice closing in, massive stores of Tabun were ordered removed from Dyhernfurth and transported into the Bavarian Last Redoubt for use as a last resort to save the Reich. But before any of the chemical weapons could be employed, the war ended.

Lieutenant Colonel Paul Tarr, the intelligence chief for the Chemical Warfare Service, knew about the new, deadly German gases. He even knew approximately where they had been produced and who had been involved in their production. The secret deals made by certain highly placed individuals on both the American and German sides had taken care of that. Even Military Intelligence, which had remained ignorant of the facts concerning the nerve gas program, did not know of this higher echelon of communications.

Leading a team of fifty chemical warfare experts, Tarr raced across France toward his objectives: the I.G. Farben factories in the Ruhr valley. He reached his destination just as the German army collapsed. But what he found was disheartening. The Ludwigshafen nerve gas facility had been almost completely destroyed. No one remained to be captured and the condition of the equipment appeared to be almost worthless. But Tarr did not give up. Instead of moving on, he ordered his men to round up every German technician and factory worker that could be found and bring them in for interrogation. Through these efforts, Tarr and his staff managed to intimidate the frightened prisoners sufficiently enough to have them lead the Americans to the homes and hiding places of the scientists. One of the first captured was Gerhard Schrader.

Schrader proved more than willing to help the Americans. Anything to keep safe from the Russians. Within a day of capture Schrader provided the formulas of both Sarin and Tabun to Tarr, who quickly dispatched the valuable documents to the rear.

At the same time Tarr and his interpretors were questioning the German scientists, another team of investigators arrived on the scene. Only this group had not come to glean technical information. Their purpose was to gather evidence for the Nuremberg trials. Information and confessions from the I.G. Farben scientists and directors would help hang certain Nazis—and maybe even some of the personnel of Farben. One of the scientists they were looking for was Otto Ambros, the mastermind of the I.G. Farben factory at Auschwitz who was an integral part in the decision to use Zyklon B in the gas chambers. It was also at Auschwitz, and at Natzweiler, that the Tabun and Sarin gases were fatally tested on prisoners by Professor August Hirt and Dr. Karl Wimmer who had supervised the painful deaths, then conducted the morbid dissections on the still-warm bodies. But Ambros was not in the Ruhr. He had made his way to Gendorf in Bavaria, and was not found for several weeks.[35]

When he finally was located, it was not by the criminal hunters who desperately wished to drag him to Nuremberg to answer for his crimes, but by Tarr, who spirited him away to a safehouse in Heidelberg. Then, after hiding Ambros, Tarr flew to London, Paris, and back to Frankfurt, in a frantic attempt to negotiate for not only Ambros, but all Nazi chemical warfare scientists held by the military authorities. But before he could complete his mission, Ambros disappeared. He was not to surface again until he had been gainfully employed—and guaranteed protection—by the French. Ambros was one of the few Nazi scientists the French managed to steal away from the British and Americans.[36]

Ambros was eventually tried for his crimes, but was given only a token sentence. Then, before he could even finish the sentence, he was released by the High Commissioner of Germany, John J. McCloy—who later became president of the World Bank and served on the President's Commission on the Assassination of President Kennedy—the Warren Commission.

Ambros, who after being released traveled to America, was extremely fortunate in finding post-incarceration employment. He was immediately hired by W.R. Grace and Company, then by Dow Chemical. Many of his cohorts, similarly fortunate, had already been hired by American firms. And those who were not found a home at Edgewood.

The German scientists who arrived at Edgewood discovered that their assignment was to continue what they had been doing in Germany. They were to carry on with testing both Tabun and Sarin. According to the Edgewood chemical corps officers, the reason was two-fold: to learn how the gasses effected humans, and to develop defenses against the chemicals.

Tabun and Sarin were the most deadly chemical agents the American military had every encountered. If the Russians had captured the Dyhernfurth plant's scientists and records, as intelligence said they had, then developing protective clothing, gas masks and antidotes was essential. The only way to do this, according to the chemists, was to experiment on humans.

To determine how the chemical mixtures effected soldiers, hundreds of volunteers—who had no idea exactly what they were volunteering for—were selected and sworn to secrecy. Though the captured German documents dealing with the gases were scrutinized by American army chemists, including the Tabun human experiments performed at Auschwitz, it was not enough to satisfy the military. At first, the tests were performed on cats, dogs, rabbits and mice. But after the data proved insufficient, soldiers were locked into the Edgewood gas chamber with the animals. Each soldier was given a mask, told to go inside and sit down, then wait for the order to unmask. Different strengths of the gas were then administered as scientists watched though an air-tight window.

Don Bowen, who participated in the experiments, later related what it was like inside the sealed chamber along with several cages of test animals. "I waited five minutes and took off the mask. The plastic covers were ripped off the animals, and they went wild. They ran around the cages, whimpering and shrieking, and finally stumbled to the floors of their cages. My immediate response was not to breathe. When I finally did take a deep breath, the gas burned my nose, my lips and throat." The gas was carefully measured: enough to kill the animals, but not the man.

Other soldiers at Edgewood underwent mustard gas experiments. Mustard gas is a blister agent which causes blisters on any skin or organ it comes in contact with. The gas itself is actually a fog or mist of liquid droplets. Each droplet that lands on the skin, or is breathed into the lungs, burns through the outer layers of epidermis or lung or nasal tissue and creates open, painful running blisters. In the eyes, mustard gas causes blindness. In the lungs, provided the quantity is sufficient, it causes the lung tissue to rupture and bleed, creating a horrible burning sensation until the victim dies gasping from asphyxiation. In two instances, soldiers were exposed to mustard gas up to fourteen times before finally being hospitalized.

The gas experiments tapered off in 1949 when, at the direction of the Central Intelligence Agency, a new program was initiated. From inside the Iron Curtain, information was emerging that the Soviets were experimenting with mind control drugs. If this was so, and the Russians could control someone's mind through chemicals, then the danger was obvious. The masses could be controlled, enemy troop formations could be made combat ineffective, and certain people might even be able to be programmed to kill. The program, already discussed, was MK/ULTRA.

Chapter 10

Atomic Guinea Pigs

There is one last group of government guinea pigs that must be mentioned. As a whole, they are called The Atomic Veterans. They are the soldiers, sailors, Marines and airmen who both knowingly and unknowingly participated in the nuclear radiation experiments conducted between 1945 and 1962. According to the Disabled American Veterans organization, "somewhere in the neighborhood of 200,000 and 250,000 veterans were exposed to nuclear or ionizing radiation during their military service, most with no more protection than a rifle and a helmet."[37]

These experiments, conducted in remote desert locations and faraway Pacific island atolls, were performed to test the military's preparedness for war. If the U.S. were to become involved in a nuclear war, just how would blast effects and radiation contaminated battlefields effect combat troops and the crews of ships at sea? That was the question asked by the Pentagon war planners. It was answered by the scientists who had no qualms about using humans as test subjects.

To find the answers, U.S. infantrymen were transported to test areas during nuclear bomb detonations and purposefully exposed to the resultant radiation. One such place was Yucca Flat in Nevada where a 44-kiloton device was exploded during the "Smokey" tests. Then within three hours of the blast, some 1,000 G.I.s were marched to within varying distances of ground zero to see if their physical fighting ability would be immediately effected. Then, for weeks and months afterwards, they were both overtly and clandestinely monitored for symptoms of radiation sickness.

At sea, sailors and Marines were ordered on deck on naval vessels to observe atomic bomb detonations in the Pacific. Then, after the blast had occurred and the radiation cloud had drifted away, they were ordered to swim in contaminated lagoons. In one documented Pacific experiment, servicemen were ordered onto a large, flat barge, then towed out to sea to watch a mushroom cloud blast of a 15 megaton hydrogen bomb that was detonated 100 miles from the Bikini atoll. Afterwards, they were towed in to the blast site and ordered to bathe in the contaminated waters.

In all of the above experiments, servicemen unwittingly breathed and ingested deadly radioisotopes.[38]

To understand the long term effects of these experiments, one only has to read material readily available in any public library. According to a study published in the Journal of the American Medical Association, workers involved in the Manhattan Project at Oak Ridge National Laboratory, Tennessee, who supposedly were exposed to very low levels of radiation during the war, developed cases of leukemia far in excess of the general population. In the study it was determined that the Oak Ridge employees had a 63% higher rate of leukemia than the civilian population.[39]

And in Los Alamos, New Mexico, a study of 18,000 people who lived in the vicinity produced a startling percentage of brain cancer. Though the general rate of this disease among the normal population is 6 in every 100,000 people, the residents of Los Alamos had 48 brain cancers—9 of them primary.[40]

Dr. Helen Caldicott, author of *Nuclear Madness*, wrote, "Today, almost all geneticists agree that there is no dose of radiation so low that it produces no mutations at all. Thus, even small amounts of background radiation are believed to have genetic effects." Yet the U.S. government, to this day, as in the cases involving the Unit 731 survivors and the MK/ULTRA experimentees, continues to deny claims—and quite often, any knowledge that these events even occurred. Of the 12,147 radiation exposure claims filed by atomic veterans, only 1,067 were granted compensation by the VA. Veterans

Administration Compensation and Pension Service Director J. Gary Hickman, when asked by the DAV why there was such a discrepancy in awarding disability claims to the veterans, responded, "Our grant rate is low because the amount of radiation which the DoD (Department of Defense) indicates to us these people were exposed to are very low."

This statement, according to the results of tests conducted by the National Science Foundation, is further evidence of the government's failure to publicly recognize past misdeeds. In the research, known as the BEIR (Biological Effects of Ionizing Radiation) study, the foundation reported that amounts of ionized radiation not considered hazardous in the past are now considered quite dangerous.

But even if the government openly acknowledged the various experimental programs that involved testing on human subjects, it is doubtful at this late date that the extent of such operations could be exposed and proven. Most of the records have been purposely destroyed.[41] And even if any records do remain, both the intelligence services and the Pentagon are reluctant to make them available. According to W.J. Layer of the VA's public Affairs office, "The VA has no way of knowing who is part of an experiment and who is not until the individual comes forward. Services don't turn over their records wholesale. The record always has to be requested."[42]

The Committee on Veterans' Affairs agreed. In a Senatorial investigation conducted in 1994, the Committee reported that: "From 1945 to 1962, the United States conducted numerous nuclear detonation tests: Crossroads (Bikini); Sandstone, Greenhouse and Ivy (Eniwetok Atoll); Castle (Bikini Atoll); Pacific Ocean 400 miles southwest of San Diego; Redwing and Hardtack I (Eniwetok and Bikini Atolls); Argus (South Atlantic); and Dominic (Christmas Island and Johnson Island). The main goal was to determine damage caused by bombs; however, as a result, thousands of military personnel and civilians were exposed to radioactive fallout. Similar tests were conducted within the continental United States, including sites in New Mexico and Nevada. Veterans who participated in activities that directly exposed them to radioactive fallout are referred to as 'Atomic Veterans.'

"Data obtained on some military personnel who were exposed to radioactive fallout were collected after these men were unintentionally exposed. However, some atomic veterans believe they were used as guinea pigs to determine the effects of radiation from various distances, including those at ground zero, on human subjects. Their suspicions are supported by a 1951 document from the Joint Panel on the Medical Aspects of Atomic Warfare, Research and Development Board, Department of Defense, which identified general criteria for bomb test-related 'experiments' and identified twenty-nine specific problems as 'legitimate basis for biomedical participation.'"

The report continues with the sub-heading "Radiation Releases at U.S. Nuclear Sites." It states "In addition to detonation testing, radioactive releases were also intentionally conducted at U.S. nuclear sites in the years following World War II. According to the U.S. General Accounting Office, at least twelve planned radioactive releases occurred at three U.S. nuclear sites during 1948-52. These tests were conducted at Oak Ridge, Tennessee; Dugway, Utah; and Los Alamos, New Mexico. Additionally a planned release occurred at Hanford, Washington, in December 1948, which has been referred to as the Green Run test. *It is not known how many civilians and military personnel were exposed to fallout from these tests.* "[43]

According to fallout maps, giant clouds of nuclear fallout have been born in the easterly winds of the Jet Stream across the United States, from Nevada and Utah to the Mississippi River Valley. Depending on the time of year, the clouds have been plotted as far north as South Dakota and as far south as Central Texas. There is no way to tell exactly where these deadly clouds have deposited their radiation over the civilian population. And not one word from our watchdog agencies regarding this abuse of power and technology.

The DAV, as late as 1995, has continued to fight for the rights of disabled atomic veterans. DAV legislative counsel, Joseph A. Violante, told one House Veterans' Affairs Committee panel: "The issue of ionizing radiation and its potential adverse health effects have been present for more than 50 years. Atomic veterans and their loved ones have been patiently waiting for answers from the scientific and medical communities, as well as response to their continuing concerns from Congress and the VA. Unfortunately, all too often those answers were not forthcoming. Nor does it appear that definitive answers will ever be known. For each study done concluding one point, another study surfaces to discount the findings of the prior report. Thus, the debate rages, with no apparent end in sight."[44]

The VA, now known as the Department of Veteran's Affairs, has finally begun building a data base concerning the drug, gas and atomic experimentation victims. But it took congressional action, and, after great pressure from veterans organizations, an investigation by the General Accounting Office. It is feared by the DAV, VFW and American Legion, however, that anything done now will be too little, too late for the 222,968 military personnel who participated in nuclear tests after World War II.

The World War II years, and the first decade of the Cold War that followed, proved to be a valuable learning experience for the military, the scientific community, and the intelligence services. They discovered just how powerful an organization can become—and just how much they can get away with—if they have the capability to secretly circumvent the law—for purposes of "national security."

Chapter 11

Agent Orange

One of the main problems faced by American commanders in Vietnam was the Vietcong and North Vietnamese Army's ability to hide in the countryside. By constructing massive tunnel complexes for base areas, and linking them with a myriad of well-hidden jungle trails, the enemy could hide from reconnaissance flights and aerial search missions, then come out to strike at will, retreating back into the jungles to again disappear.

The solution to the problem, reasoned the American military, would be to remove the jungle hideaways. In the first efforts, vegetation was cut back away from U.S. firebases to clear open areas called "fields of fire." Next came engineer battalions that bulldozed the jungle back from main roads, and finally, in 1962 the American military began spraying the suspected enemy base areas and supply networks with defoliant.

Designated 2-4-5T and 2-4-D, the chemicals used were not actually a defoliant. Instead, the chemicals, dubbed "Agent Orange" because of the orange stripe painted around the 55-gallon drums as a means of identification, were actually a super-potent fertilizer. But because of the strength that was used, the plants that were sprayed simply grew so large and so quickly that they virtually exploded in their cell structure. The synthetic growth hormone contained in Agent Orange could, for example, cause the typical six to eight-inch Vietnamese bananas to grow to a length of two feet—then burst.

Part of the effective ingredients in Agent Orange were dioxins. Dioxin, considered a deadly poison, is so powerful that three ounces placed in the New York City water supply could kill the entire population of the city. In Vietnam, it was sprayed in thousands of gallons.

By means of specially equipped C-123 cargo planes flown by the USAF 12th Air Commando Squadron operating under Operation Ranch Hand, 11,000,000 gallons of Agent Orange was sprayed over hundreds of square miles of jungle and inland waterways. Unknown to the crews who flew the planes, and the 60,000 ground troops who were inadvertently sprayed or had to later walk though the dead forests, the dioxin would take its toll.

Within eight years of the American withdrawal from Vietnam, thousands of American veterans began experiencing the aftereffects of Agent Orange. Symptoms ranged from strange skin rashes to liver disorders, numbness in the limbs, impotence, fatigue, cancer, and finally, children born with unexplained deformities. Studies showed the only common denominators for this segment of the civilian population were that they were all Vietnam veterans—and they had all been exposed to Agent Orange.

When the veterans began showing up at their local Veterans Administration offices, they were rebuked and turned away. The VA, claiming that no scientific proof was available that Agent Orange could be the culprit, denied the veterans medical care and benefits. When the vets fought back, they ran into two legal obstacles. First, by law, the Veterans Administration is the only federal agency who does not have to answer to any court concerning its decisions; and second, a 1950 Supreme Court ruling denies military personnel the right to sue the government for service connected disabilities—no matter how incurred.[45]

A long battle followed. The Vietnam veterans, who had faced not only the enemy's bullets and booby traps, but lack of support from the government they fought for, and the apathy—and often hostility—of the American people, would not let the issue die without a fight. In 1978, a group of Agent Orange vets sued Dow Chemical and six additional companies that included the huge conglomerates of Uniroyal and Monsanto. The suit charged that the defoliants contained unsafe levels of dioxin, which was known by the manufacturers to be 170,000 times more deadly than cyanide,[46] and that the companies involved knew of the danger and did not warn users in the field. The court battles lasted six years, finally being settled out of court in May of 1984. Though not admitting liability, which according to the *Washington Post* would have been "a forum to probe corporate officials on what they secretly knew or didn't know about the dangers of their chemicals," the companies involved settled for $180,000,000—enough to pay 16,000 veterans represented in the suit $11,125 each.

The money, however, was a case of too little, too late. Most veterans effected by the herbicide felt that they had been thrown a bone and been told to go away. Former Marine David Martin told the *Post* that "We wanted our day in court...I want the truth to be told and the truth to come out." The *Agent Orange Dispatch*, a newsletter for dioxin-effected veterans, wrote "We want the world to hear how Dow Chemical poisoned Americans in Vietnam. No amount of blood money could ever be enough to repay what the bastards did to us and our children."

The out-of-court settlement came on the heels of a 1983 New York court case that produced evidence that Dow knew from the very beginning that the defoliant sent to Vietnam contained levels of dioxin that was harmful to humans. According to a 1965 company memo written by Dow's toxicology director, the dioxin contained in the product could be "exceptionally toxic." In another memo written by the company's medical director, dioxin-related "fatalities have been reported in the literature."

Of question at this point is the loyalties of the U.S. government. Unlike the Atomic Veterans and the veterans used as human guinea pigs at Fort Detrick and Edgewood Arsenal, the government was not the primary target of the Agent Orange veteran's organizations. Though the government's evident lack of support, failure to investigate, and failure to provide benefits and medical care made it appear guilty by association, the actual parties targeted by the groups were the manufacturers. The only plausible explanation for what appeared to be a lack of action on the part of Washington would be a fear of discovery by behind-the-scenes high-level individuals involved in the issue. If this were the case, if certain individuals were guilty of covering up the effects of Agent Orange during the war—and the aftereffects—then they were now guilty of conspiracy. But why would anyone in the government that existed in the 1980s go out on a limb for those who served in Washington during the Vietnam war? The only answer could be that some of the same people still held power, and money was still changing hands.

But what evidence is there?

In 1990, a House subcommittee chaired by Representative Ted Weiss investigated the Agent Orange situation. What the committee found was damning.

In 1982, the U.S. Congress ordered a study of the effects and possible aftereffects of Agent Orange. The investigators discovered that the Reagan administration, who promised support for the veterans in the media, actually "had secretly taken a legal position to resist demands to compensate victims." Rep. Weiss went on to state unequivocally that "While the Reagan administration defended the Vietnam conflict as an honorable war, it worked behind the scenes to deny benefits to the very people who sacrificed their health for their country."

After spending more than $40 million, the study was suddenly cancelled by the White House in 1987—just after the above report was issued.

Not everyone in the upper echelons of military power surrendered to the White House. Admiral Elmo R. Zumwalt, Jr., the former Chief of Naval Operations (CNO) in Vietnam, testified to the Weiss Committee that Dr. Vernon Houk, the Center for Disease Control (CDC) representative in charge of the study had "made it his mission to manipulate and prevent the true facts from being determined. It was pointed out that Dr. Houk was a former member of President Reagan's Agent Orange study team.

Adm. Zumwalt stated that "more than enough verifiable, credible evidence [exists] linking certain cancers and other illnesses with Agent Orange," and that government officials were purposefully ignoring it. He went on to say that "government and industry officials [responsible for] examining such linkage intentionally manipulated or withheld compelling information of the adverse health effects."

It is obvious that a great deal of money could have been involved in dealing with the liability of manufacturing, using, and aftereffects of

Agent Orange. The product liability of the manufacturers, the veterans compensation by the VA, and the responsibility for the malformed children born to the veterans could conceivably run into billions. And possibly more important to those involved in the coverup, the criminal conspiracy surrounding their negligence in warning the users what could happen in advance could have serious repercussions. Those responsible decided early on to first not mention any health risks, then later to deny any risks existed. When this did not work and the veterans continued their fight, it was decided to cover up the entire affair as well as possible by denying lab information to the veterans groups, then finally to stop the congressional investigation by way of an order from the president. No better example can be given that exhibits the power of major corporations and their links to the highest levels of government.

Admiral Zumwalt had a very good reason to come forward and confront the government. As CNO in Vietnam, he was in charge of all naval operations in the theater of operations. Part of these operations were the naval river patrols that constantly plied the various inland waterways of the country. These patrols, which were conducted by lightly armed river patrol boats known as PBRs, penetrated the farthest reaches of the various rivers and streams in search of Vietcong. These patrols were extremely dangerous. Because the jungle vegetation grew right to the edge of the banks, and often into the rivers themselves, the VC could lay in ambush right at the water's edge and not be detected until the first shots were fired. In an effort to deny the enemy this advantage, Admiral Zumwalt ordered the VC-controlled areas of the Mekong sprayed with Agent Orange.

Admiral Zumwalt's son, Elmo Zumwalt III, was a commander of one of the PBRs who patrolled the Mekong. He died of an extremely rare form of lymphoma in 1988—just months after Reagan cancelled the Weiss study.

Chapter 12

The Gulf War Syndrome: Business As Usual

It was like the beginning of no other battle in history—at least prior history. Instead, it was like a scene out of the Book of Revelation, for the sky had indeed turned as black as sackcloth and there was fire upon the land.

For the Marines poised to breach the Iraqi army's trench system and mine fields in southern Kuwait, it was like a scene in Hell. According to one Marine first lieutenant, "We moved into the oil smoke about one o'clock in the afternoon, and it was pitch dark. Like something out of a sci-fi movie. Like a scene out of Dante's inferno...it was an eerie situation. I think it was the day the Marine was quoted as saying 'this ain't hell, but you can see it from here."

Further west, along the advance route for their "end run" around Kuwait to entrap the Republican Guard Division, Lieutenant Colonel Gregory Fontenot of the U.S. 1st Infantry Division, recalled another odd and terrible scene, one that sent chills up the necks of the troops as they advanced.

"It was a combination of a sand storm and a world class biblical thunderstorm," said Fontenot, "It looked like the end of the world. It was sort of greenish and black on the horizon with sand in your face one minute and rain pelting you in the face the next. It was unbelievable. It was part of being in something you couldn't imagine. Salvador Dali couldn't have made it up. It was kind of a strange surreal atmosphere of electrical charges and sheet lightning across the sky. We were between the Iraqi main defense and the guys we thought would give us the biggest fight, the Republican Guard. We moved all day in this thing. You could only see 800 to 1000 meters. You thought you were alone."

Another battalion commander, this one a Marine, remembered the feelings he had as he rode atop his command vehicle across the Kuwaiti border into the smoke and flames and darkness as "...something evil, just plain bad. If there is a feeling as a condemned soul descends into Hell, this was it. Your hair stood up on your neck and you had a feeling of stark terror grip you like you've never witnessed before. Not a shot had been fired yet, and it wasn't the anticipation of battle that grabbed you. It was something else, something evil, like the Devil himself lived here."

These men and thousands more would not realize how true their premonitions would become—but not because of a demonic presence or something out of the Twilight Zone, at least not working alone. It would be something else, something they could not see or sense, something very small and unnoticed until it was too late.

It began slowly at first, almost insignificantly, when the problem surfaced and began to get the world's attention in 1992. It was then that members of two Indiana Army Reserve units began showing symptoms of something terribly wrong with their physical conditions. They reported that they had begun suffering headaches, memory loss, bleeding gums, skin lesions and rashes, hair loss, muscle aches and extreme fatigue. Over the next several months even more Gulf War veterans began arriving at various medical institutions with similar complaints. Neither the military or civilian doctors could provide answers to the Gulf War vets complaints.

Since then, over 20,000 veterans have complained of strange physical disabilities, and over 7,000 have died from what has been dubbed "Gulf War Syndrome." But the Pentagon's official stance from 1992 until late 1996 was that there was simply no such thing as "Gulf War Disease," and further, that no chemicals or biological weapons were used by either side in the war that would provide an explanation to the strange disease-like symptoms exhibited by the vets. It was another case of "standard denial."

But there were far too many incidents of veterans reporting to doctors that they had similar symptoms, and more were coming forward every month to add fuel to the fire. Then, even worse as time went on, spouses of veterans began complaining of similar symptoms, indicating that the condition was transferrable. And as if this were not enough to convince medical personnel that a problem existed and should be investigated, pregnant wives of veterans began to give birth to deformed babies—far in excess of the rest of the population. According to Dr. Alan Cantwell, Jr., a medical researcher and author, veterans claim that one third of Gulf War babies have been born with abnormalities, ten times the normal rate. Dr. Francis Waickman, an environmental pediatrician, stated that the syndrome can be passed on, creating an infant whose immune system does not function normally.

Eventually theories began to form as to the cause of this strange epidemic that appeared to originate after the return of the Gulf War service personnel. Most of these theories centered around three schools of thought. First were those that supported what became known as Multiple Chemical Sensitivity (MCS). MCS is defined as an allergic reaction to chemical agents that can range from household chemicals to various forms of plastic and petrochemicals.[47] Though the Veterans Administration does not regard MCS as a disease, many researchers think that heavy exposure to various chemicals in a wartime environment, such as diesel fuel in shower water and handling various explosives, can become compounded later when a victim handles other chemicals at home or on the job. The combination of such chemicals, plus the body's inability to cleanse them from the system, creates a toxic build-up. One particular military chemical agent that was used extensively in the war was CARC, or Chemical Agent Resistant Coating, that was sprayed in the thousands of gallons on vehicles and equipment.

To support this theory Dr. William Johnson of the Dwight David Eisenhower Army Medical Center in Fort Gordon, Georgia, told a congressional sub-committee that soldiers worked twelve-hour days spraying CARC in poorly ventilated tents, and some inhaled so much that they were literally coughing it up. Dr. Charles Hinshaw, Jr., president of the American Academy of Environmental Medicine, analyzed data on twenty-five Persian Gulf veterans who had been exposed to "low levels of various petrochemicals" and stated that all but one showed signs of MCS.

The second theory concerns depleted uranium, or DU, which was used in tank and artillery shells, 30mm A-10 cannon rounds, and armor plating on tanks. According to the Army, more than 4,200 DU rounds were fired in the war, and the anti-tank cannons of the A-10s fired thousands more. When fired against armor much of the round shatters into a radioactive dust that, according to experts, can cause health problems similar to heavy metal poisoning. The Army maintains that no soldiers are believed to have ingested dangerous amounts of DU, and that none have tested high in uranium levels in their bodies.

The third theory is the most plausible. It addresses Chemical and Biological Weapons (CW and BW) which were available to both sides during the war. It also addresses the preventative medicines given to our soldiers and Marines—often against their wishes—to counteract such agents.

In 1993, two U.S. Navy Seabees from the 24th Naval Construction Battalion in Columbus, Georgia, testified before a Senate Armed Services subcommittee that their unit was hit by chemical weapons on January 20, 1991. They also testified that everyone knew it and that they were all ordered to "keep it quiet." Their statements were backed up by other reports from multi-national forces that did not "keep it quiet," and the Pentagon had to do some back pedaling while they retreated to plan future damage control. One report came from a Czech chemical detection unit that detected mustard gas and the nerve agent Sarin. These agents were discovered after allied air strikes hit Iraqi munitions arsenals and ammo dumps. The Czechs later reported that ten of the soldiers from the detection unit later began suffering "mysterious ailments." In other sectors the British also detected chemicals, and U.S. forces had numerous instances of chemical alarms going off. Unnamed Pentagon spokesmen simply dismissed the latter as "defective equipment." Yet, according to the French forces on February 4th, 1991, thirteen days after the Czech and British units reported the BW indications, chemical fallout was being detected throughout Iraq. This was just after General Schwarzkopf announced that allied forces had attacked 18 chemical and 10 biological plants.[48]

The German newspaper *Frankfurter Rundschau und Handlesblatt* reported that allied raids had caused the release of toxic chemicals that were killing scores of civilians, and that Michael Sailer of the Ecological Institute in Darmstadt told the paper that sections of Iraq would remain polluted and unusable for years after the war.[49]

Contrary to the Pentagon stance, a report issued in September of 1993, by the staff of Senator Donald W. Riegle, Jr. (D-Mich.) and the Center for Disease Control affirmed that an Iraqi SCUD missile, capable of carrying BW and CW agents, landed near an ammunition supply unit stationed near the Saudi-Kuwaiti border, and since the war, 85 of the unit's 110 members have exhibited GWS symptoms, many described as debilitating. Soldiers of this unit were warned not to mention this missile strike to anyone.

A second missile struck near the Navy Seabee unit where the members were instructed not to talk about it. This begs an answer to the question of what the officers of that unit already knew about the missiles prior to their impact. Normally, receiving incoming fire would simply be a basis for harmless war stories. What was it about these missiles that the chain of command knew in advance that made them secret?[50]

For the Army, the coverup of what really happened began early. When the first indications surfaced with the Indiana reservists that something was wrong with our Persian Gulf returnees, the Pentagon immediately concluded that they were simply suffering from "stress," probably due to problems of readjustment to civilian life. One Indiana reservist countered with "when people were coming back from Vietnam, wringing Agent Orange out of their clothes, they were told they were under stress. The Army took almost twenty years to settle that one, so I don't think they have a real good record of letting the troops know what might be going on."

One victim that definitely was not "under stress" was Indiana Congressman Steve Buyer who developed respiratory symptoms and repeated bouts with influenza, and kidney problems after returning from the Gulf. He is also afflicted with prostrate infections, spastic colon and multiple allergies.

These symptoms, plus more, have surfaced in an Alabama reserve unit which has experienced a two-thirds GWS rate among its members. One of the reservists, William Kay, blames his sickness on an Iraqi SCUD missile that hit near his unit which he believes was loaded with either chemical or biological agents.

The military takes credit for doing its best to protect against chemical and biological weapons. One of the methods consisted of a series of injections of drugs that were thought to counter CW and BW agents. The problem at the time is that the drugs had not been proven effective or safe.[51]

The Los Angeles Times reported on May 10, 1994 that experimental and unapproved vaccines and drugs were given to all personnel who fought in the Gulf War, and that these vaccines were prescribed to protect soldiers against anthrax and a nerve disease called myothenia gravis. It was also hoped that these drugs would prove effective against other biological warfare agents, but "In an effort to protect the health and lives of uniformed personnel, the U.S. military may have inadvertently done some of them serious injury."[52]

It did not matter to the military hierarchy whether or not the soldiers and sailors in the Gulf consented to being used as guinea pigs for untested vaccine. They simply were ordered to line up and take shots. When some refused, they were forced to submit to the injections. One Army Reserve doctor, Dr. Yolanda Huet-Vaughn, protested that it was her duty under the Nuremberg Code of Justice not to vaccinate personnel with experimental vaccines without their consent. The Army's answer was a courts martial for the doctor wherein the military judge ignored the considerations of international law and medical ethics. He sentenced the mother of three children to 30 months in prison.[53]

Soldiers who refused the vaccinations were given them forcibly. One female reservist reported after her return that she was held down against her will and injected. When her second shot came due a few weeks later, someone came up behind her and injected her before she could resist.

One soldier refused to buckle under the Army's weight and filed a lawsuit against the government regarding "unethical and unlawful use of people as guinea pigs in medical experiments without their informed consent." When the case went to court, however, U.S. Court District Judge Stanley S. Harris dismissed the law suit, citing the necessity of the military to "protect" the health of its troops. The fact that the vaccines and drugs were untested and unapproved by the FDA was irrelevant.[54]

By 1994, even members of Congress began to take note of what appeared to be a significant problem that was spreading in the civilian population. In the staff report prepared for the Senate Committee in Veterans' Affairs (December 8, 1994), Section III outlined the findings and conclusions of the Committee:

A. For at least 50 years, DOD has intentionally exposed military personnel to potentially dangerous substances, often in secret.

B. DOD has repeatedly failed to comply with required ethical standards when using human subjects in military research during war or threat of war.

C. DOD incorrectly claims that since their goal was treatment, the use of investigational drugs in the Persian Gulf War was not research.

D. DOD used investigational drugs in the Persian Gulf War in ways that were not effective.

E. DOD did not know whether pyridostigmine bromide would be safe for use by U.S. troops in the Persian Gulf War.

F. When U.S. troops were sent to the Persian Gulf in 1994, DOD still did not have proof that pyridostigmine bromide was safe for use as an antidote enhancer.

G. Pyridostigmine may be more dangerous in combination with pesticides and other exposures.

H. The safety of the botulism vaccine was not established prior to the Persian Gulf War.

I. Records of anthrax vaccinations are not suitable to evaluate safety.

J. Army regulations exempt informed consent for volunteers in some types of military research.

K. DOD and DVA have repeatedly failed to provide information and medical followup to those who participated in military research or are ordered to take investigational drugs.

L. The Federal Government has failed to support scientific studies that provide information about the reproductive problems experienced by veterans who were intentionally exposed to potentially dangerous substances.

M. The Federal government has failed to support scientific studies that provide timely information for compensation decisions regarding military personnel who were harmed by various exposures.

N. Participation in military research is rarely included in military medical records, making it impossible to support a veteran's claim for service-connected disabilities from military research.

O. DOD has demonstrated a pattern of misrepresenting the danger of various military exposures that continues today.

Pyridostigmine bromide (PB) is a drug often prescribed to victims of myasthenia gravis, a degenerative nerve disease. According to medical sources, PB has been shown in animal experiments to provide some protection against Soman nerve gas. Because of this, the military administered PB to almost all personnel stationed in the Gulf. However, Air Force personnel reported serious side effects from the drug. Pilots reported impaired breathing, blurred vision, short term memory problems, and decrease in stamina. And it was not until later that it was discovered that PB actually increased the effects of nerve gasses other than Soman, such as the indications of Sarin that were discovered by the British and Czech units.

Life magazine reported in an article about the GWS that "Czech and British governments say their troops detected both kinds of gas, presumably released during allied bombing of Iraqi chemical plants. And veterans' advocate Paul Sullivan recently obtained 11 pages of a secret Defense Department log revealing that U.S. chemical alarms went off repeatedly during the war. Pentagon spokesmen blame those alarms on faulty equipment and note that there have been no reports of massive Iraqi gas deaths near the bombed factories. But former congressional investigator Jim Tuite speculates that gases were blown straight upward, then settled miles away as fallout. And, he says, Iraqis are suffering health problems 'similar to what we're seeing in our veterans.' Ironically, much of Iraq's chemical arsenal was made by

U.S. companies—80 of which face a class-action law suit by 2,000 ailing vets."

There is much more to the story regarding U.S. participation in arming the Iraqis with biological and chemical weapons. What few investigators know concerning the background of this topic is the collusion of certain U.S. government officials with the chief arms buyer for Saddam Hussein, a mysterious man named Ihsan Barbouti.

Ihsan Barbouti was Hussein's chief architect on many interesting projects. First, he owned an engineering company in Frankfurt that had a $552 million contract to build airfields in Iraq. At about the same time, he designed Moammar Khadaffi's German-built chemical weapons plant in Rabta, Libya, while buying various businesses in the U.S. that were capable of producing war materials.

Of the latter, Barbouti invested in two companies in the U.S.: Pipeline Recovery Systems of Dallas, Texas, which made an anti-corrosive chemical that coats and preserves pipes such as those used in nuclear reactors, and Product Ingredient Technology of Boca Raton, Florida, which makes food flavorings. Barbouti also attempted to buy an Oklahoma City company, TK-7, which had formulas that could extend the range of jet aircraft and liquid-fueled missiles such as the SCUD. This deal fell through at the beginning of Operation Desert Shield when Iraq invaded Kuwait and Iraqi assets were frozen in the U.S. But not before many other items of concern had exited the country through the "smugglers underground."

Product Ingredient Technology made cherry flavoring, which used ferric ferrocyanide, a chemical that's used to manufacture hydrogen cyanide, which can penetrate gas masks. This is the chemical used against the Kurds in northern Iraq when Saddam Hussein bombarded a village, killing all men, women and children.

According to a Nightline broadcast, a New Orleans exporter who was a business associate of Richard Secord assisted Barbouti with "exporting" the products. Barbouti, according to the broadcast, met with Secord in Florida on several occasions, and phone records show that several calls were placed from Barbouti's office to Secord's private number in McLean, Virginia. Secord was reported to have been in business with James Tully and Jack Brennan (former aide to Nixon) who were involved in a $181 million business deal to supply uniforms to the Iraqi army, which they contracted through Nicolae Ceaucescu's

Romania prior to his execution. The partners in this particular deal were former U.S. Attorney General John Mitchell and Sarkis Soghanalian, a Turkish-born citizen who had been Saddam Hussein's leading arms procurer. It was Soghanalian who introduced Super Cannon builder Gerald Bull to the Iraqis, and who later sold 103 military helicopters to Iraq illegally, was caught and served six years in prison in Miami.

Barbouti managed to secretly remove more than 2,000 gallons of ferric ferrocyanide from the Florida plant and ship it to Iraq. It is also been reported that Barbouti bought from high-level American sources biological weapons. It is now maintained by experts in the Gulf War Syndrome investigation that a biological weapons laboratory in Houston supplied Barbouti with basic bacilli and virus cultures from which biological warfare agents could be manufactured. This would follow suit to the fact that Barbouti designed the Libyan "pharmaceutical" plant in Rabta, Libya, and had met with former Nazi scientist Volker Weissheimer to recruit other former Nazi scientists to work in Libya and Iraq. These were some of the same scientists that had worked on chemical and biological weapons during World War II for Hitler.

Barbouti was part of a CIA operation to "improve relations" with Saddam Hussein by supplying his armed forces with "special weapons." This was done under the guise of providing Iraq with agricultural loan guarantees, with the U.S., through arms dealers like Secord, funnelling millions of dollars of biological and chemical weapons technology to Iraq. These business maneuverings were handled through the Department of Agriculture's Commodity Credit Corporation, and the loans channeled through the Atlanta branch of Banco Nazional Lavaro in Italy. This enterprise became part of what later was dubbed "Iraqgate."

Barbouti allegedly died in London of a heart attack in July, 1990. However, this is the second time he has died, as he faked his own death previously in 1969. His grave in London is covered by a huge concrete monument and is registered as Moslem holy ground and cannot be disturbed. Conveniently, Barbouti's corpse cannot be exhumed for identification.

The bottom line is that all of these technology transfers concerned the highest levels of government. Key individuals from the White

House on down knew of these sales to Iraq, but were not concerned as long as the weapons were used against the Iranians. It was not until the Gulf War that we began to face our own weapons, and any deep investigation into how Hussein got them would expose too many politicians and bureaucrats, thereby influencing their political futures.

Still, the government continued to deny that Gulf War Syndrome existed. In an Associated Press article titled "No Mystery Ailment Found in Gulf War Veterans, Study Says," the author wrote that "A study of more than 10,000 veterans and family members suffering post-Persian Gulf War medical problems found no evidence of any unique disease or disorder, the Pentagon's top medical official said Tuesday. The study turned up instances of back pain, headache, alcoholism, depression and other ailments, but no mystery illness stemming from the desert war."

The article went on to note that according to Dr. Stephen Joseph, assistant secretary of defense for health, "We do not find a single or unique illness responsible for a large or even significant proportion...of illness. Rather, what we find are multiple illnesses with overlapping symptoms and causes." The article then audaciously stated that "Tuesday's announcement marked the first categorical rejection by the Defense Department of the existence of an unknown malady stemming from the 1990-91 war." Dr. Joseph concluded in the article that the Defense Department researchers found "not a single mystery illness or unique Gulf War illness but rather a combination of symptoms and illnesses...that you would particularly expect to find in a population that was exposed to the kinds of stresses that people were exposed to in the Gulf."

By 1995, however, the mounting evidence and the public outcry began to draw political blood. A November 6th article in *Air Force Times* titled "Raids May Have Released Iraqis' Nerve Gas" pulled the curtains back on the fact that the Pentagon was beginning to weaken in their denials that anything unusual had occurred. The article stated that "The Pentagon is investigating whether allied bombings of an Iraqi chemical weapons depot inadvertently exposed some U.S. troops to nerve gas during Operation Desert Storm, says a top investigator of Persian Gulf War illnesses. The investigation, however, does not change the Defense Department's position that U.S. forces were not exposed to chemical or biological warfare agents, whether through SCUD attacks or inadvertent releases from allied bombing, said Air Force Colonel Ed Koenigsberg, a doctor who directs the department's Persian Gulf War Veterans' Illnesses Investigation Team." Koenigsberg went on to say that "To date, we have not found anything to change that policy."

Interestingly, the exposure being investigated occurred in late January, 1991, when the Czech experts in chemical warfare detected traces of Sarin in areas occupied by Allied forces. Still, the coverup continued with the government spokesmen espousing other theories as causes for Gulf War disease. Sand fleas, Saudi desert hygiene, health hazards due to the fine grain Saudi sand, and even breathing fumes from SCUD missile fuel were mentioned as possible culprits. Though the Department of Defense was beginning to waiver it was still not ready to admit that "something" happened during the active duty service of the veterans that would cause communicable life-long illnesses, which they brought home to pass on to their families.

Veterans organizations, involved in exposing the truth, fought an uphill battle with the government. Arthur H. Wilson, Executive Director of the Disabled American Veterans, wrote that the "Pentagon has shown an absolute reluctance to openly discuss these concerns with the DAV. It is also a complete mystery why we haven't had an answer to a strongly worded letter we wrote on this subject to Secretary Aspin on October 25, 1993." Mr. Wilson went on to write "Following World War II, the Korean War, and especially the Vietnam War, didn't we hear the same words from our government as we fought to find the truth and struggled to rebuild our lives? Only later, in some cases 20 years after the fact, did we learn the truth about 'mystery' illnesses like shell shock and war neurosis. And worse yet was the awful truth that some disabilities may be directly related to exposure to dangerously high levels of radiation and Agent Orange by our own government."

Mr. Wilson summed up his article in *DAV* magazine "Remember that during and after World War II the Department of Defense concluded there would be no significant long-term health effects from the mustard gas or atomic radiation tests they performed on unsuspecting soldiers and sailors. Remember that in the late 1950s and

119

early 1960s the Department of Defense concluded there would be no significant long-term health effects for soldiers and airmen who were given multiple doses of the powerful hallucinogenic drug LSD. And remember, if you will, that during the Vietnam War the Department of Defense concluded there would be significant long-term effects for troops exposed to dangerous herbicides like Agent Orange."

As time passed the government became more nervous about the failure of damage control to sweep the issue under the carpet of the collective consciousness. When CBS newsman Ed Bradley interviewed Undersecretary of Defense John Deutch, who later became Director of the CIA under Clinton, in March of 1995, it was obvious a few nerves were struck. The line of questioning centered around "Were American forces exposed to chemical, biological or radiological weapons during the Persian Gulf War?"

Deutch denied any such events had occurred. But as the questions became increasingly tougher and more pointed, Deutch began to sweat and grow increasingly nervous. His eyes began to shift rapidly between Bradley and the camera as he attempted to fend off each question. Finally, Bradley asked if there was a "possibility" that BW or CW weapons "might" have been used, and Deutch simply dodged and evaded the question. This interview was aired on March 12, 1995.

Two stalwart doctors have relentlessly continued research on GWS. Doctor Garth L. Nicolson and his wife, Dr. Nancy L. Nicolson, have isolated a laboratory "engineered" microorganism known as Mycoplasma Fermentans. This strain of microplasma, according to the Nicolsons, is what causes most of what is now known as Gulf War disease. Dr. Garth Nicolson is professor and chairman of the Department of Tumor Biology at the world's largest cancer facility at the University of Texas in Houston (the same city from which Barbouti bought BW ingredients). His wife, Nancy, is president of Rhoden Foundation for Biomedical Research in Houston.

Dr. Nicolson has published more than 400 scientific papers and serves as the editor or associate editor of 13 scientific and medical journals. According to him, "the mycoplasma that we have found in Desert Storm vets has very unusual retroviral DNA sequences; thus in all probability it was 'engineered' and did not evolve naturally." The Nicolsons believe that since the microorganism was probably illegally developed and tested in the United States, then illegally sold and transferred to Iraq prior to the Gulf War, there is a major coverup being conducted by the Clinton administration. This coverup, however, started before Clinton came to office and can be traced back to the Bush administration in which the major players resided.

In a letter written to former army chaplain Col. James Ammerman of Dallas, Texas, Dr. Nicolson wrote "We have possibly uncovered one of the messiest controversies and coverups since Watergate. This one makes Watergate seem like a tea party."

The heat from the fire of public sentiment continued to burn until August 19, 1996, when the Associated Press published an article titled "Pentagon Admits Chemical Weapons Reached Soldiers." In the article the Pentagon finally admitted that it knew as far back as November 1991 that chemical weapons had been stored at an Iraqi ammunition depot that U.S. troops had demolished just months earlier. According to the article, "The Pentagon and other government agencies aware of the presence of chemical weapons at Kamisiyah ammunition storage facility did not realize in 1991, however, that American troops had been there, spokesman Captain Michael Doubleday said. So a November 1991 intelligence report indicating the presence of chemical shells at Kamisiyah—including one described as leaking—essentially was filed away and forgotten even as the U.S. government continued to deny it had any evidence that large numbers of troops might have been exposed to chemical weapons."

Something else that was not mentioned by the government was the fact that an engineer unit, the 37th Engineer Battalion, demolished the facility with explosives, sending clouds of chemical agents into the air to disseminate for miles over American units. Directly underneath the cloud as it rose were 150 U.S. troops who did not know that chemical weapons were stored there. It was not until much later, when home videos taken by the engineers showed the shells in bunker 73 to be 122mm chemical rockets, that the munitions were positively identified.

A further twist to this story is that a chemical officer told the engineers that he detected the nerve agent Sarin, but the officers in charge of the soldiers told them not to don their chemical protective suits and gas masks. The chemical officer, Dan Tipulski, ignored the order and put on his MOPP suit. Now he is the only man from the unit not afflicted with the syndrome.

Another break in this case is the fact that the *New York Times* reported that an intelligence memo had been circulated in 1991 concerning this event, and the routing marks showed it to have traveled to not only the Pentagon, but also the White House, State Department and CIA. Even when the U.N. weapons inspection teams reported to the U.S. government that the 37th Engineers had blown up a bunker with chemical weapons inside, it was dismissed because "it was thought they [the Iraqis] were feeding the United Nations disinformation in order to hide or obscure their weapons arsenal."[55]

On September 3, 1996, another torpedo of truth was fired at the Pentagon bureaucrats when the AP released an article titled "Part of Log Of Gulf War Data Missing." In the article, Gulfwatch, a Gulf veterans watchdog group, discovered that log pages were mysteriously missing from a diary kept for General Schwarzkopf that covered the dates in question regarding the Kamisiyah ammunition depot demolition by the 37th Engineers. "Entries are missing for March 4-11, the week troops and engineers spent examining the Kamisiyah ammunition depot and blowing it up," said the article, "...Several gaps exist in the 36 pages of logs that were declassified and turned over to Gulfwatch."

Exposing the coverup at this late date will have little effect for those already effected by the physical aftermath of the Gulf War. Especially for those who have died of these strange ailments. There will be no more waiting for recognition or proper treatment for former Army Specialist Michael Adcock, who died on April 23, 1992—only eleven months after returning home. But his last words ring in our ears: "Mama, fight for me. Fight for my comrades. Don't let this happen to another soldier. Don't let this be another Agent Orange."[56]

Part III

The Boys We Left Behind

"The [POW] problem becomes almost a philosophical one. If we are 'at war,' cold, hot or otherwise, casualties and losses must be expected and perhaps we must learn to live with this kind of thing. If we are in for fifty years of peripheral 'fire fights' we may be forced to adopt a rather cynical attitude on this for political reasons."

Classified Pentagon
policy on POWs.

"You're talking about people who have no feelings whatsoever about the individual soldier in the field. Their answer to all this is to build a black wall in Washington and put all their names on it to pacify you and I. Do they care about soldiers? They could give a damn about soldiers!"

Major Mark Smith
Former Green Beret
Army Intelligence on POW/MIAs

"As far as I'm concerned, the Pentagon is nothing more than a lair of liars."

Diane C. Renselaar
National League of
Families

Chapter 13

Casualties Of War

They had held for 54 days. But now the little men clad in black and khaki were among them, running in small groups or charging singly at wire entanglements with explosives strapped to their bodies, shooting at any position where resistance was found, and overrunning the remaining outposts. It was the 55th day of the siege, and it would soon be over.

Dien Bien Phu, a battle that became legend, started with a simple mission assignment given General Henri Eugene Navarre on 28 May, 1953: protect the little kingdom of Laos, which had remained loyal to France, from a threatened invasion from the east by Ho Chi Minh's Viet Minh guerrillas. To do this would take a blocking force of considerable strength occupying a key position on the most logical access route. Upon studying the map, it was determined that the most effective choke point would be in a valley straddling the Nam Yum River near the village of Dien Bien Phu. At this point, Route 41 entered the valley from the northeast and followed the Nam Yum River south along its east bank. This is where Navarre decided to stop the enemy.

The valley was surrounded by mountains. No modern army would attempt to cross such rough terrain with heavy equipment, and without artillery an invasion would surely fail. They would have to pass through the valley.

Instead of one central fortification, a series of strong points were established. Each small *herisson* (hedgehog) was positioned to cover others with fields of fire. One breach in the lines would not cause the garrison to fall. Throughout the winter, the French built their fortress.

But fall it did. By 13 March, 1954, the Viet Minh leader, General Giap, stood poised with 43,000 men and over 200 artillery pieces and heavy mortars in the mountains surrounding Dien Bien Phu. The French garrison numbered fewer than 11,000 men supported by only seven batteries of artillery, two mortar groups and 10 American-made M-24 Chaffee light tanks.

Once surrounded, the only relief forces and supplies that could be sent had to come by air. Landing on the airstrip was disastrous, as it was well within range of the Viet Minh artillery, so most supplies and reinforcements were dropped by parachute—many drifting into the hands of the Communists.

As the battle progressed, Viet Minh troops dug "saps" to within yards of the French perimeters. Mortars and rocket launchers moved forward and machine gun positions appeared on all flanks, pouring withering fire into the defenders trenches and bunkers. Finally, on May 7th, the final assault began.

Suicide troops with explosives strapped to their bodies charged forward from the Viet Minh trenches and threw themselves into the French wire, blowing gaping holes in the entanglements. Masses of waiting soldiers stormed through and were soon within one strong point, then another. The French fought valiantly, but the outcome was inevitable. One weapon after another ran out of ammunition. Dead and wounded were everywhere. Medical supplies were almost non-existent. Only one tank remained operational, and the reserve forces had been used up five days before. By 1740 hours, the Viet Minh flag hung over the main command post.

In the end, over 10,000 French and colonial prisoners were taken by the Vietminh—many of which would never be released.[57] By the end of the French Indochina War, 39,888 prisoners were held by the Vietminh. Of these, 29,954 were *never* repatriated. Many were local Vietnamese troops, but according to French military records, 2,350 were French nationals, and 2,867 were Legionnaires.[58]

Of those that were repatriated, some did not see French soil until as late as 1962. In that year forty French POWs were returned to France. But after their return, instead of being greeted as long lost sons, they were labeled by the French government as *"ralliers"* (deserters). Then, in an attempt to discredit any testimony they might produce about being abandoned by their government after being taken prisoner, the army court martialed them, found them guilty of desertion, then gave them lengthy prison sentences and loss of all back pay. Twenty other POWs, after hearing of this "welcome home" decided to remain in Vietnam. They were court martialed in absentia, charged with various capital crimes supposedly committed during the war, and should they ever return, faced execution.[59]

Writer William Stevenson, co-author of *Kiss the Boys Goodbye,* and a noted BBC correspondent who covered the French Indochina War, testified before the Senate Committee on Foreign Relations in 1991 that he had interviewed French soldiers held as POWs, and that due to their long incarceration, seemed to be "mentally deficient." It was believed that this was due not only to the passage of time, but to brainwashing and harsh treatment by the captors. Still, it had been years since their war had ended and they were still alive and in captivity.

Robert Garwood, an American Marine taken prisoner during the Vietnam War, stated that he had personal knowledge—and had seen—French prisoners in the 1970s that were being used as slave labor at a North Vietnamese dairy farm. This was after the French government, in an effort to resolve the lingering problem over the unaccounted-for POWs and MIAs taken in Indochina, declared them all dead.[60]

The French experience with the communist ideology concerning prisoners of war was not the first time such treatment by a communist government had been encountered by Western governments. Nor would it be the last.

As the Allied vice closed in on Hitler's Germany in the waning days of World War II, a decision was made by the Allied High Command—Supreme Headquarters, Allied Expeditionary Forces (SHAEF)—commanded by General Dwight D. Eisenhower, that the U.S., British and French forces would stop short of Berlin. Instead of linking up with the Red Army at the *Reichstag*, the Russians would be permitted to take Berlin on their own. According to Eisenhower, it would save American lives. In actuality, the Russians had demanded the exclusive right to swarm into the Nazi capital in retribution for the death and destruction vested upon the Russian people by the Nazis during Operation Barbarossa.

As each army made their way through Nazi-occupied Europe on their trek to Berlin, they overran German POW and concentration camps along the way. At first, the Germans evacuated the camps and transferred the prisoners farther into the Reich. In the west, American prisoners were moved into eastern Germany and Poland, and in the east, Russian POWs were transferred to western Germany, France and Austria. In the end, the American forces liberated camps that contained thousands of former Red Army soldiers, and the Soviets occupied camps that contained thousands of captured American soldiers and airmen. The repatriation of prisoners from both sides should have been a fairly simple manner. But it wasn't. There was a third, very significant group of prisoners in the scheme of affairs that would surface as a detriment to prisoner swap negotiations.

Besides the Red Army POWs from the liberated Nazi camps, the western armies also captured hundreds of thousands of anti-communist Russian nationals who had fled the Soviet Union and had joined Hitler's army to fight Stalin. This fact was not lost on the Soviets, and as soon as Germany surrendered, inquiries were made by the Red Army staff concerning the disposition of such captured enemy prisoners. Stalin wanted them turned over to Red Army authorities for transport back to Russian-occupied territory to answer for their treachery. The punishment for treason was summary execution.

But Stalin took treachery a bit further when he condemned not only those who had turned against Mother Russia, but anyone who had refused to fight until death and had managed to either get captured by the Germans or had surrendered while still able to fight. In Stalin's mind, this covered virtually every prisoner taken.

The American high command was deluged with pleas from Soviet prisoners who refused to be repatriated. Each man knew that to return to Russia meant death. In one document of the period which describes the efforts of Allied soldiers to repatriate 399 Soviet soldiers, the feelings of the prisoners were quite evident:

"All of these men refused to entrain. They begged to be shot. They resisted entrainment by taking off their clothing and refusing to leave their quarters. It was necessary to use tear gas and some force to drive them out. Tear gas forced them out of the building into the snow where those who had cut themselves fell exhausted and bleeding in the snow. Nine men hanged themselves and one had stabbed himself to death and one other who had stabbed himself subsequently died; while 20 others are in the hospital for self inflicted wounds. The entrainment was finally effected of 368 men who were sent off accompanied by a Russian liaison officer on a train carrying American guards. Six men escaped enroute. A number of men in the group claimed they were not Russians."[61]

In another instance, one which occurred in occupied Austria, British Field Marshal Harold Alexander, commander for Austria and Italy, received a message from American Twelfth Army Group, signed by Omar Bradley:

"Still at large in lower Austria are surrendered forces comprising approximately 105,000 Germans NOT yet totally disarmed and 45,000 Cossacks who are fully armed and may NOT submit to being disarmed until after evacuation. The latter are accompanied by an estimated additional 11,000 camp followers (women, children, old men) who until segregated and disposed of as DPs, will be given same treatment as forces they accompany. To assist AFHQ forces these groups will be accepted by 12th Army Group units which will be responsible for any necessary disarmament and turned over to control of Seventh Army which will designate an assembly area in its name for their reception."

In the case of the Cossacks, who had fought against any mainstream government in Moscow since the days of the Czar, and especially hated the centralist thinking of the communists, being turned over to the

Soviets after fighting against them meant death by firing squad or shipment to Siberia to die in a slave labor camp.

The Cossacks, who were wearing German uniforms when captured by Allied forces, demanded to be considered Prisoners of War under the Geneva Convention. Under these rules, they could legally, as *German* soldiers, refuse to be repatriated. They would then have to be treated as displaced persons and provided for in the country they were currently in, or in another suitable country that would agree to take them. But they could *not* be forced to return to the USSR.

To deal with this problem, the Allied command issued written orders to its officers: "Under no circumstances will those [Cossacks] captured serving in enemy forces be referred to as prisoners of war." Instead, they would be given the designation of Surrendered Enemy Personnel, or SEP. In one Top Secret message sent to V Corps by the Eighth Army headquarters, "Ruling now received 15th Army Group. All Soviet citizens including arrestable categories will be treated as surrendered personnel [SEP] and will therefore be handed over to Russians...Please take action accordingly."[62] The change in terminology was semantical, but by changing the wording, the Geneva Convention could be conveniently circumvented.

What happened next was disgraceful. Both the United States and Great Britain had committed themselves to enforcing repatriation. This was done for two reasons: to placate Stalin, and, in accordance to the Russian interpretation of the Yalta Agreement, to trade Russian POWs for the American, British and Commonwealth POWs Stalin now held hostage. To clarify the orders issued by the military government and SHAEF, Eisenhower's staff replied to an enquiry by Lieutenant General Courtney H. Hodges (Commander, 1st U.S. Army) with: "...as to how much force an Army Commander should use in the control of displaced Russians...Talking with Judge [John J.] McCloy today, he agreed that of course an Army Commander could use any force necessary to insure the success of this operation."

Field Marshal Alexander protested, but to no avail. In the last week in May, 1945, the British forces, in accordance with SHAEF directives, began forcefully repatriating the Cossacks. The orders issued to the troops stated, "...any attempt whatsoever at resistance will be dealt with firmly by shooting to kill."[63] During the process, hundreds of Cossacks soldiers and their families either committed suicide, or were murdered immediately upon being handed over to Red Army political commissars.

One unit of Russians expected to be forced to return at gun point was the *SS Galizien*, the Ukrainian Waffen SS Division. This unit was of particular interest to Stalin, for he had marked them to serve as an example of what would happen to Soviets who take up arms against their country.

The division had fought with the Nazis against the Red Army in 1942-43, but had been withdrawn from the front in 1944 due to heavy casualties. While they were in the process of regrouping away from the battle zone, the Germans were forced out of the Ukraine. Indigenous personnel who had served in Nazi-controlled local police and civil action units—many of which were used by the SS in hunting down and exterminating Poles and Jews—were no longer needed in that capacity. They were pulled out of Russia and transferred to the SS Galizien division which in turn brought the division's strength to a total of 9000 Russians.

But the Galiziens, purposely labeled POWs by the OSS, would not be forced to return to Russia. Instead of being labeled SEP, they were marked by the OSS as future assets and secretly smuggled into Italy where they were hidden until other arrangements could be made for them. The American and British intelligence communities had hand-selected this particular group as future agents and paramilitary operatives for Eastern Europe and Russia in the projected Cold War against the Soviets. They were clandestinely hidden from military authorities, and in 1947, over 8,000 Galiziens were quietly slipped into Canada, many of which eventually entered the United States.

As the Galiziens were in the process of disappearing into the netherworld of the OSS, over 50,000 Cossacks were being forcibly returned to Russian control. In return, the Soviets traded only 2,000 POWs—all British.

In another incident, where U.S. prisoners *were* traded for Russian POWs, Americans witnessed first-hand the fate of those unfortunates who took their places. In Reisa, where the American POWs that had been held by the Germans in Stalag IVB had been moved by the

Russians, a prisoner swap took place between SHAEF personnel and the Russian NKVD under General K.D. Golubev. In this exchange, which occurred on May 25, 1945, only 3,000 of the known 6,000 American and British prisoners that were held in the camp were turned over to SHAEF.

The Russians, using this exchange as a propaganda opportunity, lined the American and British POWs up in ranks in a large field near a rock quarry. Soviet army cameras ground away as the hostages were released to American control and began boarding a convoy of trucks that lined one side of the field.

But as the Russian POWs, which had been brought to the scene by buses, were herded away by the Russians, the cameras ceased operation and stood silent. Instead of a joyous reunion with their comrades, the solemn-faced Russian prisoners were marched down into the rock quarry, out of sight of the observers. Within minutes several machine guns opened up. For ten minutes their staccato bursts of fire echoed off the canyon walls. Only the gunners and officers returned.

When the American and British POWs began to protest loudly at what they had just witnessed, they were told by Allied officers to "keep your heads down, your mouths shut, and get on the trucks."[64]

The Allied High Command had realized from the beginning—VE Day—that gaining the return of the American POWs held in Russian territory would be difficult at best. Five days after VE day, the Associated Press from Allied Advance Headquarters in Reims, France, reported that "Nearly half of the estimated 200,000 British and 76,000 American prisoners of war still in Germany are believed to be within the Russian zone of occupation and Supreme Headquarters has twice requested a meeting or an agreement to arrange their return.

Ten days later, a meeting between representatives of SHAEF under Assistant Chief of Staff (G-1) Major General R.W. Barker and Lieutenant General Golubev, who served as Soviet Assistant Administrator for Repatriation, took place at Halle, Germany. Of major concern to the Americans and British was the Soviet refusal to provide a complete accounting of American and British servicemen held within Russian-occupied territory. In a cable from British Marshal Tedder, Deputy Commander of SHAEF under Eisenhower, sent to all major Allied Command officers and officials, Tedder exposed the Russians deceptive actions. The secret cable, S-94080, dated June 29, 1945, was addressed to "AGWAR FOR WARCOS," and was signed by Tedder at "SHAEFMAIN"

> "Before the HALLE Conference we had made numerous attempts to visit PW Camps in the Russian Zone and always met a firm refusal. After HALLE Conference General GOLEBEV [sic] asked to visit Camps where Russians were being kept. We agreed and asked him for permission to visit Camps in the Russian Zone. He agreed to allow 1 of our Officers to visit 5 camps. One of my representatives started on the trip accompanied by a Russian Major who stated he had the necessary orders. After visiting the first and nearest Camp the Russian Officer produced orders signed by General GOLUBEV restricting our Officer visit to the one Camp. This is the only instance of Soviet authorities permitting US or British Officers to visit Camps in their area, which is in sharp contrast to the liberal policy pursued by us."[65]

It quickly became apparent that the Russians had their own agenda concerning repatriation. In a show of force during the conference, the Russian delegation set the stage for what was to come. According to Major General Barker, "When the Russian mission was finally assembled, it numbered some forty officers and forty to fifty enlisted men. Among the Russian officers were one Lieutenant General and six Major Generals. The Russian party arrived in requisitioned German vehicles of all makes, and [an] American type armored car, fully equipped [armed], and a radio truck, which was in operation most of the time. All Russian male personnel were heavily armed with pistols, sub-machine guns and rifles."[66]

When the meeting started, the Allied staff requested that teams of American and British officers be allowed to go to the camps, speak with the prisoners, make rosters of personnel for accountability, and prepare the groups for repatriation. They also asked that permission be granted for U.S. air transport aircraft to be allowed into Soviet airspace, and for permission to land at the nearest air field facility to provide transport for the POWs. The first request was quickly vetoed, and the second, regarding air transport, is described by Barker:

"I proposed the immediate initiation of steps looking toward prompt release and return to Allied control of all British and American prisoners of war then in Russian custody, using air and motor transport. This proposal was firmly resisted by General Golebev [sic], who cited all manner of local administrative difficulties which precluded the operation. I so informed him. The Russian position was very clear that neither now, nor at any time in the future, would they permit Allied airplanes to be used for the movement into or out of their territory of prisoners of war or displaced persons, except "Distinguished persons, sick and wounded."[67]

After the first meeting in Halle, Barker wrote that SHAEF: "...came to the firm conviction that British and American prisoners of war were, in effect, being held hostage by the Russians until deemed expedient by them to permit their release." It was estimated at that time that the Red Army held over 344,000 Allied servicemen of U.S., British, French, Dutch and Belgian forces. In addition to these, it was estimated that they held an additional 1,100,000 "Displaced Persons" of French, Dutch and Belgian origin.[68]

Six days after the first report issued by Barker describing his findings that the Russians were going to hold hostages, he wrote that: "There is every indication that the Russians intend to make a big show of rapid repatriation of our men, although I am of the opinion that we may find a reluctance to return them all, for an appreciable time to come, since those men constitute a valuable bargaining point. It will be necessary for us, therefore to arrange for constant liaison and visits of inspection to 'uncover' our men."[69]

The dilemma faced by SHAEF quickly became a monster that was growing by leaps and bounds. The war was over, the U.S. military forces were being sent home, families awaited the return of their brave fighting men, so why the delay? Why could not the powerful American military machine that had defeated the Nazis and was on the verge of defeating the Japanese, find and return our POWs?

What both the American public and the Allied field officers did not realize was the fact that the intelligence services—especially the OSS and British Intelligence—were entering the scene through the back door.

Anticipating the "Cold War," and having already decided that the Russians would be the next world threat, preparations using both indigenous and captured enemy personnel were already being taken to field the next decade's spy and sabotage apparatus. As already described in previous chapters, hundreds of war criminals were being hidden—and subsequently saved from prosecution—by the OSS and the British, and as with the Galizien SS veterans, a private army was being rescued for future use.

At the upper levels of SHAEF and the U.S. and British governments, a decision had to be made. Massive numbers of Allied prisoners remained in Russian control, obviously held hostage for bargaining chips, and the Russians were making demands that were impossible to grant if the multi-faceted juggling act between the intelligence community, the military/industrial complex, and the Geneva Convention were to continue. The OSS wanted the German Armies East spy network under Reinhard Gehlen and their various indigenous expatriate assets; the military/industrial coalition wanted the German scientists and their technology, already being transported out of Europe by the PAPERCLIP teams; and the Geneva Convention explicitly forbade forced repatriation.

The forced return of unneeded Russian and enemy personnel was quickly handled by the change of designation to SEP. But the repatriation of the Western forces personnel held by the Russians was another matter. If the Soviets would not give them back willingly—and it appeared that they would not—then the advantages of keeping the Ukrainian, Yugoslav, Hungarian, Serbian and other east-bloc nationals, and the German spy apparatus, scientists and other Nazis, would have to be weighed against regaining possession of the western forces POWs.

For the American and British intelligence services, who stood the most to gain in "to the victor go the spoils," the answer was plain. The POWs had to be sacrificed to benefit National Security. But how could this be done? The American and British people would never stand for such a thing. No one would be willing to trade their son, husband or other relative for a Nazi scientist, spy or some Russian or east-bloc ethnic tribesman. Not even for the national interest.

The answer came in a game of numbers. It was a simple matter of accountability. The plan would have to do three things: 1) It would have to be shown that the Russians, over a period of weeks or months, had repatriated all Allied POWs in their control; 2) Allied forces would have to be shown as expending an all-out effort in searching out, locating and returning both incarcerated POWs and those "lost and wandering" in groups; 3) Any POWs not returned would have to be carried on the lists as either Missing in Action (MIA), or Killed In Action-Body Not Recovered (KIA/BNR). Simply put, any POWs not recovered would be written off.

Chapter 14

Into The Gulags

On May 19, 1945, four days before the Halle meeting took place, Eisenhower sent a cable to field commanders that stated: "Numbers of US prisoners estimated in Russian control 25,000."

The message was written as a statement of fact. Eisenhower, by whatever means, had obtained solid information concerning the rounded-off number of American prisoners taken by the Russians. But this message was written and transmitted *before* it was realized how obstinate the Russians would be in the coming months.

With this number now released and known by all, something had to be done to reduce the amount of personnel noted in the original message as held inside Soviet-controlled territory. It was essential that the strength of Stalin's bargaining position be reduced, and at the same time the American public had to be placated.

On June 1st, SHAEF message FWD-23059 was transmitted by Eisenhower:

1. Due to local transfers of US PW from Russia area to US control immediately prior to and during discussions with Russians which ended 22 May, it is now estimated that only approximately 15,000 US PW were held by the Russians as of 21 May, and not 25,000 as quoted in our cable G 88613.

2. Of these 15,000 there have been transferred to US control 12,400 since 21 May.

3. It is estimated that not more than 2-3000 US PWs still remain in Russian hands. These no doubt are scattered in small groups as no information is available of any large concentrations of POWs in any one camp.

In this one message, written only 10 days after the initial Halle Conference to discuss repatriation, the number of prisoners reported held by the Russians now numbered less than 3,000. The problem with this message, unforeseen by the senders when it was written and transmitted, was another message that had just entered the system from the other end—Moscow.

In a Top Secret letter dated May 31, 1945, sent to Lieutenant General Slavin, Assistant Chief of the Red Army in Moscow, by Major General John R. Deane, U.S. Army Commanding General of the U.S. Military Mission in Moscow, Deane stated:

"I have had a cable from General Marshall in which he states he has received information which indicates that 15,597 United States liberated prisoners of war are now under control of Marshal Tolbukhin.[70]

The next day, Eisenhower signed a cable to AGWAR that stated:

"It is now estimated that only small numbers of U.S. prisoners of war still remain in Russian hands. These no doubt are scattered singly and in small groups as no information is available of any large numbers in specific camps. They are being received now only in small driblets and being reported as received ...Everything possible is being done to recover U.S. personnel and to render accurate and prompt reports thereon to the War Department."

This message, another work of disinformation by the SHAEF staff, was remarkable in that at this same time, the Russians had admitted that they held large numbers of Americans in several camps. In the southern zone alone, Allied prisoners had been moved out of the German *Stalags* to Reisa, Dessaw, Magdeburg, Parchim, Torgeau, Wismar and Crivitz. And they were still there.

To add further problems to the too-hasty concoction of disinformation being released by the High Command, another message, written by Theater Provost Marshal Major General Milton A. Reckord on May 30th, entered the message traffic at a very inopportune moment. In it, it asked that SHAEF make arrangements for shipping between 10,000 and 15,000 American POWs home when they were released from Russian control.

On the same day that Eisenhower's cable "explained" that only small numbers of U.S. POWs still remained at large, the *New York Times* reported, via the War Department, "...substantially all of the American soldiers taken prisoner in Europe are accounted for, Under Secretary Robert P. Patterson said 'This means that it is not expected that many of those who are still being carried as missing in action will appear later as having been prisoners of war.'"[71]

This is a remarkable bit of evidence. For if this information was printed in New York on June 1st, the very day Eisenhower's explanatory message—labeled Secret—went out to his commanders, then how did the *New York Times* get the same information the day before when it would have to be in the press room in time for the next day's edition?

It was because the official U.S. Government's position, on May 31st, 1945, was that no prisoners, other than whatever stragglers might crop up, remained unaccounted for.

The key to the numbers game being played by the U.S. Government, instigated by the OSS in their efforts to hide the loss of the American prisoners, and to buy time for Operation Paperclip, the absorption of Gehlen's organization, and the massive movements of the anti-communist Russian expatriates, was a simple change of designation on status lists. The POWs were broken down into three categories of missing, and one of "Returned to Military Control." Of the three missing categories, the first was "POW (Current Status)" which undoubtedly covered any embarrassing stragglers that might surface later; the second was "Other Missing in Action," which was divided into two sub-categories: "Declared Dead," and "MIA (Current Status)."

And it was very easy to declare a man dead.

In a report issued by Lieutenant Colonel L.L. Ballard, Jr., Chief of the Strength and Accounting and Statistical Office, Office of the Chief of Staff, dated February 26th, 1946, 90,937 personnel were shown as "Returned to Mil. Control," 2,997 as MIA (Current Status), and *11,753* as "Declared Dead."

And then the report indicates that 5,414 were still carried as "POW (Current Status)." Where did Ballard get these figures, if all U.S. personnel—with the exception of stragglers—had either been returned or were dead, as reported by SHAEF seven months previous?

In actuality, of the more than 25,000 Americans held by the Russians at the end of the war, only 4,165 ever came home. This count is the total of figures from the Daily Evacuation Cables that covered the period from the end of the war until all Americans had been declared repatriated, KIA/BNA, or MIA. This left over 20,800 still unaccounted for—all known to have been taken alive by the Red Army as it advanced across Eastern Europe.

Stalin's doctrine concerning captured prisoners, both friend and foe, remained constant throughout the Soviet theater of operations. As thousands of German POWs were being transported eastward toward the Siberian gulags, even more Japanese were being brought into the Asian Soviet Union. Imperial Japanese Army soldiers, captured in the last few weeks of the war in Manchuria and Korea in the last-minute Russian push into East Asia, were being herded aboard box cars or forced marched to holding camps in southeastern Siberia near the Russian city of Khabarovsk.

In Tokyo, General Douglas MacArthur and his Allied administrators had been advised by the Japanese government of the Japanese POWs being removed from Manchuria and Korea, and had been asked to intercede in their behalf. On December 21, 1945, the Four-Power Allied Council—the military government of Japan—met and discussed the issue. The Russian delegation walked out.

Lieutenant General Kusma Derevyanko, leader of the Russian group, refused to take part in any debate concerning the American allegation that over *376,000* Japanese POWs and civilian detainees had been taken into the Soviet Union and had not been repatriated.

140

MacArthur's staff made offers of "assistance" to the Russians in returning the Japanese, even offering help in utilizing American assets to transport the prisoners if the logistics were beyond Russian capabilities. The Soviets refused all offers.

Part of the reason the Russians, who had not entered the war against Japan until the last few weeks, kept custody of the Japanese, was because they discovered what was happening in secret in Tokyo. In anticipation of the Cold War, the Americans, using the intelligence operatives from Fort Detrick's chemical warfare unit, were making secret deals with former members of Unit 731—Col. Shiro Ishii's biological warfare unit.

When the Soviet Union finally entered the war against Japan, Russian units that had been poised *en masse* just across the Manchurian/Soviet border raced south in a pall mall effort to obtain as much Chinese and Korean territory as possible before Japan surrendered. In their advance, they captured Harbin, Ping Fan, and Mukden. Though the American, British and Australian POWs held in these locations were released within a few weeks, the Japanese that had been left behind—and the few records that remained of Ishii's experiments—had been seized by the Red Army. It was then that they discovered that BW experiments had taken place, and that the majority of Ishii's group had evaded capture and had evidently made it back to Japan. These findings were further reinforced when several captured members of 731 were tried in Soviet war trials at Khabarovsk. These men, "pleading guilty" to lessor war crimes, stated that the principle 731 staff had successfully retreated from Manchuria and had probably made it home.

If this was so, then the information they had was invaluable to whoever caught them first. But the majority of the troops that occupied Japan were the Americans. That meant that unless the Russians could force the Ishii people into public light and to divulge what they had discovered to one and all, then the information—if the Americans got to them first—would be proprietary. The Russians would be left in the cold.

Derevyanko demanded that Ishii be found and brought to trial. Unless he and all of his 731 personnel were apprehended and tried—and the information concerning their experiments exposed—the

Japanese government would find that it would be hard to negotiate for the return of their prisoners.

When pressed for numbers, the Russians admitted having 95,000 Japanese prisoners of war and "other war criminals." In actuality, by the best estimates available at the time, they held over 376,000. By 1949, even though the Japanese government and newspapers protested vehemently and continuously, almost none had been returned.[72] Those that remained in the slave labor camps of Siberia, and would remain so until they died, had, like their American and British counterparts taken in Europe, been sacrificed for intelligence purposes.

By the end of 1946, scores of eyewitness reports surfaced describing large numbers of Americans and other Western POWs still being held by the Russians. Though the Pentagon, under orders that originated from the OSS, whose European office was headed by Allen Dulles, had created paperwork to cover the loss of more than 20,000 Americans, the varied reports indicating they still existed continued to trickle in. One German returnee, who managed to escape Soviet control in May of 1945, identified three American paratroopers: Corporal Bucki Okhane, PFC Olen Taylor, and Pvt. Billy Hafers, as being held prisoner in a Russian camp near Dresden. The German, who stated that the men had been put aboard a train and sent east, produced a photograph of Taylor in his army uniform—signed by Taylor. None of these men were ever repatriated.[73]

Another photograph of an American serviceman, Victor Boehm, was smuggled out of a Russian camp and eventually surfaced in the summer of 1945. The information that came with it reported that Boehm had been transported to Siberia, where he was put to work in a Russian tank factory with 200 other Americans.

Then in December, message S-34414 was sent to the American Embassy in Moscow from U.S. Forces, Europe, who evidently did not yet understand the official U.S. position on the matter:

> "Information received here that as of 30 August 1945 the Russians were holding prisoner approximately 45 American enlisted men and two officers, one captain and one lieutenant, at Rada near Tambov in the Stalingrad area. Prisoners were reported in barbed wire under guard."

THE BOYS WE LEFT BEHIND

The headquarters of U.S. Forces, Europe, was not the only player left in the dark on how to treat live sighting reports of Americans being held by the Russians. Even isolated OSS teams provided information. In a report from one such team, dated December 18, 1945, several allied prisoners were reported still being held in a camp inside Russia:

> 1. Informant, a Pole forced to serve in the German Army was taken prisoner by the Russians in 1944...at the end of 1945—April, he escaped and tried to get to Europe. He was, however, arrested by the NKVD after he had got beyond Moscow, and placed in the P.O.W. and Internee Camp in TAMBOV....
> The prisoners numbered, in the informant's estimation, well over 20,000; they were both military and civilian, most likely over-run by the Russians during the offensive. When informant left the camp there were...Englishmen and several score Americans...When he was leaving these Englishmen and Americans asked him urgently to notify the Allied authorities of their plight."[74]

And there were hundreds of other leaks that testified to the existence of Americans being held in Russia long after the cessation of hostilities. Ironically, the one organization that *could* glean the most up-to-date information and form a complete picture of what was happening inside Russian-controlled territory and inside the Soviet Union itself, was the network of agents employed by Reinhard Gehlen. This, however, was an obvious conflict of interest. If Gehlen's people provided such information, it would be apparent to the Russians where the information came from. Gehlen, and his OSS protectors, would have been exposed.[75]

In the end, the OSS, and its newest and largest intelligence network inside eastern Europe and the USSR, kept silent.

And over 20,000 Americans disappeared forever into the gulags.

Chapter 15

Abandoned In Korea

On June 15, 1950, 10 divisions of North Korean troops swarmed into South Korea. Their goal: unify the country under one government. A communist government.

In the narrowest sense, the invasion marked the beginning of a civil war between peoples of a divided country. But in actuality, it represented a break in tensions between the two great power blocs that had emerged from World War II.

The North Koreans felt confident they could capture all of South Korea before any outside power could intervene effectively. This confidence was based primarily on the strength of the North Korean People's Army, which had been formed around a hard core of veterans who had fought with the Soviet and Chinese forces during World War II, and afterward, as part of the Chinese Communist armies against Nationalist China. Equipped and trained by the Soviets, the NKPA was, with the exception of naval and air power, an extremely efficient Third World ground combat force.

The South Korean Army, on the other hand, consisted of 95,000 ill-equipped and poorly trained peasants that represented more of a militia and constabulary than an army. Though the Korean-based American military attempted to assist the South Koreans in organizing and training their army, limited equipment, restricted command authority, and a policy that allowed the South Korean military establishment to become no more than an internal security force made it almost impossible for American staff and trainers to create an army capable of meeting a modern, well-equipped and led force.

On that warm June day they paid the penalty for their unpreparedness. Three days later, after smashing through the weak South Korean lines at the 38th Parallel, a tank-infantry force leading the main North Korean thrust entered Seoul, the capital of South Korea located on the west coast only 35 miles south of the parallel. On the same day, secondary North Korean spearheads raced into central and eastern Korea to keep pace with the main drive.

In the face of this onslaught, the beaten and disorganized South Korean Army retreated in full disorder, abandoning most of its equipment as it recoiled to the South. After pausing briefly to regroup, the North Koreans began hot pursuit intending to totally annihilate the rag-tag South Korean military.

Stunned by this planned Communist aggression, the free world turned to the fledgling United Nations. For the first time since its founding, it was faced with a major conflict requiring massive intervention. Its very existence depended upon how well it met the challenge.

On the 25th of June, the United Nations demanded a cessation of hostilities and the complete withdrawal of North Korean troops from the South. When that failed, the Security Council requested, on the 27th, for UN member nations to furnish military assistance to the South Korean republic.

President Truman had already anticipated the call. On the 26th, he authorized U.S. air and naval forces to attack North Korean troops and installations located in South Korea. Then on the 29th, he broadened the range of U.S. air and naval targets to North Korea and authorized the use of U.S. Army troops to protect Pusan, Korea's major port at the southeastern tip of the peninsula.

Meanwhile, Douglas MacArthur, from his headquarters in Tokyo, flew to Korea to reconnoiter the battle scene. After watching South Korean troops flounder in attempts to organize defenses south of the Han river, MacArthur recommended to Washington that a U.S. Army regiment be committed in the Seoul area at once and that this commitment be built up to two divisions as soon as possible. In response, Truman, on June 30th, authorized MacArthur to use all forces available to him.

MacArthur found his assets sadly lacking. At hand, he had the 1st Cavalry Division, the 7th, 24th and 25th Infantry Divisions—all under the U.S. Eighth Army in Japan—and the 29th Regimental Combat Team on Okinawa. None of these were ready for battle. Each division lacked a third of its organic infantry and artillery units, and almost all of its armor. Besides these shortcomings, these divisions were only 60-70 percent strength. The 29th RCT was proportionately short.

Weapons and equipment were war-torn remnants from World War II, and some weapons—tanks and artillery pieces in particular—could hardly be found by the various commands. (The commanders of these units had no way of knowing that thousands of tons of equipment had been prepositioned in Korea by the OSS/CIA at the end of World War II, and had disappeared ostensibly into the international arms market. This massive quantity of war material was half of the stockpile that had been gathered in Okinawa at the end of WWII for the aborted invasion of Japan. The other half, coincidentally, was secretly sent to Vietnam by the OSS/CIA in 1946-47 to equip Ho Chi Minh's Viet Minh guerrilla force. Examples of this shipment showed up in Dien Bien Phu in the Viet Minh's artillery—American 105mm howitzers and 75mm pack howitzers).[76]

Some weapons, medium tanks and artillery pieces in particular, could scarcely be found in the Far East. Most of these items, along with thousands of tons of other war industry produce, had been dumped in the ocean at the end of World War II. This was done, according the the Pentagon, to keep from flooding the civilian market with returning war surplus materials.[77]

To compound this situation, ammunition reserves were suddenly found to amount to about 45 days supply. As for combat readiness, the U.S. occupation troops had neglected field combat training and were found sadly lacking in war-fighting skills.

All of this, plus a serious deficiency in tactical leadership skills within the company and battalion-level chains-of-command, became readily apparent upon deployment to Korea. Instead of utilizing the principle of mass, the American units were sent in piecemeal. On July 2, only two rifle companies from the 24th Division were flown to Pusan, where they moved by train and truck to Osan, 30 miles below Seoul. The mission of this tiny force was to fight a delaying action against the might of the NKPA divisions and all of their artillery and tanks until more troops could arrive from Japan.

Almost before the Americans could dig in, the NKPA, supported by 30 tanks, renewed their drive to the south. On the 5th, the two forces met. The Americans held on for five hours, but the onslaught quickly proved too much for the tiny band. They were outflanked and shoved back with heavy casualties, and within minutes of breaking contact, retreated pall mall away from the zone of action leaving all equipment behind.

By the 6th, the remainder of the 24th Division had arrived and had taken blocking positions along the Kum River north of Taejon, 60 miles southeast of Osan. Strung out to the east, remnants of the South Korean Army held positions 50 miles above Taegu. And by the 14th of July, the 25th Division had landed and occupied defenses east of the 24th. The 1st Cavalry arrived four days later.

And so it began. Over the next three years, the U.N. and Communist forces would battle the length of the Korean peninsula, stopping just short of Manchuria. In late October of 1950, China entered the war on behalf of the North Koreans, and by the 27th of November, four Chinese armies had joined the fray. This massive addition to the North Korean side forced the U.S. X Corps to withdraw, leaving the 1st Marine Division and the U.S. Army 7th Division encircled at the Chosin Reservoir. The Marines and their Army counterparts managed to break out, fight their way 75 miles to the sea, through sub-zero temperatures, bringing their dead, wounded and equipment with them. Still, men were lost and never recovered—as was the case in every major action of the war.[78]

The war became a series of attacks, withdrawals, and counter attacks. Finally, by June of 1951, the policies governing the conduct of the war began to change. The pendulum movements of the armies had grown smaller and smaller as each force established and strengthened its positions and defenses. Bloody hill fights ensued in which the same ground was taken and re-taken over and over. But the line seldom changed. The war was becoming stagnant. It appeared impossible for either side to win. As a result, the U.N., and especially U.S., objective in the conflict shifted from military victory to political settlement. The U.N. and the North Koreans and Chinese began to negotiate a peace.

But there were many problems. Before a truce and ceasefire could be negotiated, boundaries had to be established. This called for each side to continue to jockey for position in the mountains along the 38th Parallel. But for the U.N. forces, the issue became almost tactically impossible. For by June 1st, all U.N. ground forces could not, without approval from Washington, make a general advance north of a meandering east-west line that had been established along the parallel. The only tactical operations permitted were those necessary for self defense against an attacking force. In the field, the commanders helplessly bore the weight of frustration as the war immediately bogged down. From this point, the troops were prohibited by the politicians from applying the principles of war beyond the tactical level, involving small units only.

Finally, on July 27, 1953, after a series of "peace talks" at Panmunjom—and hundreds of bloody skirmishes and a few outright battles—armistice was declared and hostilities "officially" ended. But as in World War II, there were a few items on the agenda that remained to be cleaned up. One concerned the fate of American troops captured by the North Koreans and Chinese.

It was called Operation BIG SWITCH. It began on August 5th, 1953 and continued to September 6th. It was the largest—and the final—exchange of prisoners between the U.N. forces and the Communists.

In the beginning, the North Koreans and Chinese demanded an "all-for-all" prisoner exchange. But the United States was reluctant to agree to such a wholesale swap. Based on its World War II experience, and knowing that mandatory repatriation did not work in Europe—especially with the behind-the-scenes intervention of the clandestine services—the North Koreans and the U.S. finally agreed on voluntary, or "non-forcible" repatriation that would permit each side to release only those prisoners who wished to return to their respective countries.

The problem with this plan, after a half-century of dealing with the Communist mind, is now obvious. But in 1953, diplomats and soldiers alike still attempted to permit the Communists a certain degree of latitude—saving face, so to say—in agreements. This plan of voluntary repatriation worked to the advantage of the Communists. By simply stating that someone does not wish to return, that particular individual could disappear forever.

According to official documents, approximately 14,200 Communist Chinese POWs elected *not* to return to the Peoples Republic of China, while only 21 Americans are known to have actually, beyond question, elected to remain voluntarily in Communists hands.

But there is still a question concerning over 8,000 other U.S. MIAs, many of which were known to be held captive after Operation Big Switch and never repatriated. In one article of the period, the *New York Times* reported that "...General James A. Van Fleet, retired commander of the United States Eighth Army in Korea, estimated tonight that a large percentage of the 8,000 American soldiers listed as missing in Korea were alive."[79]

This was not the result of findings after Big Switch; the U.S. military and intelligence services knew something about what was happening—and possibly the end result—five days into the month-long Big Switch operation. In a report by the U.N. Combined Command for Reconnaissance Activity, Korea, it was stated that: "Figures show that the total number of MIAs, plus known captives, less those to be US repatriated, leaves a balance of 8,000 unaccounted for." The report goes on to state that many of this number had been transported to Manchuria, China and the Soviet Union during the span of the war, and that: "...many POWs transferred have been technicians and factory workers."[80]

In a secret memorandum written by Hugh M. Milton II, Assistant Secretary of the Army in January, 1954—four months after the conclusion of Big Switch—a clandestine plan to recover lost Americans held by the Communists is mentioned:

B. THE UNACCOUNTED-FOR AMERICANS BELIEVED TO BE STILL HELD ILLEGALLY BY THE COMMUNISTS (SECRET).

1. There are approximately 954 United States personnel falling in the group. What the Department of the Army and other interested agencies is doing about their recovery falls into two parts. First, the direct efforts of the UNC Military Armistice Commission to obtain an accurate accounting, and second, efforts by G2 of the Army, both overt and covert, to locate,

identify, and recover these individuals. G2 is making an intensive effort through its information collection system world-wide, to obtain information on these people and *has a plan for clandestine action to obtain the recovery of one or more to establish the case positively that prisoners are still being held by the Communists.* No results have been obtained yet in this effort. The direct efforts of the UNC [United Nations Command] are being held in abeyance pending further study of the problem by the State Department...

2. A further complicating factor in the situation is that *to continue to carry these personnel in a missing status is costing over one million dollars annually. It may become necessary at some future date to drop them from our records as 'missing and presumed dead."* [Author's emphasis]

The Defense Department, as the War Department before it, took this advice handily. As with the missing prisoners—the "non-repatriated POWs"—of World War II (and World War I), the men were simply written off as "missing and presumed dead." In an April, 1954, memo to Milton written by Major General Robert Young, Assistant Chief of Staff and G-1 of the Army, Young states:

2. Under the provisions of Public Law 490 (77th Congress), the Department of the Army, after careful review of each case and interrogation of returning prisoners of war, has placed 618 soldiers, known to have been in enemy hands and unaccounted for by the Communist Forces in the following categories:

313 -Finding of Death- Administratively determined, under the provisions of Public Law 490, by Department of the Army.

275 -Report of Death- reported on good authority by returning prisoners.

21 - Dishonorable Discharge.[81]

4 - Under investigation, prognosis undecided. Missing in Action for over one year.

2 - Returned to Military Control.

These numbers total 615 personnel, a significant drop from the original report that 954 Americans remained in Communist hands. This discrepancy occurred during the preceding months when a series of "presumed findings of death for unaccounted-for Americans" were utilized to cut the numbers down.

Of considerable note is the first category of this report, "Administratively determined under Public Law 490, by Department of the Army." How does one "administratively determine" that a missing soldier, known to have been taken into captivity and still be alive at the end of the conflict, to now be dead? Such a finding on the government's behalf is simply a matter of convenience and economics. By removing someone from the MIA status and placing them on the KIA list, there is a one-time insurance payment to the survivors. This saves the government hundreds of thousands of dollars of monthly service pay, which includes promotions and pay raises, over the life of the POW. And it saves a great deal of embarrassment for helpless military officers and politicians who fail to secure the return of their lost men.

But what *really* happened to them?

As with the World War II prisoners, most appear to have been evacuated out of the war zone. According to several documents, the majority of missing men went to China and the Soviet Union. In one report from the Office of Special Operations of the Central Intelligence Agency:

"At the time of the official repatriation, some of our repatriates stated that they had been informed by the Communists that they (the Communists) were holding 'some' U.S. flyers as 'political prisoners' rather than as prisoners of war and that these people would have to be negotiated for through political or diplomatic channels. Due to the fact that we did not recognize the red regime in China, no political negotiations were instituted, although State did have some exploratory discussions with the British in an attempt to get at the problem. The situation was relatively dormant when, in late November 1954, the Peking radio announced that 13 of the 'political prisoners' had been sentenced for 'spying.' This announcement caused a public uproar and a demand from U.S. citizens, Congressional leaders and organizations for action to effect their release."[82]

But there were many more than the thirteen airmen reported here. Canadian Squadron Leader Andrew R. MacKenzie, who had been captured, transported to China and held in the same camp for two years, reported after he was exchanged that he had been held with a number of United States airmen and that none of the Americans in the camp were on the list of eleven whose sentencing had been announced by the Chinese on November 23, 1954.[83]

And there were other reports. Every time the government felt that it was succeeding in damage control and the issue could be put behind, other reports of sightings or information regarding live POWs being held in Russia or China surfaced. In one shocking report that arrived in Washington by Foreign Service Dispatch cable, dated March 23, 1954, sent from the U.S. diplomatic post in Hong Kong, the live sighting of hundreds of American POWs was reported:

American POWs reported en route to Siberia.

A recently arrived Greek refugee from Manchuria has reported seeing several hundred American prisoners of war being transferred from Chinese trains to Russian trains at Manchouli near the border of Manchuria and Siberia. The POWs were seen late in 1951 and in the spring of 1952 by the informant and a Russian friend of his. The informant was interrogated on two occasions by the Assistant Air Liaison Officer and the Consulate General agrees with his evaluation of the information as probably true and the evaluation of the source as unknown reliability. The full text of the initial Air Liaison Office report follows:

First report dated March 16, 1954, from Air Liaison Office, Hong Kong, to USAF Washington, G2.

"This office has interviewed refugee source who states that he observed hundreds of prisoners of war in American uniforms being sent into Siberia in late 1951 and 1952. Observations were made at Manchouli (Lupin), 49 degrees 50' - 117 degrees 30' Manchuria Road Map, AMSL 201 First Edition, on USSR-Manchurian border. Source observed POWs on railway station platform loading into trains for movement into Siberia. In railway restaurant source closely observed three POWs who were under guard and were conversing in English. POWs wore sleeve insignia which indicated POWs were Air Force noncommissioned officers. Source states that there were a great number of Negroes among POW shipments and also states that at no time later were any POWs observed returning from Siberia...."

...[according to source] POWs wore OD outer clothing described as not heavy inasmuch as weather considered early spring. Source identified from pictures service jacket, field, M1943. No belongings except canteen. No ornaments were observed.

Condition appeared good, no wounded all ambulatory.

Station divided into two sections with tracks on each side of loading platform. On Chinese side POWs accompanied by Chinese guards. POWs passed through gate bisecting platform to Russian train manned and operated by Russians. Russian trainmen wore dark blue or black tunic with silver colored shoulder boards. Source says this [is] regular train uniform because ["but"] he knows the trainmen are [actually] military wearing regular train uniforms.

...Source states [his] job was numbering railroad cars at Manchouli every time subsequent POW shipments passed through Manchouli. Source says these shipments were reported often and occurred when United Nation forces in Korea were on the offensive....

...Further information as to number of POWs observed source states that first observation *filled a seven passenger car train* and second observation about the same....

"...Comment Reporting Officer: Source is very careful not to exaggerate information and is positive of identification of American POWs."[84]

And the reports kept coming. From returned POWs, who reported comrades left behind and never brought home, to escapees and late repatriates who described camps, conditions and personnel, the information continued to leak out from behind the Bamboo Curtain. For the politicians and peace-time military bureaucrats, the issue had to not only be addressed for this war, but all future wars as well.

In a report titled "Recovery of Unrepatriated Prisoners of War," the Defense Advisory Committee on Prisoners of War provided a list of solutions to the problem that ranged from instilling in soldiers a "don't get captured" attitude, to more flexible response by field commanders in dealing with the enemy on prisoner exchange proceedings. But one part of the report stood out from the rest—and became the standard mindset of the United States Government for not only Korea, but World War II, Vietnam and very probably, all future conflicts.

"...The military courses of action apparently cannot be taken unilaterally...The problem becomes a philosophical one. If we are 'at war,' cold, hot or otherwise, casualties and losses must be expected and perhaps we must learn to live with this type of thing. If we are in for fifty years of peripheral 'firefights' we may be forced to adopt a rather cynical attitude on this for political course of action something like General Erskine outlined which would (1) instill in the soldier a much more effective 'don't get captured' attitude...."

As these whispered-behind-closed-doors courses of action were being presented, the public face of government continued to present a more acceptable front. In an attempt to resolve the problem—in plain sight of the media—the United States Department of State sent an official U.S. diplomatic note to Moscow:

"The Embassy of the United States of America presents its compliments to the Ministry of Foreign Affairs of the Union of Soviet Socialist Republics and has the honor to request the Ministry's assistance in the following matter.

"The United States Government has recently received reports which support earlier indications that American prisoners of war who had seen action in Korea have been transported to the Union of Soviet Socialist Republics and that they are now in Soviet custody. The United States Government desires to receive urgently all information available to the Soviet Government concerning these American personnel and to arrange their repatriation at the earliest possible time."

The reply from the Soviets, dated May 12, 1954, was short and to the point.

"In connection with the note of the Embassy of the United States of America, received by the Ministry of Foreign Affairs of the Union of Soviet Socialist Republics on May 5, 1954, the Ministry has the honor to state the following:

The United States assertion contained in the indicated note that American prisoners of war who participated in military actions in Korea have allegedly been transferred to the Soviet Union and at the present time are being kept under Soviet guard is devoid of any foundation whatsoever and is clearly far-fetched, since there are not and have not been any such persons in the Soviet Union."

As the years went by, the issue of the Korean War POWs rose on occasion. Each time it was addressed with official voices of concern and sympathy on behalf of the government, and brief attention in the media. But little else. Between the two wars—World War II and Korea—the government had learned how to shove the POW/MIA issue under the rug and go on with life as usual. And they were getting very good at it. In one memo dealing with Korean war and Vietnam POWs, dated January 21, 1980, written by Michael Oksenberg and sent to Zbigniew Brezezinski, the National Security Advisor under President Jimmy Carter, the attitude is plainly seen:

"...a letter from you is important to indicate that you take recent refugee reports of sightings of live Americans 'seriously.' This is simply good politics; DIA and State are playing this game, and you should not be the whistle blower. The idea is to say that the President is determined to pursue any lead concerning possible live MIAs."[85]

The lives of these missing men were now simply a matter of politics. Even though the Chinese, in 1973, released two American POWs that had been captured *during* the Korean war, along with an American pilot shot down during Vietnam, little action was taken to ascertain if the Chinese held any more. As for the Russians, *detente* would have suffered if the bothersome POW/MIA issue was pursued. It was simply more expeditious to write off one's casualties, count your losses, and drive on.

In the process of this developing political ideology, over 8,000 Americans were, by manipulation of figures on reports, abandoned to a life of slave labor by the very government that had sent them into harm's way.

And they would not be the last.[86]

Chapter 16

Plausible Deniability

Though the Soviets denied the existance of American POWs in the Soviet Union, the White House knew better. President Dwight D. Eisenhower, already a veteran of Soviet POW-holding tactics from his World War II experience, was privy to highly classified intelligence reports that not only mentioned the numbers of prisoners held, but exactly *where* they were held. And in many cases, specific names, ranks, units and hometowns of the reported hostages.

In several instances, Gulag internees of other nationalities that were released by the Soviets came out of Russia with information describing Americans by name, physical description, and often, details about the person's background that only that individual would know. Still, the bureaucrats, the Pentagon, and the American intelligence community refused to act. Instead, a policy of downplaying the POW issue became prevalent in 1954—and lasted all the way through the post-Vietnam war years.

In 1954, Colonel Philip Corso, an intelligence adviser to Eisenhower, was ordered to investigate the POW issue in regard to the information that hundreds of Korean War soldiers were still being held inside Russia. Corso, working at the behest of Eisenhower's chief national security aide C.D. Jackson (an old OSS hand-turned CIA and senior editor at *Life* magazine), concluded that the most expeditious way to approach the subject would be to interview someone who had recently been released from the Gulag, or who had at least spent time in the region and could shed light on the situation. He found that the CIA had such a person, a Soviet defector named Yuri Rastvovrov.

Corso contacted the CIA and set up an interview with Rastvovrov. By the conclusion of the meeting, Corso had his answer. Rastvovrov had not only seen trainloads of American servicemen being transported to the Soviet Union, but described one particular train as containing over 400 U.S. prisoners.[87]

Corso continued to investigate, and by the time his report was completed, it stated that "The conclusion was that Korean War POWs by the hundreds, perhaps thousands, had been sent to the Soviet Union."[88]

He reported to the President that the prisoners would probably be used for intelligence purposes, and that when their usefulness was past, they would disappear into the Gulag forever as the Soviets would never admit their existance. They were, as far as the outside world would ever know, dead men. And it would be in the government's best interest to consider them so—and to hide the knowledge of their existance from the public.

Eisenhower, having already been involved in much the same issue in 1945, agreed. "I think you're right. I accept your recommendation...thank you colonel, you did a fine job."[89]

This policy became the official stance in 1955. All POWs, whether they were in North Korea, China, or the USSR, were written off. The Government's slate was now clean.[90]

Until the next time.[91]

Between the end of the Korean War and the beginning of the war in Southeast Asia, other Americans fell victim to the government's policy regarding captured Americans. These "Cold Warriors," mainly consisting of airmen from the various services who overflew—or flew too close to—Communist countries, often found themselves in the same predicament as their WWII and Korean War counterparts.

As the Cold War grew in intensity, it became a deadly game of spy-versus-spy. The Russians, lacking the capabilities to keep up with the West in modern technology, sent armies of agents abroad to obtain by whatever means necessary the various items of interest. The West, on the other hand, spent the majority of its time trying to find out what was going on behind the Iron Curtain. The majority of this concern originated with the reports being generated by Reinhard Gehlen and his spy network.

In the early days, prior to the entrance of the Lockheed SR-71 reconnaissance jet and the spy satellites, airborne intelligence was gathered by intrepid airmen who penetrated deep inside Communist air space on a routine basis. Not all of them came home.

The fate of these men was not only downplayed by the government, but was covered up as a matter of policy. The main motivator for this, according to declassified documents of the period, was the sensitive nature and secrecy of their missions. This may have been true at the time, but does not explain why their stories are still classified. The "secrecy" element fades when one reasons that: 1) the Soviets knew who they held and what they were up to, and 2) the U.S. Government could not hide their activities from the Russians or Chinese, who held the evidence. Secrecy fell by the wayside at the moment of capture. So who was the government trying to hide the existance and circumstances of the shotdown aviators from?

General Graves B. Erskine, assistant to the secretary of defense under Eisenhower, wrote a memo to Walter Robertson at the Department of State that sheds some light on the official attitude concerning how the government would handle the Cold War POW situation:

> "...Your attention is again invited to the undersirability of providing any information through any source which might lead the next of kin of these armed forces personnel discussed herein to assume or believe that these personnel might still be alive and held unless the communists are prepared at some point to document such information."[92]

As the Cold War progressed, the U.S. government continuously denied the existance of any programs of aerial spying wherein U.S. aircraft were entering Soviet or Chinese air space. In actuality, an entire covert high-altitude spyplane program was in full swing. CIA-run Operation OVERFLIGHT brought in reams of photographic, communications, and electronic intelligence (Photint, Comint and Elint) from all parts of the Soviet Union and China. Flown at first by U.S. Air Force crews utilizing highly modified aircraft containing sophisticated electronic gear and powerful cameras, the operation progressively grew more "black" when these aging aircraft became vulnerable to Soviet air defense systems. The result was the covert high altitude program that resulted in the development of the Lockheed U-2 and a team of pilots that "contracted" to the CIA as civilians. In actuality, they were Air Force officers that had been "sanitized" by transfering them to civilian status for an indefinite period of time, then returned to Air Force status at a later date. This process eventually became known as "sheep dipping." An individual who was sheep-dipped was discharged from the military on paper, but during his absence his time in grade, promotions, retirement years and other perks continued just as if he had never left the service. After serving with the CIA, the person could return to his regular branch and continue just as if he had never left. Sheep Dipping was to become a common practice later during the Vietnam/Laotian war years for almost everyone who "left" the regular military for service in Laos. During the Cold War, and later Vietnam, it was done to provide the CIA—by now referred to as "The Company" because of the number of contract agents being handled—with a system of "Plausible Deniability." Simply put, any pilot captured could, with a certain degree of plausibility, be denied as an member of the U.S. military or a representative of the United States Government. In the case of the U-2s, the cover was very simple. The pilots were contract "weather" pilots. Their mission was high altitude weather research.

The Russians knew better, but because of the ineffectiveness of their surface-to-air missiles, could not gather any evidence that these embarrasing overflights by U.S. spyplanes were just that. Until Francis Gary Powers was shot down.

Previous to May of 1960, the Soviet air defense forces had been unable to obtain the performance characteristics and altitude envelope of the U-2. U-2 pilots often reported looking down upon swarms of MiG interceptors who could not attain the height of the long-winged spyplane, referring to the cluster of aircraft far below as "aluminum clouds." SAM missiles of the time were ineffective as well, due to an inability to properly set the altitude setting of the proximity fuses.

But on May 1, 1960, Francis Gary Powers, flying from Peshawar, Pakistan on an overflight of the USSR to Bødø, Norway, was hit near Sverdlovsk, USSR, by the concussion of a SAM missile that had somehow managed to find his range. The blast, which occurred behind him, pitched the U-2 forward so violently that the wings were ripped from the fuselage. Powers found himself struggling to exit the inverted, spinning fuselage. The G-forces were incredible, and Powers, encased in a cumbersome space suit, barely managed to escape. He was captured shortly after landing in a muddy field.

A trial was held in Moscow for all the world to see. Powers was accused of being a spy—his "survival kit" even contained poison suicide devices—and he was sentenced to a lengthy prison term.[93] But fate intervened after almost two years and he was exchanged for KGB Colonel Rudolf Abel, a more important (to the Soviets) Russian spy. The end result of the incident was a cessation of overflights of U.S. spyplanes in Soviet air space until the advent of the SR-71 and the satellite program.[94]

But for the majority of those crews who had been shot down and captured between 1955 and 1960, the Cold War would never end.

Chapter 17

Secret Losses

The war in Southeast Asia was actually two wars. To the American public, there existed only one war: the war in Vietnam. But there was also a second, very secret, war going on at the same time. And both were very closely interrelated.

The second war was the CIA's secret operation in Laos. The only American military forces involved were a few hundred U.S. Army Special Forces personnel that had been sanitized and assigned to CIA case officers in Vientiene, the country's capital city. Working under the operation moniker of WHITESTAR, these personnel were responsible for setting up and training a guerrilla army of Meo and Hmong tribesmen under a Laotian warlord named General Vang Pao. Their enemy was the communist Pathet Lao guerrillas of Northern Laos—and later the North Vietnamese Army on the Laotian side of the Vietnamese border.

To run this operation, the CIA sent former Operation 40 and Operation MONGOOSE[95] case officers and field agents that were no longer needed in Miami for anti-Castro operations. By this time Cuba was beginning to take a back seat to the developing war in Southeast Asia and the CIA had agents to spare. Eisenhower had already established Laos as the next "domino" targeted by Moscow, and if Laos fell, in his opinion, both Cambodia and Vietnam would follow. The Pentagon, on the other hand, was given Vietnam as its place to make the stand against Communisim. The CIA, though operating in both countries, concentrated its initial activities in Laos.

For the CIA, Laos represented fertile ground to expand and reinforce its concept of paramilitary and covert action activities, and such activity there was supported by Eisenhower. Vietnam, in the meantime, had been programmed for conflict at a later date and would be ripe for intervention by both the CIA and the U.S. military whenever the decision was made to enter that smoldering conflict.

The Vietnam scenario was not something that occurred entirely due to North Vietnamese Communist expansion. According to Colonel Fletcher Prouty, Kennedy's director of covert action in the Pentagon, the troubles in South Vietnam were due to political intervention by the U.S. government shortly after the fall of Dien Bien Phu. After the French pulled out of Indochina, the inland infrastructure collapsed. Several things happened within short order: The constabulary, consisting mainly of French colonial forces, pulled out of the countryside and eventually Vietnam; The Chinese merchants, who formed the bridge between the rice-growing peasants and the cities and provided the marketing resources for the product, were forced out of the country, thereby breaking the link between the countryside and the cities; and millions of non-Communist North Vietnamese refugees were forcibly removed from their ancestral lands in the North and transported south for relocation. This latter event was a major foundation stone of the Vietnam war.

The North Vietnamese refugees were mainly Catholic of Tonkinese descent, whereas the majority of South Vietnamese were Annamese Buddhists. The refugees, having no family in the south to provide land or jobs, had no one to turn to for help except the government. The South Vietnamese government, now saddled with the American relocation program, was forced to provide jobs for the new "citizens." The only jobs available were government jobs.

The villagers of the South now found that their tax collectors, government agents, police officers, teachers and other government functionaries were Catholic Tonkinese who held few attachments and little sympathy for their age-old enemy, the Buddhist Annamese. When problems arose, such as who would transport the rice crop to market now that the Chinese merchants were gone, the new government functionaries could provide few answers—and in many circumstances did not care. Problems increased and tensions worsened. Finally, conflicts arose in the countryside between not only the villagers and the government, but between villages. This later series of events occurred over water.

Because the ground water in Vietnam is extremely polluted with the run-offs of rice paddies, the only potable water supply comes from rain water that is caught during monsoon and stored in huge earthen jars. Each household has such a container, handed down from generation to generation. Without a way to capture and store water, a family could not survive.

As punishment for infractions, or to force people to move out of villages during the "Strategic Hamlet" relocation program, the new representatives of the Saigon government would break the water jars. The people then had little choice but to give up the ancestral farm and move on to the government hamlet. Those that did not succumb to these tactics became, essentially, bandits who roamed the countryside attacking other villages at will for food and water. These people, living in the jungles and marshland of the Mekong Delta, became known as the Viet Cong. Eventually they began to receive support from the very homeland of the new government agents—North Vietnam.

The relocation program was the brainchild of the CIA. Through its Saigon Military Mission, run by Colonel Edward Lansdale, the Central Intelligence Agency was able to foment a veritable revolution in South Vietnam. At the same time, they were also able to ensure that the logistical supplies and weapons for the new guerrilla force that was spreading through the hinterland came from—and could be traced to—Communist North Vietnam.

As these events were occuring, other CIA covert paramilitary activities were taking place across the border in Laos. But instead of using the media to gain attention to a volatile political situation that would very probably demand U.S. military intervention, such as was occuring in Vietnam, the war in Laos was kept secret from prying eyes. The reason for this, though never admitted, more than likely had to do with the way that particular operation was financed. Instead of going through normal channels for budgeting, the CIA instead elected to utilize the region's main cash crop to finance their secret war. That crop was opium.

Under Vang Pao and his Hmong army, the operatives formed an extensive distribution network. By using CIA assets in the form of aircraft and other vehicles, tons of opium were shipped out of the mountains of Laos to Vientiane, where it was processed into heroin, then flown on to Hong Kong and Singapore. From these two locations it entered a distribution network that took it to Europe (via the Corsican Mafia in Marseille) and the United States (via Santos Trafficante). More on this later.[96]

As the war in Laos heated up, Vang Pao's CIA-led Hmong army, using weapons and equipment purchased with drug money, expanded its actions against the communist Pathet Lao. In Vietnam, the situation also continued to escalate. And by 1965, with Kennedy's program of pulling American "advisors" out of Vietnam canceled by a bullet in Dealey Plaza sixteen months previous, and with LBJ's "Tonkin Gulf Incident" as a catalyst, the 9th Marine Regiment landed its first Battalion Landing Team (BLT 1/9) on Red Beach at Da Nang. The war in Southeast Asia had begun in earnest and would last ten years.[97]

Chapter 18

Moscow Bound

Five days after the signing of the Paris Peace Accords, Secretary of State Henry Kissinger hand-carried a letter to North Vietnamese Prime Minister Le Duc Tho which promised that the United States would assist the government of Vietnam in post-war reconstruction. In the body of the letter, two paragraphs held particular significance to the North Vietnamese.

1) The Government of the United States of America will contribute to postwar reconstruction in North Vietnam without any political conditions.

2) Preliminary United States studies indicate that the appropriate programs for the United States contribution to postwar reconstruction will fall in the range of $3.25 billion of grant aid over five years. Other forms of aid will be agreed upon between the two parties. This estimate is subject to revision and to detailed discussion between the Government of the United States and the Government of the Democratic Republic of Vietnam.

The problem with this letter is that it was secret. None of the commitments it implied were revealed to anyone in either the Congress or the Senate. That means that the letter was worthless. Unknown to the North Vietnamese, the Constitutional process required to appropriate funds from the U.S. government to fulfill such a promise had never been initiated. Without Congressional approval, no funds would be forthcoming. But the North Vietnamese were ignorant of American Constitutional law.

According to the Senate investigation on POW/MIA affairs, this letter and its promises would not have stood a chance of passing in Congress even if Nixon or Kissinger had made the proper overtures. "...Congress knew nothing of the Kissinger commitments," the report explains. "Had key Senators and Congressmen been told of the policy, they would have had the opportunity to tell the President that voting for billions of dollars of aid or funds for North Vietnam would have been an admission of culpability. The United States had failed in its mission to protect South Vietnam from the totalitarian Communist regime in the North.

"The suffering, brutality, death and dehumanization borne by the Vietnamese people since the war is proof that the American goals in Vietnam were correct. However, the failure of the civilian leadership to achieve those goals had to do more with the collapse of political leadership in the United States than with the morality of the goals. Congress realized full well, if Kissinger did not, that the soothing word 'reconstruction' actually meant 'reparations.' The American people would never pay reparations when no crime had been committed. Congress saw Kissinger's plan as a betrayal and an admission of guilt.

"However, there is no doubt that the North Vietnamese concluded that the President's emissary had pledged billions of dollars in reparations to the Democratic Republic of Vietnam."

Twelve days after the Nixon/Kissinger letter was delivered to the North Vietnamese, Operation Homecoming, the final repatriation of U.S. POWs by North Vietnam, began. It lasted until March 29, 1973, barely six weeks after the $3.25 billion dollar promise was made. In that time only 591 American servicemen, out of over 3,000 missing, were returned.

During the 60 day ceasefire instituted by the Paris Peace Accords, Americans were still flying combat and reconnaissance missions over Laos—and being shot down. In one particular instance, a special operations electronic surveillance EC-47Q was downed in Laos with all aboard. The EC-47Q was a modified C-47 "Gooney Bird" twin-engine transport that contained a cargo compartment full of highly sophisticated electronic monitoring and communications equipment. In a very suspect set of circumstances, this particular aircraft, carrying a "sheep-dipped" sterile U.S. Air Force crew of electronics technicians, was ordered to fly this "one last mission" before the war officially ended. It never came back.

Nine days after the Paris Peace Accords and the ceasefire took effect, the EC-47Q took to the air on its last clandestine mission over northern Laos. One crew member, Sergeant Peter R. Cressman, knew after reading the accords that the mission was in violation of the agreements. Therefore, should something happen and they were shot down and captured, they would be tried as war criminals. But realizing that the chance of getting shot down was only speculative, and the probability of getting court martialed for refusing to obey orders was a definite probability, the crew decided to fly the mission.

Somewhere over northern Laos their aircraft entered what was known among pilots as a "Flak Trap." A Flak Trap is basically an aerial ambush wherein ground anti-aircraft guns, commonly known as "Triple A" (Anti-Aircraft Artillery), are concentrated in one location where false targets are set up to entice unsuspecting fighters, bombers or recon planes in. Many of these ambush sites were established in locations where certain types of aircraft were known to fly. Specifically, the primary prey of the ground gunners were the sophisticated versions of reconnaissance and fighter-bombers that contained high-tech electronic systems—and systems operators.

Of particular interest were such aircraft as the EC-111, an electronic countermeasures aircraft; the RB-66, an electronic reconnaissance aircraft that specialized in jamming SAM radar sites before a raid; the F-111, which contained a new terrain following radar system; the E-6B, a Navy communications jammer, the F-4 "Wild Weasel" SAM suppression jets; and virtually any other specialized aircraft containing modern surveillance, jamming or SAM suppression equipment—such as the EC-47Q.

The reason these particular aircraft were primary targets over the bomb-laden strike aircraft was very simple. The North Vietnamese and Pathet Lao, for the entire span of the war, were armed, equipped and supplied by the Soviets and Chinese. The war material delivered to the war zone could not be paid for in cash, for North Vietnam was a very poor country, and the Pathet Lao had little internal financial means of support. But the weapons had a price, and the price was technology.

Both the Soviets and Chinese handed the North Vietnamese and the Pathet Lao shopping lists. The lists identified the above aircraft—and certain members of their crew. Even though most of the airplanes that were shot down ended up little more than twisted aluminum wreckage, many of the "black boxes" containing the solid-state electronic components would remain virtually intact. And so did most of the crewmembers who successfully ejected from their stricken aircraft.

Jerry Mooney, an analyst for the National Security Agency during the war, was tasked with tracking the airmen who were shot down once they had been captured. This was done through analysis of enemy communications. He had also intercepted Soviet shopping lists for specific items of equipment and particular crewmember specialists who knew how the systems worked. These men, known as "EWOs" (Electronic Warfare Officers), "WSOs" (Weapons Systems Officers), and "Backseaters" (communications interception and jamming specialists), were the brains that made the systems work. By capturing the equipment and piecing it together, then picking the operator's brain, the Soviets could discover not only how to design their own countermeasures to the devices, but duplicate them for use in their own aircraft.

Mooney kept a very special roster of such captured specialists. The pilots, everyone knew, were taken to such places as the Hanoi Hilton to be used later as bargaining chips. The specialists, dubbed Backseaters, Rightseaters, or Backenders by pilots, spent only a brief time in North Vietnamese or Pathet Lao prison camps. For beside each name on this roster, Mooney wrote the letters "MB"—Moscow Bound.

In the camps, the pilots and other prisoners who were not deemed technically valuable, used the phrase "on the train." This meant that if someone was said to be on the train, or to have taken the train, they had been shipped out to Russia or China. Such was probably the case of survivors of Cressman's EC-47Q.

The "Flying Pueblo," as it was dubbed, entered a flak trap over northern Laos on February 5th, 1973.[98] The enemy gunners, laying in wait with massed AAA, opened up on the lumbering 30 year-old propeller driven aircraft and delivered enough punishment to shoot it down. But it did not fall in a twisting, turning ball of flame. Instead, it must have been disabled and managed to crash-land in the jungle. For a few days later the wreckage was located by a search team who found no sign of bodies. At about the same time another U.S. recon plane intercepted enemy radio messages and discovered that at least four crewmembers from the EC-47Q were being held in captivity. This information was relayed to Washington—and Jerry Mooney.[99]

On February 17th, these men were spotted and identified by a clandestine source about eighteen miles away from the crash site and reported to be under guard and in good health. Mooney, in the days ahead, tracked more than just the original four crewmen, he located and tracked three others. Yet on February 22nd, this information not withstanding, the Air Force declared all personnel aboard the fated ship dead.[100]

When questioned why he did not come forward later and announce publicly that this finding was incorrect, Mooney articulated that he had assumed that after submitting his report either military action, or covert action by the CIA's special rescue unit would take place to recover the prisoners. But that did not happen. Instead, the issue died with all crewmembers written off as KIA/BNR. Yet two months after the shoot-down, four of the men were again spotted and identified, still in reasonable health, about sixty-five miles further away from the wreckage. It was apparent that this crew of specialists were being moved ever closer to North Vietnam for the "train ride" north. None were ever heard from again, and their names were never included on any prisoner list produced before or during Operation Homecoming.

In another instance, an FB-111 was shot down north of the DMZ in Vietnam by a SAM missile that exploded close enough to cause the engines to flame out. The crew, Majors Robert A. Brown and Robert Morrissey, ejected and were captured. The airplane crashed, but was recovered in a remarkably intact condition. According to NSA analysis, the aircraft was located by the North Vietnamese and within four days was in transit to the Soviet Union. This prize, along with the two crewmembers, would greatly benefit Soviet designers and systems technicians. For they were working on their own version of the F-111, the Sukhoi Su-24 swing-wing fighter-bomber. Other offshoot designs from the American swing-wing technology that had been developed from the F-111 appeared in the MiG-23 and MiG-27. It has also been reported that the high altitude supersonic MiG-25 owed its design features to the U.S. Navy's A-5 Vigilante.

To serve as an example of what happened to American aviators that had been sent to the Soviet Union, the Patterson case is enlightening. According to a former Red Army major, one U.S. POW, believed to have been Navy Lieutenant Commander Kelly Patterson, was transported across China to the Soviet border where he was transferred to Russian control and moved to the Red Army air defense base in Sary Sagan, Kazakhstan (Siberia). The reason he was selected was because of his expertise in the electronic jamming systems and tactics of the F-4 Phantom fighter-bombers. Like Cressman and his fellow crewmembers, Patterson never returned. Instead, he was shown as KIA/BNR on the Air Force records.

Through the efforts of analysts like Mooney, at least 65 American specialists were positively known to have been moved to the Soviet Union. In all probability there were more. One source states that an additional 90 to 180 men were removed from Vietnam and Laos and taken to various locations, mainly testing and research centers, inside Russia. According to Khamaou Boussarath, Chief of Security for the non-communist Laotian government during the war, "The Russians wanted the technology...they were having trouble in the Mideast. MiGs were all the time getting shot down by American-built planes flown by Israel. They wanted to know why."[101] For if the Israelis could shoot down the Soviets first-line fighters, then so could the Americans should World War III ever occur.

In the end, the Soviets and Chinese were trading obsolete arms and weapons systems for state-of-the-art American technology, and at the same time testing their latest weapons in a real-world war environment. Intelligence wise, it was not a bad tradeoff. Very few Soviet lives were lost in the war—the Vietnamese and Laotians were doing all the dying—and the return was a treasure trove of technology.

Throughout the post war years, American intelligence tracked live American POWs throughout Vietnam and Laos. Though reports of Americans being sighted in the USSR surfaced on occasion, the majority of what little effort was expended, was on Southeast Asia. According to DIA reports, Americans were still being "debriefed" by Soviet officers (probably KGB) as late as 1983. In one DIA "Stony Beach" report, missing Air Force member Patrick Martin Fallon was reported to have been interrogated by 12 Soviet agents in the old

USAID compound in Vientiane, Laos, between September 17, 1983 and October 13, 1983—ten years after Operation Homecoming and Nixon's statement that all American POWs had been returned.

In another intelligence report, 26 American specialists and special forces troops were transported to the USSR between December 1977 and January 1978. According to intercepted radio communications, Soviet Ilyushin IL-62 transport aircraft carried the POWs out of Gia Lam airport in Hanoi, across Tibet, to Russia. On the last flight the NSA picked up signals emanating from inside North Vietnam that "There are no more SIGINT [signal intelligence] specialists in country."

Terry Minarcin, an NSA analyst in Vietnam, heard from one of his sources that these Americans, after arrival in Russia, were broken down into groups and put on airplanes and trains of the Trans-Siberian Railroad for transport to Sokol, the forward deployment base for the Soviet strategic bomber force.

The U.S. Government, and the various agencies concerned, have all fallen into lockstep with the official policy that 1) there are no more prisoners in Southeast Asia. They are all dead.[102] and 2) no American POWs were transferred to the USSR or China.[103] [104]President Reagan promised voters that the POW situation was of "the highest national priority," and this was parroted by the Bush administration. President Clinton has been very careful not to address the issue in any form. Yet the preponderance of evidence proves beyond doubt that U.S. POWs *were* left behind and kept by Hanoi and the Pathet Lao *after* Operation Homecoming. The Pentagon finally admitted, in 1992, that at least 100 men were known to have remained in North Vietnamese custody long *after* Nixon announced that all American POWs had been returned. But they never have admitted any knowledge of POWs being transferred to Russia.

A classified CIA report disagrees:

Report No. CS-311/044439-71
Date Dist. 10 June 1971
Country: North Vietnam
DOI: 1965-June 1967

Subject: Preliminary debriefing site for captured U.S. Pilots in Vinh Phu Province and presence of Soviet Communist and Chinese Personnel at the site.

1. A preliminary debriefing point for U.S. pilots shot down over Vinh Phu Province, North Vietnam/NVN/, was located at the Lam Thao district, Vinh Phu Province. Two U.S. pilots were taken to a debriefing point on one occasion in 1965; eight in 1966; and unknown number in 1967. The prisoners were escorted to the site by personnel of the Armed Public Security Forces/APSF/, and students from a nearby school served as perimeter guards. Each time prisoners were brought to the site they rode in an open car of Chinese origin resembling an American Jeep. Some of the escort guards rode in a lead car and others rode in two cars following the prisoners. Upon their arrival at the plant, the guards lined up, forming a corridor through which the pilots entered the building. At this point a Soviet, a Chinese, and a Vietnamese greeted the pilots and led them into the building. The pilots usually remained in the building for several hours. When they emerged they had changed from uniforms into civilian clothing. [deleted] said [deleted] had told him the foreigners were Soviet and Communist Chinese. Soviet personnel had been stationed at the plant since its construction in 1963, but in 1965 the number of Soviets was reduced to three or four, and it remained at that level as of June 1967. About 20 Communist Chinese personnel arrived at the plant in 1966 and there were still about 20 there as of June 1967....

2. After shaking hands with the Soviets and Chinese, the prisoners were led to a different vehicle from the one which brought them to the site. They were escorted from the plant by a different set of guards who wore yellow and white uniforms and were armed with rifles and pistols. [deleted] did not know the destination of the prisoners.

Regarding those that were not transferred to the USSR, but were retained by the North Vietnamese as hold cards against the Kissinger/Nixon promise of reparations, Lt. Col. Stuart A. Harrington, who worked on the POW/MIA issue as a military intelligence and liaison officer with the North Vietnamese and Red Chinese, wrote in his book *Peace with Honor? An American Reports on Vietnam, 1973-1975*: "U.S. casualties under North Vietnamese control would be accounted for and prisoners returned *after* fulfillment of the promise." [Emphasis added].

But on April 6, 1973, an 88-3 roll call vote in the Senate against paying any type of reparations to the North Vietnamese—especially after the public outcry over the reports of barbaric torture of American prisoners that had been held by the North Vietnamese—sounded the death knell of the secret Kissinger/Nixon deal. Then a week later, Armed Services Chairman F. Edward Hebert announced he would introduce a proposal to prohibit any U.S. aid for Hanoi. He also said justification for Nixon's request for $1.3 billion aid to North Vietnam was either "nebulous or nonexistent." The very next day the Nixon administration and the Pentagon announced that there were no more Americans alive in Southeast Asia and that "rumors did the families a disservice."[105]

Immediately the coverup began. The word went out to stations near and far that barring any blatant publicly exposed evidence of live American POWs surfacing, the issue was to be discretely buried. In a message sent from the American Embassy in Saigon to the Secretary of State in Washington, attempts to cover up the fact that the U.S. abandoned U.S. POWs in Southeast Asia is apparent:

Subject: PW REPORT BY NVA DEFECTOR
REF: STATE 112133
1. NVA Rallier/Defector Nguyen Thanh Son was surfaced by GVN to press June 8 Saigon. In follow on interview with AP, UPI and NBC American correspondents, questions elicited information that he had seen six prisoners whom he believed were Americans who had not yet been released. American officer present at interview requested news services to play down details: AP mention was consistent with embargo request, while UPI and NBC after talk with Embassy press officer omitted item entirely from their stories.

2. Details on rallier's account being reported SEPTEL, through military channels by BRIGHTLIGHT message today WHITE HOUSE.

But no matter how much damage control the government attempted, annoying reports of live Americans being held by the Communists continued to appear. In 1975, the CIA reported that:

"...A number of Americans were being held in Hanoi pending agreement on American reconstruction aid...The Vietnamese were not stupid and would hold the Americans until three billion dollars in promised aid was received."[106]

Still, the government entities that drew the job of covering up the POW/MIA situation, mainly consisting of compartmentalized elements within the DIA and the Department of Defense (DoD), continued to debunk any evidence of the existence of live POWs still remaining in Communist hands.

The coverup continues to this day at the highest levels. When former CBS executive Ted Landreth was preparing to broadcast *We Can Keep You Forever*, the BBC/Lionheart/Landreth documentary on the POW/MIA situation that presented dramatic evidence that MIAs and POWs were still alive in Southeast Asia, Landreth discovered that the stations that had agreed to carry the broadcast had suddenly backed out. Landreth began to investigate and quickly learned that the reason was coercion at the highest level. One station manager reported that he had received a call from the White House that threatened, "If you put that British program on the air, you can forget about coming around the White House for the rest of the Reagan Administration."

Other attempts at coverup were discovered by the authors of *Soldiers of Misfortune* when they went to the National Archives in Washington, D.C., where they had been conducting research, and discovered that an Army colonel in full uniform had visited the Military Reference Section in Room 13W and had demanded the Reference Section to "stop leaking World War II documents related to prisoners of war kept by the Soviet Union." They then found that someone had also tampered with the very files the authors were using for research by inserting several new pages into Military Mission to Moscow files, Box 24. The pages had not been there previously, and had been inserted in the middle of a bound metal document holder. The new pages contained false information that were an apparent attempt to change the information that 20,261 Americans were never returned from the Soviet Union after World War II.

Among other recent attempts to cover up information regarding Americans missing in action or taken prisoner and never returned are the following events:

* In 1991, Brent Scowcroft, National Security Advisor to the White House, blocked the release of a 36 year-old White House document requested by Mark Sauter, co-author of *Soldiers of Misfortune*, regarding evidence provided by Yuri Rastvorov that U.S. POWs were transported from Korea to Siberia. Scowcroft, on White House stationary, ordered the National Archives not to release the report, as it was still considered "Secret."[107]

* The Bush administration, on numerous occasions, had hidden or censored many other documents regarding POWs and MIAs dating back to World War II. On one occasion in 1989, the DIA stated that they held no record of those missing or captured in the Korean conflict. It was later discovered, however, that just such a report existed. Titled "Alleged Sightings of American POWs in North Korea from 1975 to 1982," the memo mentioned American POWs from the Korean war.

* In an incredible twisting of logic, the administration refused to deal with reports of Americans from the Korean war still being held in Siberia because *it would be a "violation of their privacy"* for the American people to know that they had been abandoned.[108]

* Concerning media attention to the POW/MIA scandal, the major networks and newspapers all know of the information presented in the recent disclosures but as if in concert, have failed to react. In the case of *Soldiers of Misfortune*, according to the authors, "CBS Evening News," "60 Minutes," "Nightline," *Time* magazine, the *New York Times*, and *The New Republic* all knew of the information presented by the authors but refused to pursue the story.[109]

* CBS TV's "60 Minutes," after assigning Monika Jensen-Stevenson to do a segment on the POW/MIA affair, refused to air it when it was discovered that she had uncovered unrefutable evidence of Americans

still being held in Vietnam, Laos and the Soviet Union. She chose to leave her job and pursue the story along with her husband, William Stevenson (author of *A Man Called Intrepid*). The result was the bestseller *Kiss The Boys Goodbye*.

* On one occasion, Richard Armitage, who was at one time civilian attache to the Department of Defense in Saigon under Erich von Marbod, (both identified in a civil lawsuit filed by the Christic Institute as being involved in the CIA/Laotian opium racket) appeared on *60 Minutes* and stated that there was no proof that any U.S. POWs or MIAs were alive in Southeast Asia.

* Former U.S. Marine POW Bobby Garwood, who managed to escape captivity in Vietnam in 1979, instead of being welcomed home as a hero who managed to survive fourteen years as a prisoner of the Vietnamese, was court martialed as a defector. This action by the government followed the precedent set by the French when the survivors of Dien Bien Phu were finally repatriated. By charging, court martialing and disgracing such a person, their credibility on statements concerning what they had witnessed—such as seeing other live countrymen—could be dismissed as lies and fantasy. Bobby Garwood was never debriefed by any intelligence service of the U.S. Government.

And the coverup continues. As late as 1992, after reports of live Americans being held inside the Soviet Union by former Soviet intelligence agents and military officers, and a report from retired KGB Major General Oleg Kalugin that stated KGB agents had interrogated American POWs in Vietnam in 1978—three years after the fall of South Vietnam and five years after the withdrawal of U.S. troops—Russian and American officials continue to deny allegations that such was the case. It was also reported in an interview between a former KGB interrogator and a reporter for Australian television, Jeff McMullen, that nine U.S. pilots, after being interrogated by the KGB in North Vietnam, had their throats cut by the North Vietnamese. Still, no mention in the major networks or publications of these incidents even though they have received wide coverage overseas.

Why would the U.S. Government not pursue any and all leads of live American sightings in Southeast Asia? And why such an effort to

177

disavow the 30,000 plus Americans that had been spirited into Russia?

The answer to the second question is fairly obvious. As explained in previous chapters, Cold War politics, coupled with political embarrassment and a "National Interest" need by the covert intelligence services (mainly the OSS and CIA), the American prisoners from World War II and Korea were simply written off in the interest of National Security.

The answer to the first question is more complicated. It has nothing to do with National Security, nor is it an issue of the $3.25 billion dollars Nixon and Kissinger promised the North Vietnamese. It goes much deeper than that. And it is directly related to two subjects that are never addressed by either the Executive Branch or the Judicial Branch of the U.S. Government: Black Operations in Laos during the war—and drugs...yesterday, and today.

Chapter 19

"They Could Give A Damn About Soldiers"

To the Meo, it was a sacred mountain—a mountain of spirits and magic. To the CIA and the U.S. Air Force, it held a more earthly value. Known as a *karst*, a mountain formed by the upheaval of the earth during an ancient earthquake, the mountain of Phou Pha Thi jutted up from the earth's surface with sides so steep that it was virtually impregnable to ground assault. A military garrison stationed at its summit could only be expected to be resupplied by air. And it was because of this, and its strategic location near the border of North Vietnam in northern Laos only 160 miles from Hanoi, that it held its value.

Known to the military and the CIA as Site 85, the "Rock" was a natural fortress. Phou Pha Thi was a razorback ridge with one side consisting of a very steep incline heavily defended by Thai mercenaries and Meo soldiers of General Vang Pao's small army of hill people, and the other a sheer cliff. On top was a tiny landing strip, a small community of bunkers and other buildings, an antenna farm of various radio antennas, and the region's main TACAN site.

The TACAN, or Tactical Air Navigation beacon, was the critical link between the fighters and bombers coming out of the U.S. air bases in Thailand and the Steel Tiger operational zone of North Vietnam—and Hanoi. The TACAN, a UHF omnidirectional beacon transmitter, provided course, bearing, and distance information to the swarms of aircraft flying to and from North Vietnam high over the monsoon clouds. And the communications relay equipment at Site 85 formed a vital link for not only intelligence purposes, but life and death radio relay for rescue missions of downed pilots inside North Vietnam.

179

For the military and the CIA, Site 85 was a critical part of the war in the north. For the North Vietnamese, it was a threat to be dealt with. For as long as the American navigational and communications site on top of the 5,600 foot Phou Pha Thi was permitted to exist, the convoys on the Ho Chi Minh trail, the troop movements on the Plain of Jars, and Hanoi itself remained accesible targets for American bombers. Site 85 had to go.

Site 85, as far as the outside world was concerned, did not exist. Its location, its mission, and the people and equipment located there were all classified. It was what the intelligence and military communities referred to as a "black operation." Built in 1967 over the objections of the U.S. Ambassador to Laos, the site was staffed by a handful of U.S. Air Force technicians that had been sheep-dipped into "civilian" status. As far as their official positions, they had been discharged by the Air Force and had been hired by Lockheed Aircraft Systems on a one year contract. This reclassification conveniently side-stepped the Geneva Peace Accords of 1962 that prohibited any foreign military presence in Laos. It did not, however, fool the North Vietnamese or local Pathet Lao communists—whose capital, Sam Neua, was only 25 miles away.

On March 10, 1968, North Vietnamese and Pathet Lao forces attacked the mountain. The attack was well-conceived and carried out with speed and force. As Pathet Lao and NVA troops fought their way up the incline-side of the mountain, creating a diversion, specially trained North Vietnamese commandos—reputedly led by Soviet *Spetsnaz* troops—scaled the cliffs.

The small garrison was caught in a pincer movement. Quickly realizing that they were vastly outnumbered and that the force of Meo defenders would not be able to hold out for long, the American contingent called for help. Helicopters belonging to Air America, the CIA's proprietary "airline" in Laos, and airborne forward air controllers, codenamed Ravens, responded. As the Ravens, flying their light single-engine Cessna 0-1 Birddogs circled the mountain, directing fighter strikes against the advancing communist forces, Air America Hueys did their best to evacuate the friendlies.

But all could not be rescued. Of the fifteen U.S. Air Force personnel listed as manning the site, only four were located and pulled to safety. The remaining eleven were unaccounted for.

As soon as the top of the mountain had been evacuated, the friendly Thai and Meo defenders were ordered to destroy all of their heavy weapons and equipment, break contact and abandon their positions. The site, and its secret communications gear, had to be destroyed to keep it from falling into enemy hands.

American A-1 Skyraiders, summoned to support the withdrawal, now rolled in to deliver their bomb loads on the mountain top. Bunkers, now occupied by North Vietnamese and Pathet Lao, exploded in balls of flame. Concussion from the blasts sent deadly shards of rock ripping through the air causing secondary casualties. When the Skyraiders had expended their loads they headed for home.

The next day U.S. fighter-bombers were called in from Thailand to finish the job. Thousands of pounds of bombs rained down on the mountaintop, virtually destroying what remained of the site. As this was happening, the Meo and Thai defenders had managed to break contact and had reached a rally point where heads were counted. After a complete accountability, it was determined that none of the eleven Americans were there. However, one Thai sergeant reported that he had seen three of the Air Force technicians at the site being taken prisoner and led away by the North Vietnamese attackers.

Though this report was given to U.S. intelligence almost immediately, and no bodies were ever recovered, the U.S. Ambassador declared the eleven missing personnel to be dead.

But merely declaring a man dead does not make him so. CIA reports of the incident surfaced in 1978 under the Freedom of Information Act that stated the three American prisoners from Site 85 were brought to a village near the mountain by NVA troops, and after parading them in front of the villagers for propaganda effect, had been taken back to a cave near Phou Pha Thi. They were later moved to other caves near Sam Neua where they were guarded by the NVA, and later the Pathet Lao.

But their captivity in Northern Laos was apparently short-lived. In September of 1990, an Air Force captain who was traveling in Laos while conducting research for his doctoral degree, managed to interview a former Pathet Lao general. The general claimed to have been involved in the attack on Phou Pha Thi, and related the fact that three American technicians had indeed been captured and had eventually been turned over to North Vietnamese troops. The NVA, according to the general, spirited them away to North Vietnam. None of them were ever heard from again.

The Air Force losses at Site 85 were only one example of American personnel that disappeared during covert or classified military operations. Other Black operations, such as the covert border crossing activities of the U.S. Special Forces recon and prisoner snatch teams, the Army Long Range Reconnaissance Patrols (LRRP), and Marine Force Recon scouting missions, occasionally resulted in some of their members being lost and presumed captured by enemy forces. Other highly dangerous, and often semi-clandestine activities also added to the toll of MIAs. Navy SEAL teams, PBR Swift Boat crews, Army Riverine forces, and secret aerial reconnaissance flights all produced figures on the MIA and KIA/BNR lists.[110]

But it was in Laos, outside of the Republic of Vietnam, where no foreign forces were to tread, that Americans disappeared with the least chance of being recovered. For in Laos, no one taken prisoner ever came back.

Known as the Kingdom of Lan Xang—the Land of a Million Elephants—the tiny key-shaped country of Laos (pronounced *louse)*—was considered by the Chinese, Soviets and Americans to be the key to Southeast Asia. Because of its strategic location, Laos commanded the entire western border of North Vietnam and half the border of South Vietnam. It was also the gateway from China to Cambodia and Thailand.

President Eisenhower considered Laos to be a more important domino than Vietnam. In his transition briefing to President-elect Kennedy, he pointed out that if Laos fell, so would Southeast Asia. Kennedy believed him.

Laos after World War II was a weak, land-locked, peaceful country that just happened to lie between much stronger, perpetually warring neighbors. To the north was Burma and China, borders that meant little to the tribes of mountain people who for centuries have wandered back and forth as if no border existed. To the south is Cambodia, and to the west, Thailand.

The eastern border, largely drawn along the flow pattern of the Mekong River, shared 1,324 miles of mountainous jungle with North and South Vietnam. And it was this border, and its geopolitical values, that brought the peaceful, backward kingdom of Laos into 20th century war.

In 1953, the importance of Laos, which was at that time part of French Indochina, did not escape the French. Because the rugged terrain of Laos, Ho Chi Minh's Viet Minh guerrillas could move the length of Vietnam undetected by merely crossing over into the Laotian provinces. And of further concern to the French was the expansionism of Ho's Asian Communist Party. Should Ho begin moving his political commissars and fighting forces into Laos in large numbers, the French reasoned that it would not be long before he would be able to rally support from the Laotians against the French. This was a major factor considered by the French when they chose Dien Bien Phu as a strongpoint and blocking position against the Viet Minh advance. According to the map, the valley was well-situated to keep the Ho Chi Minh's guerrilla army from having unfettered access to nearby Laos.

Dien Bien Phu fell after a siege lasting 56 days. And with it, the world received its first lesson on how the Asian communists handled prisoners of war, both physically and politically.

But while Dien Bien Phu was under siege, a young Meo lieutenant named Vang Pao was desperately attempting to reach the beleaguered garrison with his small contingent of Meo soldiers. He had volunteered to lead a relief expedition to the valley, but before he could arrive, the French garrison had been forced to surrender.

The Viet Minh captured over 16,000 men, and almost immediately began marching them east toward hastily-built prisoner holding compounds located closer to Hanoi. Of this number, only 78 managed to escape into the jungle and make their way to Laos and safety. Only 19 of these were Europeans.

Vang Pao's fellow Meo tribesmen found the escapees wandering the forests and provided them with protection, shelter, armed guides, and rafts to navigate the Mekong downriver to Saigon, and safety. It was the last the majority of the Meo would see of the European colonists.

In 1954, a settlement in Geneva resulted in the division of Vietnam at the 17th parallel. Laos was left as a separate entity to serve as a buffer between pro-western Siam (Thailand) and communist China. But this effort at geographical separation soon proved a failure. Repeated invasions by the North Vietnamese through the Plain of Jars into the northern provinces of Laos forced the Laotian government to concede the two northern provinces, Sam Neua and Phong-Saly, to Pathet Lao control. What was actually happening behind the scenes was something else. The communist-backed Pathet Lao were almost non-existent in numbers. Instead, the two provinces actually came under North Vietnamese administration and the Pathet Lao were merely used by the Viet Minh as a front.[111]

The French had no sooner left when the United States took over support of the pro-western southern half of Laos. By supporting the economy with millions of dollars of U.S. aid, the U.S. managed to buy its way into the government. Within a year the Laotian army began to swell, eventually reaching a manning level of 50,000 troops. It became the only foreign army in the world completely financed by the U.S. government.

As would later happen in Vietnam, the money—over $300 million—did little more than corrupt government officials and the officer corps. Most of the funds went into the pockets of the upper level benefactors and little results were seen in the field. In the end, the heavily financed Royal Laotian Army and Air Force rarely left their contonement areas. Especially to fight the much more motivated—and dangerous—communists.

The CIA, who had by now entered the scene, saw what was happening. In an attempt to gain control of a bad situation, the Agency shifted U.S. backing to Phoui Sananikone, an anticommunist politician who appeared more aggressive than his predecessor, Prince Souvanna Phouma, who was a devout neutralist. But the new prime minister did not last long. An army general, Phoumi Nosavan, took over the capital, and the government, in a military coup. The CIA had to quickly change horses.

By 1959, the U.S. State Department had managed to set up a clandestine military mission in Vientiane. Dubbed the Program Evaluation Office, or PEO, it became the headquarters for an American staff of military officers and NCOs whose mission was to form, equip, and train an operational army that would not only be field deployable, but would fight. The personnel on this team were mainly American army infantry officers who wore civilian clothes and were carried on the roll as "technicians."

Meanwhile, General Phoumi Nosavan had proved to be less of an anti-communist strongman than originally anticipated by the CIA. He even refused to go to the capital for swearing-in after an election rigged by the CIA legitimized his position because a fortune-teller told him he would be killed if he went. Another Lao officer—one that had guts—would have to be found to lead the new clandestine army.

The search did not take long. Vang Pao, who was by this time a major in the Royal Lao Army, had built a reputation for being a fighter. Even though he was of Meo descent, which is looked down upon by the lowland Laotians as being little more than uneducated savages, he had managed to attain the highest rank ever held by a Meo and had successfully led some of his countrymen against the Viet Minh. Besides these attributes, Vang Pao had an additional qualification: he was the same race as most of the soldiers being recruited for the new fighting force by the CIA.

The Agency approached Vang Pao and offered their support if he would agree to lead the new army. He agreed, and within days orders were cut authorizing massive arms shipments to Vientiane to equip the Meo force. Major Harry "Heinie" Aderholt, who was responsible for USAF support of CIA operations in Southeast Asia was ordered to send 1,000 weapons to Vang Pao which included rifles, machine guns, hand grenades, 60mm mortars and enough field gear to supply 1000 men. These supplies were quickly loaded aboard C-46s and flown out of a secret cache at Tahkli, Thailand, to Padong, Laos, where Vang Pao established his initial headquarters.

Aderholt then received orders to open up a network of landing strips, known as Lima Sites, across Laos to provide staging and resupply points for the covert army. Vang Pao's people had been programmed to conduct a highly mobile guerrilla war against the NVA and Pathet Lao, fighting them the same way the communists had fought the French. To do this required numerous points of resupply and aerial support within the area of operations. The Lima Sites, each identified by a number on the map, were to provide such logistical support.

As Aderholt and Vang Pao flew over the countryside looking for suitable locations for airfields, the PEO in Vientiane was in the process of being replaced by 400 Special Forces personnel that had been moved in from their home station in Okinawa. In an operation codenamed WHITESTAR, the Green Beret "Mobile Training Teams," as they were dubbed, donned civilian clothes, bogus titles and job descriptions, and quickly faded away from the city to the countryside to train the Meos.

This activity did not go unnoticed by the Soviets and Chinese. Each began bolstering the Pathet Lao and NVA forces with arms and equipment, often flying loads into, and out of, Vientiane in broad daylight aboard their own cargo transports. One Air America veteran recalled drinking with Soviet air crews in the evening, then waiting in line with them the next day on the Vientiane taxiways in their various arms-laden aircraft for take-off clearance. Each would depart Vientiane in a different direction, drop their loads to their respective clients, then return unmolested to Vientiane for another night of drinking.

Resupply by air was the only means of supporting the army in the field. There were only 470 miles of paved road in all of Laos. If Vang Pao was to receive arms, ammunition and food, it had to come by air. But the U.S. Air Force, because of the Geneva accords, could not be based in or officially operate inside Laos in support of military forces. To overcome this, the CIA formed its own cargo airline, appropriately named Air America.

Air America, utilizing Short Take Off and Landing (STOL) airplanes such as Helio Couriers, Pilatus Porters, DeHavilland Caribous, and cargo planes such as C-46s, C-47s, C-119s and C-123s, and H-19 and UH-1 helicopters, all flown by "contract" pilots, delivered thousands of tons of "soft rice" (food), and "hard rice" (arms and ammunition) during the war.

Air America would before long, however, find itself carrying much more than rice and weapons.

As the war against the PL and NVA intensified in ratio to the war in Vietnam, the CIA presence in Laos grew. Air America and the main contingent of the CIA up-country team quickly outgrew their small Lima Sites and were forced to relocate to a new base of operations that was both handy to the war, and not susceptible to the prying eyes of the media or other undesirables. The new station would have to be naturally protected by the terrain, be within Meo territory, provide enough real estate to build hangars, quarters, offices and admin facilities, and enough room to construct a large all-weather runway.

THE BOYS WE LEFT BEHIND

The CIA, by way of one of its agents, Edgar "Pop" Buell, located such a place at Long Tieng (pronounced Long *Cheng*). Long Tieng, surrounded by the rugged karsts of Northern Laos, provided a natural bowl within the mountains large enough for the CIA's requirements. Within weeks construction was begun and aircraft began arriving, and before the year was out, Long Tieng would become the CIA's largest field headquarters in Asia. After Vientiane, this secret installation became the largest city in Laos.

A macadam runway was built that was capable of handling everything from small single-engine bush planes to the largest four-engine transports, and was long enough to handle a jet fighter should the need arise. The buildings, each with a shiny tin roof, reflected the sun from what the journalists eventually began to call "Spook Heaven."[112]

By 1964, the CIA had, under its Air America cover, one of the largest air forces in the world. It also had, under the leadership of Vang Pao, the second largest guerilla army in Southeast Asia. And it had the expenses of operating both.

The war in Laos was a secret war. It was so secret that it could not be financed in the conventional manner of going to Congress for a budget. Instead, it had to be financed from a "black" budget within the annual operating expenses of the CIA. The problem with this was that the war in Laos quickly outgrew what the CIA could provide through in-house means.

Upon examining its resources, the CIA turned to the Laotian government for the needed additional financing, but it was quickly determined that there were virtually no export products that could be used as a means of finance—except one. Opium.

The tri-border area of Laos, Thailand, and Burma, known as the "Golden Triangle," was the Asian center of the opium trade. Within this region, over 1000 tons of raw opium was produced each year by the nomadic hill tribes of the Hmong, Meo, Yao, Lisu, Akha, Lahu, Shan and Karens. These tribes had for centuries collectively tended thousands of acres of opium poppies, using the product in tribal rites and as a cash crop for the local economy.

187

From the Golden Triangle, the raw opium, resembling a black sticky substance packed in bamboo tubes, or formed in bricks, or packaged in several other ways, entered the Asian market through two routes. The first led through Thailand to Bangkok and came under the control of the remnants of the Nationalist Chinese Khoumantang Army that had fled China in 1949. The second route passed through northern Laos and South Vietnam. It was in both that the CIA found its means of providing its additional funding for the war.[113]

A strange and remarkable set of circumstances melded at this point. The raw opium, which was being grown in northern Laos and the Golden Triangle, was flown to Vientiane for processing into heroin. The facility used to process the heroin was a Pepsi Cola bottling plant that had originally been established prior to the massive U.S./CIA build-up during the time that Richard Nixon's law firm was representing Pepsi. It was built shortly after Nixon's visit to Dallas for a meeting of the Board of Directors of Pepsi Cola—which he does not remember, nor is there any record of a meeting occurring on that date, November 21, 1963, the day before JFK was ambushed in Dealy Plaza. But Nixon *was* there, and an article in a Dallas newspaper makes note of the event.[114]

Another meeting occurred in which other players came together in Southeast Asia. According to sources that have only recently surfaced, a meeting took place in Saigon in which a network was established for the world-wide distribution of raw heroin. At this meeting, which was set up by CIA operatives Theodore Shackley and Thomas Clines, were Nguyen Cao Ky, head of the Vietnamese Air Force under Prime Minister Thieu; Vang Pao; a representative of the Corsican Mafia; and *Santos Trafficante*, the Miami mafioso who had been instrumental in forming the ZR/RIFLE assassination team that the CIA attempted to use against Fidel Castro.

The meeting, which took place in Saigon in early 1968, established a division of responsibilities, property and profits. Though what actually was decided in the secret meeting is not known, the results bear witness to the event. Vang Pao, by way of Air America and his own private airline, Xieng Khouang Air Transport, would supply the opium to the Pepsi Cola lab at Vientiane. His airplanes would then fly the pure heroin to Bangkok, where it was divided into three lots. One lot would go to the United States, where Santos Trafficante and the American Mafia would handle distribution, and the other would be flown out by the *Union Corse*—the Corsican Brotherhood—to Marseille, France. Once in France, the Corsican Mafia would have the franchise for all of Europe and North Africa.[115] A third shipment would be provided to Nguyen Cao Ky and would be flown to Da Nang. From Da Nang, Vietnamese Air Force planes would distribute it to the various cities of South Vietnam. The "customer" in the form of the end user in South Vietnam was the American serviceman.[116]

The money that was made was to be split between the traffickers and certain individuals within the CIA in Laos. The latter would supposedly use their share to finance the covert war.

The enterprise proved so profitable that Vang Pao was forced to open a second, larger laboratory in Long Tieng.

The participants of the meeting are well known government officials and organized crime figures. But who were Theodore Shackley and Thomas Clines?

Clines and Shackley had been integral players in the JM/WAVE CIA operations against Cuba. Shackley was chief of station for Miami, and Clines worked under Shackley as case officer for the Cuban-era Operation 40 and directly supervised many of the Cuban exiles, including Felix Rodriguez, Raul Villaverde, and Rafael "Chi-Chi" Quintero. Another operative, Edwin P. Wilson, also worked under Clines and would be exposed later in the Iran/Contra scandal.[117]

When the attention of the CIA was shifted from Cuba to Laos, Clines and Shackley, along with key members of Operation 40, were transferred to that country. Shackley became Chief of Station in Vientiane. Clines functioned as Shackley's deputy, and as base chief at Long Tieng. Air support for their operation was provided by Richard Secord, who like Wilson, would surface again during the Iran/Contra affair.[118]

Felix Rodriguez was an interesting character. He had been part of the Operation 40 team—very probably a member of the ZR/RIFLE team—who specialized in commando, sabotage and counter-guerrilla operations. After his time in Laos, he would go on to hunt down Che Guevara in South America, support the Contras in

Nicaragua/Honduras, and perform other clandestine paramilitary missions for the CIA until becoming disgruntled with the upper level bureaucracy. Of note during his Laotian tour is his relationship to one such bureaucrat. Rodriguez was one of the principle contacts between the Laotian field team and Donald Gregg, National Security Advisor to then Vice-President George Bush.

Theodore Shackley would eventually leave Laos for a promotion. In 1969, Shackley would be transferred to Saigon to become Chief of Station for all of Vietnam until 1972. Clines followed soon after, and together, they directed the CIA's Operation PHOENIX, the assassination program run under MACV-SOG (Military Assistance Command, Vietnam—Studies and Observations Group).

By June of 1971, the heroin addiction problem in South Vietnam among U.S. troops had garnered national attention. President Nixon, realizing that the media had discovered that U.S. troops were dying at the rate of two a day from heroin overdose in Vietnam, declared a "war on drugs." But such a war would never occur. There was simply too much money involved.

The amount of return on investment for the CIA was in the multi-millions. Some estimates put the yearly take on opium to be in excess of $3-$4 *billion* dollars. To handle such sums of money, and turn it into funds that could not be traced, taxed or even discovered, took an additional organization. This organization, set up in the form of a "bank," became the money laundering mechanism for the insiders within the Agency who knew of the operation.

The enterprise, not officially founded until 1973, was the Nugan Hand bank of Australia. It derived its name from Francis John Nugan, an Australian attorney, and Michael Jon Hand, a former member of the Special Forces who worked under Clines and Shackley. The Nugan Hand bank eventually set up offices and affiliates—or at least addresses—in thirteen separate countries, including the United States, Hong Kong, Taiwan, the Philippines, Thailand, and the Cayman Islands. But the "bank" never seems to have done any banking. According to Jonathan Kwitney, who has written a book on the bank's activities,[119] the organization busied itself in moving funds between countries and various accounts. This operation lasted seven years, and at the end of that period, when the Australian government began to investigate the organization, Michael Hand declared the organization bankrupt and shut down operations.

But by that time, it had been determined that the drug profits from the Laotian war zone had been deposited in the Nugan Hand banks and had been eventually laundered through the Bangkok branch. It had also been discovered that several other conduits for the money had been established and that one branch, Chiang Mai, handled nothing but drug money and served as the personal bank for local drug warlords of the Golden Triangle.

Chiang Mai, a city located on the edge of the Triangle in Thailand, based its entire economy on the opium trade. (Incredibly, the Nugan Hand branch at Chiang Mai had adjoining offices with the local Drug Enforcement Administration (DEA) office and even shared the same secretary).

In one seven month period, the Chiang Mai branch handled $2.6 million in deposits from six major drug dealers.[120] This was only their share, and amounted to less than 5% of the total capital gain received abroad.

But did the CIA, as an agency and institution of the Federal government, know of the drug trafficking that it would one day be accused of conducting? According to Victor Marchetti, the CIA's involvement in drugs was not something that just happened to appear in, or was unique to, Laos. It went back further than that.

"It goes back to the predecessor organization, OSS, and its involvement with the Sicilian Mafia and La Cosa Nostra in southern Italy during World War II," explained Marchetti. "Later on, when they were fighting the communists in France, they got in tight with the Corsican Brotherhood. The Corsican Brotherhood, of course, are big time dope dealers. Things changed in the world and the CIA got involved with the Kubla-Khan types in Burma. The same things happened in Southeast Asia, and later Latin America. Some of the very people who are the best sources of information and who are capable of accomplishing things happen to be the criminal element."[121]

William Colby, Director of the CIA from 1973 to 1976, countered with: "The CIA has had a solid rule against being involved in drug trafficking. That is not to say that some of the people the CIA has used or been in touch with over the years may well have themselves been involved in drug traffic, but not the CIA."

The people on the ground in Laos differed in their statements concerning the official U.S. government position. The airfield operatives and the pilots, those who flew the dangerous missions carrying rice and ammunition to Vang Pao's troops—and the opium back to Long Tieng—told a different story. Ron Rickenbach, who worked for USAID in Laos from 1962 to 1969, stated, "I was on the airstrip. That was my job, to move in and about and go from place to place. I was in the areas where opium was transhipped. I personally was a witness to opium being placed on aircraft—American aircraft—I witnessed it being taken off smaller aircraft coming in from outlying sites."

Neal Hanson, a former senior Air America pilot, confirmed Rickenbach's observation from the aircrew end. "I've seen the sticky bricks come on board," he explained, describing the opium being brought aboard by various passengers. "And no one was challenging their right to carry it. It was their own property...We were sort of a freebie airline in some respects there. Whatever the customer, or the local representative put on the airplane, we flew. Primarily it was transported on our smaller aircraft: the Helios, the Porters and things like that which visited the outlying villages. They would [bring the] opium to market."

The smaller STOL planes covered the countryside, carrying whatever was required by the "customers," whether they be pig farmers or opium producers. The pilots, after dealing with the local attitude regarding opium shipments for a few flights, became numb to the situation. In the words of Ron Rickenbach, "Raw opium was a natural agricultural enterprise for these people, and they had been doing it for many years before the Americans ever got there. When we got there, they continued to do so."

Fred Platt, a former pilot for Air America, explained what it meant to the farmer: "When a farmer raised a crop of opium, what he got for his year's worth of work was the equivalent of thirty-five to forty dollars. That amount of opium, were it refined into morphine base, then into morphine, then into heroin, and appeared on the streets of New York—that thirty-five dollar crop of opium would be worth fifty, sixty, maybe one hundred thousand dollars. That was 1969 dollars. Today? Millions."

As the war in Laos began to take a turn for the worse, and Vang Pao's Meo army was forced to withdraw from the theater of action, it would appear that the amount of drug money required to run the war would decrease. But that did not happen. Though the fighting was slacking off as the NVA and Pathet Lao advanced and took site after site, pushing the Meo back, the flow of opium continued unabated. But where was the money going, if not to the war effort?

According to Frank Terpil, CIA agent Edwin Wilson's former business partner, who was interviewed in 1983 by journalist Jim Hougan, the operation continued long after the Americans had pulled out of Vietnam, and Laos, and even after the date when there was supposedly no American involvement in the conflict in Southeast Asia at all. According to Terpil, the convenient business arrangement with the Miami Mafia (Trafficante) continued long after the fall of Vietnam to the communists.

"The significance of Miami is the drug syndicate," explained Terpil. "That's the base. Shackley, Clines, the Villaverde brothers, Rodriguez...all these people that I hired to terminate other people, from the Agency, are there. They get involved in the biggest drug scandal going on, which is whitewashed.[122] Who is the guy behind the scandal? Clines. Who's the boss of Clines? Shackley. Where do they come from? Laos."

Terpil then addressed the flow of money. "Where did the money come from? Nugan Hand. The whole goddamned thing has been moved down there...Clines was running drugs." Terpil went on to state that the drug lords percentage of the profits returned to the Golden Triangle was flown to them aboard American-owned aircraft. "What was on the plane? Gold! Ten million bucks at a time, in gold." The planes would return loaded with new shipments of opium. "Now what do you do with all that opium? You reinvest it in your own operations...Billions of dollars—not millions—*billions of dollars!*"[123]

The opium was carried south, to Bangkok, where it was sold to drug merchants from Singapore, Hong Kong and New Delhi. The money received was then laundered through the Nugan Hand Bank in Bangkok.[124] [125]

By 1975, the Nugan Hand banking network had drawn the attention of various governments around the world. The Australian government, investigating information that the bank was linked to numerous groups known to be associated with drug trafficking, discovered that several Australian mobsters had dealings with Nugan Hand and were directly linked to Santos Trafficante and his U.S. drug network. The senior officials of Nugan Hand, many of which by now were retired admirals and generals, began to feel the heat.[126] But the banks remained open for business and managed to cover their activities until 1979. At that time, when more investigations began to home in on the operation, the bank was declared insolvent. Francis John Nugan was found dead on a deserted Australian country road, mutilated by the blast of a shotgun. Among his possessions found on what was left of his body by the police was the business card of William Colby, Director of Central Intelligence from 1973 to 1976.[127] Jon Michael Hand, the former Special Forces trooper, simply disappeared.

The cartel did not suffer any great setback because of the closing of the Nugan Hand system. Instead, they had learned a great deal about money laundering and merely shifted the operation to a deeper level—the investment game.

A new firm was established in Honolulu. Serving as a front for the money laundering operation, the financial firm of BBRDW—for Bishop, Baldwin, Rewald, Dillingham and Wong—came into being almost overnight. But questionable financial dealings and poorly run operations eventually brought the BBRDW organization, and fifty of its subsidiaries, into the spotlight of both the Internal Revenue Service and the media. A scandal erupted and 43-year-old Ronald Rewald, who had no past experience or qualifications in the financial world, was indicted. But when the case came to trial, a strange thing happened. A former CIA agent was appointed as Assistant District Attorney for the case, and the first thing he did was cut off all lines of questioning and evidence that led to the CIA. Of specific note in the evidence were documents that related to POW and MIA affairs in Southeast Asia. BBRDW, according to several sources, had been involved with financing one—and probably up to three—aborted POW reconnaissance and rescue missions. According to the court transcript, Chief District

Judge Harold M. Fong, after reviewing the documents before they were sealed by the court, explained, "...they relate to the highly emotional issues of the missing-in-action and prisoners-of-war."[128]

What they actually related to were missions that were programmed to fail from the beginning. One mission, which was to consist of a handful of Americans and Laotian mercenaries, who were to enter Laos by crossing the Mekong from Thailand to search for a suspected Pathet Lao POW camp containing "caucasians," failed to leave Bangkok. Before the personnel, who believed they were on a legitimate cross-border POW search operation, could leave the city, their arms and equipment were seized by the Thai police and they were evicted from the country. Someone had made special efforts to inform the Thai authorities of their planned activity. According to the team leader, the local CIA station, located in the U.S. Embassy, was the culprit.

Another mission, which did make its way into Laos, reportedly *found* Americans being held prisoner. According to Scott Barnes, a controversial figure who had connections to Vang Pao and Lt. Col. James "Bo" Gritz, the reconnaissance patrol he accompanied into northern Laos managed to locate a suspected POW camp being guarded by asians in military uniform. Upon examining the camp with high-powered binoculars and cameras equipped with telephoto lenses, prisoners were spotted that were not only caucasian, but were identified as Americans. The team leader, Michael J. Baldwin, was apparently taken aback. He exclaimed, "My god, look! They *are* here! And they're *caucasians*!" Baldwin then employed a long-range high-gain parabolic microphone to listen to the sounds of the camp. "They're American!" The voices that came across the listening device were not only speaking English, they were speaking with an American accent.

Baldwin quickly set up a compact satellite radio used by Special Forces and long-range reconnaissance patrols. Dialing in the frequency of the CIA station in Bangkok, he reported what they had discovered. After a few moments a startling message came back: "*Liquidate the merchandise.*"

Baldwin and Barnes were shocked. They could not believe what they had heard. The message told them that they were to use their sniping equipment to kill the American POWs. Why?

Both men refused to carry out those orders. Instead, they began frantically snapping photographs as proof of what they had seen. Surely there was a mistake in the radio-transmitted orders.

But there wasn't. When Operation GRAND EAGLE, the patrol's codename, returned to Bangkok, the film was confiscated by the local CIA. It disappeared, never to be seen again. Barnes and Baldwin, mystified over the turn of events and disappointed that the American POWs had to be left behind, renamed the mission BOHICA—Bend Over, Here It Comes Again.

Barnes later discovered that the mission leader, "Michael J. Baldwin," was in fact, Jerry Daniels—a former CIA and Special Forces operative who worked under Clines at Long Tieng and served as Vang Pao's case officer.[129]

In a later attempt to locate American POWs in Laos, former Green Beret Lt. Col. James "Bo" Gritz led a three-man team into the Golden Triangle section of Burma. He had been told by a member of the National Security Council that an opium warlord named General Khun Sa might know of, or even have control of, American POWs captured during the Vietnam war.

In 1983, Gritz's team managed to make their way through the jungles and virgin teak forests of northern Thailand to Burma to meet with Khun Sa. What they found was that once again, the POW/MIA situation was directly linked to drug trafficking. Though Khun Sa told Gritz that he did not have, or know of, any Americans held within the Shan state (his territory), he did want Gritz to take back to Washington an offer that he felt the Reagan administration could not refuse. The offer was this: The Shan people would reduce—and within five years quit—the production of opium if the U.S would simply give Khun Sa one tenth of the money that was sent to Thailand to fight the reputed "war on drugs" being supposedly conducted by the U.S. Government under Vice President George Bush.

Gritz was excited. Though he did not succeed in gaining information regarding U.S. POWs, he did manage to return home with an offer that would definitely impact the drug scene, and subsequently, the crime rate at home. The mission, Gritz felt, was not a total failure.

Khun Sa's motivation for such and offer was simple. He wanted the Shan State, and its people, recognized by the U.S. government. If this occurred, Khun Sa's people (and his private 40,000 man army) would be legitimized in the eyes of the Burmese government. Secondly, he wanted the U.S. to send Peace Corps volunteers to show the Shans how to grow crops other than opium, and for the proper equipment to be provided to do so. If the U.S. agreed, he would reduce the opium production over a five year period to zero. This would account for over 1,000 tons of opium that was being brought down the infamous "Heroin Highway" to Bangkok. It would also have an impact on the receiving end—and all the people involved in the chain who were making billions of dollars on the product world-wide.

Gritz returned to the U.S. and delivered Khun Sa's message to his contact at the White House, NSC advisor Tom Harvey. Harvey called Gritz later with a "well done" message concerning his successful infiltration and exfiltration of Khun Sa's hideaway. When Gritz asked about the heroin deal, Harvey turned cryptic.

"What about the 900 tons," asked Gritz, referring to the 1986 quantity of opium that was due to be sent to Bangkok by Khun Sa.

"Bo," said Harvey quietly, "there's no interest here in that."

Gritz was taken aback. "Tom, what do you mean 'no interest'? Didn't President Reagan appoint Vice President Bush to be the top cop and keep drugs out of the U.S.?"

"Bo, what can I tell you? There is no interest here in doing that."[130]

Gritz continued to press the issue and returned to Burma to conduct a second interview with Khun Sa. This time he took a video camera and filmed the entire meeting. After returning to the U.S., he delivered copies of the tape to several members of the written and electronic media and to numerous congressmen and senators. But he received almost no coverage in the press, none on television, and almost total silence from Washington. Finally, when a few smaller newspapers whose circulation is outside of the Beltway wrote lengthy articles naming certain high government officials as being conspirators, Washington reacted. Especially when one of those accused was the Assistant Secretary of Defense.

"A drug warlord in Burma has accused Assistant U.S. Secretary of Defense Richard L. Armitage and former American officials of trafficking in drugs to raise money for anti-Communist operations," began a June 4th, 1987 article in a Riverside California newspaper written by David E. Hendrix. "In a three-hour videotape interview smuggled out of Southeast Asia within the past week and given to the Press-Enterprise yesterday, Khun Sa said high-ranking American officials were involved in drug trafficking between 1965 and 1979."

1979. Five years after the Paris Peace Accords were signed, and the same time span since American forces were pulled out of Southeast Asia. Still, the drugs flowed out of the region and the money flowed into certain, clandestine bank accounts. The article went on: "Khun Sa, who says he directs an army of 40,000 attempting to form an independent nation from part of Burma, said Armitage controlled the finances of the alleged American drug operations. 'After the Vietnam War, Richard Armitage was a prominent trafficker to Bangkok,' a Khun Sa aide said. 'Between 1975 and 1979 he was a very prominent trafficker. He was one of the embassy employees.' The aide said Armitage established the Far East Trading Co. after leaving the embassy, and used the company as a cover for drug traffic."

Armitage, previous to being appointed to the Reagan administration, had served in the Defense Attache's office in Saigon during the war, then between 1973 and 1975 served as a consultant with the Department of Defense in Washington. In 1975, he became an "export agent" in Bangkok. This lasted until 1978, when he became an aide to Senator Robert Dole.

Various offices in Washington played down the tapes, making statements ranging from "we haven't seen the tapes yet, so we can't comment,"[131] to "These are old allegations, but without having viewed the videotapes, it's hard to address the current allegations. Regarding the old allegations, they have been looked into and have been found to have no substance."[132]

And so it went. No one wanted to address the content of the tapes, or even acknowledge receiving them or viewing them. In typical political/bureaucratic fashion, the issue was down-played for the moment with the hope that it would become "yesterday's news" tomorrow. And to the media, as every government official knows, old news is no news.

Even so, the article did drive several names home to the American people. According to the report, Khun Sa's staff stated that former CIA official Theodore Shackley was the central figure in the American-controlled Laotian drug business, and later had been considered as a candidate for Director of Central Intelligence. He was also later discovered to be a key player in the Iranian arms-for-hostages dealings that would expose the CIA, the NSC and secret underworld dealings with international arms dealers to the American congress.

Gritz's reward was to be indicted by a federal grand jury for doing exactly what every clandestine agent working for any government does on a routine basis: he used a bogus passport to enter and leave Thailand. Gritz's attorney, Lamond Mills, the former U.S. Attorney for Nevada, told the press that "If...the United States government tries Col. Bo Gritz, believe me, he won't be the only one tried. I'm not going to stand there and let him take the fall on a technical violation when all he was doing was acting for the American government in trying to find POWs...I've got three hours of video tape I'm going to use."

The charges were dropped by the government.

H. Ross Perot, who became very involved in the plight of U.S prisoners of war in Indochina and their families, was named by President Reagan to assist in the hunt for POWs. However, when he brought his massive assets to bear, he discovered basically what Gritz and Barnes and already learned. The POW affair was meshed with the drug scene like the teeth on a zipper.

Upon traveling to the White House to meet with the Vice President, who Reagan had directed to lead the war on drugs, Perot felt that there was less concern over the drug problem than he was originally led to believe. It was obvious that he was becoming disheartened by the whole affair when he told Bush, "Well, George, I go in looking for prisoners, but I spend all my time discovering the government has been moving drugs around the world and is involved in illegal arms deals...I can't get at the prisoners because of the corruption among our own covert people."

Shortly thereafter Perot was removed from the position as presidential investigator for POW/MIA affairs. In a heart-rending statement made to the POW/MIA families in 1987, he said simply, "I have been instructed to cease and desist."

According to Gritz, the Pathet Lao continue to hold 308 American POWs. "They have stated that they want to negotiate, and that they had 'tens of tens' of POWs, and they could not understand why the

Americans would not negotiate with them like they did the Vietnamese," said Gritz. "I found out why...when the war ended, the communists consolidated Laos and Cambodia. The 'Secret Team' that trafficked in drugs during the war continued to do so—supposedly to continue to finance covert operations inside Southeast Asia. But the funds went also to wars all over the world."

And they went into private bank accounts. The "Secret Team" continued to operate into the 1980s, and with a few new faces, surfaced again during the Iran/Contra affair, known in the media as "Contragate."

But why was so much clandestine attention focused on Laos in reference to the POW/MIA affair? Why not North Vietnam, who held hundreds more Americans prisoners than the Pathet Lao? The answer is simple. The Vietnamese, in their consistent Asian play on words, have stated over and over that "No live American POWs are in Vietnam." To them, this may be a factual statement for two reasons: 1) some of the Americans held inside of Vietnam, like their Korean War and World War II predecessors in the USSR and China, have been designated as "war criminals." This removes them from POW status. 2) Most of the American POWs have been transferred out of Vietnam to Northern Laos, where Washington's investigative teams sent to Vietnam will never find them.

These men have been held amid the poppy fields in Laos long enough to have intimate details of the drug trade. Should one come out, the entire affair would unravel. And for those within the government who have, for economic and political reasons, consistently stated that no live Americans still exist in Southeast Asia, one live American returnee would be politically embarrassing at the least, and result in criminal prosecution, followed by lengthy prison sentences, as the most likely scenario. Sadly, the entities assigned the tasks of resolving the POW/MIA issue have historically contained, or answered to, the very people who are personally concerned or involved in both aspects.

"[They] would not want the American POWs to come home," explains Gritz. "Because when they do, there will be an investigation as to why they were abandoned. At that time we will uncover this secret organization and its illicit drug money and financing. The Secret Team would then be exposed."[133]

As of 1993, the coverup and the damage control continues at the highest levels. Senator Bob Smith, Vice Chairman of the Select Committee on POW/MIA Affairs, stated in a Committee meeting that took place on December 1, 1992:

> "The Select Committee meets today, one year after its first round of hearings into the POW/MIA issue to consider the fate of unaccounted for American servicemen from the Vietnam conflict. These hearings have been dubbed the 'Wrap-Up Hearings.' Frankly, I am disturbed that we are perceived to be wrapping up this investigation when there is so much more *unwrapping* we should be doing...I have found that the more research we do, the more questions we find. That task was to learn everything our government knows about the fate of our missing men. Mr. Chairman, I regret to say that this Committee does not yet have everything our government knows on the fate of our men..."

> "For the last 19 years, we have been told by both our government, and the Communist governments in Southeast Asia, that no American servicemen were kept back or left behind at the end of the war. Indeed, just this past August at the Committee hearing, the Defense Intelligence Agency POW/MIA Chief informed us, and I quote, '...Through the debriefings at Homecoming, we accounted for everybody who was known to be in captivity.'[134] The facts, as our government has known them, tell a different story. In my own review of MIA files, intelligence reports, and other information, I have come up with a universe of over 300 American servicemen who were last known by our side to be alive, many of them in captivity in both Laos and Vietnam—all of them still unaccounted for...."

> "The list includes references to information from the National Security Agency which confirms the capture of U.S. servicemen from incidents in Laos and Vietnam, where the individuals have previously been simply listed as missing by our government. These men are still unaccounted for, yet we know many of them were captured.

"This listing of over 300 persons is also based, in part, on information contained in the debriefs of POWs who returned in 1973, and who reported that others were last seen or known to have been alive. These men are also still unaccounted for. Incredibly, the Department of Defense, for the last 12 months, has denied access by professional Committee staff members to the relevant portions of these debriefings—even though we have been receiving permission from the returned POWs themselves to review the information they provided upon their return. This is but one more example of the way this investigation is being obstructed."

"...When you consider the number of MIAs at the end of he war, currently 1,117, where we had no information on the fate of the individual, it is probable that even my number of over 300 is at best conservative."

"...the staff also found over 920 accounts of reported American POWs sighted or said to be detained in captive environments in Laos and Vietnam. More importantly, they found that these accounts clustered in geographic locations where, in many cases, our own intelligence agencies confirmed the presence of detention facilities.

"In April of this year, the staff, after having plotted all of these sightings on a map, tried to brief the members of this committee on their findings. Regretfully, that briefing did not take place in an independent and objective manner because the Defense Intelligence Agency, with the cooperation of certain members and senior staff of this committee, badgered and insulted the Committee's investigators. Some obviously did not agree with those findings, as is their right, but to this day, I remain shocked at the manner in which both investigators and their findings were treated.

"For the record, let's be clear what those findings were. After spending over 2,000 man-hours reviewing these selected reports, staff investigators concluded, and I quote, that 'the intelligence indicates that American POWs have been alive in captivity in Vietnam and Laos as late as 1989, and that no POWs are in captivity in Cambodia.'"

THE BOYS WE LEFT BEHIND

Senator Smith, during his presentation, made some very bold statements. One regarded recent distress signals picked up by aerial photo reconnaissance:

> "As late as June, 1992, next to a prison in North Vietnam...the markings 72-TA-88 and a name are stamped out next to a prison facility, and this name and the code letters 'TA' do in fact correlate specifically by name to an unaccounted for serviceman shot down in '72, and the National Security Agency indicates this individual may have been captured during the end of the war in Vietnam."

He went on to mention that:

> "...on at least four occasions, the Vietnamese reportedly indicated to the United States, through third parties and third countries, that there were live American servicemen in Vietnam and Laos who could be returned through negotiations with the United States...[these were] in January, 1977;...January, 1981;...November 1984 and early 1985;...and in the 1989/1990 time frame."
>
> But no one seems to have wanted to negotiate for "live American servicemen."

Smith's investigative staff, in their report, described their frustrations in dealing with the American intelligence services and requested help in forcing the various entities to cooperate with the investigation:

> "Mr. Chairman...I ask your support to immediately issue subpoenas for the documents we have not received from the Executive Branch [President Bush's administration] including 60 boxes of intelligence reports from the National Security Agency, operational files from the Central Intelligence Agency, the relevant portions of the debriefing reports from our returned POWs, and over 500 DIA intelligence reports which our investigators say indicate POWs have been alive in captivity in Vietnam and Laos as late as 1989.

"I also call on this Committee, as I indicated in writing last week to immediately vote to declassify, as we are empowered to do under our authorizing legislation, all the live-sighting and hearsay reports that have been in our possession for the last six months...The American people are entitled to have these reports publicly released *by the Senate in a coherent fashion*. Last week I made one last appeal for the Defense Department to come to the Senate and physically declassify these reports. They denied my specific request in writing. They won't come here. So I call on this Committee to do it ourselves."

"...In conclusion, Mr. Chairman...we have hundreds of questions yet to be answered, thousands of documents that this Committee has not seen and that this government refuses to provide. This Committee must have the will to get those documents, and to get those questions answered, and to get all the information declassified for the American people...

"There should be no final report until there is a final accounting."

The Senatorial investigation, though far from complete, ended before Christmas, 1992. The POWs, if any are still alive, remain in captivity in Southeast Asia.

And not one government official has faced trial for drug trafficking.

As for the feelings of the veterans who fought in Vietnam and Laos, former Green Beret Major Mark Smith, who was privy to live sighting reports through Army intelligence channels, sums it up: "You're talking [about] people who have no feelings whatsoever about the individual soldier in the field. Their answer to all this is to build a black wall in Washington and put all their names on it to pacify you and I. Do they care about soldiers? They could give a damn about soldiers."

Part IV

Manipulating The Third World

"The underdeveloped world presents greater opportunities for covert intelligence collection simply because governments are much less highly orientated; there is less security consciousness; and there is apt to be more actual or potential diffusion of power among parties, localities, organizations and individuals outside the central governments."

> Richard Bissell
> Deputy Director of Plans
> (1958-62)
> Central Intelligence Agency

"The most obscene haste with which the West has rushed to pour arms into Zaire reinforces the argument of many Africans that behind every attempted or successful coup on this continent is the hand of a foreign power."

> The Zambian government
> concerning CIA activity in
> Africa—1975

"Certain covert operations have been incompatible with American principles and ideology and when exposed, have resulted in damaging this nation's ability to exercise moral and ethical leadership."

> Senate Select Committee
> On Intelligence

Chapter 20

A Profitable Adventure

Following World War II, the United States became increasingly concerned with the fact that underdeveloped countries of the Third World were rapidly becoming targets for Soviet expansionism. The Russians, already having gained control of the Eastern European countries, and successfully pushed communism into mainland China, North Korea and Vietnam, quickly turned their eyes to other strategically located or resource-rich countries that might expand the Soviet sphere of influence in the world.

As one country after another began to show signs of internal turmoil instigated by external sources, the U.S. government found itself in the position of having to guard its interests abroad in manners that would not be considered acceptable by the American people at home. It was one thing to assist a legitimate government in protecting itself from communist aggression, but quite another to remove an existing government and replace it with one more favorable to American interests—especially if done with violence. But between 1951 and 1978, this is exactly how business was conducted.

Often it was exactly that. Business. American "interests" went far beyond world politics and national security. In too many instances, staged *coups*, covert military action, popular revolutions, and assassinations conducted under the guise of national security were in fact motivated by the business interests of major corporations—and the investment bankers that backed them.

To the average American, the forty years following World War II were a very confusing four decades. The media spoke of countries few people had ever heard of, much less understood the significance of, and described bloody revolutions, terrorist activities, bombings, kidnappings and murders on an ever increasing scale. But for the most part, the public paid little attention to these events occurring in remote countries half a world away. After all, what bearing did these events have on the United States? Little of it seemed to concern America.

Or did it? What the American public did not realize was to what extent the U.S. government, by way of its clandestine services, participated in the bloody events transpiring in the Third World.

Iran

Between 1951 and 1953, while world attention was focused on the fighting in Korea, other key geopolitical events were occuring that drew little if any press from the media. An entire government was in the process of being targeted for change, and it was to be done with as little attention as possible being drawn to the event. The target was Iran.

In that time frame, the actual power in the Iranian government rested with the Prime Minister, Mohammed Mossadegh. Though the Shah, the traditional king of Persia, held the throne, his power had been systematically reduced until he was little more than a figurehead. The young Shah, Mohammed Resa Pahlavi, had very little experience in government and no motivation to regain the reins of power from the Prime Minister, who held great popularity among the people after nationalizing the British-owned Anglo-Iranian Oil Company. The Iranians, believing the British had been bleeding the nation of its main source of wealth for decades, considered this a move of nationalistic patriotism.

The British, of course, were outraged. But there was little they could do about it other than request American support in mounting an economic blockade. The support was given and the pressure that was brought to bear began having a critical effect on the Iranian economy. But for Winston Churchill, that was not enough. He wanted more direct action, and in 1952 he ordered his intelligence personnel to make contact with the CIA to see if there might be "other" activities mounted against Mossadegh.

President Truman, after getting wind of the request, refused to allow the CIA to participate in such an adventure for British interests. The U.S. had its hands full in Korea and the Iranian situation was a British problem.

One year later this changed. John Foster Dulles was appointed as Secretary of State—the same year his brother, Allen Dulles, was named to head the CIA. To the Dulles brothers, both Wall Street lawyers who had represented the Rockefeller family's oil interests, Iran appeared to be a plum ripe for the picking. The Iranian oil assets, should they fall in to American hands, would benefit not only the nation's economy, but certain large oil companies as well. Though the Iranian oil fields had traditionally been an all-British preserve, that could now be changed.

Declaring Mossadegh a member of the Iranian communist party—the Tudeh—the State Department and the CIA began making plans for his ouster. With Mossadegh removed from the scene, power would fall back to the young Shah who could be controlled by the American government. The end result would be a subservient country that was strategically located, held tremendous oil reserves that could be exploited, and would provide the CIA with an excellent base of operations along its northern border for monitoring Soviet communications. Everyone would get what they wanted. Except the British.

To head up the operation, Allen Dulles picked Kermit "Kim" Roosevelt, grandson of President Theodore Roosevelt. Kim Roosevelt was an old hand with the CIA by this time, having left Harvard during World War II to work with the OSS, and had become an expert on the Middle East. He was given a budget of $2 million, his choice of team members, and a mission objective to topple Mossadegh from power. He had been briefed that this would be a dangerous assignment, that they would have to operate outside the protection of the U.S. Embassy, and that they would have to supplement their tiny force with local agents of their own choosing. All in all, it was to be a risky business.

The plan developed by the CIA was simple. The Shah, assured of American support, was to order Mossadegh replaced by the interior minister, General Fazollah Zahedi. Mossadegh, once removed from power, would not be able to stop Zahedi from restoring power to the Shah. The plan was sound in theory. In actuality, it was a dismal failure.

The planned coup was initiated in August of 1953. Shah Pahlavi did what he was told, but Mossadegh did not go out the door as easily as the CIA had hoped. Instead, confident of popular support, Mossadegh had the colonel who delivered the message arrested, then declared the Shah's decree illegal. He then removed the last vestiges of power from the Shah and assumed full control of the country himself.

Massive demonstrations erupted in the Streets of Teheran in support of Mossadegh. The Shah, fearing for his life and realizing the CIA could not protect him as they had promised, took his family and fled the country. After a brief sojourn in Baghdad, Pahlavi went on to Rome where he met CIA Director Allen Dulles.

Dulles, contrary to being depressed about the turn of events, assured the Shah that the situation was far from over. It was only a matter of adjusting the plan to handle Mossadegh in a different manner. The CIA had simply misjudged Mossadegh's personality. He was a bit more stubborn—which meant he didn't take the hint—than they had originally anticipated.

As this meeting was taking place, Kermit Roosevelt was working quickly in Teheran to take advantage of the destabilized state of affairs. By bribing the proper officials, and printing and distributing propaganda leaflets which included the text of the Shah's decree, a counter-demonstration erupted in the streets. This demonstration, outnumbering the pro-Mossadegh mobs, was extremely successful and was soon joined by the majority of the military whose officers had previously been bribed by Roosevelt's team.

Bloody fighting broke out, leaving several dead in the streets. The Tudeh and pro-Mossadegh force, reinforced by a few faithful army elements, was quickly outgunned and forced to flee. Zahedi was then installed as the Prime Minister and Mossadegh was arrested. As Mossadegh stood trial for various trumped-up offenses, Zahedi invited the Shah to return to Teheran.

Within a year, American oil companies—principally Standard Oil—were given 25-year contracts by the Iranian government that allocated them a forty percent share of the country's petroleum; CIA communication monitoring stations were constructed along the northern (Iranian/Soviet) border; American arms manufacturers and aerospace corporations flooded into the country to equip and train the Shah's armed forces; and the CIA began recruiting for and training the Shah's secret police, the notorious Savak.

Over the next twenty years, the Shah proved to be a valuable asset to the U.S. The listening posts along the Soviet border continued to pour reams of intelligence into the CIA coffers; American oil companies and arms companies had made, and continued to make, millions; and the communist advance through the Middle East had been stopped short of dominating the Persian Gulf region. But the rule of the Shah was not a popular one. His secret police, the Savak, had been responsible for keeping any political opposition to a minimum and had done so with morbid enthusiasm, using murder, kidnapping, terror and torture as their tools.

After the 1976 election of Jimmy Carter to the Presidency, the State Department and the CIA (now under retired navy admiral Stansfield Turner) made overtures to the Shah to change the ways in which the Savak conducted itself. Turner, who was not a proponent of the CIA and did not place a great deal of faith in the HUMINT (Human Intelligence) sources, quickly set about reducing the CIA's agent strength almost as soon as he had taken over from the previous DCI, George Bush. Under Turner, who had specific orders from Carter to curtail certain CIA activities, the Agency was cut from several thousand agents to just over 300, the lowest it had been since the Truman years. Covert operations were reduced to two or three each fiscal year, and the operating budget was cut to just 40% of the previous year's allocation. The old hands around the Agency, who had operated with little, if any, supervision and previously had millions of dollars from the "Black Budget"[135] at their disposal, found themselves being forced to retire, resign, or fall into step with the new concepts of how the CIA should be run. Turner, who did not trust intelligence developed by field agents, built up a new program that utilized electronic devices such as spy satellites and communications monitoring systems to provide up-to-the-minute intelligence. Though he did manage to bring the CIA into the cutting edge of technology, he failed to realize that no amount of equipment, no matter how sophisticated, could replace people in the field. Observations of an activity first-hand by an experienced field operative could not be replaced by intelligence analysts who studied satellite photos and radio communications from the safety of their offices in Washington. And ironically, because the CIA was now, at the insistence of Carter, "more open" in their activities, allied countries ceased sharing their secrets with the U.S. Instead of making the CIA more efficient and trustworthy, Turner and Carter only succeeded in defanging the beast on the exterior, and causing the secret cells of the good-old-boy network in the inside to bury themselves—and their secret activities—deeper. To those who were to survive the Carter purges, Turner was only a bureaucrat to be tolerated and out-lived until a new President could replace Carter and a new DCI could be appointed.

It was during this time that three of the key players of the CIA's activities in Laos and Vietnam again surfaced. In 1975, after the fall of Saigon, DCI William Colby reassigned Theodore Shackley back to Washington and promoted him to Associate Director in the Directorate of Operations. This was a major position that put him in charge of such divisions as the Covert Action Staff, Special Operations, Counter-Intelligence Staff, Counter-Terrorism, and ironically, Counter-Narcotics. Shackley's old Southeast Asia and Cuban venture partner, Thomas Clines, was brought in to head CIA operations and training.

Another interesting character entered the scene at the same time. Edwin P. Wilson, a former CIA agent who worked under Clines, had been operating in Iran since 1975 as an agent of the super-secret Naval Intelligence Task Force 157. Clines, who had arranged Wilson's transfer in 1971, reestablished contact with Wilson and began utilizing his talents in the CIA's efforts to prop up the Shah's failing regime. Wilson's specialty was establishing proprietary companies to act as fronts for clandestine operations. For what Shackley and Clines had in mind, Wilson would be the perfect choice. He had already set up commercial fronts such as World Marine, Inc., Maryland Maritime, Inc. and Consultants International. Under Clines direction, he would become an "advisor" to the Savak and act as a double agent to keep Clines and Shackley advised on what the Savak was up to. For it was actually the Savak who controlled the country, and the Shah, as he had been before, was only a figurehead. Whoever controlled the Savak controlled Iran—and the billions of dollars of oil and drug money generated by the country.

Wilson would not be operating in Iran by himself. Following the fall of Saigon, Richard Secord was promoted to Brigadier General and sent to Iran to serve as Chief, U.S. Air Force Military Assistance

212

Advisory Group (MAAG).[136] As such, he was in position to represent U.S. contractors in the sale of arms to the Shah. He was also responsible for training Iranian military personnel in the use of new weapons, equipment and aircraft. That same year, Erich von Marbod, who had served as Nixon's Operation 40 covert operations advisor, was sent by the Defense Department to monitor all U.S. military contracts inside the country. The old crew from the anti-Castro days and Southeast Asia was back together again.

Once the Savak discovered Wilson's ties with Secord, von Marbod, Clines and Shackley, they began pressing Wilson to increase the flow of arms and equipment to Iran. Wilson was only too happy to comply and the profits from the sales, many of which had been conducted through one of his front companies, began to soar.

Some of the equipment the Savak purchased through Wilson was electronic surveillance and location systems. By using such equipment, the Savak was able to home in on clandestine radio transmitters that broadcast anti-Shah messages and subsequently close them down. In one instance that was reported to Wilson, nine such dissidents, after having been apprehended and handcuffed, had been shoved to their knees and summarily shot. Wilson passed all this information up the chain, but it had no impact on the continuing operation.

In 1976, Carter's new head of naval intelligence, Admiral Bobby Ray Inman, disbanded Task Force 157 and removed its personnel from Iran. Wilson chose to remain in the country as a "civilian," however, and continued to do exactly what he had been doing all along in his "advising and consulting" capacity.

According to Wilson, who is now serving a lengthy prison sentence after being convicted of several international crimes, the Savak began providing him with lists of names of anti-Shah activists that needed to be eliminated. Wilson would then pass them along to Shackley through Rafael "Chi Chi" Quintero (a Cuban CIA operative from the Miami station and the Bay of Pigs days). The anti-Shah dissidents were later found executed by hired assassins.[137]

In August of 1976, Shackley recruited the Iranian-born head of the Stanford Technology Corporation, Albert Hakim, to play a pivotal part in the Shah's purchase of American technology. Hakim had major contacts within the Iranian military and the Savak and could further arms sales and obtain more lucrative contracts. Shortly after taking the job, he was introduced by Wilson to Secord, who along with von Marbod, succeeded in using Hakim's contacts to sell the Iranians $5.5 million worth of electronic monitoring equipment built by Rockwell International, and $7.5 million worth of telephone monitoring equipment. This last deal was cut by bribing General Mohammed Khatemi, commander of the Iranian Air Force—and an associate of Hakim.[138]

That same month three top managers for the Rockwell IBEX project were murdered. William C. Cottrell, Donald G. Smith, and Robert R. Krongard, all involved with the IBEX surveillance equipment project being set up for the Savak, were assassinated in a road ambush. The former IBEX Director of Security, Gene Wheaton, investigated the murders for ten years. His conclusion was that the trio had been eliminated because they had discovered profit skimming going on within the project and that Secord, Clines, Hakim, Shackley and Quintero were linked to the assassinations. The only people eventually accused of the murders were two Iranians who were killed during shootouts with the Iranian police when they came to arrest them.[139]

As all of these business dealings were transpiring, the political problems within the country were being neglected by the CIA. Instead of attempting to win the hearts and minds of the people, as they did with the Meo in Laos and the Montagnards of Vietnam, they simply let the Savak continue its programs of oppression, brutality and torture. One former CIA intelligence analyst, Jesse Leaf, recalled that the Savak established special facilities where cells contained some of the most horrible torture devices ever devised. "The ones [methods of torture] that I saw reported on were hot tables, which were metallic tables hooked up to electricity, and people would put the juice through it and it would burn parts of their back or whatever; [other torture methods included] boiling water up the rectum; heavy weights on the genitals; beatings with wire ropes; nail pullings; tooth pullings and so on. The CIA's attitude to Savak torture was 'their enemy is my enemy.' If Savak wanted to torture somebody, some communists or somebody who was anti-Shah, or who was ultimately detrimental to our world interests, well, fine, go ahead and let them do it. The Agency's official position was that it was not our problem."[140]

This attitude, plus the lack of good human intelligence being developed from inside Iran—particularly due to the lack of field agents inside the country since Turner and Carter had reduced the CIA to a shadow of its former self—caused the greatest intelligence failure in modern history to occur. While business dealings took up the time of those who were sent to keep tabs on the situation and make corrections as needed, the fundamentalist Moslem religious sects were rallying the people to revolution. In January, 1979, Iran was again cast into massive demonstrations. Within days the people began disarming the military and taking over government buildings. Instead of reacting with force, which the Shah certainly had, he panicked and once again fled the country. This time he would not return.

The CIA listening posts were abandoned, each wired to high explosives should anyone tamper with the sites, and the CIA technicians began making their way out of the country any way they could.

The fanatical anti-American Khoumeni regime came to power almost immediately, flying the Ayatollah Khoumeni back to Teheran from Paris after years in exile. Within days a rag-tag band of Moslem fundamentalist militia, posing as students to the world press, stormed the U.S. Embassy in Teheran. The Marine guards, who could have defended the Embassy, were ordered not to resist by President Carter. Even though forcibly entering and capturing the embassy of a foreign country is an automatic act of war, Carter failed to react accordingly. This failure to respond resulted in the Embassy staff and the CIA station personnel being taken prisoner and held hostage for 444 days.[141]

The Iranian crisis could have been averted had the United States understood sooner the injustices perpetrated by the Savak and intervened. But neither did the State Department, or the CIA, report to the President what was actually going on in Iran behind the Savak's prison doors. Nor did either do anything to correct the situation before it got out of hand, or failing that, support a democratic change in power to salvage a weakening situation. The end result is that the U.S. lost a vital ally in a part of the world that would become ever more important to U.S. interests as time went by.

But for some of the participants, it had been a profitable adventure.

Chapter 21

Guatemala: The Banana War

One year after the war in Korea ended in stalemate—and just ten months after the successful reinstallation of the Shah in Iran—the American government turned its attention to regions of influence much closer to home: Central and South America. It was as if it were time for a bit of prophecy to be fulfilled. In the words of Simon Bolivar, who brought revolution to South America: "America..is the highest and most irrefutable assignment of destiny..The nations I have founded will, after prolonged and bitter agony, go into an eclipse, but will later emerge as states of the one great republic, *America.*"[142]

In relation to the engineered takeover conducted in Iran, the coup that took place in Guatemala in 1954 was considerably more audacious. Where the public excuse for being involved in Iran was thinly disguised as being an anti-communist operation, no such excuse existed in the tiny Central American country of Guatemala.

In 1951, Jacobo Arbenz Guzman, a pro-trade union reformist, was elected as the country's president. His platform consisted of redistributing the land, of which two percent of the population owned 70%, and labor reforms for an impoverished population whose main source of income was derived from the American-owned United Fruit Company. For decades the UFC had dominated Guatemala—the original "Banana Republic"—and exploited the cheap labor of the semi-literate population. Arbenz was determined to change that.

But Arbenz's problem, as seen by the CIA, was that he not only tolerated, but cooperated with the local communist party. Though he, himself, was not a communist, and he had none in his cabinet, the mere fact that he did not actively suppress them made him intolerable to Washington. Especially after the United Fruit Company utilized its powerful contacts in Washington to influence Eisenhower to do something to protect UFC interests in the country. Arbenz became a two-fold threat. He not only gave the appearance of providing communisim with a foothold in North America, he threatened the economic dominance of influencial and powerful private interests.

Eisenhower decided Arbenz had to go. He issued marching orders to Allen Dulles, whom he had just appointed Director of Central Intelligence after moving General Walter Bedell Smith, former DCI under Truman, to his personal staff. Dulles turned the Guatemalan operation over to his Deputy Director of Plans, Frank Wisner. Wisner, following standard procedure, began searching for a Guatemalan national of sufficient rank and stature to become the figurehead for a coup, and quickly found him in Carlos Castillo Armas, a right-wing colonel in the Guatemalan army. As would be the trademark in all CIA-involved coups in the Third World, the Guatemalan operation would be staged as a revolt by disatisfied elements of the Guatemalan military, assisted by right-wing exile groups.

Guatemalan expatriots, led by mercenaries recruited from both inside the United States and abroad, were assembled at training bases in Nicaragua. An air force, consisting of C-47 transports and World War II vintage Republic P-47 Thunderbolt fighter-bombers, began staging at Managua airport. Along the Honduran/Guatemalan border, clandestine radio transmitters and communications stations were set up to handle both inflamatory disinformation and military communications.

By the Spring of 1954 all was in order. The small army had been trained, the air force equipped and staffed, and the radio transmitters had begun transmitting anti-Arbenz propaganda. All that was needed for the next phase of the operation—the military uprising—was an excuse to escalate. The plotters didn't have to wait long.

In May, the CIA discovered that a shipment of arms had been sent to Guatemala from Czechoslovakia. This was all that was needed to spur a counter-action by the U.S. government. Almost immediately, fifty tons of military equipment and ammunition was flown from U.S.

bases to the "exile army" in Nicaragua. This was followed by a release of several news stories describing links between Arbenz and various European communist countries, magnifying and escalating the incident into an international confrontation. To blockade such shipments—to cut off Guatemala's trade with the outside world—ships of the U.S. Navy were dispatched to search all foreign vessels enroute to the tiny country. The French and Dutch, after discovering that their ships had been stopped on the high seas, protested loudly that such activities were, in effect, an act of piracy. The British, flatly refusing to allow their ships to be detained or boarded, notified the U.S. government that such action was tantamount to a "technical act of war." One British official, realizing who was behind all of this, sent a memorandum to another government official that stated "I have written a private letter to Sir R. Makins asking him whether Mr. Dulles is going fascist. I can think of no other explanation [for this conduct]."

By June, the propaganda campaign against Arbenz began to show its effects. The Voice of America, operated by CIA agent David Atlee Phillips, had conducted a day and night blitz campaign of disinformation against Arbenz, accusing him of being a devout communist, of disloyalty to his own people, and of ties to the Eastern European bloc.

Arbenz, sensing a change in the attitude of his military, grounded his own air force and began watching his army generals carefully for signs of treason. The air force commander, fearing further actions by Arbenz, defected to the CIA-backed mercenary army in Nicaragua. The time was ripe for invasion.

Eisenhower, in a last meeting prior to sending the rebels into Guatemala, stated: "I'm prepared to take any steps that are necessary to see that this mission succeeds. For if it succeeds, it's the people of Guatemala throwing off the yoke of communism. If it fails, the flag of the United States has failed." No mention was made of the fact that Arbenz had been elected in a democratic election by the people.

On June 18th, 1954, Colonel Armas took his "Army of Liberation" across the Honduran border into Guatemala. As they made their way toward Guatemala City, the squadron of P-47s bombed San Jose, the major Guatemalan port on the west coast located fifty miles southwest of the capital. While both of these events were transpiring, the Voice of America filled the air waves with false news flashes of battles and skirmishes—in which Armas was consistently the victor—that were total fiction. The effects of the broadcasts were spectacular. Each hour that went by, with its announcements of additional Armas' victories, the Guatemalans became more demoralized.

As the population sat glued to their radio sets, the C-47s took advantage of the fact that the Guatemalan Air Force remained grounded and began dropping propaganda leaflets over the capital. These flights were interspersed with sorties of bomb-dropping P-47s that added weight to the claims of the radio stations.

Arbenz, by way of his representative in the United Nations, immediately accused the United States of being actively involved in the attack. The United States delegate countered with the programmed response that the uprising "does not involve aggression but is a revolt of Guatemalans against Guatemalans."

The invasion was going well, but the CIA feared that the small rebel air force would not be able to counter the Guatemalan *Fuerza Aeria Guatemalteca* if Arbenz lifted the order grounding it. Allen Dulles, in anticipation of such an action, managed to talk Eisenhower into releasing more fighters from U.S. military (Air National Guard) inventory. The airplanes could not simply be transferred to a rebel army, which would immediately implicate the U.S. government, but could be moved through a "cut-out," or middleman. This was effected through the Nicaraguan Air Force, which "bought" the planes for next to nothing, then passed them on to the rebel squadron.

By the end of June, Arbenz, suffering from almost six weeks of military and propaganda assault, could no longer stand the pressure. On the 27th, he turned the reins of power over to the head of the Guatemalan armed forces, Colonel Carlos Diaz.

But instead of buckling and suing for peace, as the CIA had anticipated would happen in a power shift, Diaz announced that he would continue the fight. It was obvious to Dulles and Wisner that resistance would require further persuasion and additional bombing raids were ordered. This time, the headquarters of the Guatemalan military was targeted—and hit. Diaz, after holding the office of president for only one day, was ousted by a junta of other officers who saw no reason to resist further. Six days later an agreement was signed between the junta and Armas, which eventually led to Armas becoming president.

What followed was a textbook reversal of nationalism. Armas began a reign of terror that disenfranschised over 70% of the population by denying voting priviledges to anyone who could not read or write; repealed the laws permitting unions; and returned almost 800,000 acres of land to the United Fruit Company. For the CIA—and American business—the status quo had been restored in Guatemala. For the bureaucrats of the covert intelligence agencies and the State Department, who had kept the American people in the dark concerning the actual machinations behind the coup, the facade continued. John Foster Dulles, reinforcing the secret on Amercan television, said: "...the struggle in Guatemala exposed the evil purpose of the Kremlin to find nesting places in the Americas." He went on to state, "Led by Colonel Castillo Armas, patriots arose in Guatemala to challenge the communist leadership and to change it. Thus the situation is being cured by the Guatemalans themselves."

Nothing was said about the interests of the United Fruit Company—or the $20 million cost to the American taxpayers.

Chapter 22

Cuba: Assassins and the Bay Of Pigs

After Fidel Castro managed to overthrow the dictatorship of Fulgencio Batista in 1959, the CIA was shocked to find that this charismatic guerrilla fighter, whom they had backed, intended to establish friendly relations with the Soviet Union. They were further taken aback when he stated that he would support guerrilla activities against U.S.-backed dictatorships thoughout Latin America. The final straw came when Castro nationalized all foreign interests inside of Cuba and seized all U.S. business assets.[143]

By December, the CIA had decided that Castro had become a detriment to U.S. interests not only in Cuba, but Central and South America as well. If he aligned himself with the Soviet Union, massive shipments of arms, military equipment and "advisors" could completely destabilize the region and threaten the United States itself. The last thing Eisenhower wanted was a physical Soviet presence in the Americas.

Colonel J.C. King, director of the CIA's Western Hemisphere Division, sent a memo to Allen Dulles noting the dangers of having such a character as Castro residing only ninety miles from Miami. He recommended that "thorough consideration be given to the elimination of Fidel Castro—the disappearance of Fidel would greatly accelerate the fall of the present government."

Dulles concurred and called a meeting of the National Security Council to discuss various means of dealing with the situation. The

Council, headed by Vice President Richard Nixon, decided to form a special task group to deal with Castro. National Security Council memorandum 5412 was drafted, creating the infamous "5412 Committee."[144]

The 5412 Committee, whose members considered the elimination of Fidel Castro, his brother Raul, and Ernesto "Che" Guevara to be in the national interest, met on several occasions to discuss various means of effectively dealing with the situation.[145] From one of these meetings emerged the decision to form a sub-group whose existance could be disavowed if discovered. Any link between the 5412 Committee and this secret operation could be plausibly denied, and at the same time, its existence could be blamed on someone outside the Agency. The cut-out for this operation, codenamed Operation 40, would be Miami Mafia boss Santos Trafficante—the same mobster who would surface later in the Kennedy assassination and in the Laotian/CIA heroin smuggling operation. Trafficante was picked because of his former personal interests in the Cuban casinos, his current ties with the Cuban exile community in Florida, and his friendship with former Cuban dictator Fulgencio Batista. And above all, Trafficante, after being promised that Mafia holdings would be restored, would be agreeable to serving in this capacity.

All that remained would be the financing of the operation. According to the brief on the Avirgan/Honey vs. Hull and Vidal lawsuits,[146] "...Richard Nixon and other members of the endeavor, on information and belief, agreed to use the color of their authority as officials of the United States Government...[to divert]...funds appropriated by the U.S. Congress for foreign intelligence gathering, comingling such diverted funds with the income generated through the criminal activity of Trafficante's organization and laundering these funds through foreign and domestic banks, in violation of federal banking and currency laws of the United States."

Irregardless of how the funding mechanism was established, sufficient monies were provided to finance a huge operation against Castro. This operation, was divided into two branches: the formation of a paramilitary brigade of Cuban exiles, to be trained by CIA case officers for both covert and overt military action against Castro, and a top secret, highly trained, specially equipped team of assassins. This team, codenamed ZR/RIFLE, received the assignment to eliminate the three targets: Fidel, Raul and Che.

The ZR/RIFLE team, according to the Avirgan/Honey lawsuit, consisted of Rafael "Chi Chi" Quintero, Raul Villaverde, Luis Posada Carriles (aka Ramon Medina), Felix Rodriguez (aka Max Gomez), Francisco Fiorini (aka Frank Sturgis), Ricardo Chavez, Joaquin Sanjenis (who directed Operation 40 for ten years) and eight others not named. This team was placed under the direction of case officer E. Howard Hunt, codenamed "Eduardo."[147]

Another sub-unit that was organized under Operation 40 consisted of a group of exiles who had a very special and devious mission. Equipped with Cuban uniforms and arms, they would be put ashore prior to the Bay of Pigs invasion at the east end of the island near Guantanamo naval base. Their mission was to attack the American naval base. Kennedy, being led to believe that Castro's forces were attacking the installation, could be expected to respond accordingly. This act of war, it was thought, would ensure that Kennedy would land the Marines at the Bay of Pigs in support the small *Brigada* after it had gained a foothold and declared itself a legal government-in-need.[148]

Eisenhower had been completely aware of what had gone on at the CIA during his tenure. He wrote: "On 17 March 1960, I ordered the CIA to begin to organize the training of Cuban exiles mainly in Guatemala against a future day when they might return to their homeland." He had also attended several of the NSC meetings where the proposals to assassinate Castro were discussed. Kennedy had not been so included.

Of the master plan that dealt with the overall situation in Cuba, the initial action would be to discredit the popular Fidel in they eyes of the Cuban people. For this, a whole series of "dirty tricks" were considered. But the ideas the Agency came up with bordered on the ridiculous, some actually comical. One concerned the CIA's MK/ULTRA experiments with LSD. In this one, agents would spray a Cuban television studio with the hallucinogen prior to Castro making an appearance to give a speech. The object was for Castro to somehow injest enough of the LSD to hallucinate and appear to hundreds of thousands of watching Cubans to be uncontrollable and unpredictable.

This idea was abandoned when no one could guarantee that the LSD droplets would stay in the air long enough to have the desired effect.

The second plan involved doctoring the dictator's cigars with LSD. This scheme was cast aside when no one could figure how to get the chemical into Fidel's cigars, or to get cigars that had been prepared in advance to Castro.

The next idea was to put thallium salts into his shoes, hopefully during an upcoming trip to Europe when he was expected to leave them in the hallway outside his hotel room in the European fashion. These salts are a debilatory. After being absorbed into the skin they are supposed to make one's hair fall out. In Fidel's case, it would be his beard. This trick fell through when Castro cancelled all scheduled foreign trips.

As these schemes were being considered by the Agency, the Operation 40 staff continued to pursue the demise of the Castro brothers and Che Guevara in a more serious vein. In July of 1960, one of their agents inside of Cuba reported that he might have access to Raul on a given date. He was immediately told to make the hit, but before it could be carried out, plans were changed and the agent was told to disregard the previous orders.

Marita Lorenz, Castro's girlfriend, had by this time been recruited by the CIA. Frank Sturgis, who had been on Castro's staff during his Escambray Mountains guerrilla days, but had defected to the CIA when Castro announced his intent to deal with communists, talked Lorenz into murdering Castro, then joining the CIA in Miami. The actual job was to be done with poison capsules that she would drop into his drink. But Lorenz made the mistake of hiding the capsules in a jar of cold cream, and when she tried to retrieve them in the bathroom of her and Fidel's hotel room in Havana, discovered that they had dissolved. She took this to be an omen, and was greatly relieved when the plan failed. I her words, "I'm just not a murderer. I looked at him in there [laying on the bed of the hotel room] and asked myself 'what's he doing? Nothing.' I just couldn't carry it out. I don't kill people for governments. I'm a lover, not a killer."

In another attempt, the Mafia was recruited to try to poison Castro. The CIA sent former FBI agent Robert Mayheu to Las Vegas to meet with Mafia member Johnny Roselli to ask for help in killing Fidel. Mayheu told Roselli that the government was behind the operation, that it was part of a planned invasion of Cuba, and that they needed the help of the Mafia in pulling it off. Roselli agreed to help—for a fee of $150,000—and contacted Chicago mafioso Sam Giancana, who made arrangements for the operation. Giancana in turn asked for a poison pill that could be dropped in a glass of liquid that was tasteless, odorless, and would not take effect for at least four or five days. The CIA complied with the request, and Mayheu delivered the pills to Roselli and Giancana in a sealed envelope. But the Mafia contacts, for some reason, failed to deliver the pill to Castro.

Richard Bissell, Head of CIA operations from 1958-62, recalled: "Several of the attempts to assassinate Castro using Mafia types took place before the actual Bay of Pigs landing. I knew of these and encouraged them. I felt that if just before the landing, Castro had disappeared from the scene there would be a great deal of disorganization and it would be vastly easier to break the will of any successive regime."

No attempt to assassinate the Castro brothers or Che Guevara (while he was in Cuba) succeeded.

In November of 1960, John F. Kennedy was elected President. By that time the Cuban exile force of CIA-trained soldiers had grown to a full 1300-man brigade. Known as the *Frente Revolucionario Democratico* (FRD), it was equipped with World War II weapons, munitions and field gear, and funded by a budget of $13 million previously approved by Eisenhower. Its support inventory included six small (2,400 ton) freighters, leased for $600 per day per ship, six C-47 transport aircraft, and sixteen clandestinely-procurred B-26 attack bombers for air support. Its pilots were being trained by sheep-dipped members of the Alabama Air National Guard, and its commandos by military officers and NCOs of both the army and the Marines.[149]

Virtually the same players behind the Guatemalan operation were involved in the Bay of Pigs invasion, now codenamed Operation ZAPATA.[150] David Atlee Phillips, the mastermind of the radio disinformation program in Guatemala, now manned the anti-Castro transmitter on Swan Island off the coast of Honduras. Richard Bissell, and second-in-command Richard Helms, were now focusing on the coming Cuban venture. Allen Dulles, the old spy master, was in overall control as usual.

The entire operation was being controlled by Theodore Shackley and Thomas Clines at the Miami CIA station. Several businesses were set up in Miami and surrounding communities—gunshops, hardware stores, even coffee shops—to provide fronts for the various activities of the operation. In New Orleans, where the second training site was located, the Guy Bannister Detective Agency was such a front. In this particular case, almost everyone who worked in the vicinity knew what was going on. Cubans, dressed in green fatigues and spotted camouflage uniforms, went in and out of the building in droves, often carrying large boxes full of weapons or explosives. The training site was located in the marshland on the north side of Lake Ponchartrain. In all, it was hard for the CIA to keep a secret with so much activity going on along the Gulf Coast. Castro himself announced on a continuous basis that the Yankees would invade any day.

When the invasion finally came it was a disaster. Not because it was ill-concieved or meekly carried out, but because it was defanged early in the game. The key to the invasion plan lay in the Brigade's ability to knock out the Cuban Air Force. Castro's air force at that time consisted of 15 B-26 bombers, 10 Hawker Sea Furies, and 4 T-33 jet trainer/fighters. The T-33, a two-place version of the Korean War-era Lockheed F-80 Shooting Star fighter, was by jet standards, a slow, easy to hit target—at least up against the more modern supersonic jets of the time. But for ground troops, the T-33 could be devastating. And for ships, deadly. The key was to knock out the T-33s on the ground. This job fell to the FRD's B-26 Invaders (actually A-26 attack versions that were equipped with eight .50 caliber machine guns in the nose).

The problem that confronted the tiny anti-Castro air force was two-fold: they had to go all the way back to Nicaragua to refuel and rearm, and they were no match for the T-33 in the air should any get off the ground. The only solution would be to hit the jets on the ground, early in the operation, and hope to get them all.

It did not happen. After a dawn raid, in which only six B-26 bombers were allowed to participate instead of the planned 16, only a small part of Castro's air force was destroyed. Castro, anticipating an invasion, had dispersed his airplanes to outlying airfields and had used non-flyable hulks as decoys. U-2 photographs taken later verified that only five flyable airplanes had been completely destroyed. The surviving planes that were still airworthy were quickly scrambled in a effort to repulse the invasion force, both in the air and at sea. As the FRD B-26s returned to Nicaragua to rearm and refuel, Castro's pilots homed in on the Bay of Pigs.

Unknown to the FRD pilots, strange machinations were taking place behind the scenes in Washington. The Assistant DCI, General Charles Cabell, who was running the show from the Washington end (Dulles was in Puerto Rico at the time), arrived at the Air Operations office at Quarters Eye.

"What are you doing," he asked the Air Ops officer-in-charge.

"Readying the follow-up strike, sir. We have to finish them off."

"Seems to me," intoned Cabell, "that we were only authorized one strike at the airfields."

"Oh, no, sir," replied the officer, "There are no restrictions on the number of strikes. The authorization was to knock out the Cuban air force."

Cabell's neck muscles tightened. "I just don't know about that. So to be on the safe side, I'm going to ask [Secretary of State] Dean Rusk about it. Cancel that strike order...until I can get someone to approve it."

Approval never came. JFK, though permitting the amphibious assault to contine, cancelled the follow-up air strikes.

For the Cuban and sheep-dipped American pilots revving up their engines in Nicaragua, the word came like a thunderbolt from hell. Major General George "Poppa" Doster, the American commander of brigade pilot training, was livid. "There goes the whole goddamn war!"

As these events were transpiring, Castro's wounded air force, consisting of nine surviving combat-capable aircraft, began to gather over the small invasion fleet. Rapidly picking their targets, each plane began a dive toward either the open beach where supplies were being offloaded from landing craft, or the ships resting close offshore. The ships, containing the heavy weapons, six Sherman tanks, ammunition, and medical supplies for the Brigade were the primary targets for the initial onslaught.

The *Houston*, laden with ammunition, was struck repeatedly and began to sink. The *Rio Escondido*, which contained the bulk of the Brigade's fuel, ammunition and medical supplies, was hit by rockets from a Sea Fury and exploded in a massive eruption of flame. Those on deck on each vessel fought back valiantly, but such fast-moving targets were hard to hit. CIA "advisor" Grayston Lynch, who was in command of the ships once the Brigade was ashore, manned a .50 caliber machine gun and fired until the barrel turned white hot. He later described what happened to one attacking bomber after it was struck by anti-aircraft fire: "We shot down one B-26 that hit the water, skipped, and bounced over our ship." Other airplanes were shot down, but the advantage of air superiority could not be overcome by the lightly armed ships. Next to go was the *Marsopa*, from which the invasion force was being coordinated, and immediately thereafter the smaller vessels being used to ferry the supplies ashore came under attack.

Lynch, aboard the *Blager*, was assaulted by messages from the shore. "Go to sea! Get out of here! Come back after dark!" Lynch, reluctantly, gave the order to the captains of the vessels to abandon landing activities and flee for international waters.

Finally sighting part of the eight-ship naval task force—six destroyers and the U.S. carrier *Essex*—Lynch felt relief that the plan was finally beginning to come together and help was at hand. "We arrived at the twelve-mile limit and there were two destroyers on the horizon. I called them and said 'well, here we are, we're in international waters, we're under air attack. Can you help us?' I'll never forget the destroyer captain came back and said, 'my heart is with you, but I cannot help you. Our orders are not to become involved.' And I asked him, 'did you receive any orders to give us air cover or support out here? And he said, 'no, I did not.'"[151]

Something was drastically wrong. The plan had started to unravel at the seams and was rapidly becoming unmanageable. In the worst possible scenario, the landing forces had managed to reach the beach and had made their way inland, but their supplies had been cut off with the withdrawal of the remaining support ships; the U.S. Marine Battalion Landing Team, which stood just offshore outside the twelve-mile-limit, was ordered not to debark in support of the free Cubans; and most of all, to the shock of the CIA advisors caught on the beach with the Brigade, the promised additional air power—the "umbrella of air cover" originally promised by Eisenhower—had been cancelled by Kennedy. This lack of air support manifested itself one more time that day when the C-47 cargo planes, which had taken to the air loaded with paratroopers, came under attack over Cuba. Captain Eddie Ferrer, pilot of the lead ship of a flight of six lumbering transports enroute to drop 177 paratroopers northeast of Blue Beach, had his confidence shattered after he made the drop on the San Blas road, then spotted Cuban B-26s roaring in on the flight. As he watched helplessly, the nose guns of one of the attacking bombers began to sparkle as they opened fire on the unarmed transports. One of the C-47s began to stream smoke from one engine, then winged over and spiraled into the ground. Only by diving low and skimming the waves back to Nicaragua did he manage to escape. At that point it became "every man for himself."

Infuriated by the orders to cancel further air attack missions, some of the aircrews chose to ignore the orders and rejoin the fray. But as they approached the combat zone, Castro's T-33s were waiting. No match for the jets, five of the remaining FRD B-26s became easy prey and were shot from the sky—including one flown by American pilots Leo Francis Baker and Pete Ray. Baker and Ray managed to crash land, but were killed on the ground during their escape from the crash site. (Their bodies, recovered by Castro militia, were kept frozen in an Havana morgue for the next 18 years).[152]

By midnight, 20,000 Castro soldiers had managed to trap the 900 surviving members of the Brigade in a small pocket in the swamps north of the beach. Communist tanks and infantry battered the brigade with artillery and mortar fire for the next 48 hours, and after enduring over 2,000 artillery and mortar rounds, the *Brigada 2506* was forced to surrender. They had fought heroically, but they had been let down. The battle was lost.

Richard Bissell summed up the CIA feelings concerning the overall picture in Washington: "In the utterly vain, and foreseeably vain, efforts to maintain the disclaimable character of the operation, all kinds of sacrifices in operational capability were made. We were not allowed to use U.S. territory. This meant that the starting base had to be in Central America. We weren't allowed to use more modern aircraft, that perhaps would have meant they had greater range. We should have had twenty American air crews instead of four, and we should have had another thirty B-26 bombers available to us. So the myth that the operation could be disclaimable cost us a decisive capability in the conduct of the operation."[153]

After the operation failed, the politicians and bureaucrats in Washington began fortifying their individual positions to weather the coming storm. The American people, surprised by the invasion attempt at first, now began to ask what had happened, and why did it fail? Kennedy, on whose shoulders the decision rested concerning the failure to provide the promised air support and landing of the Marines, decided that the most important thing to do at the moment was to salvage the presidency. At all costs.

After conferring with his staff—all of which had talked him into cancelling the additional air support and intervention of the fleet—made a decision. Allen Dulles, who bore overall responsibility for CIA activities, and therefore the Bay of Pigs debacle, had to take the blame. This meant one thing: he had to resign. In Kennedy's words, when he contacted Dulles, "If we had a parliamentary government, I would have to resign. We don't. We have a presidential government, and that means that you, and several others directly reponsible for the operation, will have to resign."

Kennedy, because of the embarrassment caused by the failed invasion, declared that he would "tear CIA into a thousand pieces and throw it to the winds." Then, before these words were cold, he promised the Cuban community in Miami during a massive rally in which he was presented a Brigada battle flag that "I can assure you that this flag will be returned to this brigade in a free Havanna."

But this was never to happen. The Bay of Pigs defeat changed the course of world history, for out of it grew the Communist perception that America no longer possessed the moral courage to face down aggressors or violators of the Monroe Doctrine. And to the Third World, it appeared that the United States could not be trusted to honor its commitments.

Evidence of these perceptions was exhibited four months later when the Soviets began emplacing missile batteries in Cuba, then in the following months and years when the Berlin Wall was raised, revolution broke out in the Dominican Republic, guerrilla warfare intensified in Latin and South America, and Nicaragua fell to

Communism. All of these events transpired after, and arguably because of, the Bay of Pigs.

Though Kennedy considered the elimination of Castro his number one priority during this time frame, he no longer trusted the CIA to do it. But he found that getting rid of the CIA, as he had threatened, was almost impossible. The Agency had built strong proponents outside of, and above, the White House. The independant back-room power of the CIA reached from the meeting rooms of Washington to the board rooms of major corporations, and from allied intelligence organizations to international bankers. Kennedy had little choice but to allow the CIA to try yet again to eliminate the Castro regime.

Kennedy may not have been able to destroy the CIA—at least not at the moment—but he could at least control its operations by appointing a new director he could trust. His choice was John A. McCone, a bespectacled grandfatherly type who was loyal to the Kennedys. Under McCone, the operations against Cuba took on a different approach. Instead of a frontal assault on some beach, Castro would be eliminated by subversion and saboutage. This new onslaught, codenamed Operation MONGOOSE, began in October of 1961 when the remnants of the Brigade, bolstered by a few new recruits, started training in the Florida Everglades.

Coordinated out of Miami Station, Mongoose conducted 2123 missions into Cuba. They consisted of commando raids, saboutage attacks, propaganda efforts, intelligence missions, and supply missions to indigenous guerrilla groups. But over the life of Mongoose, the end evaluation was that it was too small, too late, and had too little bang-for-the-buck.

During these trying two years, ZR/RIFLE had continued to play its part. Richard Bissell, who was instrumental in the formation of the ZR/RIFLE assassination team, admitted: "From time to time individuals would appear on the scene, and it would be very important to have them dissappear from the scene. I came to believe it was desirable to have a very small office that developed the techniques and methods for Executive Action—actions targeted toward a very threatening and dangerous individual in some other country, action designed to demobilize him."[154]

The main target during the Mongoose operation continued to be Castro. In some of the ZR/RIFLE schemes, bizarre plots surfaced on just how to conduct an Executive Action hit on Fidel. One example concerned booby-trapping an exotic sea shell with high explosive and placing it on the ocean bottom in one of Castro's favorite scuba diving spots. When Castro picked up the shell, it would blow up. This suggestion was discarded when the planners realized that anyone who dove in that location might pick up the shell, and there were no guarantees Castro would ever see it to begin with. Another suggestion involved hiding an automatic pistol inside of a movie camera, then sending a team in to "film" Castro at some opportune moment during a public appearance. But this plan's weakness was the fact that it would be impossible for the team to escape afterwards.

In another instance, a team of Cubans under Thomas Clines managed to smuggle a 3.5" rocket launcher, popularly known as a "Bazooka," into a building overlooking a plaza where Fidel was to address a huge crowd that was to be on hand to welcome the first Soviet Cosmonauts. But they managed to get the electric firing mechanism wet and the weapon malfunctioned. They were spotted by Cuban security forces and captured, much to the embarrassment of the ZR/RIFLE case officers.

Rolando Cubela, a later recruit of ZR/RIFLE, recalled one device that had been issued that was reminiscent of the World War II OSS days. "They sent me a pen with a very fine needle," he recalled. "The pen could be filled with poison, just as if it were a syringe. I found it quite unpleasant. I did not believe it to be something feasible. We were not accustomed to having such instruments. I had asked for explosives, a rifle, a silencer. We were fighting men...I was not a fanatic."

Cuban security officer Israel Behar, who was instrumental in arresting Cubela on one failed attempt that netted Cubela fifteen years in prison, was involved in foiling twenty-six attempts on Castro's life. In one, the plan was to take advantage of a massive rally that was going to be held in front of the Presidential Palace. The team had positioned itself across the huge plaza in a multi-story apartment building that overlooked the square. But unknown to the hit team, Behar's people had discovered that this particular apartment was much smaller on the inside than any other apartment in the building. When they began to investigate, they found a false wall behind which were two Czech Skorpion submachine guns, a Thompson submachine gun, a bazooka, and a supply of rockets. The would-be assassins were taken into custody when they showed up to take their positions before the rally.

Justification for these activities, according to the retired CIA officials who were in charge of these operations at the time, allegedly came from the White House. According to William Colby, who became DCI in 1973 under Nixon, "I'm sure that Bobby Kennedy was aware of some actions being taken. And if Bobby was aware, I'm sure the President was aware. Bobby wouldn't have done it without the President's awareness."

This statement cannot be verified, however, since both individuals referred to by Colby, who mysteriously drowned in a canoeing "accident" in 1996 after his retirement from CIA, were later assassinated themselves. And dead men tell no tales.

Chapter 23

Africa: Murder on the Dark Continent

Of the CIA's forays into Africa during the early 1960s, the first attempt at manipulating a native government occured in the Congo. On the target agenda was the newly elected prime minister, Patrice Lumumba. And American commercial interests would once again be represented by the bullet instead of the ballot.

Lumumba, a pro-Marxist trained in Moscow, found himself suddenly in control of a small country that was rapidly becoming a bone of contention between western powers. The Congo had just been granted independence by its former colonial master, Belgium, but the country had not been prepared for self-government prior to independence. Lumumba found himself trying to run a country splintered by rival factions that went back to tribal days; an the economy on the verge of collapse; and communications and transportation systems rapidly deteriorating. Adding to Lumumba's troubles was the southeastern province of Katanga, which had just seceded from the Congo under the leadership of a pro-Western Katangese named Moshe Tshombe.

There was little Lumumba could do about the problem. His "army" was a rag-tag group of uneducated warriors that teetered on the edge of mutiny; his president, Joseph Kasavubu, was of little help in restoring order in a rapidly deteriorating situation; and Belgian troops, which had been temporarily left behind to assist the new government, were too few and scattered to be effective. Kasavubu, realizing that the

234

situation was beyond local control, appealed to the United Nations for intervention until the new government could get on its feet.

The UN sent a force to restore order, but the UN commanders were not authorized to interfer in the Katangan situation. For Lumumba, the secession was intolerable. Half of the country's mineral wealth lay within the region, and the tribes of the area were the age-old enemy of his own people. If he did not conquer them, he would lose respect throughout Central Africa.

To rectify the UN's lack of action in Katanga, Lumumba called upon his old friends, the Russians. On August 26th, 1960, ten Iluyshin Il-10 transports arrived in Leopoldville carrying 100 Soviet "technicians," the lead element for a larger force that would follow. For the CIA, once again the picture became clear. Lumumba would have to go.

But there was more to it than a simple matter of a backwards Third World country that just might swing into the communist camp. This factor, though exploited in the press, took a back seat to the real reason. Of major significance to American commercial interests were the copper mines, located in the Katanga province, and industrial diamonds—of which the Congo produced half the world's supply. Also of importance was cobalt, gold, manganese, tin, zinc, cadmium and coal. In all, the Congo was a wealth of mineral deposits that were of considerable "strategic" importance to American companies.

Lumumba, who was considerably outspoken in his anti-American sentiments, played right into the hands of the CIA. The CIA station chief in the Congo, Lawrence Devlin (*nom d'guerre* Victor Hedgman) sent a report to Washington describing "a classic communist takeover government." He ended the cable with: "There may be little time left in which to take action to avoid another Cuba."

That was all it took to get the attention of the CIA bureaucrats. They replied: "You are authorized to proceed with operation." The operation referred to was the result of a planning session that took place between Allen Dulles, Gordan Gray (Presidential Assistant for National Security Affairs), John Irwin II (Assistant Secretary of Defense), Livingston Merchant (Under Secretary of State for Political Affairs), and CIA African desk officer Thomas Parrot. In this meeting they agreed that "any planning for the Congo would not necessarily rule out consideration of any particular kind of activity which might contribute to getting rid of Lumumba."[155]

Dulles sent a cable to Devlin in Leopoldville giving him "wide authority for even more aggressive action if it can remain covert." Devlin was further authorized to spend up to $100,000 on "the program"—a huge sum by African standards.

The "program" was initiated and Devlin began by recruiting anti-Lumumba factions around the Congo. By September, Kasavubu, fearful that too much anti-government sentiment was building, removed Lumumba from his post. In his place he appointed army colonel Joseph Mobutu. The CIA approved of Mobutu, but realizing that things change quickly and unexpectedly in Africa, feared that Lumumba, who held favor in the Congolese parliament, could conceivably come back. The only way to assure his demise was to have him assassinated.

The Agency began to look for a means to this end. As with Castro, the weapon of choice was poison. For this they turned to Dr. Sidney Gottlieb (of MK/ULTRA fame), an expert in bio-organic chemistry and special assistant for scientific matters to the Director of Plans, Richard Bissell. Gottlieb was asked to develop a poison that would show the symptoms of some common African disease, then personally deliver it to Devlin in the Congo.

Gottlieb managed to work up a chemical compound that fit the specifications and, as requested, personally carried it to Devlin and issued instructions concerning its use. As these affairs were being consumated, the Agency recruited two professional hit men, codenamed QJ/WIN and WI/ROGUE, to serve as backup in case the poison caper failed.[156]

After several planning sessions, Gottlieb and Devlin decided that getting the poison to Lumumba would be difficult at best, impossible in all probability. Lumumba, who was being protected by UN security personnel, was not accessible and his inner circle was unapproachable. Further, Gottlieb became growingly concerned that the poison, even if administered, might not work. It had been unrefrigerated since it had left the U.S. and Gottlieb began to worry that the poison had lost its strength. Devlin scrubbed the plan and sent Gottlieb back to the States.

Devlin then shifted gears and began planning a more overt action—a commando raid. He reasoned that a small, well-equipped elite force of men might be able to assault Lumumba's house, kill him, then escape before anyone could react. Barring that, it might be possible, as a back-up plan, to draw Lumumba outside where he could be eliminated by one well-placed sniper bullet.

Devlin notified the Agency to send him a precision sniper rifle—the same as had been issued to the ZR/RIFLE team members—and a shooter to man it. The sniper picked by the Agency was one Justin O'Donnell. But O'Donnell, upon arriving in the Congo and finding that he was to be part of an assassination plot, refused to be the trigger man. Instead, he asked the Agency to send QJ/WIN over to take his place. He agreed to help lure Lumumba out into the open, but QJ/WIN would have to take the shot.

But before either plan could be put into motion, Lumumba escaped UN custody and began making his way toward Stanleyville, where he could link up with members of his tribe and plan a counter-coup against Mobutu.

Mobutu, prodded by Devlin, alerted troops to block the roads between Leopoldville and Stanleyville and to search the countryside for the fugitive. This move was successful and Lumumba was recaptured, returned to Leopoldville, then moved to a prison in Thysville, fifty miles southwest of the capital.

The CIA now had Lumumba where they wanted him. He was away from UN custody, accessible to the Congolese government—i.e. Mobutu—and it was now simply a matter of arranging his demise. This, however, had to be done quickly. The CIA sensed a great deal of dissention rising among the Congolese troops, who, should they decide to change sides, might rescue Lumumba and overthrow the Mobutu government.

Secret meetings were held and it was decided to move Lumumba to Bakwanga prison, which at that time was nicknamed "The Slaughterhouse" by those familiar with it. No one who went in came out.

On January 17th, 1961, Lumumba was scheduled to be moved by air. But before the airplane could reach its destination, it received orders to divert to Katanga—Tshombe's tribal city. As soon as it landed Lumumba was murdered. No unclassified records exist concerning who was responsible for the killing, however the Church Commission on Assassinations stated that "the testimony is strong enough to permit a reasonable inference that the plot to assassinate Lumumba was authorized by President Eisenhower." This being the case, the financial backing, planning, and instigation had to have originated with the CIA.

Mobutu stayed in power and became one of the world's richest men. His personal fortune eventually exceeded $3 billion dollars—much of which was provided by U.S., British and French commercial interests and funneled through the Congolese (now Zaire) treasury. Ironically, the punishment for the crime of embezzlement in Zaire is death.

Angola

Unlike other colonial powers in Africa, Portugal refused to allow its colonies the independence being granted to other European powers. Antonio de Oliveira Salazar, prime minister of Portugal in 1961, told the United States that "the only nationalism in Angola and Mozambique was Portuguese."

With the Portuguese refusal to grant independence and give up its colonial and commercial holdings in Angola, bloody revolts broke out in the capital city of Luanda and in the militant anti-colonial north country. But each revolt was crushed in turn by the Portuguese-controlled government and armed forces, and martial law was declared.

In the United Nations, the U.S. castigated Portugal for refusing to give up its colonial holdings and for the violent manner in which the uprisings were handled. The UN, following the American lead, called for Portugal to grant independence to Angola and initiate a peaceful transition of power to the black nationalists.

The CIA began playing its part as well. By supplying "financial non-military aid" to the Leopoldville-based Revolutionary Government of Angola in Exile (GRAE), the Agency began ingratiating itself to its leader, Holden Roberto—who just happened to be Mobutu's brother-in-law. The CIA anticipated that the Portuguese would either give in to UN pressure or be overthrown by one of the Angolan nationalist groups—hopefully the GRAE—and they wanted to be in on the ground floor when a new government took over. But the Kennedy administration looked at the Angolan situation in a more global light. The U.S. military was dependant on Portugal for strategic military ficilities in the Azores, and Kennedy did not want to upset the boat. This, coupled with pressure from the Portuguese, forced Kennedy to order support for Roberto to cease.

Throughout the 1960s rebel factions continued to resist Portuguese rule. The U.S., unsure of what the future would hold and afraid of finding itself on the losing side should allegiance be wrongly placed, began playing both sides. While overtly providing the Portuguese with aircraft suitable for counter-insurgency to be used against the nationalists, the CIA was covertly consorting with Roberto. The GRAE, with the backing of the CIA, had free use of the Congo as a base for mounting guerrilla activity against the Angolan government. But Roberto was too timid to do so. Instead of fighting, Roberto showed little inclination to take on the Portuguese. Even after being recognized by the Organization of African Unity (OAU) in 1964 as the legitimate government of Angola, the GRAE under Roberto refused to become involved in any military action against the Luanda government. By 1966 the GRAE had lost credibility with the nationalists to the point that an alternative independence movement was formed. Under former GRAE member Jonas Savimbi, the National Union for the Total Independence of Angola (UNITA) began operations in southern Angola.

A third nationalist movement, the Popular Movement for the Liberation of Angola (MPLA), had existed in the central and east sections of the country since 1956, but had little support until the mid-1960s when it aligned itself with the Soviet Union. Operating from its base in Zambia, the MPLA grew rapidly and by 1969 was considered by the Portuguese to be the most dangerous guerrilla element in the colony.

By 1971 the OAU, fearing repercussions from the Soviets within their own countries, withdrew support from UNITA. Roberto split from UNITA, taking most of his loyal followers with him and named his new organization the Front for the Liberation of Angola (FNLA). The MPLA, which had grown steadily under Soviet guidance, had by then threatened the Portuguese to the extent that the Luanda government established liaison with both non-communist organizations, FNLA and UNITA, in an effort to neutralize the MPLA.

Portugal's efforts to counter the MPLA came to an end in 1974 when a group of left-wing army officers in Portugal staged a coup and overthrew Marcello Caetano, Antonio Salazar's successor. One of the objectives of the new government was to cease Portuguese involvement in colonial wars, which meant that Angolan independence was assured.

The Portuguese forces in Angola ceased all military action and withdrew to their bases to await further orders. With the colonial military out of the picture, the three rebel factions began a race for power.

The CIA, who had been waiting in the wings, made its move. With $32 million authorized by President Gerald Ford, the Agency began supplying and advising both the FNLA and UNITA. FNLA, however, received the bulk of the aid since it was headquartered in Zaire (formerly the Congo) where the CIA maintained its African base of operations. UNITA had by then moved out and taken its forces into southern Angola, which made it more difficult for the CIA to provide covert aid. Support for UNITA was left to South Africa.

Of the $32 million, more than half was spent on arms and military equipment, but Mobutu, who served as middleman on the CIA/FNLA dealings, skimmed a large portion off the top of all transactions. Less than half of that spent ever reached the UNITA.

Independence was finally granted by the Portuguese, with the date set for November 11, 1975. In the interim a provisional coalition government was formed that incorporated representatives from the three factions. But the MPLA, being the strongest group militarily, established its dominance and began shouldering the other two groups aside. Fighting broke out in the streets and each organization began jockeying for strategic position in the countryside. Within days the situation deteriorated into a full-scale civil war, with the FNLA invading Angola in force from Zaire, and UNITA, backed by the South African Army, driving toward Luanda from the south.

In order to save the MPLA, the Soviets responded by flying in a large force of Cuban infantry, backed by tank and artillery brigades. These expendable Cubans were in turn backed up by a massive airlift of equipment and arms from the Soviet Union.

Wary of a direct confrontation with the Soviets, and fearing detrimental action by the U.S. Congress over the amount of money being expended on the war in Angola, the Agency was forced to take the issue abroad. But little help was to be found. Most countries shied away from becoming involved in an issue in which the Soviet Union appeared to be so interested. Only in Britain, where a few mercenaries were recruited in a effort to bolster the anti-communist forces, did the CIA receive any positive response. But the effort was a matter of too little, too late. By February of 1976, both UNITA and the FNLA had failed in their efforts to oust the MPLA. Cuban troops, utilizing Russian armor and artillery, controlled northern and central Angola—including the capital—and the MPLA was recognized as the government of Angola.

The CIA was incensed, but there was little that could be done. Congress, upon recognizing the MPLA, cut off all funding for covert operations. This action caused South Africa to officially withdraw, but due to its close proximity to the Marxist nation, continued to covertly support Jonas Savimbi's UNITA in southern Angola.

The CIA, in deference to the loss of funding, managed to continue supporting Roberto for a brief period. But the FNLA faded away into obscurity in the face of the overwhelming Cuban and Soviet presence and the CIA was forced to shift what support it could muster to UNITA.

Other than brief incursions by the South African defense forces into southern Angola, little changed between 1975 and 1990. But with the fall of communism in the Soviet Union, and Castro's inability to supply his own troops in a land so far away without Soviet air transport (especially after Operation *Urgent Fury* in Grenada eliminated the Point Salines refueling stop), Cuban support for the MPLA has become almost non-existant.

As a whole, the Angolan operation was a failure. Though American intervention in the Congo and Angola was viewed in some quarters as essential to counter a Soviet threat, the majority of political analysts maintain that the end result was a high cost fiasco which jeopardized relations with neighboring moderate countries. The U.S. Congress also came to the conclusion that the Soviet threat was vastly overdramatized by the intelligence services, and that on many occasions throughout CIA African involvement, grassroots freedom movements were actually chased *into* the Soviet camp.

Meanwhile, half a world away, another government had drawn the attention of the CIA. And the outcome would be far different.

Chapter 24

South America: The Beat Goes On

The CIA was involved either directly, or indirectly by means of forces trained by CIA instructors, in successfully manipulating the affairs of almost every major South American government. These interventions included the installation of a military government in Brazil in 1964, the defeat of Che Guevara's guerrillas and the subsequent execution of Che Guevara in Bolivia in 1967, and the campaign against the Tupamaros guerrillas in Uraguay between 1968 to 1973. But the classic case of CIA intervention in Latin American affairs was undoubtedly Chile.

Chile, during the Kennedy era, had been selected by the U.S. Government as a bastion against Castro's spreading communist influence in Latin America. Traditionally a democratic country, Kennedy considered Chile to be the best bet for establishing a pro-American foothold in South America that could be controlled by both Washington and private U.S. corporations who, with the proper encouragement, would invest in the country's economy.

Solid relations were established with the right-wing government in 1962, and U.S. corporations began moving into the country that Kennedy promised would never expropriate them. These infiltrations by American business were assisted by a grant of $135,489,000 in aid by the U.S. Government. But after Kennedy's assassination Lyndon Johnson became concerned that the situation in Chile would deteriorate in the upcoming 1964 Chilean election. According to the intelligence reports given Johnson by the CIA, a Marxist of considerable political

242

experience, Salvador Allende, was planning on running for president to replace right-wing President Jorge Alessandri Rodriguez who was ending his six-year term. If Allende were to be elected, American business interests would be threatened with nationalization.

It became imperative to U.S. interests that Allende should lose the election. Allende's opponent, Eduardo Frei Montalva, was a Christian Democrat who was considered somewhat liberal by Latin American standards—but not a Marxist or communist. The CIA, unknown to Frei,[157] began an operation that would assure his election. It began with massive amounts of money being infused into Frei's election campaign, actually providing over half of his war chest. The next step, propaganda against Allende, began almost simoultaneously. Both in print and over the radio, Allende was depicted as a Stalinist who would virtually become a tyranical dictator. The campaign worked and Frei was elected.

But the two major U.S. businesses in Chile, International Telephone and Telegraph (ITT) and Pepsi Cola, were not convinced that Frei could be trusted to honor Kennedy's promise to leave their concerns intact. And when Frei began mentioning ideas of establishing profit sharing for employees, the two corporations decided the Frei would have to be replaced in the next election, scheduled for 1970, in which Allende would again run.

Making this decision and having the CIA carry it out was no problem for the two companies. ITT was now headed by former CIA Director John A. McCone, and Pepsi Cola was being run by Donald Kendall, Richard Nixon's personal friend and former client when Nixon was working as a Wall Street lawyer for John Mitchell's law firm (who also represented Nelson Rockefeller).

When Richard Nixon was inaugurated in January of 1969, the Business Group for Latin Amerian instructed him to support Jorge Alessandri in opposition to Allende. The business conglomerate at first attempted to donate $500,000 to Alessandri's campaign through the State Department, but the State Department did not want to get involved. Instead, this money, along with an additional $200,000, was delivered to the CIA. Of the $700,000 passed to the Alessandri campaign, $350,000 came from ITT alone.

By July of 1970, ITT had paid the CIA an additional $1,000,000 to assure Allende's defeat, and this sum was increased by a further

$500,000 by Nixon's National Security Council. But even these massive infusions of funds did not accomplish the mission. Despite the pressure, Allende managed to gain 36.9 percent of the electorate to Alessandri's 34.9 percent. A third candidate received the remaining 27.8 percent.

Needless to say, ITT panicked. CIA Director Richard Helms was summoned to the White House. When he left, he carried these notes jotted down in his brief case:

"One in 10 chance perhaps, but save Chile!
Worth Spending
Not concerned risks involved
No involvement of Embassy
$10,000,000 available, more if necessary
Full-time job—best men we have
Game plan
Make the economy scream
48 hours for plan of action. "

His comment later was "If I ever carried a marshal's baton in my knapsack out of the Oval Office it was that day."

After several brainstorming sessions, the CIA came up with a plan. Specifically, it called for a military coup to be carried out before Allende could be inaugurated. To lead the coup, ex-Chilean general Robert Viaux was selected. He agreed to the plan, but could not guarantee its success without support of the Chilean Air Force. But when General Rene' Schneider, commander of the air force, was let in on the plan, he refused to become a co-conspirator.

The CIA, undaunted, continued to plot. All agreed that the Chilean Air Force was necessary to the operation, and therefore Schneider would have to be removed from the scene and replaced by someone more ammenable. Conspiring with Viaux and two others—military attache to the U.S. embassy Colonel Paul Wimert and Chilean Army General Camillo Valenzuala—the CIA funded a kidnapping mission with $50,000 provided by the White House.

On October 23rd, a snatch-team attempted to kidnap Schneider. But the attempt was unsuccessful. Instead of making the grab without incident, Schneider was wounded and later died. His successor, General

Carlos Prats, took over in his place and continued to support the Chilean democratic order. Allende was confirmed as president the following month.

The CIA began an immediate propaganda onslaught against Allende. As before, local journalists were bribed to write anti-Allende articles, and newspapers and periodicals abroad were fed supporting propaganda. Even *Time* magazine changed an article written by a Santiago correspondent that supported Allende to an article that showed Allende to be a communist threat.[158] The Chilean newspaper, *El Mercurio*, received over $3.5 million over a three year period after 1970, and further funds were given to the Christian Democrat Party and the right wing National Party to permit them to buy radio stations and newspapers to step up the attacks on the Allende government. In all, over $8 million was spent.

After sufficiently tempering the minds of the population, the CIA launched its planned coup. On September 11, 1973, CIA-backed General Augusto Pinochet Ugarte led Chilean Army elements in an attack upon the Presidential Palace. Allende was killed in the assault.

Pinochet moved immediately to wipe out all vestiges of Allende's left-wing power structure. Utilizing secret police tactics, Pinochet rounded up thousands of Allende supporters and confined them inside the national stadium. Over the next few days, large numbers were interrogated, tortured and executed. It is estimated by one eye witness that over 500 pro-Allende leftists were shot in the week following the coup.[159]

The end result was a military dictatorship that owed its creation and allegiance to the Central Intelligence Agency. In a country whose constitution limits the term of the president to six years, and prohibits two consecutive terms, Pinochet has been President for over twenty years. Opposition to Pinochet results in mandatory prison sentences, torture and often, death.

But as promised by the U.S. Government, American corporations have remained free to expand and profit in Chile without fear of nationalization. Pinochet is considered one of the richest dictators in the world.

In a continuing game of chess, the United States and the Soviet Union, by means of their covert intelligence and military organizations, continued to manipulate Third World countries until the fall of communism. It was often hard to tell exactly who was doing the manipulating. The tactics were all the same.

Part V

Guns, Drugs and Politicians

Chapter 25

The Enterprise

The imperial and globalist line of thinking exhibited during the Truman, Eisenhower, Johnson, and Nixon years, temporarily checked by the outcome of the Vietnam war and the Watergate scandal, reemerged during the Reagan administration. In a world that was increasingly being consumed by Third World actions, terrorism, and the expansion of Soviet and Chinese communism, the assets of the covert intelligence community once again became the primary behind-the-scenes foot soldiers for those who manipulated countries and governments.

In the 1980s, President Ronald Reagan introduced a new, much tougher, foreign policy that virtually flew in the face of the detente and liberalism that was prevalent during the previous administration under Jimmy Carter. In the new doctrine, the Soviet menace was to be aggressively confronted and resisted wherever it was found, by the use of covert aid when possible, and military intervention when necessary. Operation *Urgent Fury*, the massive invasion of Grenada, and the peacekeeping mission in Beirut were examples of the latter. Afghanistan and Nicaragua would be examples of the former.

In Afghanistan, the Afghan *Mujihadin* tribes valiantly resisted the superior Soviet invaders who propped up Moscow's puppet Kabul government. In the end, the Soviet commanders bogged down in a counterguerilla war much like the U.S. had encountered in Vietnam fifteen years before. The constant monetary support and infusion of weapons to the *Mujihadin*, particularly the Stinger anti-aircraft missile, turned the tide and the Soviets were forced to withdraw in defeat.

Nicaragua would be different.

One of Reagan's first efforts on becoming president was to begin rebuilding the CIA. Under Carter and Stansfield Turner, the CIA had been reduced to a shadow of its Vietnam-era strength. Hundreds of field agents had been fired or forced to retire—which created an overnight surplus of freelance spies and paramilitary types who sought employment elsewhere, often becoming very mercenary in their endeavors. Under Reagan, who promised during his campaign "to provide our government with the capability to help influence international events vital to our national security interests, a capability which the United States alone among major powers has denied itself," the worm was about to turn.[160] Covert action, and manipulating other governments "for reasons of national security," was back on the agenda.

One of Reagan's first actions was to get rid of Admiral Stansfield Turner and appoint his own Director of Intelligence. His choice was William Casey, a millionaire securities lawyer and former OSS agent, who had just happened to have served as his campaign manager. Casey, who was no stranger to the CIA, immediately began rebuilding the Agency's strength in manpower and increasing its budget. By 1982, the Agency was once again a force to be reckoned with.

It was in Central America that Casey found a cause worthy of his new organization. Two countries: Nicaragua, where the communist Sandinista movement under Daniel Ortega had come to power after overthrowing Anastasio Somoza in 1979, and El Salvador, where leftist guerilias threatened the U.S. supported government.

The Reagan administration regarded Nicaragua as a second Cuba, and Ortega another Castro. Having a leftist regime between Mexico and the Panama Canal, a bare four hours flying time from the United States, was unacceptable. Reagan, who was determined to be more successful at ridding the Western Hemisphere of Ortega than Kennedy was with Castro, authorized covert military operations in Central America. The mission was to train, arm and support an army of anti-Sandinista Nicaraguans. This army, made up mostly of former Somoza national guardsmen and rural Moskito indians from three separate regions, were known as "Contras," for contra-revolutionaries.

In November 1981, using as arguments the increasing Sandinista support for the guerrillas in El Salvador and the mounting oppression in Nicaragua by the Sandinistas, Reagan persuaded Congress to approve $19.5 million for CIA efforts to establish and equip the Contra force. It was a start, but it would not be enough.

To form the nucleus of the leadership and cadre for the fledgling Contras, members of Somoza's old National Guard (*Guardia Nacional*) were selected from those that had fled Ortega's Nicaragua and taken up residency in neighboring Honduras and Costa Rica. To supplement these forces, the CIA called upon a few old contacts in the anti-Castro Miami Cuban community and some faithful Cuban/American contract agents that had continued to work with the Agency long after the failed Bay of Pigs endeavor. To organize and lead the efforts, the Agency would rely upon some very interesting old standbys.

Among the people selected to handle the Contra operation were none other than:

Major General John Singlaub, an OSS veteran and CIA officer responsible for China and Korea during his time in Asia. Singlaub's OSS team, which operated in Kunming in China—the very center of KMT drug trafficking during World War II—consisted of E. Howard Hunt, Paul Helliwell, Lucien Conein and Mitch WerBell. According to the *Wall Street Journal*, OSS payments at this base often consisted of five-pound bundles of opium. One of Singlaub's teammates, Lucien Conein, went on to be the CIA's liaison with the Corsican Mafia of Saigon and had intimate knowledge of drugs being shipped to Europe by the Corsicans.

During the Vietnam war, Singlaub directed clandestine infiltration of secret recon and prisoner snatch teams into North Vietnam, Laos and Cambodia. While in Southeast Asia, Singlaub worked with Richard Secord and Oliver North.[161]

Major General Richard Secord, who flew more than 285 combat missions in Southeast Asia between 1963 and 1968, most of which were in Laos in support of the CIA/Meo operation. He served as commander of all air operations in Laos, which included all sorties flown by Air America. These missions, as previously shown, included transporting opium and heroin. Secord "resigned" from the Agency in 1983 after being linked to renegade CIA operative Edwin Wilson, who was convicted of smuggling explosives to Libya. Secord's part in the Contra supply operation involved secretly moving high-tech weapons systems to Iran where they were sold to the Khomeini regime for use against the Iraqis. The profits of the sales were deposited into secret international bank accounts, then utilized to support covert military actions directed by the National Security Council. Within two years, these funds had also provided "The Enterprise," as it became known, with numerous shell companies and front organizations, two airfields, five airplanes, twenty contract pilots, a boat and huge stockpiles of guns, ammunition and other military equipment. Secord is also credited with milking funds from the Saudi Arabian government for use in the Nicaraguan campaign in return for promised favorable consideration in future military equipment purchases from the U.S. Government. Key in these purchases were sophisticated AWACS early warning planes.

Theodore Shackley, former head of the anti-Castro operation at the CIA's Miami station (codename JM/WAVE), where he served as chief of station, and director of Operation 40. From 1966-68, Shackley, who was sent to Laos by Richard Helms when the Miami station was closed down, served as chief of station in Vientienne. Here, he conducted the CIA covert war—and its creative financing by drug trafficking. While in Laos, Shackley worked closely with Singlaub, Thomas Clines, Felix Rodriguez, and Richard Secord. In 1968, at the height of the Vietnam war, Shackley was transferred to Saigon where he became chief of station and directed Operation Phoenix—the CIA's and Special Forces assassination program in Vietnam. From 1976 to 1977, Shackley worked as Director of the CIA's worldwide covert operations under DCI George Bush. According to reliable sources on Capital Hill, Shackley had been programmed to become Director of Central Intelligence under Gerald Ford if Ford was reelected in 1976. Shackley's role in the Iran/Contra affair was two-fold. First, he had long-standing contacts with Iranian arms dealers that gave the "Enterprise" inroads to the Teheran regime, and at the same time paved the way for the arms-for-hostages tradeouts. Second, he was instrumental in assembling the team that trained, equipped and ran the Contras.

Thomas Clines, Shackley's second-in-command at the Miami station, and deputy in Laos who became head of the Long Tieng CIA base and supervised the creation of the Hmong/Meo army under General Vang Pao, helped Secord arrange clandestine arms deliveries to the Contras. Clines had put together a private aid network even before Reagan had ascended to the Presidency. In 1978, he and Edwin Wilson reportedly began negotiating a $650,000 deal with Nicaraguan dictator Somoza to create a hunter-killer organization to be used against Somoza's enemies. Along with Israeli arms merchants, Clines, who left the Agency on bad terms under the Carter/Turner realm, was operating in violation of Carter's official policy toward Nicaragua.

Felix Rodriguez, a "retired" CIA officer who had served under Clines in Operation 40 as an alleged member of E. Howard Hunt's ZR/RIFLE assassination team, then worked in the Congo, and finally Vietnam, went to work for Clines again in the late 1970s as a representative of his Latin American arms sales business. It was Felix Rodriguez who tracked down Che Guevara in Bolivia and, after capturing him alive, relayed orders from headquarters to the Bolivian soldiers for his execution. In the Contra operation, Rodriguez served as the main supply officer at Ilopango military airbase in El Salvador where arms and drugs were transhipped between the Middle East, Europe, South America, and the United States. In this role, he has been credited with being the Contra's logistics mastermind.

Lt. Col. Oliver North, a decorated Vietnam veteran and National Security Council Coordinator, served as the link between the CIA (William Casey) and the White House. He had worked in Vietnam in counterinsurgency operations and served with both Secord and Singlaub. North also worked with Secord during Operation *Rice Bowl*, the failed hostage rescue attempt in Iran. North's link to the Iran/Contra affair was as fund raiser, fact finder, and Enterprise/Middle East connection.

Donald Gregg served in Saigon under Shackley and Clines. A seasoned CIA veteran, Gregg was appointed to Carter's NSC as CIA liaison in 1979, then became National Security Advisor to Vice President George Bush during the Reagan years. In the Iran/Contra operation, Gregg served as the NSC-CIA liaison and worked closely with Oliver North and Felix Rodriguez. According to *The Iran-Contra*

Connection: Secret Teams and Covert Operations in the Reagan Era,
"Between 1983 and 1986, Felix Rodriguez had 17 meetings with
Gregg, three of which included Vice President George Bush." It was
Gregg who introduced Oliver North to Rodriguez.

William Casey, former OSS agent during World War II, became
DCI under Reagan. Casey was the architect of the Contra/CIA war
against the Sandinistas. According to material developed during the
congressional investigation of the Iran/Contra affair, Casey was the
mastermind behind obtaining illegal funds when Congress voted to end
the CIA's arms shipments to the Contras. In one example, Casey
managed to convince the Pentagon to give the Contras $12 million in
"surplus" military equipment. When Congress discovered this, they
prohibited any and all military aid shipments to the Contras. It was at
this time that Casey suggested to Oliver North that he should hire
Richard Secord to keep the war alive.

Albert Hakim, an Iranian-born business partner of Secord from his
earlier Teheran days, managed the private supply network for the
Contras under North's supervision. For this, he used Saudi and Iranian
oil money deposited in Switzerland in secret Enterprise accounts.

A host of other, less significant, covert operators joined these
players in carrying out the aims of the Reagan White House. These
included many more of the old anti-Castro hands, veterans of the
Shackley/Clines/Hunt/Miami Station days, former Pentagon special
operations officers, and ex-CIA/Air America pilots and crews from
Laos and Vietnam.

In early 1981, the CIA set up military training camps in California and
Florida reminiscent of the anti-Castro training bases created in Florida
and Louisiana during the late 1950s. These camps soon began training
anti-Sandinista guerrillas, and by the middle of the year, arrangements
had been made for these groups to begin raiding Nicaragua from secret
bases in Honduras. Funding at this early date was given to the Miami-
based Nicaraguan Democratic Union (UDN) led by Francisco Cardenal,
who agreed to join the newly formed Nicaraguan Democratic Force
(FDN). The last of the three regional commanders, Eden Pastora
Gomez, however, refused to join forces with the others due to their
links with the Samoza *Guardia Nacional.* Pastora, a former Sandinista,

found such allies totally unacceptable. Still, he pursued his part of the war and was supplied accordingly.

In 1982, with funding increasing to over $60 million, the war heated up. Under 150 CIA operatives and trainers, the FDN reached a strength of almost 10,000 and were conducting commando raids both across the border and into Nicaraguan ports by sea. Contra aircraft supplied by the CIA, and contract agents such as Southern Air Transport (based in Miami), flew both supplies and bombing missions into Nicaragua in support of Contra operations, and boats were supplied for mining operations of Sandinista harbors.

These operations finally brought world attention to the region and eventual exposure of the CIA's involvement. The Nicaraguan government filed an action against the United States in the World Court in the Hague accusing the U.S. of participating in combat inside Nicaragua, and with substantial proof available after the shootdown of a Southern Air Transport C-123 and the capture of crew member Eugene Hasenfus, managed to force a clampdown on CIA activities. In 1984, Congress blocked President Reagan's request for further funding of the Contras. If the CIA was going to continue to assist the Contras, another source of funding had to be found.[162]

In order to get the fast, massive infusion of cash required to continue the war, the Enterprise once again turned to what had kept the war in Laos alive: drugs.

Of the major drug suppliers in the world, South American cartels rank among the largest. From the coca producing countries of Columbia and Bolivia, hundreds of tons of cocaine are produced and smuggled each year into the various organized crime networks of both Europe and North America. The end results are millions of tax-free, untraceable dollars that flow into the coffers of everyone in the drug network from drug lords to pilots to distributors. For the CIA, becoming involved in the drug trade to support a secret war was business as usual. And by 1980, the door to the world of South American drug lords had already been opened.

In 1980, the Argentine *Confederacion Anticommunista Latina* (CAL) had infiltrated into various countries in a plot to eliminate troublesome Roman Catholic priests and missions that fostered dissent against rightest dictatorships. This rise of religious militantism was not something that came into being overnight, but had been growing ever since the Operation Paperclip and Omega network days of post-war Europe. The Nazis that had been smuggled out of Germany to South America had by the 1950s become well-entrenced in government circles of such countries as Argentina, Brazil, Bolivia, Columbia, Uraguay and Peru. By the 1960s, proteges of this Nazi infrastructure, trained in SS tactics, had moved into other countries—including those of Central America—and had brought with them the Gestapo tactics they had learned. The most militant and capable of the German-trained "trainers and advisors" came from Argentina.

By 1980, CAL plotting had reached its zenith. In that year Argentine officers, bankrolled by the cocaine drug lords, installed Luis Garcia Meza as dictator of Bolivia. Two of the Argentine officers involved in the action were not actually from Argentina, but were wanted Italian terrorists named Stefano delle Chiaie and Pierluigi Pagliai. Another was someone even more villainous: veteran Nazi fugitive and drug trafficker Klaus Barbie, the infamous "Butcher of Lyons."

Chiaie and Barbie spearheaded the CAL operation to identify, locate and exterminate radical priests and troublesome leftists not only in South America, but Central America as well. For the latter, Chiaie met with Major Roberto d'Aubuisson, the Death Squad leader in El Salvador, at the CAL conference in Argentina in September of 1980. This meeting produced an agreement to send arms and money to d'Aubuisson in El Salvador.

But the main thrust of this conference, which was attended by selected rightest dictators and their senior officers, was to export the "Argentine Solution" of death squads from Buenos Aires to Central America. The first target would be Guatemala, but that country would only serve as a jumping off point for similar operations to be put in place in El Salvador, Nicaragua, Panama, Honduras and Costa Rica.

According to the authors of *The Iran Contra Connection*, the driving force behind these movements was not the Argentine government, but an international partnership that had developed between the Italo-Argentine secret—and politically militant—Masonic Lodge P-2 and the Milan Banco Ambrosiano.[163] The P2 lodge had been identified by the Italian Government as a fascist-oriented secret society of anarchists and neo-Nazis. Considered part of the infamous *Illuminati*[164] by some, and indirectly linked by others, the P-2 is little more than a front for a secret order of political manipulators independant of the more public network of Masonic lodges. P-2 has come under considerable scrutiny because of its on-going involvement in coup attempts involving covert intelligence agencies, bank manipulations, and terrorist bombings.

P-2 had strong links to the CIA and the Republican Party. Under Nixon, the CIA allocated $10 million of "black" funds, which do not require accountability, for the right-wing parties in the 1972 Italian elections. The funds went through Ambrosiano bank connection Michele Sindona, and Italian Intelligence Chief Vito Miceli—both P-2 members. It should be noted that Sindona's American investiments were handled by the Continental Illinois Bank headed by Nixon's first Treasury Secretary, David Kennedy, and his legal representatives in the U.S. was the law firm of Nixon Attorney General John Mitchell.

Finally, P-2 and CAL have one other thing in common: drugs. CAL chairman Suarez Mason, according to the Italian magazine *Panorama*, became "one of Latin America's chief drug traffickers. Italian terrorist delle Chiai is suspected of being involved in the French Connection case and the Corsican Mafia heroin trafficking. A further connection is Paraguayan Intelligence Chief Pastor Coronel, a member of CAL, who was a smuggling partner with Auguste Ricord, the main Corsican drug buyer in Latin America. Ricord was the connection, via the Corsican Mafia, to the Gambino Mafia family of New York. The organized crime connections and violent means of obtaining funds by the P-2, according to author Penny Lernoux in her book *In Banks We Trust*, is typical of the time: "the P-2 crowd obtained money from the kidnappings of well-to-do buisinessmen in Europe and from the drug traffic in South America. Sindona's bank laundered money from the notorious Mafia kidnappers of *Anonima Sequestri* [Italian Mafia family].…"[165]

After the CIA contributed the $10 million to P-2 for the Italian elections—which followed a large P-2 contribution to Nixon's CREEP (Committee to Re-elect the President) fund—and Nixon's resignation following Watergate, the dealings of the CIA came under intensive scrutiny by the Carter administration and the new DCI, Stansfield Turner. Subsequent investigations and closings of cash flow conduits effected such parallel operations as Edwin Wilson's Iran arms dealings—which forced him to move to the Libyan weapons and hit team deals for which he was eventually jailed—the drug-linked Nugan Hand Bank of Australia, and finally, the failure of the CIA-dependant Banco Ambrosiano. These upper-level CIA reforms, however, were only a temporary setback. The ousted clandestine operators simply faded into the shadows and began building a much more powerful coalition of agents, drug runners and arms merchants.

The end result was that by the time Congress cut off aid to the Contras during the Reagan administration, the means of financing further military operations was already in place. By 1986, a private aid network had been established that permitted cocaine to be smuggled into the United States and arms to be smuggled out.[166]

As the Nicaraguan campaign grew in size and intensity, even the enormous profits of drug running would not be enough to sustain operations. It was because of this that the NSC and CIA operatives were forced to look across the Atlantic for further funding.

The precedent for dealing with the Middle East, and especially Iran, Saudi Arabia, and Israel, had already been established. It merely required servicing to once again become a source of financing.

In late May of 1972, Nixon and Kissinger made the Shah of Iran an offer he could not refuse: unlimited access to America's non-nuclear arsenal in return for a guaranteed flow of Iranian oil and an agreement to serve as the U.S.'s military stalwart in Southwest Asia. The Shah agreed, and soon weapons sales began turning cash dollars for CIA front organizations, and certain U.S. oil companies and banks began generating huge profits.

The windfalls that were brought to the private sector were centered mainly on Eastern banks that specialized in dealing with international oil. Chief among these was the Chase Manhattan Bank of New York, whose chairman, David Rockefeller, was a personal friend of the Shah. The Shah, by way of the National Iranian Oil Company, agreed to recycle much of his oil earnings back into investments and long-term government securities inside the United States, by way of the Chase Manhattan Bank. It is not surprising to find that Henry Kissinger later became chairman of Chase's international advisory committee.

In 1973, Chase Manhattan loaned Teheran $250 million which went for arms and weapons systems purchases. This was the largest loan ever arranged with the Iranians up to that time, but was soon followed by more. One year later Chase established the Iran-Chase International Bank in Teheran to handle the cash flow. By 1975, Rockefeller's bank was handling over $2 billion a year in Iranian transactions.[167]

These transactions were also fortuitous to the American war material industry which was facing massive profit losses as the American military was being pulled out of Vietnam. With no war to generate a need for weapons, the military/industrial complex, along with their investors and bankers, would have to locate new clients or go broke. The Shah, with his insatiable appetite for modern weaponry, became their next client. In 1974, Iran spent 14% of its gross national product on weapons and aircraft. Three years later the annual purchases were topping $4.2 billion. The grand total spent prior to the fall of the royal family exceeded $17 billion.

The armament industry was not the only commercial sector saved by Iranian oil money. The construction companies that had built the ports and airfields of Vietnam were also benefactors to the Shah's generosity. The largest of these, of course, was Lyndon Johnson's old supporters, Brown & Root. It should be mentioned that Brown & Root received the enormous Cam Ranh Bay contract, among others. In Iran, Brown & Root managed to glean an $8 billion contract to build a huge port facility at Chah Bahar—without the annoyance of competitive bidding. The Chah Bahar port was to become the main Iranian naval base for a fleet of vessels to be built by Litton Industries.

The Rockwell International IBEX project has been discussed in a previous chapter, but of interest at this point are the huge bribes paid to Iran's air force commander, General Mohammed Khatemi (the Shah's brother-in-law), to win approval for the $500 million project. Other companies that did business at this time inside Iran and followed the bribes-for-contracts procedure of doing business included Grumman, Northrop and Bell Helicopter.[168]

Not everyone in Washington was happy with the events transpiring in Iran. In 1975, Defense Secretary Schlesinger drafted a memo to then-President Gerald Ford questioning whether "our policy of supporting an apparently open-ended Iranian military buildup will continue to serve our long-term interests." The memo never reached the president. It was blocked by Henry Kissinger, and two months later Schlesinger was fired.

That same year the U.S. established a Military Assistance Advisory Group (MAAG) in Iran consisting of 201 personnel. Two years later, almost 8,000 Americans were working in Iran on military contracts. Among these were Edwin Wilson, Thomas Clines, Theodore Shackley, Richard Secord, and Secord's old Laotian contact, Eric von Marbod. Von Marbod would later become the key player in the Carter administration's proposal to sell eight AWACS to Iran, and Shackley would pave the way for the Reagan administration's arms-for-hostages trades with the Khomeini government.

In Teheran, Shackley was a consultant for an arms company called Stanford Technology Corporation. STC was founded by an Iranian-born arms dealer named Albert Hakim, and did business with the Shah by selling military equipment manufactured by Hewlett-Packard, Olin Corporation, and various smaller companies. Hakim was introduced to Richard Secord by Edwin Wilson, who did business in Libya out of Hakim's offices in Switzerland. One of the contracts handled by this group was STC's $5.5 million deal to supply electronic equipment to the IBEX project—which Secord oversaw. Hakim would eventually work with Secord and others in laundering funds involved in the Iran/Contra arms deals.[169]

The continuing bribes, scandals and exposure of corruption, coupled with the heavy-handed oppression of the Shah's secret police, the CIA-trained SAVAK, eventually contributed to the downfall of the Shah and the reestablishment of Moslem fundamentalism under Ayatollah Khomeini.

David Rockefeller and Henry Kissinger, who both realized what could happen should the Shah's money in the Chase Manhattan Bank become nationalized by the Khomeini regime, moved to block any such attempt on the part of Iran to obtain possession of the assets. With the help of a former ARAMCO attorney—who also happened to be a former chairman of Chase Manhattan—Rockefeller and Kissinger mounted a campaign to grant the Shah asylum in the U.S. for "medical treatment." The attorney who joined Rockefeller and Kissinger to handle the legal aspects and add weight to the case was, not surprisingly, John J. McCloy. McCloy was the architect of the Nuremberg trials, served as former High Commissioner of Germany (HICOG), headed the SWNCC during WWII, served on the Warren Commission and presided over the Council on Foreign Relations—some of whose members owned the major oil companies such as Standard Oil and Texaco.

In the end, President Carter, after being told that the Shah would cash in billions of dollars in U.S. government securities if not allowed admittance, agreed to take the Shah in. The consequences, as far as American/Iranian relations, would prove disastrous.[170] But for Chase Manhattan, the main objective was accomplished. The Iranian oil money stayed.

The overthrow of the Shah by the followers of Khomeni seriously weakened America's position in the Middle East. Besides the expulsion of CIA assets and American companies from Iran, which incited fear that pro-Soviet elements or the Soviets themselves would move into the country, and the explosion of Islamic fundamentalism and the spread of its subservient terrorist organizations, there were more highly visible demonstrations of anti-Americanism taking place. Pro-Iranian Islamic groups in other countries in the region began all-out attacks on American holdings and government representatives. In April of 1983, the U.S. embassy in Beirut was almost destroyed by a suicide attack in which an Islamic extremist detonated a bomb at the base of the building. This attack killed sixty people, seven of which were CIA.[171]

Then in March of the following year, CIA station chief William Buckley was kidnapped outside his Beirut apartment and held along with several other hostages by the Iranian-backed terrorist group Islamic Jihad (Islamic Holy War). The U.S. government, in a complete turnaround from the token way the Vietnam war POW/MIA situation was being handled, went to frantic extremes to free Buckley and a handful of international hostages.

Despite President Reagan's public stance on refusing to deal with terrorists, secret moves began almost immediately to bargain with the terrorists—or those who controlled them. In this case, it was the new Teheran government. The price of freedom would be arms and military equipment needed to keep Saddam Hussein of neighboring Iraq from invading Iran during the country's post-revolution reorganization.

But there was an official U.S. embargo on military equipment sales to Iran. A means had to be found by the secret planners to skirt the embargo, remain anonymous from all but those they were dealing with, and still recover the hostages. This means was found in Israel, who agreed to serve as middle-man. Israel was willing to provide the arms-for-hostages deliveries to Iran in 1985 in exchange for sales of some of the latest American weapons systems.[172] For the next several months Israel managed to slip some weapons systems into Iran, but by mid-1986, the NSC had established its own clandestine smuggling routes and Israel was no longer needed. The architects of the new filtering system were Lt. Col. Oliver North and retired general Richard Secord.

By this time Buckley had succumbed to the stress of incarceration and torture and had died. Still, there were other hostages to be rescued, and beyond that, the CIA was concerned that Buckley may have given his captors the names of other agents in the Middle East. The deals continued.

Three direct arms shipments were sent to Iran from the U.S. to serve as payments toward the release of the hostages. The first shipment went out in February 1986, followed by the second in May. This latter shipment was accompanied by North and national security advisor Robert McFarlane who held a bargaining session with Iranian leaders for several days. The third and final shipment arrived in Teheran on October 29th, 1986, after which hostage David Jacobsen was released. It becomes obvious at this point that the U.S. received very little in return for the massive effort put forth—except for one thing: the profits skimmed off of the Iranian deals went to the CIA's Contra program for the purchase of arms. The remaining hostages were not to see freedom until 1991, almost at the end of *George Bush's* term as president.

In late 1986, revelations of arms-for-hostages/drugs-for-money dealings, dubbed the "Iran/Contra Scandal," rocked the covert intelligence community. CIA director William Casey, who held many of the answers to the obscure affair, developed a brain tumor in December and died the following year. Deputy director Robert Gates was initially picked to replace Casey, but due to his involvement in the scandal, was not confirmed for the post. Instead, FBI director William H. Webster was selected and transferred to the CIA to succeed Casey. Gates would still manage to take over the CIA—after Webster.

The ensuing Congressional investigation brought to light some of the behind-the-scenes dealings that had transpired between the Iranians, the Israelis, the NSC, CIA, Contras, and cocaine cartels. But, partially due to Casey's death, it only scratched the surface. Almost everyone involved who testified before Congress managed to push the issue—and the blame—to a higher level. For some of the questions, especially those fielded by Oliver North who was the White House representative at the NSC, the ball was passed up to the White House and President Reagan—who conveniently could not recall anything of value to the investigators. For others, it was a case of "blame the dead guy." From his grave, William Casey continued to serve the world of covert intelligence by taking full responsibility for the Iran/Contra affair.

The majority of U.S. support for the Contras ceased during the investigation. What remained dwindled until the Contras could no longer depend on their North American allies for arms, ammunition and equipment. They eventually had to resort to basic guerrilla warfare, living off of the countryside as well as they could.

But the cocaine network, and the people who profited from it, continued to flourish. As late as 1993, the Columbian drug lords continued to grow in power and wealth, and the distribution network, and those in it, continued to operate as they had during the war. The end result is that there were more drugs on the streets of America than ever before in history—both cocaine from South America and heroin from Southeast Asia—and the organizations involved, from the cartels to the Mafia, profited in excess of $10 billion per year.

When all of the smoke and mirrors are removed, the true machinations and benefactors of the Iran/Contra affair surface: Hundreds of millions of dollars worth of weapons found their way into Iran illegally; the Contras, as a *cause celebre'*, served as a patriotic motivating factor for the players in case the affair was ever exposed; the handful of hostages in Beirut received more media coverage and financial attention than all of the POWs and MIAs of World War II, Korea, and Vietnam combined; the Chase Manhattan Bank managed to retain the Shah's wealth; and finally, the drug network established to support the Contras not only remained intact, but was by the end of the affair much more efficient and profitable than ever before.

And why not? The drug traffickers and cartels were recruited, organized and trained by people who, by then, had gained years of experience in just such enterprises.

Part VI

Unsafe At Any Altitude

"I armed my missiles and brought the nose down sharply. It worked! I saw that I had lock-on. The first missile was fired when the distance between us was about five kilometers. Only now I could really see the intruder."

Lt. Col. Gennadiy Nikolayevich Osipovich
Soviet Air Force

"Very strange people were at work very early on. Within a matter of three hours there were American accents heard in the town. Over that night there were large numbers, by which I mean twenty, twenty-five, thirty people arrived. The next day...there was a whole bevy of people walking down the main street with blue windbreakers and baseball hats with 'FBI' on them...there were a lot of other Americans there who were in town who weren't wearing FBI windcheaters...I know who some of them were, and it certainly wasn't tourists."

David Ben-Aryeah, British journalist
On the bombing of Pan Am 103

"I told them [the FBI] that it was definitely a flare type rocket heading toward the aircraft, then it exploded. It was then suggested that we did not see anything at all and that we were going along with what other people said they saw, just for the excitement of it. I told them 'no way, I know what I saw'...[other men in suits arrived later and] They gave us some money and told us 'never to mention anything to anyone about being witnesses to the crash again.'"

Anonymous letter to editor of
California newspaper regarding TWA 800

Chapter 26

Ambush Over Moneron

On the dark, cold night of September 1, 1983, a Boeing 747 Jumbo Jet carrying 269 passengers flew placidly over the Western Pacific. Its destination was Seoul, the capital of South Korea.

It would never arrive.

Unknown to the crew, the airliner had strayed off course. For some reason, the sophisticated primary and secondary navigation systems failed to alert them that their course line had altered far to the west of where they should have been, and at that very moment had put them dangerously close to the Kamchatka Peninsula of the Soviet Union. Had they received an accurate plot, they would have been alarmed to know that they were well within the Soviet Air Defense Zone—and the Russians took the presence of intruders seriously. Only five years before, another jet airliner belonging to the same company, Korean Airlines (KAL) had strayed into Soviet airspace and had been intercepted. On that occasion, the Soviet interceptor pilot had twice told Soviet ground controllers that he had identified the intruder and that it was a civilian airliner—even identifying the company and type, a Boeing 707 with KAL markings. Both times he was told to proceed with shoot-down procedures, and both times he refused. However after the third order, and probably realizing the dire personal consequences for failure to obey a direct command, he reluctantly fired a missile which killed two passengers and disabled the aircraft. The Korean crew fought desparetly to save their ship and miraculously managed to land the crippled airplane on a frozen Soviet lake. The passengers were released two days later, but the Soviets kept the 707.[173] KAL Flight 007 would not be so lucky.

Besides the error in navigation, something else was occuring. For like the fated 707, they too were being tracked by Soviet air defense radar and would soon be joined by Russian interceptors.

The Soviet radar operators had already spent the night tracking an American air force Boeing RC-135—a four-engine 707 derivative especially equipped with sophisticated radios and other electronics for reconnaissance and spy work—and were completely alert when the new blip, KAL 007, appeared on their screens. Only this time, instead of assuming the routine race-track oval flight pattern just outside their air defense interception zone (ADIZ), the new target continued southwest at an angle that would place it inside the ADIZ within minutes.

The air defense officer at the radar site made a quick decision. He would scramble the "alert" fighters. Within minutes the Soviet interceptor pilots manned their aircraft, rolled onto the runway and, shoving their throttles past the afterburner detent, roared into the night sky.

Each pilot came up on the radio in turn and was given a steer to the bogey. But for some reason, the radar vectors were faulty. For no matter how hard the frustrated controllers tried, they could not seem to vector their flight to a point of visual contact with the intruder. In the end, after searching until they were too low on fuel to continue, the MiG flight returned to base. Incredibly, the sleek supersonic fighters, even with the aid of a sophisticated ground defense radar network, which was at that time suffering problems similar to 007's navigation systems, had not come within 50 miles of the lumbering Jumbo Jet.

KAL 007, still not realizing how close they were getting to the Siberian coastline, continued on. Then, as other radar sites began to pick up the 747, another flight was ordered into the air. This time it came from the air defense station on Sakhalin, who scrambled four aging Sukhoi Su-15 "Flagon" interceptors (which were not equipped with the sensitive electronic systems of the MiGs).[174] In the cockpit of the lead Sukhoi, No. 805, sat Lt. Col. Gennadiy Nikolayevich Osipovich.

The Korean airliner, flying straight and level at an airspeed somewhere below 500 mph, had managed to fly completely across the wide Kamchatka Peninsula, the 500 mile expanse of the Sea of Okhotsk north of the Kuril Islands, and was approaching Sakhalin Island just north of Hokkaido, Japan, and had managed to do so completely unmolested—which infuriated the Soviet commanders.

The Sakhalin radar operators were more successful than their Kamchatka counterparts in tracking the bogey and vectoring their interceptors. As they were doing so, for some reason, Soviet commanders were changing the radar blip identification from "non-Soviet aircraft" to "American RC-135."

As the flight of four Su-15s converged on the 747, General Ivan Tretyak, commander of the Soviet Far East Military District, and his superior, General Vladimer Govorov, commander of the Far East Theater of Operations, decided Osipovich should maneuver his flight closer to the target for visual identification.

Fearful that pilots might defect, as had Lt. Viktor Belenko who had flown to Japan in a shiny new super-secret MiG-25 eight years before, the interceptor flight's tanks had only been filled with enough fuel for local operations. They would not have much time to loiter once contact was made with the bogey, and a decision concerning what course of action to take next would have to be made quickly by the ground staff.[175]

At 6:15 a.m. Osipovich received orders to close with the intruder and identify it. But before he could do so, he was ordered by Tretyak to "Kill the intruder." Horrified crewmen aboard the American RC-135, who had been monitoring the Soviet activities, heard this order repeated no less than five times.

KAL 007, which had unknowingly managed to evade the latest and most capable Soviet MiG fighters, was now about to leave Soviet airspace after flying completely across Sakhalin Island. Within a few minutes the huge jet would reenter international airspace and escape. Unfortunately, this was not going to be permitted.[176]

At 6:23 the four Su-15s fell into trail behind the unsuspecting 747. One minute later, Osipovich, reacting to the command to destroy the target, lit his afterburners and activated his missile system which consisted of two Anab air-to-air missiles. Almost immediately his missile seekers locked on to the heat source of the 747's engines and his armament panel began to flash. He reported back to the ground station that he had lock-on and was prepared to launch missiles. The target was now only five kilometers distant, well within range of the

Su-15's Anabs. Osipovich, in his own words later, stated: "...suddenly in my earphones I heard this: 'Abort destruction! Match altitude with the target and force it to land.' I was already approaching the intruder from below. I matched speeds and started to flash him [author's note: Osipovich was probably referring to his landing lights]. But he did not respond. 'Give him some warning bursts,' I heard from the ground. I fired four bursts, firing off more than 200 rounds. But what was the sense of that? I had armor-piercing rounds, not incendiaries [tracers]. And it was hardly likely that anyone would see them."[177]

There was no way the crew of the 747 could have seen Osipovich flashing his landing lights. The Soviet pilot was behind and below the large airliner.[178] Yet he goes on to say that "I have no doubt that they noticed me...The reaction of the pilots was unambiguous—they quickly reduced speed. Now they were moving at about 400 kilometers per hour [250 mph]. I was moving faster...I simply could not go more slowly. In my opinion the intruder's reckoning was simple: If I did not want to stall and go into a spin, I would be forced to overtake them. And that is what happened. We had already flown past the island; it is narrow at that point. And it was then that the command was given from the ground: 'Destroy the target.'"[179]

In this statement, Osipovich tells two lies. First, he states that his interceptor could not reduce speed below 400 kph and that he would be forced to overshoot or stall out. This is not true. To keep from overshooting he had two choices: First, he could retard his throttle, drop a few degrees of flaps, even drop his landing gear, and go into a "slow flight" configuration. Obviously the Su-15 could slow to a much slower speed considering that it lands at approximately 105 knots. The second choice would be to reduce his forward progress by maneuvering. Simply put, he could "S" turn while the Korean airliner continued on a straight course. The second lie concerns his use of gunfire. The Su-15 does not have an internal gun. Instead, if armed in advance, it is capable of mounting two GSh-23L 23mm gunpods. Each pod carries two cannon, with 100 rounds of ammunition for each gun in each pod for a total of 400 rounds. Because of maneuverability restrictions concerning external loads (the two gunpods are mounted on belly pylons in the center of the fuselage) external gunpods are seldom carried. Instead, the interceptors rely on the two air-to-air missiles. They can be employed from a far greater range with much more devastating effect. By Soviet doctrine, the GSh-23 gunpods were only carried in the off chance that the fighter might get into a close-in dogfight. Even at this, the Flagon was designed for straight line speed to head off intruding bombers and not for maneuverability. It therefore had to rely on stand-off distance and missile capability to make it a lethal aircraft.[180]

Osipovich chose to maneuver his aircraft in a vertical climbing turn behind KAL 007 to preclude overshooting the slowing target. "I...managed to make a sharp turn and was now above and running on to him. But then I had a thought. I dropped 2,000 [he doesn't say feet or meters—all Soviet aircraft altimeters are marked in meters, which would have him drop approximately 6,500 feet!)...I armed my missiles and brought the nose down sharply. It worked! I saw that I had lock-on. The first missile was fired when the distance between us was about five kilometers. Only now I could really see the intruder. It was larger than an IL-76 and its outline was something like a TU-16.[181] The trouble for all Soviet pilots is that we do not study civilian aircraft belonging to foreign companies. I knew all the military aircraft, all the reconnaissance aircraft. But this was not like any of them."

This last statement is also untrue. The Soviet military encyclopedia contains photographs and identification silhouettes of both military and commercial aircraft. The 747 is represented, and its distinctive whale-like shape is quite unique. Also, if the target did not resemble any reconnaissance aircraft, then why was it later stated that Osipovich confused it for a much smaller RC-135?

But the biggest problem with Osipovich's story is with his time-line of events. For as he was supposedly performing these time consuming maneuvers, the RC-135 radio operators were monitoring the Soviet radio conversations and Japanese air traffic controllers and radar operators were observing the progress of KAL 007. They had just given the KAL pilots permission to climb to 35,000 feet—which might explain why Osipovich thought the aircraft was slowing down in an attempt to evade him. It was actually climbing to a higher flight level, which caused it to slow in speed relative to the pursuers. [Author's note: Why did the Japanese controllers at this point not tell KAL-007 they were off course, far into Soviet air defense territory?]

In actuality, the time span between General Tretyak's 6:15 order for Osipovich to maneuver closer to the radar target and the receipt of the final command to "Kill the intruder," at 6:25, was only ten minutes.

At 6:26, Osipovich said he fired two missiles simultaneously. The Anabs ran true and, according to Osipovich, struck the 747 "one near the tail, and the other took off half the left wing." This would not be true if Osipovich actually was "70 right" of the plane as he reported to ground controllers. The heat-seeking missiles would have homed in on the nearest engine, in this case, number four right outboard engine.

But contrary to later reports, the missiles did not cause the 747 to explode in flight. Even though Osipovich transmitted at 6:26 that "The target is destroyed," the Tokyo air traffic controllers reported that one minute later they picked up a broken radio transmission from KAL 007: "Tokyo, Korean Air zero zero seven...fifteen thousand holding with rapid decompression! Descending to one zero thousand...[10,000 feet]. *Tokyo Radio acknowledged KAL 007 but did not advise them that they were off course because they were probably not in range of Tokyo radar which was over 900 miles away.*

This is exactly what the emergency procedures call for in such an incident. To the 747 pilots, the explosion of the missiles must have sounded like a rupture in the pressure hull of the aircraft—and possibly shrapnel from the explosive warheads of the Anabs, which homed in on the tailpipe of one of the engines, had indeed pierced the cabin of the airliner. If this occured, yellow oxygen masks would automatically be deployed from the overhead compartments above the passenger seats and the sudden decompression in the cabin would have been felt throughout the aircraft. The pilots, realizing that there is only sufficient oxygen to sustain human life below 12,500 feet, would immediately begin an emergency descent.

Had the 747 exploded, as the official version later recounted, it would have struck the surface of the ocean in less than three minutes. This did not happen. The Japanese controllers knew that the Korean crew continued to maintain control of the Boeing for another *12 minutes!*

At 6:32, KAL 007 descended from Flight Level 35 (35,000 feet) to 16,400 feet. This was confirmed on Japanese radar. Then after a couple of minutes, the big jet began another descent. It appears that the crew could not maintain altitude and was fighting valiantly to save the ship. It is not known if there was insufficient power in the remaining engines to maintain altitude, or if another engine had failed due to fuel lines being severed, or possibly there were further complications from fire. But for whatever reason, the 747 again began to descend and at 6:39 had dropped to 5,000 feet. Three minutes later it fell below 1,000 feet, and at 6:40 a.m. local time, it was lost below radar 1.5 miles from Moneron Island.[182]

Twenty-seven minutes after Osipovich fired his missiles, another Russian pilot reported that he was making "reference point circles" over the wreckage and that "rescue operations were underway." If KAL 007 had exploded, as the official Western reports stated the next day, then why would a Soviet search plane bother to make circles over the wreckage, and rescue operations initiated? What was there to rescue?

Contrary to this, later Soviet press releases explained that the Russian fighter pilots actually reported: "I don't see it" (1829:13); "No I don't see it"(1835:54); "He doesn't see anything in the area. I just looked" (1838:37). None of Osipovich's comrades could find the wreckage of his "kill" where it was supposed to be. These statement must be compared to the burning wreckage of TWA 800 which crashed into the Atlantic of East Moriches, New York, on July 17, 1996. The fuel from this incident burned for hours, marking the location of the main wreckage site.

Within two hours of the shootdown, Soviet defense stations in Sakhalin were in communication with Moscow. The information they relayed was not good. They had mistakenly downed a civilian airliner—*and some of the passengers were American*! How could anyone know that any of the passengers were American? Had they discovered floating bodies that still held readable identification papers or passports? According to both Soviet and Western press releases, no bodies were ever recovered, and no wreckage was ever found.[183] This in itself is not only improbable, it is unbelievable. As in every example of an air disaster over water, and in most instances of ship sinkings, bodies surface and are recovered. One case in point is the tragic shootdown of the Iranian Airbus over the Persian Gulf by an American missile frigate *Vincennes*. Dozens of bodies floated to the surface from the ruptured cabin and were photographed by the world press floating in clusters just below the surface of the sea. Though the colder water in the Sea of Japan would delay such an occurance due to better temperature preservation of flesh, eventually the bodies would bloat and rise to the surface. With the exception of a few body parts that allegedly drifted ashore in Japan, 250 miles away, which could not be identified as having originated aboard the fated flight, no bodies were reportedly recovered.

Four hours after the shootdown, Marshal Ogarkov could see an already negative international incident rapidly deteriorating into a world relations disaster. The only way it might be salvaged would be by a world-class deception created with layers of lies. Even as a vast armada of Soviet vessels converged on Moneron Island, Ogarkov began formulating a story of intrigue and espionage. According to the rapidly fabricated version of events, the Korean airliner had joined up with the RC-135, which had already probed Soviet airspace on several occasions that night, and then had flown on to cross over Kamchatka, the Sea of Okhotsk, and finally Sakhalin. It was obviously on a spy mission, probably had secret cameras and eavesdropping devices on board, and flagrantly ignored all warnings given by the Russians. The Russians were left with no choice but to shoot it down. The Americans, of course, were to blame. It was them who had placed the 269 innocent passengers at risk for their own selfish reasons. The Americans, by their deceitful actions, had murdered those people and would now try to blame it on the Russians, who had been forced to defend their homeland.

Moscow had a choice. The government could do one of two things: buy the tale and reinforce it, supporting the Far East Defense Command in the process, or place the blame on over-zealous officers and punish them accordingly. This latter choice would have been the easiest. There could be an investigation, a finding of a tragic mistake having been made, blame fixed on the lowest ranking officer who could be pegged as responsible, an apology issued, and life would go on. But instead, Moscow bought Ogarkov's version of the event and began an immediate campaign of disinformation.

The end result is that the world press swallowed the Soviet version and even came up with other reinforcing stories that the Korean 747 had indeed been on a CIA spy mission. *The Washington Post* headlined a six column article with "Article in Britain Links Ill-Fated KAL Flight to Intelligence Mission." The piece referred to originally appeared in Britain's *Defence Attache'* magazine. But when the author of the article, who claimed that KAL 007 was engaged in espionage, was finally tracked down, it was discovered that he was a London advertising agent with no technical expertise and no remarkable or inside knowledge of the event.

Then, in 1984, a Yale graduate student named David Pearson, wrote an article for *The Nation* that stated "...the U.S. government also must be held accountable" for the deaths of the passengers aboard KAL 007, because "It seems probable that Soviet radar systems were jammed at least on Kamchatka Peninsula and perhaps on Sakhalin Island." If this were true, the Russians would have jumped on it to reinforce their disinformation. And beyond this, if the radar was indeed jammed, then Osipovich's flight would never have found KAL 007.

In the end, even after President Reagan denounced the Soviets as murderers and called for an international investigation, the issue faded into history and was all but forgotten. General Tretyak was promoted to head all Soviet air defenses; General Govorov was promoted to deputy minister of defense; and Marshal Ogarkov became personal military adviser to Mikhail Gorbachev.

Osipovich was not so lucky. It seems that in the Russian military, as in other forces, the proverbial excretian rolls downhill. After being told by his commander, Colonel Kornukhov, that he had shot down a foreigner and to "make another hole in your shoulder boards for a new star," Osipovich was instead ostricized. After the arrival of an investigating committee, Osipovich was, in his own words, suddenly "a son of a bitch."

During the investigation, which ironically was reported after the fall of Communism by none other than *Izvestiya*, the official government newspaper, Osipovich makes a startling statement. "In the grand reckoning," he reflected, "I have no doubt that we were right. A foreign aircraft was in our airspace for two and a half hours, and during that time it covered a distance of more than 2,000 kilometers. *All the air traffic control services of foreign states said not a word, remained silent.* What order can you give in such a situation? Sit on your hands?" [Author's emphasis].

Izvestiya came out with a 17 part expose' of the Soviet cover-up surrounding KAL 007 which ran between December 21, 1990 and February 6, 1991. The series reported on *Izvestiya*'s efforts to discover the actual "truth" regarding the shootdown, and surprisingly, was considered the most accurate and in-depth version of the incident ever published. According to *Izvestiya*, the wreckage of KAL 007 was found almost immediatly and divers were sent down to examine it. Three flight recorders were found and recovered, and were quickly rushed off to Moscow. But not one body was found! According to a Soviet diver who had examined the wreck, "The main thing was not what we had seen there, but what we had *not* seen. The divers found practically no human bodies or remains." What had become of the 269 passengers and nine crewmembers?

Unless they weren't there.

If the bodies did not surface, and they were not found in the wreckage, then they had to have been either rescued or recovered immediately after the crash. If this is so, then the survivors—or their bodies—were transported to the nearby Siberian island of Sakhalin, probably to the nearest settlement: Shebunino. If not this small town, then perhaps Gornozavodsk, Nevel'sk, or the larger community of Khomnsk, all of which are along the southwestern coastline of Sakhalin facing the tiny island of Ostrov Moneron. From any of these places it would be reasonable to assume that they would be quickly transhipped to the nearest city: Kharbarovsk, on the mainland of Siberia.

It should be remembered that it was in Kharbarovsk that the Soviets held the War Crimes Tribunals for the Japanese captured at Mukden and Pingfan in World War II, and served as the primary destination for the American POWs taken in Korea—and some of those received from Vietnam—and was the city that contained the largest military installations in southeast Siberia. It was from here that thousands of people had disappeared into the Gulags.

But why would the Soviets care about incarcerating or eliminating innocent civilians? Was it because they were witnesses to the truth? That they could testify that they were ambushed and there was no warning—no gunshots across the nose, no blinking of landing lights from the interceptors?

Hardly. It was more likely that they were victims of a far greater and much darker plot than even the Soviets could father.

Only one small mention was ever made in the Western press of the importance of one of the passengers who perished aboard 007. Buried in most accounts is the fact that U.S. Congressman Larry McDonald of Georgia was aboard the Jumbo Jet. What is not pointed out is that Congressman McDonald was involved in a major investigation of the world banking cartel, the Council on Foreign Relations, the Federal Reserve Board, and other significant entities that were interrelated with each of these.

McDonald was the most dedicated anti-communist on Capital Hill, and the press had noted that "From the time he took his oath of office in 1975 until the moment of the shootdown, Congressman McDonald had systematically carried out a campaign against the Soviet communists of a sort which no other U.S. elected official had ever done on his own."[184] In *The Day of the Cobra*, author Jeffrey St. John writes: "Congressman Lawrence McDonald had spent his entire career warning against the use of terrorism as an instrument of Soviet policy, particularly the use of the threat of nuclear war by the Kremlin as a weapon to paralyze the United States and its Western allies' will to resist."

But McDonald had gone beyond fighting simple Soviet communism. He had discovered a spiderweb of hidden corridors that linked power brokers in Moscow with those in New York and Washington. This, in turn, made him a threat to the Establishment/international banking cabal. This put him at crossed swords with the Council of Foreign Relations and its international brethren of New World Order and One World Government proponents. In *The Rockefeller File*, authored by Gary Allen, McDonald wrote the foreword and railed against "the drive of the Rockefellers and their allies to create a one-world government, combining super-capitalism and communism under the same tent."

McDonald went on to establish his Western Goals Foundation, whose purpose was "to rebuild and strengthen the political, economic, and social structure of the United States and Western Civilization so as to make any merger with totalitarians impossible." It is probable that with his discovery of the shadow world of international finance and power brokers—and their goal of globalism and control of international relations—that he had gone too far. It is unlikely that the whole truth will ever be known, but one question will forever remain. Was KAL 007 misdirected over the island of Sakhalin so that an aerial ambush of Dr. Lawrence McDonald could be accomplished?

Since the original data was released and the first investigations were conducted, other information has surfaced. One FAA investigator who was working in Asia at the time discovered that the Japanese at the Tokyo radar site actually monitored the 747 below the 5000 foot level and saw it do something other than the official "crash in the ocean" version. According to them, they watched as the target turned toward Sakhalin Island, descended, and apparently landed on the island! Shortly after the attack, the Rome, Georgia office of Congressman McDonald received several calls from not only KAL officials, but from the FAA claiming they had evidence that the jet landed in Russian territory. One call was recorded by their office:

> "This is Duty Officer Orville Brockman at FAA Headquarters in Washington, D.C. We have just received information from our FAA representative, Mr. Dennis Wilham in Tokyo, as follows: He has been advised by the Japanese Civil Aviation Bureau headquarters, Air Traffic Division, Mr. Takano—T-A-K-A-N-O—who is his counterpart in Japanese aviation, as follows: *Japanese self-defense force confirms that the Hokkaido radar followed Air Korea to a landing in Soviet territory on the Island of Sakhalinska*—S-A-K-H-A-L-I-N-S-K-A—and it is confirmed by the manifest that Congressman McDonald was on board." [Emphasis mine][185]

This would explain many things, including the lack of bodies and wreckage, plus the Soviet fighter pilots not being able to locate a crash site on the water. It also would explain another cryptic event—an American reporter came out of Russia just prior to the publication of the *Izvestiya* series and stated that the series would reveal "that Moscow had ordered the bodies of the 269 victims destroyed in a local crematorium." That information did not later appear in *Izvestiya*. However, if the airplane had landed on the island safely and discharged its passengers, why would orders be given to "cremate the victims"? Considering the fact that millions of Soviet citizens, prisoners of war, and political enemies and dissidents of the communist government have "disappeared" into Siberia in the past, would it be unusual for the Russians to "disappear" a few more embarrassing foreigners? Orders from Moscow for this event to happen might simply be: "Cremate the victims."

There are many other questions that deserve answers as well. First, how could a modern airliner, which was on a routine IFR (Instrument Flight Rules) flight under positive control of the international controllers have been permitted to stray several hundred miles off course without correction? Osipovich himself reported that "all the air traffic control services of foreign states said not a word...remained silent."

Second, why had not the RC-135, which was conveniently on location—ostensibly there to monitor a missile launch—notified either the KAL crew or the Japanese air control facilities of the 747's incursion into Soviet air space? Every military flight crew realizes all too well the consequences of flying too close to the Soviet Union, and the RC-135, which had radios on board that could monitor the Soviet frequencies, had the capability of relaying the critical information to both the KAL crew and the Japanese controllers. They also knew the Korean crew did not have this capability.

Third, what happened to the 747's navigation systems? Besides on-board radar, VOR and LORAN systems, there are inertial navigation positioning systems that are accurate within a kilometer. Had they failed? If so, why had not the Korean crew notified the ground stations?

Fourth, why did the experienced crew of KAL 007 manage to go over 200 miles off course without realizing it? The obvious answer is that they were directed to do so.

When flying IFR at night, the normal procedure is to be given a steer for a course line until further advised. As an example, such a transmission would be "KAL 007, maintain flight level three-five-zero, steer two-zero-five." Translated, this tells the pilot to maintain an altitude of 35,000 feet and fly a magnetic heading of 205 degrees. What had KAL 007 been told to do?

Lastly, what happened to the bodies?

Or the survivors?

Chapter 27

The Downing of Pan Am 103: Libyans, PLO or CIA?

On the cold, windy night of December 21st, 1988, the villagers of the quaint Scottish town of Lockerbie, Scotland heard a tremendous explosion. Those that were outside witnessed the sky light up with a billowing ball of fire high overhead. Within minutes huge pieces of bent and shredded aluminum wreckage impacted in and around the village, obvious bits and pieces of an airplane.

At first, the local constabulary and the British police logically assumed this event to be either the work of terrorists, who placed a bomb aboard the aircraft—a Boeing 747 Jumbo Jet designated Flight 103—or a mechanical malfunction that ignited the fuel cells. With their extensive experience dealing with terrorists that range from the IRA to Middle-Eastern terrorist groups, most agreed it was a terrorist act.

The local emergency and police organizations organized quickly, with a command center being established within an hour of the incident by the Lockerbie police, and local residents and medical personnel gathering to form search teams. For that first hour everything appeared to be coming together logically.

But within the next hour things began to become very strange for the British participants in the search and investigative teams. Several things began to happen in various sections of the search area that were described by locals as "most unusual."

George Stobbs, a Lockerbie police inspector, remarked later "On the night I was...started to set up a control room, and by [between] eleven o'clock and midnight, there was a member of the FBI in the office who came in, introduced herself to me, and sat down—and just sat there the rest of the night. That was it."[186]

The unusual activity of this alleged "FBI" agent is striking, but not quite as odd as the fact that Lockerbie is over 350 miles from London, which is the nearest point an American FBI agent might be. To reach Lockerbie that night from London, even if traveling by air, would have taken far more than one hour considering the sequence of events that would have had to occur. Assuming a timely notification, an American agent in London would have had to have been tracked down considering the late hour, notified to pack up for an investigation, rush to Heathrow, board a waiting airplane, fly immediately to the nearest airport that could land a jet transport, obtain ground transportation from there to Lockerbie, then locate the command center. An effort that would require four to six hours at the minimum.

Not a very likely scenario to occur in less than two hours of the blast.

A Pan Am security officer, interviewed at a later date, offered one piece to the puzzle regarding the rapid response: "As far as I can recall, there were about forty people, excluding crew, on board [the Pan Am VIP flight of personnel being sent to the Lockerbie crash site], of which I would estimate fifty percent were Pan Am people. The others, I wasn't aware of their affiliation at all."[187]

The questions at this point are: Who were these people, how did they get to the airport so quickly, where did they come from, why were they in England, and what was their mission?

After arrival in Lockerbie, the unidentified Americans began to behave in a bizarre manner. Instead of organizing to investigate the crash or assisting in the search in a manner consistent with normal routine, the "Americans" made themselves busy elsewhere.

Mr. Tam Dalyell, a member of the British Parliament, related "The local police force...they were concerned. Absolutely swarms of Americans [were] fiddling with the bodies, and shall we say tampering with those things the police were carefully checking themselves. They weren't pretending, saying they were from the FBI or CIA, they were just 'Americans' who seemed to arrive extremely quickly on the scene."

Dr. David Fieldhouse, the local police surgeon, reported a strange series of events in his sector: "I was asked to go to various locations in and around Lockerbie to look for bodies...we [then went] down one large field and identified about ten bodies. We thought we ought to retrace our steps and put some form of identification on them, and so, the only thing I had with me was a block of small white labels and one hundred or so plastic gloves which I carried at all times as part of my usual police surgeon duties. I put a code on every one, DCF-1 right through to fifty-eight. All the bodies in that particular sector. I learned later that when the bodies were taken to the mortuary, all the labels which had been put on them had been removed with the exception of two...but all the rest had been removed and discarded."

Someone appears to have been very intent on disrupting the investigation by obstructing and interfering with the search and recovery process. But who? And Why?

British journalist and Pan Am 103 researcher David Ben-Aryeah answered part of the puzzle: "Very strange people were at work very early on. Within a matter of three hours [after the crash] there were American accents heard in the town. Over that night there were large numbers, by which I mean twenty, twenty-five, thirty people arrived. The next day...there was a whole bevy of people walking down the main street with blue windbreakers and baseball hats with 'FBI' on them. But there were a lot of other Americans there who were in town who weren't wearing FBI windcheaters. I don't know who they were. I know who some of them were, and it certainly wasn't tourists."

Out at the crash site, as the sun rose, small pockets of Americans, keeping to themselves, wandered among the wreckage and strewn bodies, poking, looking, searching...for something. They had been there most of the night. As one searcher, a member of a mountain rescue team that arrived within two hours of the initial explosion, related: "We arrived within two hours. We found Americans already there. The British police and military who were there are still not speaking [about this]. Because of the Official Secrets Act, they are prohibited from speaking."

But Tam Dalyell, a member of Parliament who is very suspicious about the odd activities surrounding the Lockerbie incident, refuses to be shackled by "national security." He told interviewers working on the

British documentary about the Lockerbie tragedy, *The Maltese Doublecross*, that "It was thought it was very odd and strange that so many people should be involved in moving bodies, looking at luggage, who were not members of the investigating force. What were they looking for so carefully? You know, this was not just searching carefully for loved ones. It was far more than that. It was careful examination of luggage and indeed bodies."[188]

And there was more to it than that. Someone was very concerned that Scottish searchers might find something before their own people could. One searcher, Eric Spofforth, told of a helicopter that circled his group for some time as they made their way through the wreckage: "This helicopter was overflying the area. A chap in it was looking at me out of the telescopic sight of a rifle. Probably some secret service man or other. It was a white unmarked helicopter, for all intents and purposes a civilian helicopter."

These unmarked helicopters continued their observations over the crash scene for days. Innes Graham, a local resident, reported that "These helicopters were landing just behind [my house], in the field, quite regular. It was constant, just every day for days on end flying over."

It became obvious to the British investigators at the scene that this was not just an aircraft bombing or terrorist investigation to many of the Americans who arrived so swiftly on the scene. It was something else. Something on the airplane that they were looking for. But what? What was so important about this flight, or the passengers, or what it carried that was of such interest to people who were obviously American "spooks"?

Three individuals that were on the scene or investigated later give three clues. David Ben-Aryeah noted that "The arc [of the wreckage] ran right around the crest of the hills overlooking where the cockpit fell. *There were a number of bodies which subsequently became of great interest to a lot of people.*" David Johnston, a radio journalist for Radio Forth, reported "I'd been told early on that the investigators believed the bomb had been taken onto the plane by a U.S. officer who had been seconded to military intelligence, and the bomb had been planted on him in Beirut."

Finally, there are stories of a large suitcase filled with heroin being recovered by the American searchers. A local farmer, Jim Wilson, told relatives of Pan Am 103 victims that he was there "when the drugs were found." According to *Private Eye* magazine, Wilson, of Tundergarth Farm near Lockerbie, "found a suitcase packed with drugs in one of his fields. He was worried the substances might harm his sheep and immediately informed the police. He was surprised that the police seemed to know the case was there and were under the impression that it had already been removed." When the drugs were discovered, a team of Americans rushed to the location in an all-terrain vehicle. Wilson noted that the Americans seemed extremely angry over the fact that the drugs had not been discovered earlier by their own personnel.

According to one constable who did not remain silent, the Scottish police had been told to keep an eye out for the drugs early on. He also mentioned that he had overheard the Americans say that there was a drug courier on the airplane, and heard a name: Khalid Jafaar.

In the months following the bombing of Pan Am 103 and the murder of its 270 passengers, the U.S. government broke the case. With a great deal of luck and more than a few fortunate coincidences, a searcher found a tiny bit of microchip in a wooded area that was turned in and recognized as something other than an airplane part.[189] This in itself is extremely interesting considering the amount of electronic parts aboard an aircraft that could have ruptured and scattered solid state circuit boards, microchips and other various electronic bits and pieces over the countryside. It is also interesting to note that the FBI does not have Boeing aircraft engineers or experts on staff that are capable of sorting through the debris and deciding what is and is not a part of an aircraft system. Yet, they managed to allegedly find and identify this part and determine it was suspicious. This one fingernail size piece of plastic is credited with being the key to the solution of the case.

According to the FBI, the laboratory determined the microchip to have been part of a timer built in Switzerland by a Swiss company named MEBO. The timer was sold to Libya, and two Libyan intelligence officers, Abdel Basset Al-Megrahi and Lamin Khalifah

Fhimah, used it to construct a bomb inside a tape recorder, smuggle it into Malta, then put it in a suitcase filled with various Maltese clothes, transport it to the airport, tag it for the final destination of JFK international, then place it aboard an Air Malta airplane unaccompanied.[190] The bag then managed to fly to Frankfort, change planes (also unaccompanied), then fly to London, then take off again to explode over Lockerbie. How the FBI decided that Megrahi and Fhimah were the two responsible parties has never been satisfactorily explained. However, they were put on the wanted list, exposed to international media attention, and have not left the confines of Libya since—even though they have volunteered to surrender to an international court as long as it convened in any country other than the United States or the United Kingdom. Neither the U.S. or the U.K. have ever agreed to such a neutral location for trial.

To support the U.S. government's version of the sabotage are the statements of such people as CIA veteran Vincent M. Cannistraro who was an operations officer and director of intelligence on the National Security Council staff. Cannistraro stated: "The principle avenues [of the investigation] led to identification of a foreign role in an act of terrorism was forensic evidence recovered by the Scottish police at Lockerbie themselves. Investigators and townspeople on their hands and knees, crawling along the countryside, picking up minute bits of debris. And one of those bits of debris turned out to be a microchip, which was analyzed microscopically that led to the Libyan connection."[191]

The problem with this statement is that there was not a concrete chain of evidence for the microchip. At the time of the investigation no one had been identified as finding the piece. In fact, there were attempts to make people sign statements a year later saying they had found the microchip. One Scottish searcher, identified only as "Bobby," stated that two years after the bombing a Scottish police officer visited him and asked him to sign a statement: "I got a call from a policeman asking if he could come down to my home, and would I sign to say that I picked those [items] up. He brought with him three small bags about the size of an eight-by-five piece of paper, one of which contained an item of cloth, one of which contained a brown piece which looked very much like a piece of plastic, the third piece I couldn't tell what it was."

Could the "brown piece" have been the microchip?

The U.S. government position was also backed up by the findings of the FBI lab in Washington. According to Tom Thurman, FBI forensics expert, he made the identification of the microchip and tied it to the Swiss manufacturer. He remembered that "June fifteenth of 1990 was the day I made the identification. I knew at that point what it meant, because I was an investigator as well as a forensic examiner. I knew where that would go. At that point we had no conclusive proof of the type of timing mechanism that was used in the bombing of 103. When that identification was made at the time I knew we had it." Agent Thurman does not say, however, how he determined the microchip to not have come from one of the aircraft instrumentation systems, such as the autopilot, radios, clocks, or navigation devices.

According to the FBI, the identification of the chip led to a timer manufacturer in Zurich, Switzerland, the MEBO company. Edwin Bollier, the owner of the company, stated that "Scottish and American FBI officers came to Switzerland. They showed us a photograph of a fragment of a timer. They asked if it was a timer from the O-series...of the first series from our MST-13 timer. They explained that in 1986 two of these timers were confiscated in Dakar and later on in Senegal from two Libyans. I immediately recognized from the photo that the fragment found in Lockerbie was without a doubt from a timer that we ourselves had made."

It is interesting to note here that according to the FBI, they had in their possession two timing devices two years before the bombing of Pan Am 103. That would mean they had the interior components, including the microchips, long before the Lockerbie incident. Perhaps this could explain why the lab could identify such a chip. It might also explain other things, such as how a piece of such a chip ended up in the evidence. This last statement is not unreasonable considering Edwin Bollier's next revelation.

"In 1990 or 1991 I spent a whole week with the FBI because I wanted to see the actual fragment. Then they told me they didn't have it—that the Scottish police had it. So I spent a whole week with the Scottish police, but they refused to show me the piece. They only showed me a photograph." When Bollier asked the FBI to give him more information on the chain of evidence on the microchip, and to explain what was going on, he was told that "this could be explained. Three of his people had sworn that they had found this piece in a piece of a coat and had signed a paper to this effect. I later heard that it was the Scottish police who had found the piece in a shirt that came from Malta."

The FBI was essentially telling Bollier that they had agents in place in Scotland for two years as every piece of material was discovered, turned in, and examined. Then, the Scottish police stated that it was they who found the microchip. But then, it is extremely odd that they actually attempted to have a civilian searcher sign a statement two years after the event that he had found it.

The bottom line on the government story appears to be a smoke screen for what actually happened. The government version is basically that the Libyan government—Crazy Khadaffi—sent two of its intelligence officers to Malta to build a bomb, put it in a suitcase and tag it for JFK, then wait while the suitcase made its way through three countries, in the middle of the European winter when flights are often delayed or cancelled due to weather, to explode in an American Jumbo Jet named "Maid of the Seas."

The problem is that there is another story that has begun to surface since that cold, blustery, fateful night in December, 1988.

On July 3rd, 1988, less than six months before the Pan Am 103 bombing, another large aircraft disaster occurred. On that day in the Persian Gulf, the U.S.S. *Vincennes*, an Aegis class frigate, identified an incoming bogey on its early warning radar scope. As the sailors watched, the blip continued to approach their ship from the direction of the Iranian coastline.

Fearing an attack by an Iranian F-14 fighter bomber, Captain Rogers, the skipper of the *Vincennes*, gave the order to man battle stations. As the klaxon echoed through the ship's compartments and sailors scrambled to their stations, the Aegis missile targeting system came to life.

The communications division of the *Vincennes* attempted to contact the inbound aircraft over and over, but there was no response. And when it continued in-bound and crossed into the danger area of missile launch, Rogers decided he had no choice but to protect his ship. He ordered weapons systems to fire. A few minutes later the aircraft, an

Iranian A-300 Airbus filled with 290 civilian passengers and crew, plunged into the waters of the Persian Gulf.

The Iranians held America—who they considered "The Great Satan" —responsible. And in their Islamic law, it was dictated what such an event had to be answered with "an eye for an eye."

Abulhassan Bani Sadr, who served as president of Iran from 1979 to 1981, remarked "It was a crime. The people of Iran saw this as a crime...shooting down an airplane, killing almost 300 people is a crime. The people of Iran have never forgotten. Had it involved any other country, there would have been legal proceedings. A lot of fuss would have been made all around the world. But here they destroyed the aircraft, and then congratulated themselves. They even gave a medal to the officer who fired the missile at the plane."

Pan Am 103 investigator Juval Aviv noted "After the downing of the Iranian aircraft by the *Vincennes*, everybody expected revenge. The Iranians had to, religiously, avenge what had happened. It was clear that they would teach the Americans a lesson that they can duplicate what the Americans had done to them. It was only a question of time where an American airplane would be downed in retaliation."

Aviv casts even more light onto an Iranian/Pan Am 103 connection by way of what covert intelligence agents call a "cut-out," or middle man. "Iran would never do it directly," said Aviv during an interview with the investigators for the documentary *The Maltese Doublecross*, "they would pay $10 million to a terrorist network that knew how to go about it and the contract was out. It was known at the time that the contract was out to down an American airliner."

The contract—known as a *Fatwa*—was issued to a group of the Syrian-based Popular Front for the Liberation of Palestine—General Command (PFLP-GC). The leader of this cell, one Ahmed Jibril, was a Syrian-backed terrorist who ran in the highest circles of Islamic terrorism. To him, it would serve three purposes. First, it would earn the PFLP-GC quite a sum of operational money. Second, it would be a major attack against the hated Americans. Finally, it would give him a great deal of stature in the terrorist underworld.

For this mission, Jibril established a special action cell in Neuss, Germany, near Frankfort. In this cell he provided everything his men would need to accomplish the mission, including one Marwan Abdel

Razzack Khreesat, bombmaker extraordinaire. Khreesat's specialty, besides building small, but very powerful, bombs, was modifying and incorporating very sophisticated timing mechanisms. Some of his accomplishments included timers connected to altitude detonators. Such systems would allow an aircraft to become airborne, fly a given distance over time, then the bomb would arm and only detonate when the airplane reached a certain pre-selected altitude. Such a mechanism would work in a scenario such as the bomb being loaded onto the airplane in Frankfort, then not arming until the Jumbo Jet had made a stop at Heathrow, then resumed travel to the United States. The bomb would not arm until a given time, then would not detonate until the aircraft reached a given altitude. This would allow for the stop in London, then the resumption in travel. It would also explain why the bomb did not detonate over the Atlantic. The plane was delayed two hours at Heathrow.

All did not go well for the terrorists, however. They were detected in September of 1988 by the German BKA, or *Bundeskriminalamt*—the West German criminal police—during an operation called Operation Autumn Leaves.[192] A few weeks later, in October, seventeen people were arrested, including Khreesat. The Germans found massive amounts of weaponry, explosives, and timing devices. They also found a Toshiba radio/tape player with a plastic explosives bomb inside which "was designed to blow up an aircraft."[193]

Khreesat was taken in by the BKA and held for terrorist activities. They had more on him than most of the others, for they had intercepted an international call made by Khreesat to Damascus, Syria, in which he stated: "I have made some changes to the medicine. It is better and stronger."

But Khreesat evidently had connections in high places. He demanded to make one phone call from BKA headquarters, and then refused to answer any questions afterwards. Within a couple of hours he was mysteriously released and immediately flew to Damascus.

Former CIA agent Oswald Le Winter, who helped expose the inner workings of the affair to the media, gives us a clue concerning Khreesat's connections. "I had spoken to a German reporter who refuses to go on camera, but who is very close to federal intelligence sources in Germany, who assured me that Khreesat was an agent of the

Jordanian service, and an asset of the Central Intelligence Agency." Le Winter also discovered that "pressure had come from Bonn...from the U.S. Embassy in Bonn...to release Khreesat."

The U.S. Embassy? Why would our government be interested in releasing a known terrorist bomb maker? During the course of his investigation, Juval Aviv discovered the fact that Khreesat not only served Jibril, but other terrorist networks as well. According to Aviv, "he [Khreesat] was also reporting his activities for years to Israel, Jordan, and some other countries intelligence departments." This may have included the CIA, and assuredly included the Israeli Mossad, who had infiltrators inside the PLO for years. The Israeli effort was so successful that it has been rumored that Abu Nidal himself is on the Israeli payroll, which is why he has never been picked up or assassinated by an Israeli Kidon hit team.[194]

In April, 1989, four months after the destruction of Pan Am 103, the BND raided an apartment in Neuss. Inside, they discovered three other Khreesat-manufactured bombs concealed in electronic devices. The Germans knew there was a fourth bomb, but it was not found. There were rumors of a fifth. And these bombs were so sophisticated that the top German bomb technician was killed trying to disarm one.

Amazingly, the German government would never request the extradition of Khreesat, and the Scottish police would never be permitted to talk to him. On top of this, the FBI interviewed Khreesat on November 12th and 13th, 1989, and never revealed the details of these interviews to the Scottish police. Later, an investigative journalist managed to interview Khreesat, who told him that he was a secret agent, had been sent to Germany on a mission, and had built airplane bombs for Jibril.

It appears that the U.S. government, or at least certain persons in the intelligence "community," knew in advance of the device and did nothing to stop it. In fact, as the story continues, certain American agents appear to have assisted the bombers. Another clue that the intelligence community knew what was going to happen are the facts that certain high ranking individuals from various governments were pulled from the plane. One example was a South African delegation which included South African president Peter Botha. The Botha party changed its flight booking at the last hour due to a warning from South

African state security forces, who are closely aligned with two major intelligence sources, the Israeli Mossad, and the CIA.

Others also changed their mind about flying on Pan Am 103. According to one Pan Am security officer, "It subsequently came to me on further enquiries that they hadn't ignored [the warnings]. A number of VIPs were pulled off that plane. A number of intelligence operatives were pulled off that plane."

But these events have been successfully swept under the carpet in the official American government (FBI) version of events. According to the FBI, here is what happened: Libyan "strongman" Moammar Khadaffi, incensed over being bombed on the April 14, 1986 air raid on Tripoli airport, Bab al Azzizia barracks, Sidi Bilal naval base, Benghazi city, and Benine airfield, sent two of his intelligence officers to Malta to build a suitcase bomb. They then tagged the suitcase for JFK International airport in New York City, put the bomb aboard an Air Malta flight, then sat back to wait for the bomb to make its way through three countries—and their security measures—changing planes twice (Frankfort and London), to explode after the Pan Am jet left Heathrow and flew three hours over the Atlantic.[195]

To back up the findings of this "investigation," the U.S. government relied on its pre-programmed view of Khadaffi being a crazy out-of-control terrorist-supporting killer. CIA veteran Vincent Cannistraro developed a "Libya" policy that fit the National Security Council's desire to hold Khadaffi responsible for the majority of terrorist activities. Cannistraro is quoted in *The Maltese Double Cross*, "I developed the policy toward Libya. In fact, I even wrote the draft paper that was later adopted by the President."

Howard Teicher, the senior director of the NSC between 1985 and 1987, stated, "Mr. Cannistraro and myself were the coordinators of Libya policy within the NSC, and did have a direct role in coordinating the papers written by State, with input from the CIA, Department of Defense, and *other agencies that all had a role*." Were any of the "other agencies" perhaps the FBI?

Iran/Contra affair figure Lt. Col. Oliver North, working for the Reagan administration's NSC, paired up with Cannistraro in a program meant to destroy the Khadaffi regime. Coincidentally, Cannistraro later headed up the CIA's investigation into the bombing at Lockerbie.

Cannistraro later recounted "The principle avenues that led to identification of a foreign role in an act of terrorism was forensic evidence recovered by the Scottish police...one of those bits of debris turned out to be a microchip, which was analyzed microscopically that led to the Libyan connection."

It has never been satisfactorily explained how this "bit of microchip" led to Libya, verses Syria, or Iran, or Iraq or East Germany. And considering that this vital piece of evidence allegedly found away from the main crash site, in a densely wooded area, could have easily been planted—or shown up in the evidence chain later and simply tagged "found at such-and-such location," it makes this one piece of evidence very suspect. Especially considering the fact that no one seems to know exactly who found it, and at least one Scottish searcher was approached later to sign a statement that he was the finder, even though he wasn't.

Also, we find that dealing with Libya as a terrorist state was much more expeditious and less dangerous than dealing with other, far more dangerous, countries. Howard Teicher mentioned that "Vince was quite aware of what was going on in Syria, and of the Iranian dimension and the Iraqi dimension of their role in state-sponsored terrorism. What emerged in U.S. policy was the tendency to be able to most directly deal with Libya because of Libya's geographic proximity to Europe and the United states, as opposed to Iraq, Iran and Syria. It was much more difficult to deal with other countries."

It was also much more difficult to deal especially with Syria, the host country of the PFLP-GC headquartered in the Bekaa Valley, in the days leading up to the Gulf War. Syria was needed to help oust Saddam Hussein from Kuwait, and to blame Syria for involvement in the bombing would be a political disaster for the Bush administration.

But the Bush administration *did* know who did the actual bombing. Bush's Secretary of State James Baker visited Syria in 1989, six months after the Lockerbie disaster, and met with the Syrian foreign intelligence minister. At that meeting, Baker was reported to have asked:

"What are you doing about the GLC group?"
"What are you talking about," asked the intelligence minister.

"Jibril," answered Baker. "We know they are responsible for Lockerbie. What are you doing about them?"
"How do you know that?"
"We have the evidence," answered Baker. "And the evidence is irrefutable."

Despite the fact that the U.S. government knew who was behind the bombing, official Washington put on a different face. Marlin Fitzwater, Whitehouse spokesman, announced to the press "...that the investigation has come to this [Libyan] conclusion is not a surprise. We are now actively considering what actions to take." Then the U.S. Attorney General, Robert Mueller, told the American public that "We have no evidence to implicate another country [other than Libya] in this disaster."

The British joined in the coverup with Douglas Hurd, British Foreign Secretary, releasing the news that "I understand the investigation has revealed no evidence to support suggestions of involvement of other countries." Lord Fraser, Lord Advocate of Scotland and head of the enquiry on Lockerbie, clinched the case when he stated that "the two accused are Abdel Basset Ali Muhammed Al-Megrahi, and Lamin Khalifah Fhimah."

With the exception of physically apprehending the villains, the case appeared to be closed. But was it?

It seems there was more to the case than a simple terrorist attack. What was not exposed to the press or the public at the time were the international drug smuggling and the American hostage connections.

In the Bekaa Valley, terrorist groups rub shoulders with heroin drug gangs. Often they are one in the same. According to Steve Donahue, an ex-US Drug Enforcement Administration undercover agent, "The heroin laboratories themselves were located in the Bekaa Valley. The major one is run by Jamil Hamiya who was the target of our investigation. [Jamil's activities were] a method for financing, at the first level, internal military activities within Lebanon. And at the second level, financing terrorist activities abroad."[196]

To this, FBI agent Oliver "Buck" Revell, who supervised the FBI investigation into the Lockerbie case, adds "Lebanon is a conduit for a great deal of drugs, and the organizations that are moving it through are at least supporting the movement, [and] are violent political organizations such as Hizbollah, the Iranian Revolutionary Guards, and now Hamas. They are directly connected with much of the drug trafficking through the area."[197]

In the Bekaa Valley, the Jafaar family sent one of their relatives, a boy named Khalid Jafaar, to Frankfort to stay with "friends," who would find him work in the United States then put him on a plane for America. What they did not know was that Khalid had been selected to perform a mission for the PFLP-GC. One of the members of the Jafaar family explained "Hourani family tell him 'we send you to Germany. From Germany you can go to America.' They give him this address. In Germany he stay with some friend. And what he [the friend] fix in his bag is the tape recorder. Hizbollah is behind Khalid [killing], what he done to him."

The family may or may not have known that Khalid was also taking a suitcase filled with heroin to the U.S., through a system that they thought was safe, but which in actuality was part of a DEA "controlled buy" network. Lester Coleman, U.S. Defense Intelligence Agency agent who was detailed to work with the DEA and CIA in the Lebanese-U.S. drug war, explained that "They could not eradicate the drugs in Lebanon, so they could only do two things: [one], monitor what was being produced and how it was being shipped out, and two; use DEA informants from Lebanon in drug sting operations back in the United States to set up drug buys and catch drug buyers in the U.S. That was a big part of what they were doing...It was arranged by the DIA for me to go over to work for the DEA in this Narcotics Operations Group, headed by Michael T. Hurley, the country attache. And my main responsibility was to gather intelligence in Lebanon relating to opium production and trafficking and that kind of thing."

The operation was simple. Paid DEA informants would notify the DEA teams when a suitcase shipment would leave Lebanon, the routing, and the description of the courier. The DEA would in turn make sure the courier and heroin would, by means of paid double agents and "in the know" customs agents who worked at the various airports and airlines baggage facilities, travel unmolested between destinations. After the drugs reached the U.S. they were tracked to the recipient, who was at the top of the distribution chain in this country.

Juval Aviv explained that "At least once or twice a week a courier would carry a brown Samsonite suitcase full of drugs from Cypress to Frankfort, where an arrangement in Frankfort with a baggage handler would switch the suitcase with a similar suitcase full of clothing. The suitcase would then go through the security system...then be switched by one of the Pan Am employees...back to the one with drugs. Then it would go on board the airplane, would arrive at Kennedy, and would be picked up. It would then be sold on the local market."[198]

During this time frame another political crisis was underway. Six Americans had been taken hostage in Beirut and were being held in the terrorist underground. The Reagan administration became obsessed with gaining the release of these prisoners, whether by bribery or by force. Besides attempting to gain their release by means of bribery through the Iranians, who supported and exerted a great deal of influence on Hizbollah, other plans were made as well.[199] One of these plans incorporated a military hostage rescue by a team of Delta Force personnel under a Major Charles D. "Chuck" McKee.

But as it turned out, Major McKee was extremely anti-drug. When he discovered that he would be working hand-in-glove with drug smugglers in the hostage rescue efforts, he refused to go through with the mission. Instead, he took his team out of Beirut to Cypress, where he had his commo man notify Washington that he would be returning to the States with his team—complete with all travel details—and would tell them what was going on when he got there. In other words, he was going to blow open the Mid-East international drug smuggling aspect of U.S. government operations in the Iran/Contra affair.

According to *The Maltese Double Cross*, "The DEA was watching McKee, separately telexing McKee's final travel arrangements to the CIA's Director of Operations in Washington, MI-6 (the British Secret Service), and SPAG (The CIA's Special Action Group) in Germany with overall control of the drugs-for-intelligence operation. Every spook in Europe knew that McKee was flying back on December 21st."

Traveling with McKee on his leg from Frankfort to London, then on to JFK, was Matthew Kevin Gannon, the CIA deputy station chief for Beirut, who was also evidently going to back up McKee's claims. According to a taped telephone conversation between ex-CIA agent Oswald Le Winter and a former colleague, taped after Le Winter left the CIA, the bomb went on board the "Maid of the Seas" in Frankfort—assisted by CIA operatives:

Le Winter: "Are you there?"
Confidential Contact: "Yeah."
LW: "How are ya?"
CC: "Pretty good. Where you calling from?"
LW: "I'm in Wiesbaden. I just got in to Frankfurt, from the airport. Just thought I'd chill out here for the night."
CC: "Are you alone?"
LW: "Of course I'm alone. You don't think I'd be asking you questions with someone around?"
CC: "Hold on. [tone in background of recording device] Hello?"
LW: "Now tell me where you were."
CC: "[tone] Okay.
LW: "What's that?"
CC: "I just turned it off. It was being taped. What the f__k do you want to know this for? You mean the Special Action Group in Wiesbaden?"
LW: "Yeah, yeah. I mean, you're retired from there now, but your still doing, what?, consulting work, right?"
CC: "Sure."
LW: "Alright, now look. Does the name Khalid Jafaar mean anything to you?"
CC: "Yeah."
LW: "Who is that?"
CC: "He's a local guy, man, you know who he is."
LW: "What do you mean 'local guy?"
CC: "Come on."
LW: "Who does he have to do with?"
CC: "He's the Lockerbie man."[200]
LW: "Okay. Now, when he came to Germany in '88, who met him? Who met him at the plane? Naw, when he was taken back to get on the plane to leave the country, who took him through security?"

CC: "Oh, we did. Some of my men took him out. We took
    him on the plane and turned him over to Gannon."
LW: "You mean Gannon was his keeper on the plane?"
CC: "That's right."
LW: "No s__t!"
CC: "That's right. First class. That big mother____r
    sitting right up there."[201]

Upgrading to First Class after changing planes to Pan Am 103 at
Heathrow was Major Chuck McKee. Linda Forsyth, Pan Am ground
hostess at Heathrow remembered McKee "...because he asked me for
an upgrade. He had a certificate for a program we were running at that
time, and I moved his class. He was pleased, which struck up a
rappoire over that short period of time. Then later another gentleman
came in, which I found out was Mr. Gannon."[202]

    At 7:02 p.m., on Wednesday, December 21st, 1988, Pan Am
103—the Clipper *Maid of the Seas*—had reached 31,000 feet on a
northwesterly course across Britain. One minute later, over the Scottish
village of Lockerbie, almost to the coastline, a bomb exploded aboard
the 747. The combination of airspeed, depressurization, and failure of
structural integrity caused the Jumbo Jet to virtually shred itself to
pieces as it plummeted to the ground.

We have already seen that after the tragedy many curious things
happened on the ground during the search of the crash scene and
identification of bodies and luggage by the authorities. But one oddity
that bears mentioning at this point is a very odd detail that most
historians have failed to examine.

    Dr. Fieldhouse, who was searching an area near the church,
mentioned that "I identified several bodies, amongst those were
McKee...*I knew that McKee was absolutely correct because of the
clothing which correlated closely with the other reports and statements,
and the computers that were linked up to Washington.*"[203]

    How did the computers in Washington know exactly what McKee
wore as he boarded the fateful flight? The only way was for it to be
reported by someone on a special surveillance mission whose job was
to do just that. But why?

Also of note is a paragraph concerning the victims in the Interfor, Inc. report [Juval Aviv, working for Pan Am] which states "At least five passengers were CIA: Beirut Dep. Station Chief Matthew Gannon, agents Ronald Lariviere, Daniel O'Connor and Bill Leyrer, and U.S. Army major Charles McKee, assigned temporarily to CIA. They had flown in from Cyprus to connect with Flight #103. Four U.S. Air Force scientists with secret documents were reportedly on the flight. CIA agents quickly arrived at the crash site and acted very strangely and nervously in securing the CIA passengers' luggage."

Investigative journalist David Ben-Aryeah also mentioned the unusual events that occurred around certain bodies: "There were a number of bodies which subsequently became of great interest to a lot of people. Charles McKee, a very brave man, an expert on counter-terrorism, was found just off on the ridge...Matthew Gannon, an intelligence officer...Captain Curry, Special Forces, who according to his memorial was killed in the line of duty. We've never found out what that line of duty was. There were some very strange people whose backgrounds have never really been clarified."

One thing was for sure. Neither Special Forces Major Charles "Chuck" Mckee and his team, nor CIA station chief Matthew Gannon ever had a chance to tell "Washington" what concerned them.

The destruction of Pan Am 103 that icy December night appears to have accomplished three major objectives: The Iranians got revenge for the shootdown of the A300 Airbus; the international drug smuggling and arms-for-drugs network remained intact; and the Libyans received the blame.

And the coverup continues.

Chapter 28

Gander: The Crash of Arrow Air 950JW

By 6:15 a.m., on December 12, 1985, it was still pitch dark in Gander, Newfoundland. The winter months in this near-arctic area cause the days to be short and the nights long. For some on this morning, there would never again be another dawn.

At that moment, two Canadian truck drivers, Cecil Mackie and Leonard Loughren, were pushing their big rigs along the Trans-Canadian Highway near the Gander airport when they noted something very odd happening in the dark night sky. Cecil Mackie recalled later that he watched as a large plane flew low overhead, apparently taking off from the Gander runway only 1,000 feet away, and: "...there was a flame on the bottom" of the aircraft, which was so bright that it illuminated the inside of his cab. Mackie, giving a witness report to Canadian authorities, explained that he was positive he saw flames, not just landing lights.

Leonard Loughren saw the airplane at a different angle at approximately the same time. He reported to Doreen Harty of the Royal Canadian Mounted Police that "I think the right side of the aircraft was afire. It was pitch-dark and I could see the tail and parts of the plane from the glow."

A car rental agent named Judith Parsons watched from the parking lot at the airport as the airplane, a four-engine DC-8 belonging to a little-known American firm named Arrow Air, lifted from the runway then disappear into the night as it began its climb. A few seconds later she saw a flash, followed by "a large orange oval object" moving

298

through the sky. It then "blew up, it just went into a million pieces...It was definitely not on the ground." A few seconds later she witnessed a huge fireball erupt in the distance—on the ground.[204]

What these people had witnessed would become one of the greatest aviation disasters of the decade—and one of the least investigated. Even more than Pan Am 103, which occurred almost exactly three years later, the tragic end of Arrow Air 950JW would be swept under the political carpet and buried in layered bureaucracies. The fact that the investigation was a coverup is uncontestable, for the "reason" of the crash that eventually was released to the public was that the airplane failed to go through de-icing procedures, took off with too much ice on the wings, and crashed because it was overweight and entered a fatal stall. Case closed. The problem is that the witnesses and evidence indicate otherwise. But what really caused the airplane to catch fire in midair, and why a coverup?

To understand the series of events that led up to the destruction of the Arrow Air DC-8, one must understand the international political environment of the time. America had lost its main political ally in the Persian Gulf, the Shah of Iran, and had gained a new fanatic enemy in the person of Ayatollah Khomeini. Israel and Egypt were on the verge of war, and American citizens had been taken hostage in Lebanon by an extremist terrorist organization known as the Islamic Jihad (whose sub-organization is the Iranian-backed Hizbollah, or "Party of God").

In an attempt to contain events in the middle east and Persian Gulf, then-president Ronald Reagan dispatched both military and CIA personnel to the region. Marines and CIA officers went to Beirut, where a show of force was supposed to intimidate the Bekaa Valley-based Hizbollah and Islamic Jihad, while a force of soldiers from the 101st Airborne Division, based in Fort Campbell, Kentucky, was dispatched to the Sinai Desert to participate in what had been designated "Multinational Force and Observers" (MFO). The mission of the MFO was to support U.N. activities in the Egyptian Sinai in a buffer zone between the Egyptians and the Israelis. Their job was to conduct reconnaissance patrols, man observation posts along the international boundary, and set up checkpoints for border crossings.

Though the mission was to have been peaceful, the 101st found itself targets on several occasions for hostile activities of the Shiite

Moslem Islamic Jihad. Meanwhile, the Marines in Beirut fared even worse at the hands of this same group when they became victims of a truck bomb at their airport barracks at Beirut International Airport. In that attack, an Islamic Jihad fanatic drove a flat-bed Mercedes truck stacked with 12,000 pounds of high explosive, surrounded by cylinders of compressed butane gas, into the front door of the building. The huge explosion caused the entire structure to collapsed, killing 241 Marines. This attack followed an earlier attack by the same group that set off a truck bomb at the U.S. Embassy in Beirut, killing 17 Americans and 40 other nationals. Islamic Jihad also claimed responsibility for the June 14, 1985 hijacking of a TWA jetliner enroute from Athens to Rome; kidnapping 57-year-old William Buckley, the CIA station chief in Lebanon, and twelve other hostages; and numerous other terrorist attacks.

As these attacks continued, the Islamic Jihad announced that there would be more in retaliation for Israeli incursions into southern Lebanon and American interference in the Middle East—not to mention military and financial support for Israel. In one communication an anonymous caller boasted that these attacks would no longer occur only in the Middle East, but would "be aimed at every Zionist, American or reactionary establishment in various parts of the world." He followed this with the threat that future operations would be "immediate, surprising and lightning."[205]

It was under this cloud of international terrorist threats that the 101st Airborne troopers of MFO in the Sinai were withdrawn from peacekeeping duty. For them it was none too soon. They would be exchanging a foreign desert for the hearths of home in Fort Campbell—just in time for Christmas.

But moving a large number of troops out of an operational area consists of more than simply boarding airplanes at the airport—especially when they are scattered throughout an operational area among remote outposts. There was the question of equipment, personal baggage, staging troops and gear, and ground movement to the airlift point. In the case of the Sinai troops, the air transport out of the desert was limited to a couple of small Egyptair 737s, which could not hold the troops with their luggage and the piles of unit equipment. Because of this the gear and baggage traveled by truck from their base camp at Sharm El Sheik to Cairo, where it caught up with the troops the next day. It was then loaded aboard a waiting civilian air contract carrier—a DC-8 owned by Arrow Air of Miami, Florida—for the long flight home.[206]

It was during this stage of the movement that unusual things were noted. Though customs officers from both Egypt and the U.S. searched all baggage and equipment containers at Sharm El Sheik, then sealed the containers on the trucks, the trucks left a full day early and spent the night at the airport at Cairo with only two American soldiers as guards. Then at 4:00 p.m. on December 11th, the truck drivers took over the guard detail so that the soldiers could prepare to depart.

At about 8:00 p.m. that evening, American officers broke the seals on the trucks and gave the order to load the baggage compartments. The loading was conducted not by American soldiers, but by a local Egyptian company contracted as baggage handlers at the airport. It was during this time that the Arrow Air pilot, Captain Arthur Schoppaul, noted something odd. The Egyptian guard, who was supposed to guard the baggage and aircraft, disappeared from his post several times, sometimes for as long as an hour. Then, during one of these absences, Schoppaul witnessed a fist fight break out near a baggage hold between some of the "Egyptian" loaders. This was highly unusual as Arabs almost never touched each other, and to most investigators it appeared to be a diversion. Then there was a period of time when the electricity was cut to the ramp and the lights went out, leaving the area in total darkness.

The next unusual thing that occurred happened after the cargo holds had been loaded. Still sitting on the ramp were the duffel bags of 41 soldiers, personal gear that would not have been left behind under any normal circumstance. But on this flight the bags had been "bumped," because there was other cargo that joined the battalion's gear in the Sinai base camp and took precedent in Cairo—several large wooden crates the size of coffins. These mysterious boxes must have taken priority, for the battalion commander, Lieutenant Colonel Marvin Jeffcoat, ordered the already loaded duffel bags removed to make room for what he described as "very important military material." Also odd is the fact that one of the twenty "mystery boxes" had not been transported to the airport by truck with the other gear, but had flown to Cairo in the hold of one of the 737s that brought the troops out of the desert. No one knows exactly where this box was kept after the

301

737s were offloaded and the rest of the gear was still being transported by truck from the Sinai.

Even more mysterious is the fact that numerous investigators have attempted to discover the contents of the mystery boxes, but no records or manifest exists in army records that even mention their existence.

After departing Cairo, the Arrow Air flight arrived at Cologne, Germany, for refueling at 1:21 a.m. It was on the ground for almost two hours while the troops changed uniforms (and the baggage holds were opened and left unguarded). At 3:20 a.m. it took off for the long leg across the Atlantic to Gander, the next refueling stop.

The weather in Gander was typical for December. It was overcast, and precipitation consisting of spitting snow and freezing rain cut the visibility to minimums. The airplane landed without incident, refueled and taxied for the runway at 5:40 a.m. Gander time. Five minutes later it was rotating for takeoff. Sixty seconds later witnesses watched in horror as the big airplane dove, on fire, into the woods near the shore of Gander Lake.

David Owen, a former Canadian bush pilot-turned-senior-investigator for the Canadian Air Safety Board, along with Department of Transport pilot George Dewar, arrived in Gander four hours after the crash. But before landing, they located the site and circled it to check the impact pattern and extent of ground damage from the air. What struck Dewar was that they could not identify an airplane crash as such—only a field of burning debris. Owen's participation in the investigation was short-lived, but before he was replaced by investigators from headquarters, he managed to send out the first official memo on what would become Canada's worst aviation disaster:

"JW950 [sic] crashed shortly after departure. No apparent survivors. Aircraft departed Rwy 22. Disappeared below the line between TCH and Gander Lake. Aircraft exploded on contact near the edge of Gander Lake."

It was short and to the point. But it failed to take into account the observations of the witnesses concerning an airborne fire prior to the crash. That would come later, but would still not figure in the final "official" versions of the reports regarding the crash released by both Canada and the U.S.

By 3:00 p.m., A U.S. Army major general named John Crosby arrived with a contingent of military personnel to "assist" the RCMP and the CASB in their efforts. Shortly after his arrival several members of the NTSB and FBI arrived. But before they could entrench themselves in the investigation they were advised by Canadian authorities that they had no jurisdiction there, and that the investigation would be accomplished by Canadian officials. Though agitated, the U.S. officials agreed to bide by the Canadian findings as they awaited the outcome from hotel rooms in Gander. Even though Americans were the victims, and the airplane was of American registry, the FBI remained strangely content to await the outcome of the Canadian investigation without more than token protest.

One caveat did occur regarding the bodies. Any blood and serum toxicology tests conducted had to be performed in Canada and the results sent back to the U.S. The American government agreed to this and awaited transport of the bodies to Dover Air Force Base, New Jersey.

What happened next would be a matter of contention for years. General Crosby ordered the immediate bulldozing of the crash site! No effort was made to reassemble the wreckage, which is standard procedure, nor preserve the site for future, more detailed investigation. Instead, the "crime scene" was destroyed as soon as American officials gained possession of it. Crosby was in touch with Canadian officials in Gander regarding the cleanup of the crash site, and according to witnesses, insisted that "a representative of the Army be present at all times."

Instead of a detailed investigation of the wreckage, conducted by attempting to reassemble the myriad bits and pieces of airplane to determine if there was a mechanical malfunction or sabotage, which is standard operating procedure, the evidence was covered up with little more than a hasty look-see by officials. The only hard evidence examined were the bodies.

Colonel Robert McMeekin, director of the Armed Forces Institute of Pathology, received notification of the crash at 6:30 a.m. on December 12th. He immediately began packing and by 3:30 p.m. that afternoon arrived at Gander airport. The RCMP, under a Memorandum of Understanding between the two governments, permitted Col. McMeekin access to the crash site for purposes of recovering the

303

bodies of the victims for shipment to Dover for identification. It was at Dover that the bodies would be examined, their fluids drawn for toxicology, x-rays would be taken, and identification made.

During the Dover examinations, x-rays revealed that none of the bodies appeared to have any internal indication of pre-impact damage due to explosion, and that all had died as a result of "plane crash." The problem with this finding is that it is a blanket ruling that is not acceptable in a court of law. The cause of death is always determined on an individual basis, such as "broken neck," "fractured cranium," "myocardial infarction," etc. In this case, no individual autopsy "cause of death" was recorded for each victim.

Then more problems arose when the toxicology reports came back from Canada. Dr. David Elcombe, director of the Canadian Aviation Safety Board, released the findings that conflicted with the American ruling. According to the Canadian tests on the blood of the victims each had high levels of carbon monoxide poisoning. Only by breathing smoke for an extended period, from two to five minutes, could such levels be reached. This indicates that the plane, which went down in less than one minute, and burned for hours, obviously held live victims inside that were still alive until they asphyxiated or burned to death. Another observation proves that the fire actually started in flight, filling the cabin with smoke, *before* the plane impacted with the ground. Many of the victims bodies which held high levels of carbon monoxide had been found *decapitated*! This trauma could only have occurred upon impact, not in the air. Therefore, they had ingested the gas prior to impact, revealing the plane was on fire when it went down. So much for the "icing" theory.

On June 20th, 1986, Dr. Elcombe sent a memo to Dr. McMeekin stating: "Some of the carbon monoxide and hydrogen cyanide values are striking...and I look forward to meeting with you...to consider their significance." The outcome of such a meeting, if one was indeed held, has not been reported.

There had to be something else that worried the military and the government besides an on-board fire as the cause. Simply trying to hide the fact that something went wrong while the plane was airborne would not justify such extreme measures in covering up the cause of the crash as burying the wreckage without detailed investigation, or trying to hide the cause of death of the 248 servicemen and women. The answer has to lie in the mission of the 3rd Battalion, 101st Airborne—and their mysterious boxes and "add-on" personnel.

It has been speculated by various investigators that the boxes loaded in the hold contained items ranging from HAWK missile system parts rejected by the Iranians during the Oliver North/Bill Casey Iran/Contra dealings, to dead members of a failed hostage rescue attempt by Delta Force. What is known is that twenty members of the elite Task Force 160 were also on board the flight. TF-160, based in Fort Campbell, is the Army's special operations aviation battalion tasked with support of not only Special Forces, but Delta Force and CIA. Dubbed "The Night Stalkers," TF-160 has a huge budget that permits them to have virtually any piece of equipment they want. Items ranging from night vision equipment to exotic weapons to just about every helicopter in military inventory are at the beck and call of the group. Hauling paratroopers around the desert during U.N. operations are not what TF-160 would be deployed to accomplish. Their missions are much more serious, more specialized, more secret.

Paired up with Delta Force, TF-160 would be the air support unit that would participate in any hostage rescue attempt. For this mission they would not only ship their helicopters and support equipment across the Atlantic in C-5A Galaxy aircraft, but would box up and take any specialized equipment—especially that which would give away the mission or current technology—in sealed containers that would stay with the personnel as they went through their movement stage. This would include weapons and explosives. Could it be that TF-160 and Delta Force were using the 101st base camp as a jumping off point for commando operations in the vicinity? Or possibly simply linking up with them for the return home after their secret mission was accomplished or aborted?

Lt. Col. Oliver North had been negotiating with the Iranians for several months regarding their "assistance" in convincing the Jihad terrorists to release hostages in Lebanon. Most of this "negotiating" revolved around arms shipments to Iran consisting of TOW anti-tank missiles from the European "Reforger" stocks and HAWK anti-aircraft missiles. But when the HAWKs arrived, the Iranian technicians determined that they were an outdated model, not dependable, and not up to engaging some of the latest generation of Russian jets supplied to the Iraqis. The Iranians were extremely upset, feeling that North and his Israeli contacts had betrayed them and tried to cheat them. North had to agree to take the missiles back and replace them with newer, updated models. It is not known outside of the most inner circles where the old HAWKs and their spare parts went. Could they have been what were in the boxes?

The Iranians, however, felt they had to teach the Americans a lesson. According to the Islamic law, something had to be done in revenge that was much greater than the original "crime." North knew this, and when told that the Islamic Jihad might condemn some or all of the hostages to death, remarked that the deaths of the hostages would be our "minimum losses."

Realizing this, did North plan a covert hostage rescue attempt? If so, is it possible that he knew exactly where the hostages were located? Or was he relying on the CIA/Bekaa Valley heroine connections to provide unreliable intelligence?

If a hostage rescue attempt had indeed occurred, but failed, did the boxes contain the remains of those killed during the attempt? Would these make up the "maximum losses"? If this was the scenario, then an Islamic Jihad retribution for the rescue attempt, committed on our withdrawing troops by planting a Marwin Khreesat-type bomb in the 101st's baggage, might have been the answer. It must be remembered that the Pan Am 103 bomb managed to be put on the aircraft in Frankfort, take off, fly to Heathrow, land, change planes, then take off to become armed at a given time, past a given altitude as the airplane climbed for the skies over the Atlantic. A similar device would have accomplished the same mission on Arrow Air—without having to change planes. A simple timer permitting a pre-set number of hours of flight time would have done the trick.

Had the Arrow Air flight been on time, the airplane would have caught fire or exploded on its approach to Fort Campbell, sending a terrible message to the "infidels" of America.

Whatever the actual reason Arrow Air 950JW flamed out of the sky at Gander, Newfoundland, on that cold December morning, the official version is a lie.

Chapter 29

Fire On The Water: TWA 800

A controller working Departure Control at John F. Kennedy International Airport saw it first: something on the radar screen that shouldn't be there. Near the "target" blip of a TWA 747 that had just taken off from JFK a few minutes before, which now winged its way over the Atlantic paralleling the coast as it climbed toward its cruising altitude, was another blip. The controller examined the scope, wondering if there was another aircraft in the area that might pose a hazard to the TWA jet since the secondary target was not "squawking" a transponder code, which meant it was not under control of any air control facility, and it seemed to be moving rapidly toward the big transport as the big Boeing joined its designated course for Paris.

Then, before any more analysis could take place in the FAA control room, something happened to the tiny double-bar radar blip that was designated TWA flight 800.

The coastal residents of East Moriches, Long Island, first noticed something in the sky when there was a sound that some later described as "fireworks" over the ocean. Looking up, many noticed that there was a small glowing ball of reddish-orange light high over the ocean. Closer examination showed it to be an airplane. But something was wrong with it.

As they watched, they saw the small glow become engulfed by a huge fireball. Then, what was curiosity at first rapidly became a state of shock for some and horror for others as the airplane seemed to break up into two large flaming "comets" and fall for several horrifying seconds until it hit the surface of the ocean. Many could not believe what they had just witnessed, but the lake of fire that floated on the surface of the sea proved that the nightmare was reality.

Hundreds of witnesses along the shoreline and in boats later reported what they had seen. A fisherman recalled that when he looked up what he saw "...started off like a little ball, like a flare. It came down for a few seconds and all of a sudden burst into flames, a big ball of flame."

An unidentified man said that he "...saw a big fireball with pieces coming off of it. I heard two big explosions, like two big firecrackers going off."

A New York Air National Guard colonel flying a C-130 nearby caught the 747 just after the second explosion. He reported that he witnessed "...two large orange fireballs. They looked like comets, coming straight down into the water."

An unidentified woman interviewed by reporters saw more: "There was a loud explosion, which was followed by a fireball. The plane literally dropped out of the sky...and it hit the ocean, sort of like the space shuttle [Challenger] did, and there were five more explosions."

Vic Fehner, a fisherman, said "it started off like a little ball, like a flare. It came down for a few seconds and all of a sudden burst into flames, a big ball of flame."

Jason Fontana, who was standing at John Scott's Raw Bar in Westhampton Beach, saw "a big fireball with pieces coming off of it. You heard two big explosions, like two big firecrackers going off."

Craig Squires, surfing when the plane blew up: "I looked up and saw a trail of fire, and then it disappeared, and I heard an explosion.

Finally, Eileen Daly, a local resident, summed up what many saw and felt when she said, "My first reaction is fireworks, then 'Oh my God, it's an airplane.'"

Almost immediately boats began racing toward the impact area, which was easily marked by a virtual lake of fire as tons of fuel burned on the surface of the water. Residents raced to their telephones and began dialing police, the fire departments of the various beach towns, ambulances, and the Coast Guard. At the same time radio calls began to fill the air waves requesting assistance in search and rescue operations. Like any accident scene, no one seemed to know exactly what had happened, but everyone began trying to do what they could to notify authorities to lend help.

Among the first of hundreds of rescue craft, airplanes, ships and helicopters to reach the site was a U.S. Coast Guard plane practicing search-and-rescue operations nearby, whose pilot witnessed the horrific crash and immediately circled the area, identifying the wreckage and reporting back to his commanders.

Two other aircraft quickly joined the search: an Air National Guard C-130 that had been conducting a "flare dropping exercise" nearby—and ostensibly was the same C-130 whose crew that witnessed the tragedy—and a U.S. Navy P-3 Orion submarine hunter who reportedly heard the radio traffic regarding the explosion and offered to assist.

Rescue craft began arriving immediately, consisting mainly of boat-owning local residents, fishermen and Coast Guard cutters. According to media reports "six Coast Guard helicopters and cutters" joined the search, and throughout the night other vessels arrived to lend assistance in searching for victims, recovering bodies, and eventually recovering wreckage.

By the next morning, Thursday, July 18, 73 bodies had been pulled out of the water. Unlike KAL-007, where no bodies were recovered, many were found floating in the area—none of which wore a life jacket! Many of the bodies had been badly burned, some beyond recognition.

One private boat that arrived early on the scene found among the debris a yellow TWA life vest, inflated and buckled...but no body. According to Jimmy Vaccaro, who hooked the empty jacket into his boat, "It was inflated and it was buckled. These things don't light and inflate by themselves—you have to pull on it or blow through the tube." The reference to a "light" may be to a strobe light attached to the vest that had been activated. This discovery lended credence to an observation that some of the passengers had time to reach for life jackets before they died—but not enough time to put them on. Evidently one such individual inflated the jacket before trying to pull it on, or the CO_2 cartridge activation lanyard had somehow snagged on something after being pulled from under the seat and inflated before the jacket could be donned.

The Coast Guard said none of the bodies recovered wore life preservers, suggesting that the explosion came without warning and there was no time to pull out life vests before impact.

As fishermen and other local residents helped recover the bodies of the victims, a temporary morgue was set up near the beach near the little town of East Moriches close to the crash site. As this was being accomplished, local officials cautioned residents to report any wreckage or bodies washing ashore in the next day or so, but not to touch anything that may serve as evidence that could explain what made the jumbo jet suddenly disintegrate into the darkness.

Of note regarding the wreckage and flotsam that was being found along the beach was a special notification from federal officials on the 18th that if anyone came upon any boxes on the beach, not to open or tamper with them because there were two boxes of AIDS-infected blood *unaccounted for*. No one in the media seemed to ask the sources why anyone would be shipping AIDS-infected blood anywhere, nor was this event followed up on later. In fact, only a short mention was made in the media when CNN aired the statement of a pool reporter who was aboard a Coast Guard 33-foot rescue boat who said that the boat crew retrieved several State Department pouches and seven packages that were labeled as HIV-infected blood (Biohazard)—plus instructions on how to use the blood to infect children! Though these alleged "instructions" were not displayed on camera, it should be noted that one of the victims on the flight was the son of the president of a French pharmaceutical firm, Merieux, who is one of the leading researchers in AIDS. It is also pertinent to note that this same firm had earlier been accused of desiring to use unwilling human test subjects, including military personnel, as guinea pigs for their vaccine experiments. None of this seemed to trigger questions in the national media regarding the finding of the blood. The crash itself was the story.

Almost immediately a media feeding frenzy ensued concerning the cause of the explosion. The major networks scurried about, madly racing to interview any think tank or terrorism "expert" they could find. As a sample, among the interviews conducted and broadcast nationwide to explain what "probably" happened were:

James Donoghue, editor-in-chief of *Air Transport Magazine*, who said "It's got the hallmarks of a bombing, but it could be all kinds of things. Of the number of 747s that have descended in flames, the vast majority have been because of bombs."

Michael Barr, director of aviation safety programs at USC, spoke against mechanical failure when he stated: "Airplanes don't blow up just like that. I've been following 747s since 1970 and I've never seen one blow up like that."

Robert McGuire, president of Kroll Associates of New York, a highly regarded consulting and security firm, and former NYPD police commissioner—who obviously had not heard the eyewitness statements regarding the "small glow" that preceded the huge fireball—said, "The nature of the incident appears to be traumatic explosion. There were no reports of a burning engine, smoke or the normal stuff that happens to these planes before an accident. Because there was no transmission back to the tower, there seems to have been immediate or overwhelming trauma."

Philip Stern, the managing director of the Fairfax Group, hinting he suspected possible terrorist involvement, mentioned that the original departure point of Athens, where the TWA jet had flown into JFK from, was "troublesome" to him. Athens, according to Stern, has long been known to act as a gateway to the Middle East, and Greece has a history of "radical politicians sympathetic to Middle Eastern causes."

Robert Kupperman, senior advisor to the Center for Strategic and International Studies in Washington and well-known terrorism expert, said that he noted several pieces of evidence that made him believe that this was a likely terrorist bombing. He said the signs indicating a terrorist incident were: All of the eyewitnesses describing a fireball and subsequent explosion; it was a U.S. aircraft enroute to Europe; terrorists in late June attacked a U.S. military facility in Saudi Arabia; and the Summer Olympic Games were starting two days later in Atlanta.

Jack Barker, retired FAA spokesman, said that it was quite likely a bomb, but "You don't want to speculate about what has happened until the NTSB and the FBI have made their investigation, but it certainly is reminiscent of the Lockerbie explosion and in the realm of speculation. The explosion in the air, the fire—there had to be some kind of ignition in the air, and that could be caused by only a very few things. A bomb being on board could be one of them. The other has already been ruled out by the FAA—a collision with another aircraft.

311

Aside from those two things, for anything else to cause an explosion would be very, very rare."

Amazingly, two spokesmen for the TWA 800 disaster were the same "experts" that handled Pan Am 103, Oliver "Buck" Revell (FBI) and Vincent Cannistraro (CIA). Buck Revell told the press that such a jet had never been destroyed in the air by an explosion that was not sabotage, and Vincent Cannistrano said that if it was a bomb "this is another notch up the ladder of terrorism...in the past year domestic aviation security has been tightened considerably." [Because] He said that terrorists have never blown up an airliner with a bomb planted in the U.S.

The government spokesmen were being much more cautious about jumping to conclusions, however. White House spokesman Mike McCurry and others, including President Clinton, refused to comment on whether they felt it was a terrorist event or a catastrophic failure of an aircraft system. Noncommittal, they developed for the media a "wait and see" stance.

But behind the scenes it appeared that other lines of communication between government agencies were being developed and a different message was being sent. There appeared to be drastic discrepancies between what many eye witnesses saw and what the government— especially the FBI—was willing to recognize as a possible cause of the explosion.

Early on many witnesses stated that they saw something that appeared to them to be a flare or a streak of light that seemed to arc up and hit the jumbo jet. Variations of these sightings match what the FAA radar controllers saw on their scope at JFK Departure Control, and what three crewmen on the C-130 witnessed as they flew their "flare dropping exercise."

But the FBI and other federal agencies, up to and including the White House, though not ruling out the "possibility" of a missile attack, consistently attempted to debunk any reference to a surface-to-air missile as a viable cause worth investigation. According to FBI Agent Jim Margolin, when questioned about the three possibilities—a bomb, a mechanical malfunction, or a missile: "Along with a mechanical malfunction, the missile theory rounds out the known universe of potential causes."

Special Agent in Charge (SAC) of the New York office of the FBI James Kallstrom, however, was not quite as dismissing. He appeared to be walking a political tightrope when he told the media that [paraphrased] "Widespread attention being given to the crash may make many eyewitness reports related to the missile theory suspect." He conceded, however, that with similar accounts reported by "numerous citizens" of "events, things in the sky" meant the missile theory could not be discarded.

Then, a mysterious "unnamed Pentagon Spokesman" offered this for mass consumption when the subject of shoulder-launched missiles, such as the Stinger or the Russian SA-7, might be the culprits: "There is no way a Stinger or other hand-held shoulder-fired missile could take down a 747—and *a Stinger does not have the range to hit TWA 800 at the altitude it was at.*" This same spokesman went on to state unequivacably that the plane could not have had a fuel explosion because it was fueled with JP-8. This means the "spokesman" was a Navy man because only the Navy uses JP-8 fuel, and then only on carriers because of its high flash point. Two things immediately discredited this learned source. First, TWA 800 was well within range of a Stinger if it was fired from a boat, and second, the airplane was fueled with Jet A fuel, which is the commercial jet fuel that all civilian jets and commercial airlines use. When this information was brought to the attention of SAC Kallstrom's office by the author no more was heard from this "unnamed Pentagon source."

By Day Three it became evident that there were three powers at work fighting over the bone of contention of TWA 800 and the cause of its demise. First, it became apparent that the National Transportation Safety Board (NTSB) spokesman, Robert Francis, was trying to walk a non-committal line between the FBI, TWA, Pratt & Whitney (the engine builder) and the Boeing Airplane Company. He had by then hunkered down to weather out the storm of controversy by repeatedly announcing that "we are moving slowly forward," and "it's just too early to tell."

The FBI, and the Anti-Terrorism Task Force, however, reminded reporters that though they were not officially taking over the investigation, they were watching for any evidence of a bombing or terrorist involvement. At that time, according to Kallstrom, they would assume the responsibility for the investigation and it would take a new course. Hints over the next week leaned toward nudging the public mind toward acceptance of a probable bomb aboard the airliner— probably in the forward cargo hold or the passenger section just above that location.

TWA, however, did *not* want the outcome to point to a bomb as that would open the company up to lawsuits by relatives of the victims who would blame lax airport security as the major contributing factor.

The Boeing Airplane Company did not want the investigation to point fingers at a design flaw of the airframe or fuel system as they would then become the object of a massive law suit, and Pratt & Whitney did not want the blame placed on a catastrophic engine failure for the same reason.

In all, it appeared that everyone was choosing up sides and going to their corners to await the outcome of the investigation of the wreckage that was being retrieved by the Navy salvage ship, U.S.S. *Grapple.* The odd-man out in all of this, however, was the "missile theory." A shootdown by terrorists at sea, using a surface-to-air missile, would leave TWA, Boeing, and Pratt & Whitney out of any subsequent lawsuit regarding negligence. It would not, however, let the government off the hook.

The idea that someone high in government was becoming very nervous about the possibility of a missile strike became increasingly evident as the investigation continued and witnesses were discovered and interviewed. The FBI located and questioned hundreds of local residents, ostensibly to find out what they might have witnessed that night. But they evidently did not like what they were hearing, for as they found witnesses who reported aerial objects striking the jet, or smoke plumes, or flares, or fireworks, or strange lights in the sky, the agents immediately began intimidating the witnesses by telling them that they could not have seen a missile. They told them that none of them knew what a missile looked like, that what they saw was simply "falling debris" and not something that came *up* from the water. To many of these witnesses, it appeared that the FBI had orders to make the incident a bomb if possible and debunk any missile story—no matter what the evidence or witnesses saw. This falls in line with what the FBI and Justice Department did after the Oklahoma City bombing a year earlier when they dropped the search for John Doe #2 within a few weeks after the event. They then intimidated every witness who reported that they saw JD#2 with McVeigh. These included eye witness sightings at the truck rental agency in Kansas; in the Ryder truck with McVeigh in Oklahoma City when he stopped to ask directions; across the street from the post office a block away from the Murrah Building; and getting out of the truck with McVeigh after parking in front of the building. The FBI then told the press seeing John Doe #2 was just a case of mass hysteria. Would finding John Doe #2 have led the investigation in the politically incorrect direction, as would a missile?

Two witnesses would not be intimidated. A husband and wife, who asked to remain anonymous, wrote a "letter to the editor" to a major city newspaper in California. The letter follows:

Dear Editor,
I witnessed the crash of TWA flight 800.

I work in a county office in California. My wife and I were on vacation in New York. We were on the beach when it happened. We talked to many other witnesses who saw the same thing that we did. A very bright firey light heading upward toward the jet. Then an explosion.

We told what we had seen to some investigators. We told them that we were on our vacation and about to continue on to Florida. They asked us to stay a while longer and said that they would pay our hotel bill until our statements as to what we saw could be taken by other investigators. We agreed.

It turned out however to be more than just our statements taken. They took our social security numbers, drivers licenses and license plate numbers. They wanted to know my place of employment and the names and addresses of our children and relatives. They questioned us in separate rooms and made us feel like criminals. They said that what we must have seen was a shooting star or some fireworks being shot from a boat. I told them that it was definitely a flare type rocket heading toward the aircraft, then it exploded.

It was then suggested that we did not see anything at all and that we were going along with what other people said they saw, just for the excitement of it. I told them "no way, I know what I saw."

After the questioning we were asked to go back to the hotel and stay there until we were cleared to leave. About three hours later two other men we had not seen before came to the hotel. They gave us some money and told us "never to mention anything to anyone about being witnesses to the crash again."

They scared the hell out of us. It was a lot of money and we accepted it out of fear.

If it was a missile that brought down the jet then I could understand that they would not want people to panic. But the way they are handling it is shocking and inexcusable.

My wife and I are outraged and we want people to know how we were treated.

This letter is not signed out of concern for ourselves and our family.

In an article published in the August 25th, 1996 edition of *The Austin American-Statesman*, three paragraphs stood out:

"In addition, the notion that Stinger missiles from Afghanistan might have made their way into the United states was a long-standing assumption within law enforcement circles.

"The presence on the crash scene of officials with the National Security Agency and the Defense Intelligence Agency reinforced in some minds that there might have been some intercepted intelligence regarding a missile attack."

On the same day, the *Times of London* reported: "U.S. officials are investigating reports that Islamic terrorists have smuggled Stinger ground-to-air missiles into the United States from Pakistan.

"Senior Iranian sources close to the fundamentalist regime in Teheran claimed this weekend that the TWA flight 800 was shot down last month by one of these shoulder-fired Stingers of the type used by Islamic guerrillas during the Afghanistan war.

"The sources said the missiles arrived in America seven months ago after being shipped from Karachi via Rotterdam and on to the Canadian port of Halifax. They claimed an Egyptian fundamentalist group backed by Iran was responsible for smuggling the weapons across the Canadian border into the United States.

The article went on to identify the group: the Gama'a al-Islamiya—the same group that attempted to blow up the New York Trade Center under the leadership of Sheik Omar Abdel-Rahman. This same group allegedly notified the White House that they had shot down the plane, and even provided a serial number of the missile used. This last information has not been confirmed as of this writing.

The bottom line is that the vast majority of witness statements support the missile contention; federal agents have been attempting to silence these witnesses; and the fact that Stinger missiles have been smuggled into this country by Islamic fundamentalist terrorist organizations is out of the bag.

In the weeks that followed the crash a great deal of wreckage was recovered by the Navy divers. The shredded aluminum and other bits and pieces, including the first three engines (1,2 &4), were transported to an empty Grumman Aircraft Company hangar in Calverton, where the wreckage was being examined and slowly reassembled. Though most of the damage appeared to come from the center of the aircraft, somewhere around the center fuel tank and behind the forward baggage compartment, virtually no chemical residue of explosives was detected that could be pinned to a bomb. There was some evidence of explosive chemicals on the wreckage, but from various locations that included the wings, wing tips, and rear fuselage area. This would not be indicative of a bomb in the cabin or baggage compartment. It would however, be indicative of something else: a missile hit on a hot engine, which then began to disintegrate and cast burning pieces into the wings and fuselage. Especially since the chemicals that were identified also match those used in military explosives—including the warheads of missiles.

For the divers aboard the *Grapple,* it was tough going. Though the wreckage lay on the ocean floor only 120 feet down, it was scattered for almost three miles in a tadpole-shaped pattern. The water was murky and dark, making it extremely dangerous to navigate through the twisted wreckage. On top of this, the local shark population had sensed the bodies and continued to school in the area as the divers worked.

Eventually the crash site became known as "Mako City" after the most numerous of the shark breeds that infested the area.

The debris fields were mainly divided into two areas of concern: the nose and forward section of the fuselage which broke loose and fell first, and the main fuselage area, wings and tail which appeared to fly for several seconds after the aircraft had been "decapitated."

As the divers worked and the debris began to arrive on shore, the investigators on land busied themselves with assembling the pieces of the puzzle. A joint task force consisting of the FBI Counterterrorisim Task Force, the New York Police Department, and the NTSB appeared to the news watchers to be working like a team. In reality, the word behind the scenes gained through law enforcement and government aviation sources is that there was pressure coming down from Washington for federal agents to cover up what really happened, and if they could not blame a bomb or mechanical malfunction, then to drag the investigation out until the public and media lost interest.

But why? Why would the government not want to have the truth come out if it was a missile? Why not warn the flying public? And could it really have been a missile, and if so what type and where did it come from?

To understand some of the past historical events that may have a bearing on the loss of TWA 800, one must dig back into the a series of events that occurred in the 1980s regarding the "loss" of several hundred shoulder-fired Stinger missiles. During the Afghan/Russian war, the CIA, in support of the Mujihadeen guerrillas, smuggled hundreds of Stingers into Afghanistan to counter the Russian MiGs and Hind helicopter gunships. The missiles were so effective that they are credited as being a major factor in the Russian withdrawal from the country. At the end of the war a few hundred Stingers were left over and were offered back to the U.S. government. But for some mysterious reason, the government did not want them back.

The missiles were eventually taken to Islamabad, Pakistan, and put on the open market. Most were bought by Israeli arms dealers and resold at a profit to the Iranians for use against the Iraqis during the border war. The Iraqi air force seldom flew, however, leaving many missiles in Iranian inventory when the border war ground to a halt.

Reportedly, these Stingers eventually found their way into the hands of two terrorist groups: Hizbollah and Hamas.

Discounting this information, even if it was not true, other Stingers remain on sale by the Afghanis for $100,000 each, a small sum for terrorist organizations who have a $1 million contract per airplane from the Iranians in retribution for the shootdown of the Iranian A-300 Airbus by the U.S.S. *Vincennes*. The contract is called a *Fatwa*, a religious order that cannot be recalled, quite similar to the order to kill author Salmon Rushdie for writing his book, *Satanic Verses*. This Fatwa was for ten American jumbo jets.

This also matches the story of Pan Am 103 being the first to be destroyed, tracing the bombers back to Syria and the PFLP-GC; and Ramzi Yousef planning to blow up a dozen 747s. Yousef, the New York World Trade Center bomber, was arrested in Pakistan before he could carry out his mission. He was also tightly connected to Islamic terrorists in the Philippines, and to Hamas cells in the United States—including New York City.[207]

CIA sources say at least 30-40 missiles are in circulation in the terrorist ranks (a very conservative estimate), and that these missiles were offered to be given back to the State Department at no charge, but the CIA and Clinton Administration refused to take them back for some odd reason. Author and investigator Rodney Stich, receiving this information from deep-cover intelligence sources, wrote a letter to Senator Arlen Specter on Oct. 20, 1995, "that this refusal suggested a hidden agenda, with possible catastrophic consequences in shooting down commercial airliners." To prove how reliable his information was, the warning even included the serial numbers of some of the missiles, which were provided by one of Stich's deep cover CIA whistle blowers. The offer to give back the missiles was made by Afghan Mujihadeen leader General Rashid Dostom.

According to Stich, the following missiles were issued to the Afghans and may have found their way into terrorist hands: GDP 84D 001-320 362956; GDP 84J 001-320 363602; GDP 86G 001-387 369587; GDP 84G 001 320 363387.

To add to this, Israeli intelligence reported that they received unconfirmed information that 50 Stingers entered the U.S. in January, 1995. They attempted to warn U.S. authorities, but were ignored.

Stingers are not the only shoulder-fired surface-to-air missiles available to terrorists. The Russian equivalent to the earlier American "Redeye" missile is the SA-7 "Grail." According to Intelligence sources, over 120,000 Russian SA-7s have been produced, and about 10% have fallen into the hands of terrorist groups—some with Russian assistance. The SA-7 is responsible for hitting a jet near Oman at a slant range of over six miles, and a British-made Hunter aircraft near Yemen was struck at a height of 12,000 feet. During the Vietnam war, NVA and VC rocket gunners engaged and destroyed aircraft at altitudes of between 11,000 and 12,000 feet with the Grail. The Russian Stinger clone, the SA-14 "Gremlin," is even more effective.

The Stinger, contrary to what the unnamed Pentagon spokesman stated, was more than capable of reaching the 747 from a boat, even if the aircraft was in excess of the latest altered altitude of 13,700 feet. But did any witnesses observe a missile trail originating from the sea below the jet?

According to an Athens newspaper, a Greek commercial pilot saw just that.

Investigative journalist David Hoffman, editor of the *Haight Ashbury Free Press,* made contact with an Athenian named Yannis Boyiopoulos who confirmed that the Athens newspaper *Elftherotypia* on August 23, 1996 reported on the front page that a Greek pilot had witnessed the explosion and described what he saw. The pilot was flying behind the 747 when he observed something come up from the water that to him resembled a "rocket." He watched it until it struck the airplane. According to Boyiopoulos "The same person has already testified three times to agents of the FBI and now he is in Greece. His name is Vasilis Bakoynis."

Still, no matter what the witnesses saw or photographed, the Government seemed intent on debunking any story that supported the missile strike scenario. Our unnamed Pentagon Spokesman advised the major media that "...there is no way a Stinger or other hand-held shoulder-fired missile could take down a 747—and a Stinger does not have the range to hit TWA 800 at the altitude it was at."

In this statement are two lies. First, an airplane is a very fragile machine which operates in a very unforgiving environment. Though large aircraft ranging from World War II bombers to the latest air buses have survived after sustaining very serious damage, others have crashed after simple failures of a single component in the flight control or engine systems, not to mention very small bombs that simply breached hull integrity, or baggage doors that blew off to be sucked into engine intakes. A number of crashes and other incidents have been linked to the latter scenario, including one in which a forward baggage door blew off of a 747 and was ingested by the number three engine, which then self-destructed, sending super-heated engine parts into the soft aluminum skin of the wings and fuselage. But the jet survived and landed safely.

This is exactly what could have happened to TWA 800—after a missile strike on an inboard engine, such as number three, but with much more catastrophic results.

Multi-engine aircraft engines are numbered from left to right as one looks down at the aircraft. The outermost left engine is number one. The next in, or left inboard engine is number two. Number three is the right inboard engine, and number four the right side outboard engine. In the case of TWA 800, engines one, two and four were raised fairly early in the search. The last engine, described in the first few days as "engine parts" was not raised until several weeks after the crash. The reason it was left on the bottom supposedly was because it had not yet been found, and that only "parts of an engine" had been located. This proved untrue when the number three engine was actually brought to the surface by the Navy.

To those who knew what they were seeing, number three engine told a dramatic story. As it was loaded aboard a flat-bed truck to be transported to the reconstruction site, the educated observer could see that there were several descrepancies. First, the fan section in the front of the engine was only about 30% intact. Most of the fan blades were absent and those that remained, a pie-shaped section on one side of the wheel, were bent at the tips, as if they contacted the engine intake cowling while still turning. The center section of the engine displayed bent and distorted connector rings over the burner can section, and most of the back of the engine was missing! The entire engine appeared to have been burned, and this did not happen underwater.

The next day the NTSB announced that all engines were up and none showed any "problems" that could have contributed to the incident.

The NTSB spokesman, Robert Francis, was quoted in a London publication as reporting that "Investigators have stripped down all four of the jet's engines but found, according to safety board vice chairman, Robert Francis, 'nothing really extraordinary'."[208]

No problems, no clues, no new evidence.

Then came the Kabot photo.

Linda Kabot, an East Moriches resident attending a party near the beach, took a photograph during the event. When the photo was developed, it showed a cylindrical object in the air with one end brightly lighted. The problem with this photograph is that according to Kabot, she held the camera facing north, away from the ocean, which means the "missile" in the photo had to come from inland—which might put it out of range of a shoulder-launched SAM unless it was fired as TWA 800 was passing nearby still climbing. Whatever the case, the photo and negatives were seized by the FBI for analysis.

The second lie told by the unnamed Pentagon source was that a Stinger could not bring down a 747. As discussed, it *could* bring down such an airplane if it hit an inboard engine, such as number three, which in turn would catch fire and begin spewing bits and pieces of flaming engine parts into the fuselage—and center fuel tank—and the wings and internal wing tanks. Within a minute or two the near empty center tank, now ruptured, might be ignited. A large fuel tank such as this, which only carried about fifty gallons of volatile fuel, is a veritable bomb.

The burned carcass of number three engine notwithstanding, the investigators still continued to deny the missile scenario. There are many plausible reasons why they would take such a stance: First, no amount of airport security could stop such an attack in the future. Next, it could possibly have a giant impact on the flying public and subsequent airline profits. Then, of course, the public would want to know where terrorists obtained such a weapon, which would eventually lead back to U.S. government figures at the highest levels. And how did it get into this country without being detected? And finally, if the word leaked out that the missiles were offered back to the government and the administration refused to take them back, what then? And in an election year?

As the bomb and mechanical malfunction aspects of the investigation began to lose credibility due to lack of evidence, the missile scenario began to build into an acceptable reality. At about this time, another rumor began circulating regarding the possiblility of "friendly fire" from a military ship or aircraft that had "accidently" loosed a missile which struck Flight 800. The day after this rumor hit the Internet and was being repeated in radio talk shows, the Pentagon sent a spokesman to squash the rumors. On CNN that day a full Navy captain appeared before the cameras to announce that [paraphrasing] "there had been no accidental discharge of a weapon that night, and there had been no military exercises in the area, and no military vessels or aircraft."

These statements were quickly countered by very simple and obvious questions: If this was the case, then where did the C-130, two Blackhawk helicopters, the P-3 Orion, and a Navy guided missile cruiser—the U.S.S. *Normandy*—come from?

This spokesman was never seen again. Nor did the military address the question of friendly fire in the electronic media.

Investigative reporter David Hendrix of the Riverside, CA, *Press-Enterprise* queried the Navy regarding the statements that there were no exercises being conducted nor military assets in the vicinity. This was done after he secured a copy of an unclassified message from Fleet Air Control and Surveillance Facility, Oceana, VA, to FAA New York Air Traffic Control that read: "Request stationary altitude reservation Tango Billy [area code name] surface to flight level 10,000 feet within (longitude and latitude) 39 degrees 50 minutes North and 72 degrees 10 minutes West, 39 degrees 50 minutes North and 70 degrees 45 minutes West, 38 degrees North and 72 degrees 10 minutes West (excluding warning areas) from 0100 Z [Zulu: Greenwich Mean Time] on the 18th to 0700 Z on the 18th July 96." The local time and date would be the 17th of July at 8 p.m. New York time until 3 a.m. the next morning. This request would take effect about when TWA 800 was taxiing to the runway at JFK.

The impact zone of the wreckage was reported by Associated Press as approximately 40 degrees 40 minutes North latitude, and 72 degrees 40 minutes West longitude. This is between 60-65 statute miles northwest of the northwest corner of the reserved exercise area. Other reports, however, state that the 747 was in close proximity—some within ten miles—of the exercise zone.[209]

Hendrix received a reply to his August 30, 1996 letter to the Navy ·from COMNAVAIRLANT (Commander Naval Air Atlantic) public affairs office via CINCLANTFLT (Commander In Chief Atlantic Fleet) Public Affairs office. In it the Navy admitted being in the area: "...As previously stated a P-3 Orion submarine patrol aircraft was operating at flight level 10,000 (approximately 3,700 feet below TWA 800) and some distance away when the incident occurred. The P-3's crew heard radio traffic discussing the incident and offered assistance. They reversed course, were vectored to the area, and remained for a short time until released by the Coast Guard. The P-3 carries no offensive or defensive weapons and would not have been capable of causing any damage to another aircraft."

Either this was a deliberate lie, or the Public Affairs officer who wrote the letter did not know, nor did he or she check, what the P-3 is capable of. After all, the Orion is an anti-submarine aircraft. This means it is capable of locating, then sinking, submarines. In actual fact, the P-3 is capable of carrying in its weapons bay one Mk-25 or 39 or 56 mine, or three Mk-36 or 52 mines, or three Mk-57 depth charges, or 8 Mk-43 or 44 or 46 torpedoes. On underwing pylons, the P-3 can carry mines and *rockets*, or can ferry torpedoes. Maximum weapons load is rated at 20,000 lbs.

The next statement, that the P-3 "heard" the radio traffic and had to be vectored to the scene is also problematic. The flames on the water from the crash could be seen from Long Island, and the P-3 would not have to be "vectored" to the site. The Navy also apparently was parroting the FBI and NTSB news releases that the altitude of the TWA plane was 13,700 feet—disregarding the official FAA radar reports on Day One of 8,000 feet, then the subsequent "corrections" of 10,300 feet and above.

The Navy letter goes on to say: "Also as previously released the guided missile cruiser USS *Normandy* was conducting routine operations about 180 miles from the crash site. It was not engaged in any weapons firing evolution at the time."

As a guided missile cruiser, the *Normandy* would carry the RIM-67 Standard SM-2ER semi-active radar homing air defense missiles. This missile has a range in excess of 93 miles and an unclassified altitude range of 100,000 feet. Its speed is in excess of Mach 2.5, and even with a dummy warhead could be deadly to an aircraft.[210]

A later story that circulated in the press was that on the evening of July 17th, the TWA jet took off for Paris, turned on course over the ocean and got too close to an exercise being conducted off shore by a joint law enforcement task force of National Guard, Coast Guard, Customs and Drug Enforcement Agency. They were reportedly practicing how to shoot down drug-smuggling airplanes with shoulder-fired missiles and were using flares dropped by the C-130 as targets. A missile was fired or "got loose accidently" and locked on to the TWA plane instead of a flare. But according to federal officials, "there was no exercise that night, the air space was available for civilian use, and law enforcement agencies do not have anti-aircraft missiles."

This, like many other government explanations regarding this incident, was not true. The Secret Service has Stinger missiles that they carry at all times when the Protection Detail is escorting the President. These missiles are carried in special boxes in the back of the Secret Service Suburban. Besides this, agents are stationed on roof tops around the White House with Stingers to protect the air space over the building. One SS agent told me when I was flying air cover over a Clinton motorcade that if we flew too close to the motorcade we would be shot down by an agent with a Stinger. He said they always carry them in the back of their escort vehicles along with other weapons.[211]

Also, there *were* exercises going on that night because we have statements made by military personnel who were involved: New York Air National Guard C-130 crew dropping flares; NY Army National Guard UH-60 Blackhawk crew who saw the explosion; P-3 Orion in vicinity; Coast Guard vessels; and the U.S.S. *Normandy* "somewhere nearby."

It is odd that the Navy spokesmen would state that the *Normandy* was 180 miles away. This is exactly twice the range of the Standard missile. This is also almost the *exact* distance between the TWA crash site and the farthest (southeast) corner of the exercise box requested by the Navy for that time frame.

In weighing the facts and witness statements, the most likely scenario to explore is that of a hand-held surface-to-air missile. This

325

would mean a Mideast terrorist organization connection—something the Clinton administration was loath to consider in the aftermath of the Oklahoma City bombing, and which has continuously disavowed or failed to recognize any domestic problems with such groups.

The missile scenario was not discounted by all media, however. According to *The Press-Enterprise* (Riverside, CA), in an article printed on August 26th, 1996, "From the beginning, intrigued by eyewitness accounts of something streaking up toward the airplane just before it began to explode, investigators considered the possibility of a missile attack, perhaps from a small boat. There has been mounting concern in intelligence and law enforcement circles that terrorists could use hand-held anti-aircraft missiles to attack civilian airliners. *A State Department report catalogued 25 incidents between 1978 and 1993 in which civilian commercial airplanes were shot down by missiles, killing more than 600 people.*"[212]

Finally, another news source, the *International Currency Review* (Vol 23 No. 4), published the following information regarding the trajedy of TWA 800: "A KGB defector has informed us that the TWA plane was sabotaged by Russian intelligence. This operation had to be implemented directly, rather than via controlled forces apparently separated from Yevgenny Primakov's global terror apparatus, because it was tightly timed to precede the Group of Seven's meeting on security and terrorism—at which it was agreed that the G-7 countries and Russia would now have access to the FBI's data base, and that a comprehensive exchange of intelligence and cooperation would ensue. Further atrocities will be staged in due course to ratchet up this process, in fulfilment of a secret Soviet sub-strategy to exploit terror and organized crime—which the successor Leninist criminal state is exporting globally—to establish 'global structures' and ultimately, a 'world justice system' which would supplant national security arrangements and legal systems, further contributing to the intended redundancy of the nation state." This falls in line with the Gorbachev Foundation's line for a new form for prosecution of "global issues" intended to render the nation-state redundant—the manipulation of organized crime and terror as weapons which could be used in furtherance of anti-state revolutionary objectives.

This explanation should not be discounted out of hand, for an agenda does exist to bring all nations into a world-wide system of government—even if the peoples of the world have to be intimidated with terror before they will accept such an Orwellian system. This is known as the "Hegelian Principle" after Professor Hegel who stated that to make the people accept a normally repugnant idea, you simply created a problem that they feared, then offer the idea as the only available—and less fearsome—solution. In this case, exhibited incidents of terrorism can be used to convince a population that more drastic "anti-terrorist" laws should be passed.

If international terrorists were responsible for this disaster, then who might they be? The list of suspects is not long:

Ramzi Yousef group (Hamas): Supporters of Ramzi Ahmed Yousef (AKA: Abdul Basit Mahmoud Abdul Karim), currently in prison in New York, was at the time of the incident undergoing trial in NYC. Yousef was trained during the Afghan War and was captured and extradited to the U.S. from Pakistan in 1995. The trial was in its eighth week when TWA 800 went down.

Hizbollah: Pro-Iranian guerilla organization, now seeking to extract revenge on the U.S. for supporting Israel.

al-Gama'a al-Islamiya (Islamic Group or IG): Egyptian terrorist group from which the U.S. imprisoned its spiritual leader, Sheik Omar Abdel Rahman. Rahman was convicted in 1995 for plotting to bomb the United Nations and several other New York landmarks. He is currently serving a life sentence in a federal prison in Springfield, Missouri.

Hamas: Hamas has vowed to attack the U.S. for agreeing to extradite a known terrorist by the name of Musa Abu Marzouk to Israel. Marzouk was arrested at JFK International Airport in New York last year, and was held and faced extradition hearings in New York. Hamas has 28 cells in the U.S., one in New York City and one in Boston.

Islamic Movement for Change: A Saudi splinter group, it is the only group known to claim any responsibility for the downing of the flight.

It supposedly has ties to Saudi Arabia, and claims responsibility for the bombing of the U.S. facilities in Riyadh in November, 1995, and in Dhahran on 25 June 1996. The question one must address regarding this group is: Could it be possible that this new, unknown group, is actually a Russian front that would match the Russian connection article? It may take years to discover the answer to this question.

This chapter was not written as an attempt to solve the mysteries surrounding the destruction of TWA 800, but to simply present evidence of what appears to support a much more complicated case than what has been reported by the controlled media. It was also written to exhibit the continued *Modus Operandi* by government mouthpieces on not only this case but the ones that came before. When one knows what to look for, it becomes apparent when a pattern of deceit develops in both the media and in the various organs of government.

Was TWA 800 shot down by a missile fired by Islamic fundamentalists as the physical evidence and majority of witness statements indicate?

Did the airplane experience a catastrophic mechanical failure?

Was there a bomb on board that exploded without leaving more than a trace of residue?

Was the plane struck by friendly fire from an aircraft or ship?

It may take years to discover the actual cause of the explosion of TWA 800. For as this chapter is being written, the FBI and other agencies continue their "investigations"....

And their damage control.[213]

But the biggest question of all is: "Why?"

Part VII

Riding The Tiger—Domestic Terror

"It should be apparent to the investigator that McVeigh and Nichols, virtually unassisted, could not have planned, provided for, financed, and executed the bombing by themselves."

Report on the Bombing of the Alfred
Murrah Federal Building
By the author.

"We seek to tell the United States and its agents that the Iraqi patience has run out and that the perpetration of the crime of annihilating the Iraqis will trigger crises whose nature and consequences are known only to God."

Iraqi newspaper *Babil*

"In the past, those who foolishly sought power by riding on the back of the tiger ended up inside."

John Fitzgerald Kennedy

Chapter 30

Terrorism—Foreign and Domestic

Ter-or-ism n. The unlawful use or threatened use of force or violence to intimidate or coerce societies or governments, often for ideological or political reasons. (The *American Heritage College Dictionary*).

It has been said that one man's "terrorist" is another man's "freedom fighter." In this modern age the truism of this statement is becoming more apparent each day. From age-old religious conflict to modern political friction, groups of people have increasingly aligned themselves through religious beliefs, political ideology, or fear of group persecution into organizations that become not only self-defensive, but oftentimes a threat to others.

There is nothing new about terrorism. It has been a political and religious means of expression, albeit violent, since the beginning of time. Examples of terrorist activity can be found in the Bible, historical texts of the middle ages, and virtually every conflict in the centuries that followed. Terrorism, in its basic definition, is a name given to the activities of either an "enemy of the state," or a weaker opponent that must rely on shock effect to gain the attention of the populace toward their cause. Examples of these "shock effect" tactics have been exhibited in virtually every historical theater of battle or conquest, and in every realm wherein one people exercised political and military control over another. From ancient Greece to modern Belfast, and from the Roman Empire's occupation of Israel to the current "Middle-eastern problems" of Israel/Palestine, events have forced certain elements of society to resist an unwanted or oppressive power by use of whatever weapons and tactics were available.

In almost every instance the only tactics available were those we now call "guerrilla warfare"—or, when civilians are involved as casualties—terrorism. For with the communications capabilities of modern technology, small groups of determined people, whether they be termed freedom fighters or terrorists, can multiply their actual influence by the use of shock tactics coupled with media exposure as a weapon. Without the media, there would be no public recognition or attention. And without civilian casualties being exhibited for the world to see in living color, there would be little shock effect among the masses. Only by using the most shocking and diabolical tactics against an unarmed civilian populace, from which no government can completely insure protection, can a fanatic terrorist (or renegade government) organization instill the public fear to accomplish their objectives.

But there is a distinct difference between what is acceptable practice in warfare and unacceptable barbarism. It is because of this that all civilized countries in this age have become signatories to such documents as the Geneva Convention on the laws of land warfare and the various agreements that limit or prohibit the use certain weapons such as chemical, biological and nuclear "weapons of mass destruction." These agreements also specify rules of engagement, declarations of war, handling of prisoners, and conduct of warfare itself. Terrorist organizations, unable to bargain from a position of strength to achieve their goals, instead disregard the "rules" and rely instead on breaking the rules to achieve attention to their causes.

As an historical example, the American colonists under George Washington could not participate in conventional warfare against the professional and mercenary troops of King George during the American Revolution. Instead of rank-and-file Napoleonic tactics of mass firepower and attrition, the colonists relied on the tactics they learned in the Indian Wars wherein they utilized camouflage, concealment, elements of surprise, and ambush to achieve victory. These tactics, to the British, not only violated the standards of European warfare they were accustomed to, but were savage and barbarian. To the British, the colonial army consisted of terrorists. But to the colonists, there was little choice. In the beginning they were outnumbered, outgunned, and did not control the urban centers where logistical assets, such as powder and shot, were located. They did, however, control part of the media—using underground printing presses to publish their own papers and flyers—and most of the rural terrain. It was not until they had captured a sufficient number of cannons, horses and rifles and enlisted a significant number of troops, that they were able to escalate from rural guerrilla warfare to more conventional engagements in major battles.

During the American Civil War, certain "raider" groups from both sides were branded as criminals. Because they penetrated deeply into "enemy territory," which took them far from the actual lines of battle and into civilian areas, where they conducted guerrilla warfare, they were condemned as rogues, renegades and outlaws. Though their main missions were to interdict enemy supply routes, capture important personages, or generally raise havoc behind the lines to draw much-needed troops away from battle, they occasionally crossed the line into what would now be termed as terrorist activities. These actions included looting and burning towns and farms, stealing horses and terrorizing the civilian populace.

Following the Civil War, organizations such as the Ku Klux Klan appeared which formulated and depended upon terror tactics in their attempts to not only intimidate the newly-freed slaves, but to influence local and regional politics regarding separation of races and classes. The hooded "Night Riders" of the KKK terrorized blacks and northern "Carpetbaggers" by burning barns, farm houses and crop fields, and shooting or hanging targeted individuals. These criminal attacks on the populace were meant to serve as examples and intimidate others into fear and submission to local thugs. Little thought was given to making any type of political statement on a national level. Still, certain segments of society today consider the actions of the post-Civil War KKK as racially nationalistic, and are sympathetic to their tactics and objectives, and indeed have patterned themselves after it.

Other violent, illegal and savage activities by secret groups, societies, and organizations that could be defined as terrorist actions have occurred since the end of the Civil War. These include bombings, arson, assassinations, sabotage of federal property, inciting riots and even conspiracies to overthrow the government. The organizations have ranged through such racially and politically diverse names as: the Black Panthers, the Weathermen, the Students for a Democratic Society, the

Jewish Defense League, the Order, and other extreme left and right wing organizations.

Domestic "terrorism" is nothing new to America. By strict definition, it has been around since the first colonists were ambushed by indians, leaving their mutilated bodies behind as a warning to others, which in turn instigated colonists to "scalp" indian bodies in reprisal. What *is* new to the American scene, however, is the influx of international terrorism coupled with mass media advertisement of their atrocities. The "combat multiplier" of the media magnifies in the minds of the populace the impact of what otherwise would be minor footnotes to history. A car bombing, a "plot" to blow up a building, or the derailment of a train is focused on by the sensationalist/tabloidist American media to the point in which the events become a major crises. Many recent events have received more press coverage today than was given in the past regarding such tragedies as the explosion of the Hindenburg, the sinking of the Lusitania, or the fact that we left thousands of American POWs behind in World War II, Korea and Vietnam. One can only ask if there is a current agenda behind what is and is not reported in the print and electronic media, and what constitutes today's "big news." By what history has exhibited, it would appear that there now is a secret agenda at work behind the scenes. But why? And who benefits?

Whether terrorism is of the domestic or imported international brand, some basic fundamentals apply. One of these fundamentals is the fact that there are only five types of ground-based terrorist targets. Every target falls under one of these categories, with the exception of what is known as the "Love Boat" scenario. The PLO assault on the Greek liner *Achille Lauro* falls into this last category, but a ship at sea is not a "land-based" target.

The five land-based target categories are:

1. A private building (or structure including bridges, dams etc.)
2. A public (government) building (or facility)
3. Mass transportation (ground)
4. Mass transportation (air)
5. Large gathering of people (or segment of the population)

What becomes immediately apparent is that between 1993 and 1996, and for the first time in American history, four out of the five listed target types have been attacked by terrorists or terrorist activities *inside* the borders of the Continental United States. These include the bombing of the World Trade Center in New York City (private building), the bombing of the Alfred P. Murrah Federal Building in Oklahoma City (public—or government—building), the derailment of the Sunset Limited near Gila Bend, Arizona (mass transportation—ground), and the destruction of TWA 800 (mass transportation—air). As of this writing the only target left to complete all five categories is the fifth: a large gathering of people, or the "Black Sunday" scenario.

Some might consider that the small pipe bomb that exploded at the Olympics at Atlanta would qualify for the fifth target category. However, this writer feels that though the Olympics themselves would qualify as a prime target with maximum media coverage for effect, and indeed were probably targeted, the effort was too minuscule and unprofessional to effectively complete the list.

The following chapters deal with three of the above tragedies: the World Trade Center bombing, the bombing of the Alfred P. Murrah Federal Building (in which the author was personally involved in the investigation), and the derailment of Amtrack's Sunset Limited. In all of these events someone benefitted and someone took the blame. But it is not who we have been led to believe by the mainstream media.

To the uninitiated—those who have not read and absorbed the preceding chapters—the true "story behind the story" regarding these events is simply incomprehensible and unbelievable. But taken in context with what has already been presented in this book, the learned reader will find the material in the following chapters little more than a continuation of "business as usual" for the powerbrokers of not only this nation, but the world.

As you read, ask yourself if the events you are about to dissect fall under the category of domestic terrorism, international terrorism, or...something else.

Here are the stories that you did *not* get through NBC, ABC, CBS and CNN....

Chapter 31

Hiding the Truth: The World Trade Center Bombing

It was just after noon on February 26, 1993, when downtown New York City was shaken by a thunderous explosion. Pedestrians who were able to see the origination point through the jungle of high rise buildings could see that black smoke was pouring from the 110-story World Trade Center building. No one realized at that moment that they were witnessing history in the making: the first known international terrorist attack on U.S. soil.

Though damage to the building was heavy, it was not as devastating as had been planned by the instigators. Had the bomb, which had been placed in a rental truck, accomplished the damage intended, and had the target "tower" collapsed, it is estimated that deaths might have exceeded 20,000. As it were, only six people were killed and an additional 1,000 injured.

The New York City bomb squad, police, emergency personnel and federal agents of the FBI and BATF immediately swarmed to the scene. Photographs were taken inside the building of a huge hole blasted through the floor of an underground parking garage, shattered columns, bent rebar rods, and fire damaged automobiles and building structure. Witnesses and victims were interviewed and statements taken from bystanders. All standard police procedures were followed, but little hope was exhibited at the time that the case would be solved because all who deal with bombings know that most of the evidence is destroyed in the blast, and the perpetrators are normally a long way away by the time the explosion takes place.

But in this case the public would be amazed at the speed in which the FBI solved the case. In less than thirty days the FBI managed to round up five suspects—all members of an Islamic terrorist cell located in a "mosque" in Brooklyn. The so-called mosque, actually a floor of rented rooms over a storefront, was headed by an Egyptian radical Moslem fundamentalist cleric named Sheik Omar Abdel-Rahman. Rahman, who delivered his anti-American "Great Satan" sermons in two locations: the Brooklyn headquarters and another mosque in Jersey City, New Jersey, had been exiled by the Egyptian government for subversive activities. Rahman, a follower of Iranian fundamentalist ideology, in which all non-Moslems were worthy only of death until no Christians, Jews or other "pagans" remained on Earth, urged his followers to "spill American blood on its own soil."

Rahman was connected to more than just a few local radical followers. His international contacts included members of the Hamas and Hizbollah, and former Afghan war vets who had served as volunteers for the Mujihadeen. Other connections ran directly to Iran, who provided over $100,000 to Rahman for anti-American domestic terrorist activities, and to Pakistan, where more than twenty former Mujihadeen training camps had been turned over to the Pakistani ISI (Inter-Service Intelligence) by the CIA after the Afghan war. These training camps were, by 1992, training up to 3,700 terrorists at a time. These Pakistani-trained zealots were being trained and armed for one thing: exporting terrorists to non-Islamic countries to carry on and expand the *Jihad*—the Holy War against non-Islamics.

Two months after the initial arrests, eight other Islamic terrorists were arrested by the FBI in connection with the bombing—five actually caught in the act of mixing explosives. With these arrests information was released that a nefarious plot that ranged far greater than the WTC bombing existed, and that other targets included the New York Federal Building, The Holland and Lincoln tunnels, and the United Nations building. Besides the bombings, the terrorists also planned to assassinate several key figures in world politics including U.N. Secretary Boutros Boutros-Ghali, and New York Senator Alphonse D'Amato.

According to the *first* official story, the FBI and BATF recovered a small piece of the truck used in the bombing and traced it to a rental agency. And, as luck would have it, one of the bombers returned to the agency shortly after the bombing to explain that the truck had been stolen and to claim his deposit. He was promptly arrested, which led to other arrests.

But according to the *second* official story, it seems that the FBI had managed to plant an informant within Rahman's terrorist cell, and that the informant secretly recorded conversations between Sheik Rahman and those arrested in a planned terror wave of bombings that were to begin on July 4th. According to the indictment which was filed by the federal court, Rahman had blessed the bombmaking plans, and had encouraged at least twenty-one followers to continue with further Jihad activities. According to court documents all twenty-one were eventually arrested or indicted. This second story, however, does not explain how the FBI lost their "handle" on the case and allowed the event to transpire without taking action to interdict the plot prior to the delivery of the truck bomb.

Even though twenty-one were arrested or indicted, according to court documents one of the main players had escaped the FBI net: Abdul Basit Mahmoud Abdul Karim—now known internationally as Ramzi Yousef.

One of the elusive ghosts of the Islamic terrorist underground network is Iraqi-trained Ramzi Ahmed Yousef. Yousef prided himself as a world-class bomb maker, capable of constructing explosives from easily obtainable chemicals and compounds that are not controlled by government authorities. Yousef is also a skilled actor, traveling around under numerous assumed names and identity cards and passports, and capable of convincing immigration and passport control officials that he was little more than a harmless refugee seeking political asylum from the evil and sadistic Saddam Hussein. Just the opposite was true, however. Yousef was an Iraqi "soldier" who traveled freely within the framework of the international Palestinian, Egyptian, Sudanese and Pakistani terrorist organizations as one of the most dangerous men on earth.

On September 1st, 1992, Yousef arrived at New York's JFK airport and presented himself to an immigration control officer as a displaced Iraqi who, if returned to Iraq, would be executed. He requested political asylum and was granted entry until an INS interview date could be established. He was photographed, fingerprinted, and run through the computer. But, because "Ramzi Yousef" was one of many assumed names, there was no computer hit on "Ramzi Ahmed Yousef."

Exactly how much Yousef had to do with the WTC bombing and the follow-on plans will probably never be publicly revealed. What is known, however, is that on December 8th Yousef requested postponement of his INS hearing because, according to him, he had not yet hired an attorney. Then on the second date—January 26, 1993—a lawyer appeared for Yousef and explained that he had been involved in an automobile accident and could not appear at that time. Another date was scheduled, but before it was reached the bombing occurred in the World Trade Center. By this time Yousef had fled the country and was lurking in the shadow world of Islamic terrorists between Pakistan and the Philippines. Yousef would next surface in 1996 when he was finally arrested in Pakistan and extradited to the United States to face trial for the WTC bombing. At the time of his arrest by the Philippine police he had been busily working on a plan to blow up twelve American 747 jumbo jets over the Pacifac.

What must be told at this point is the *third* story of the FBI "investigation" into the WTC bombing. What you are about to read is not an "official" version.

During the court hearing in New York, information surfaced that there was more to the so-called investigation than had originally been reported to the media—and the American public. It seems that the FBI actually had more than a simple "informant" inside Rahman's terrorist cell. What they actually had was an Egyptian intelligence officer named Emad Salem, who reported directly to his FBI control agent, Special Agent John Anticev. Salem, it turns out, was hired to infiltrate the Rahman group long before the bombing took place, and consistently reported on the activities of the radicals—including their plans to conduct bombings in the New York City area.

What the FBI did not know was that Salem recorded his conversations with his control agents. The tapes tell a far different story than the official versions of the "investigation." According to *The New York Times*, which managed to obtain secret transcripts of some of the conversations, the FBI knew in advance when the bomb was going to be planted, who was going to do it, the names of everyone in the terrorist cell, and where the truck was rented. But worse, one tape went even further. It seems that the FBI not only knew about the planning, they actually assisted the bombers in obtaining and constructing the bomb!

The original FBI plan was for the informant to provide a non-explosive substance that would be labled "Amonium Nitrate," then use it to construct a "bomb" that would not go off. All the FBI needed to show in court was the elements of conspiracy and intent. It would be a classic "sting" operation and the FBI would come out in the media as heros—a much-needed polishing of their tarnished image since the earlier debacle at Ruby Ridge, Idaho. (The BATF assault at Waco did not happen until two days after the WTC bombing and did not reflect on the FBI or BATF image until fifty-one days later when the final apocalypse of the Mount Carmel facility occurred).

Instead of arresting the conspirators when they received inside information that the bombing was being planned, the FBI instead kept their source in place and continued to monitor the progress of the terrorists in planning and preparing for their goal. According to the transcripts, the plan was changed and the informant was directed to provide the terrorists with *real* explosive materials. The reasoning behind this may have been simply that showing "intent" might not be enough to make a terrorism case in court, and that if real explosives were discovered then the case would make itself. But whatever the reason, the plan moved into stage two: building the bomb.

According to reports and transcripts, Salem was instructed to not only provide the materials, *but to give instruction and help in building the bomb itself*. This makes one wonder where Ramzi Yousef was during this time as Yousef was a master bomb maker, which would preclude the need for Salem to provide instruction or materials.

Part of the story regarding Salem's participation surfaced when a transcript of a secret recording he made with his handlers surfaced. According to it, he was questioned about his expenditures on his expense report to the FBI. He explained that his expenses rose during the month the bomb was built because of the cost of "building the Trade Center bomb." In the transcript he admitted that he used government funds to procure the materials and build the bomb for the Rahman group, as he was instructed to do.[214]

Emad Salem, Egyptian Intelligence, was paid $1 million for his testimony against the terrorist cell, and the Egyptian followers of Sheik Abdel-Rahman swore vengence and further violence against the U.S.[215]

In an AP article that appeared shortly after Rahman was convicted in U.S. District Court, "A militant Muslim group has threatened to attack American targets to avenge the life sentence imposed on Sheik Omar Abdel-Rahman for plotting to blow up New York landmarks. 'All American interests will be legitimate targets for our struggle until the release of Sheik Omar Abdel-Rahman and his brothers,' the *Al-Hayat* newspaper quoted the Islamic Group as saying."

The question one must ask at this point is what would be the next target of the Jihad? One must keep in mind the five types of ground-based terrorist targets. The World Trade Center fits the first category: a private building. That only leaves four: a public (government) building, mass transportation air, mass transportation ground, and a large gathering of people.

What would be next?

Chapter 32

Oklahoma City: Terrorism or Politics?

My pager went off at exactly 5:15 p.m. on April 21st, 1995. The number that flashed was that of my office at the Air Support Unit of the Tulsa Police Department. Since my work day ended at 5:00 p.m., the first thought that came to mind was that the dispatcher had issued a call-out for the police helicopter and I was being summoned to fly the mission. I could not have been more wrong. I picked up my microphone and called in to my office.

"Where are you," asked my supervisor, Sgt. Ron Moulton.

"On my way home, at least until now. What's up?"

"The FBI is looking for you," he answered. "They called the chief's office asking where you were."

"That's funny. The SAC has my pager number and office number. Why didn't they just page?"

"I don't know," answered Ron, "unless it's a different agent."

"Okay. I'll give them a call and see what's up."

This was highly unusual. Most of my experience in dealing with the "feds" occurred during duty hours. A hundred thoughts ran through my mind as I looked up the pager number of the SAC, Marty Weber. A few minutes later he returned my page.

"Hey Marty, Craig Roberts here. What's going on?"

"I don't know, why?"

"I just got a page that someone in your office was looking for me and I thought it must be you."

"No," he answered, "but I'll check it out."

A few minutes later he called back. "It's in regard to the Oklahoma City bombing. We could use some help. We haven't a clue what we are dealing with yet, and now we have this guy McVeigh. We don't know anything about him other than he's supposed to be an army deserter from Fort Riley. We know you have contacts that we don't have, and we thought you might put your mind to this and see what you can come up with."

I thought about this for a second, wondering why they wanted to bring an outsider, a local cop, into the investigation. This was highly unusual. "Marty, just exactly what do you want me to do?"

"You know...just put your head to it and see what you can find out through your own network. Just keep us advised. Who knows, maybe you can write another book."

So that was it. Marty had read two of my books, *Kill Zone: A Sniper Looks at Dealey Plaza* and *Hellhound*, a techno-thriller about middle-eastern terrorists striking a target inside the United States. Evidently some of his other agents had also read one or both, leading to my summons.

"Marty, if you'll make it an official request through the Chief's office, and he approves, I'll dig in and see what I can find out." I had just gone through a political altercation with the chief, as I had just returned from Washington, D.C., where I testified before Congress against the so-called "assault weapons" ban of the Omnibus Crime Act. Though I took vacation days for the trip, and was therefore off duty, I testified in uniform. Though there was no regulation or rule against such activity, and other officers had demonstrated or appeared on behalf of the Crime Bill in uniform, the Chief had political reservations about my trip. This resulted in a week-long media tennis match that ended in a meeting between myself and the Chief to iron out the situation. All turned out well for both sides, and the Chief issued a press release clearing me of any wrongdoing—which just happened to appear on April 19th, 1995, the day the bomb(s) exploded at the Murrah federal building in Oklahoma City. The article took a back page to this new event.

One of the items on the agenda at the meeting I agreed to was to keep the Chief advised of any outside activities that involved police work or "wearing my uniform at a political event."

The FBI request was definitely going to involve outside police work.

By 6:00 p.m. that evening I had received a phone call from the Chief's office "granting permission" to officially assist the FBI. I began the investigation the next day. Little did I realize that I would work with the FBI until April of 1996, when I retired from the police department after 26 years of service, then continue on my own to this writing—and beyond. What began as a simple call for assistance developed into another investigation on the scale of my investigation into the assassination of John F. Kennedy that resulted in my book *Kill Zone*.

What follows is my final report to the FBI that I turned in just prior to my retirement. It will serve to give the reader an explanation of many things that did not appear in the media and an idea of the scope and scale of the event as it actually happened—and was subsequently covered up—by the U.S. Government.

The Report:

THE BOMBING OF THE MURRAH FEDERAL BUILDING
Oklahoma City, April 19th, 1995

An Investigative Report by W.C. Roberts

On Wednesday morning, April 19th, 1995, at approximately 9:02 a.m., Central Time, a huge explosion rocked downtown Oklahoma City. In the minutes and hours that followed, the world came to realize that the worst terrorist strike against a civilian target in history had occurred—in almost the geometric center of the United States.

What followed became one of the greatest investigations, and by far the greatest manhunt, in American history. Only the investigation following the assassination of President John F. Kennedy, and the manhunt for John Wilkes Booth after the assassination of President Abraham Lincoln come close. No resources were spared, and even though the prime suspect, former Army veteran Timothy McVeigh, was captured within eighty minutes of the blast seemingly "escaping" from the area through rural Oklahoma, law enforcement agencies pulled out all stops in an attempt to identify and locate other possible suspects.

At first, the original reports from witnesses described two "middle eastern males" wearing blue jumpsuits or jogging suits as being spotted in the immediate area of the Murrah building. The Media picked up on this lead, and with the FBI and international law enforcement agencies rapidly becoming involved, working feverishly to track any such suspects. A single middle-eastern male was apprehended in London at Heathrow Airport, allegedly with bomb-making materials in his luggage. He had left the U.S. earlier that day and came under immediate scrutiny due to description, age, timing and profile. But within twenty-four hours, he was discarded as a suspect and the media attention immediately shifted direction and focused on "right wing extremists."[216]

Oddly, the media was evidently notified of an impending raid on a rural Michigan farm house to be conducted by federal agents. The resident of the farm was the brother of an acquaintance of Timothy McVeigh, Terry Nichols. McVeigh had been identified as "John Doe One" as he was about to make bond from the county jail in Perry, Oklahoma. He had been apprehended by an Oklahoma State Trooper as he sped north on an interstate highway just over an hour after the bombing. Strangely, his car had no license tag, and when he was stopped, even though armed, offered no resistance. Subsequent investigation led to Terry Nichols, then Nichols' brother James Nichols' farm in Michigan. At this point, a raid to serve a search warrant which should have been low key to media exposure, became a major media event. Network cameras arrived *with the raid force* and set up nearby, using telephoto lenses to record the entry and perimeter teams as they moved into position and proceeded with their search. During this "event" the various news commentators made numerous references to McVeigh's alleged "ties" with the Michigan Militia—described as "an extreme Right Wing fringe radical group."

From this point on, both the investigation and the media centered their enquiries on various right wing organizations, ranging from the Ku Klux Klan and other White-supremacist groups, to the NRA and Christian Coalition.

It rapidly became obvious that the media was being directed, and was not reporting impartially. When independent investigators began to trace the origins of the media—and henceforth the government—focus on the Right Wing (and especially Constitutionalist paramilitary groups and so-called "militia" organizations), what was discovered was self-explanatory. The so-called "experts" in the field of tracking "hate groups" that were feeding the media centered on two organizations: the Anti-Defamation League (ADL) of the B'nai B'rith (described by other Jewish organizations as extremely Left Wing), and the very liberal Southern Poverty Law Center (SPLC), who has reportedly been connected to the ADL. It began to become apparent that these two organizations were using the event in Oklahoma City to their own ends, and to further their own agenda. Evidence of this became apparent as certain liberal politicians, including vociferously anti-gun congressman Charles Schumer of New York, began a massive onslaught through the media against various paramilitary groups, so-called militias, "hate groups," and often Conservative, religious, and Constitutionalist groups in general—including the National Rifle Association, who one reporter attempted to link directly to the bombing by being financially involved.

Meanwhile, the investigation increased in intensity as witnesses were interviewed in various states. From the truck rental in Kansas where McVeigh was reported to have rented the Ryder truck, a composite drawing was made of another individual: John Doe #2. A nationwide manhunt ensued, eventually running down suspects from California to North Carolina, the Great Lakes to the Gulf of Mexico. Still, even though backed by a $2 million reward and hundreds of telephone call takers, law enforcement officers failed to develop but a few significant leads—one leading to Kingman, Arizona, and a third co-conspirator: Michael Fortier, an old army buddy of McVeigh's and Nichols. But Fortier was not John Doe #2, and this portion of the investigation ended when a soldier on leave from Fort Riley, who, with a stretch of the imagination, vaguely resembled the JD-2 sketch, was located, identified, and released as a simple mistaken identity on the part of the witnesses at the Ryder rental.

As the investigation continued, utilizing massive resources from local, state and federal law enforcement, plus independent investigators and investigative journalists, many discrepancies began to appear in the official scenario.

According to the official version of the event, McVeigh, a radical Right Wing loose cannon, planned to attack the U.S. government in revenge for the Waco debacle. He selected the Murrah building after eliminating from his target list two other federal buildings in other cities, then proceeded to recruit Fortier and Terry Nichols to assist with the preparations. Allegedly using funds obtained by selling guns stolen in Arkansas (from an alleged ATF informant who later said that the story was a fabrication), McVeigh bought plastic barrels (blue in color), tons of ammonium nitrate fertilizer, detonation cord, primers, fuse, gallons of some type of fuel oil or diesel fuel, and rented the truck. He and Nichols then took all of this material to a remote location and, by themselves, mixed 2.5 tons of ammonium nitrate and fuel oil in the barrels inside the truck, wrapped them with det cord and time fuse, then McVeigh, by himself, drove the truck to Oklahoma City, parked it in front of the Murrah building, lit the fuse, then ran away to: (1) the yellow Mercury Marquis with no license plate, or (2) a brown GM pickup truck with a smoked glass bug shield on the front end, driven by a dark complected person. All of this was recorded by an ATM video camera (or a Southwestern Bell security camera, or an apartment building camera, depending on which version one reads) and the tape was seized by the FBI and not released to the media, nor excerpts or still prints shown to the public to prove such a tape exists, to assuage any suspicions of a government coverup.

Discrepancies began to develop in the official version of the scenario, and within weeks the matter became extremely controversial in non-mainstream media such as the Internet, newsletters, independent radio shows, shortwave broadcasts, independent newspapers, and other forms of media not tied to the major networks in New York or Los Angeles.

It was at this point that this investigator began attempting to assemble the pieces of the puzzle into a logical pattern. Only by taking all of the information available, filtering out what definitely does not belong, then piecing the mosaic together can one draw a picture, albeit incomplete, of what may have happened. The remainder of this document is written utilizing myriad sources—some of unknown reliability, but many extremely reliable—and contacts both within and without of government circles at local, state and federal level.

347

Assuming there was a "conspiracy" involved, and that McVeigh and Nichols could not physically (by themselves) do all that had to be done in the time constraints of their activities from the time of the truck rental to the time of the explosion, there would have to be others involved. It would appear, from the information presented on the following pages, that McVeigh and Nichols may be only two members of a "field team" compartmentalized and organized in structured levels. If this is the case, and the following information is even partially correct, the investigation is far from over.

And it goes much higher than McVeigh and Nichols.

Investigatory Techniques Used in this Investigation

What follows is an investigative report (to date) utilizing the standards of:

    (1) Follow the money;
    (2) Follow the power:
    (3) Follow the players;
    (4) Look for Linkages, Consistences, Patterns, and Coincidences (even those that appear remote), and discrepancies that obviously create problems with a final synopsis;
    (5) Look for, and attempt to establish, a motive;
    (6) Determine who had the means to plan, conduct, and execute the crime, then have the power to possibly influence the resultant investigation;
    (7) Observe the outcome of the investigation—was it complete? Did it answer all questions?

The Scene

Shortly after the explosion in Oklahoma City, several events occurred almost simultaneously:

(1) As emergency services responded, two other "bombs" were discovered by investigators and the bomb technicians responded. The first "bomb" was discovered within minutes after the explosion as emergency workers began searching the interior of the building for

victims and survivors, and the second within twenty minutes of the first. One was deactivated on site. The status of the second device was not broadcast over television. Both were described as "military canisters," or "devices." Later explanation would be that these were "training" devices left about by the ATF. This explanation did not satisfactorily explain why they were in different spots in the building, far from the ATF offices located on the top floor. Eventually, government media releases would claim that there were no additional devices found, despite numerous eye witness accounts.

(2) Within a very short period it was announced that there had been a "car bomb," possibly filled with ammonium nitrate/fuel oil explosive mixture. But damage to the building, coupled with the size of the crater and secondary damage to surrounding structures, increased the explosive to "truck bomb size." Throughout the morning and into the afternoon, the truck grew in size from a 14 foot truck, to a 28 foot truck. The explosives grew from 1200 lbs to 2400 lbs, then 3200, then 4600. (What is disturbing about this is that in 1985, the IRA in London exploded a large "lorry" filled with over 5,000 lbs of ammonium nitrate/fuel oil explosive in front of a much older, non-reinforced structure—a stacked-block bank building—and the resultant damage was simply front windows being blown out and a much smaller crater in the street).

(3) Within three hours, a fireman on the third floor of the building noted two military box ambulances—unmarked—back up near the building, and saw several men in black or dark fatigues carrying stretchers out to the ambulances from the lower floor or basement of the building. Many of the stretchers had boxes, which appeared to contain papers or documents, and one had what were described as "some type of shoulder-fired missiles or missile tubes."

(4) Many witnesses stated that they heard two to three distinct explosions, the second more powerful than the first. To back this up, two seismograms which recorded the "event" showed three—not two as reported by the media—distinct markings of equal intensity and duration, approximately ten seconds apart, from two separate locations. A later explanation for this would be that the first event (actually circled was the second event) was the initial explosion, and the second (which was the third event on the graph) was the building collapsing. Later charts, recorded when the building was demolished, refuted this,

however. The remainder of the building, much larger than the destroyed section, made almost no marks on the graph when it fell due to demolition charges.

(5) A video tape was reportedly discovered that showed the front of the Murrah building before the explosion, then the truck driving up, then the explosion. The truck was identified as a yellow Ryder truck. The first press release explained that the tape came from a nearby ATM machine, even though no ATM machine is in the area. A separate press release was that it was from a Southwestern Bell security camera. A later report is that it was from a security camera atop a nearby apartment complex (to the west of the building). The "tape," wherever it came from, was seized and has not been shown to the media or general public, which initiated many people to speculate that it either did not exist, or that it did not portray what the media reported. This investigator also found it incredible that this same tape was not shown to the Grand Jury that was formed to indict McVeigh—even after they requested to see it.

(6) Witnesses described two "middle eastern males" wearing blue jump suits or jogging suits "hanging around" the front of the building just before the explosion. These descriptions initiated the terrorist hunt that culminated with an apprehension in London—but was then discredited with little public explanation.

(7) Some witnesses described seeing a dark colored, unmarked helicopter, leaving the rooftop of the building a few minutes before the explosion. Oklahoma City Police Department's two McDonnell-Douglas helicopters (black and silver in color) were on the ground at their base at this time. They did not respond until after the explosion. The origin of this helicopter is unknown, nor are there indications that this lead was followed up on.

(8) The only identifiable part of the Ryder truck discovered is the rear axle, which instead of being blown down into the crater, was "thrown" two blocks away. This axle, originally identified as a GM part with a VIN number, was traced through Ryder in Florida, to a truck rental/body shop in Kansas. However, when GM stated that there are no ID numbers on their truck axles, the truck was changed to "Ford."

Other conflicts arose by the hour as other discrepancies occurred. As federal authorities switched tracks from Islamics to Right Wing radicals, and began to trace McVeigh's movements and associates, outside organizations entered the picture and began to point fingers at political rivals and enemies.

(1) The Anti-Defamation League and the Southern Poverty Law Center immediately begin feeding New York City-based media organizations, including the major news networks, "information" identifying various right wing groups as "hate groups" capable of inflaming such activities, and indeed possibly "linked" to the occurrence. Both organizations historically take every opportunity to lump Conservative organizations into the same group—from the White Aryan Resistance to the Christian Coalition, and the KKK to the NRA. As each news program and news magazine interview transpired, the public began to notice more and more that the dialogue appeared to be orchestrated, and that political agendas were being served—but only on the left wing. This made many people suspect that the "government" was somehow more involved in the bombing than the media is willing to expose.

The problem at this point for the observer, is the definition of "government." Anyone who suspects involvement by any governmental agent or agency, whether directly involved, or involved by omission or failure to properly perform an investigation, becomes "debunked" as a "conspiracy theorist." The problem with this, like lumping all right wing groups together, is that a conspiracy in this case does exist, with only the extent not known. Therefore there is no "theory." The issue then becomes this: Exactly *who* is involved, and *why*?

To answer this and other questions, the search must follow the previously listed tenets of a proper investigation. To follow the money, the power, and the players, requires a great deal of research into past political events wherein the same names seem to appear, linking events. Though some of what follows does not appear at first to relate to the Oklahoma City bombing, the reader must keep the information in mind as this report progresses to gain a full understanding of the ramifications—and possibilities—of the event. For this, I have discovered that relevant events leading to the Oklahoma City bombing actually appear to have begun in the 1980s.

351

1985

When the focus of U.S. covert action paramilitary attention changed from Cuba, to Southeast Asia (Laos), to Iran, then back to Central America (where CIA paramilitary operations began in the 1950s), the covert intelligence community adopted the Nicaraguan "Contras" as fighters against Communism and the Marxist government of Nicaragua's Daniel Ortega. But with the Boland Amendment of non-interference, the Agency and NSC ran into problems of finance. This was solved in the same manner as the financing of the Laotian campaign.

In Laos, during the 1960s and '70s, a huge cartel developed around opium trafficking. From the remote tribes of Meo/Hmong who grew the opium poppies, CIA front organizations such as Air America flew the raw opium to collection points within Laos (main base: Long Tieng), then on to Vientienne, where it was processed into pure heroin at the Pepsi-Cola bottling plant (which never bottled any Pepsi). It then left the country through four routes: Hong Kong to San Francisco (picked up by Santos Trafficante's network for distribution inside the U.S.); Air Vietnam to Da Nang and Saigon by Nguyen Cao Ky's distribution network; Singapore to Australia to be handled by the Nugan Hand banking complex representatives; and Bangkok to Marseille, to be distributed by the Corsican Mafia. All proceeds were returned through the Nugan Hand banking complex, but much less actually went back into financing the war. It appears that the majority of the funds went into private accounts after being laundered through Nugan Hand.

After the fall of Vietnam and the U.S. extraction from Laos in 1975, U.S. policy attention shifted to Iran and the Middle East. The same players involved in Laos—and later Vietnam/Operation PHOENIX—showed up in Teheran and Isfahan, Iran. These individuals were instrumental in setting up the Shah's secret police, the Savak, and in selling and trading military equipment and technology for cash and drugs. Two of the individuals involved at this point, Albert Hakim and Edwin P. Wilson, later formed EATSCO (Egyptian American Transport and Services Co.), which, among other things, became involved in the arms-for-hostages efforts of NSC, William Casey, Admiral Poindexter, Richard Secord, Oliver North and others.

After Iran fell to Khomeini and the fundamentalist Moslems, U.S. foreign attention shifted farther west, to Nicaragua. Again, the method of choice for financing the operations became drug trafficking. According to a former member of the CIA team (Terry Reed) and other sources, it worked like this:

Cocaine from the Columbian cartels was flown to Panama, to a Panamanian air force base, where agents of Manual Noriega removed a percentage as their cut (Israeli colonel Michael Harare and Mossad agent Amiram Nir). It was then flown via Corporate Air Service, Ltd., to Illopango Air Force Base in El Salvador and split into three batches: One to be flown to Southern California, the second to Guadalajara, Mexico, where it was to be crated and trucked via land route to Texas, and the last to be flown to Mena, Arkansas, for further distribution. The carrier from Illopango on all three air legs was a Miami-based CIA proprietary air transport company.

It is what happened in Mena that is of interest to this investigation.

Mena, Arkansas, 1982-?

According to Reed (and other sources), cocaine was flown into Mena airport by "Enterprise" pilots coming in from Honduras and El Salvador (on some occasions, from Panama direct). The drugs were then offloaded, then loaded onto smaller aircraft for further distribution within the U.S. Almost all of these smaller airplanes, normally twin engine aircraft, were stolen from private airports and repainted with N numbers registered to similar type aircraft belonging to innocent owners.

According to Reed and other sources, payoff money to Arkansas government officials was flown at night in what were called "green flights" and dropped in duffle bags on property owned by an associate of governor Bill Clinton. The money was then picked up and transported to Little Rock, where it was allegedly laundered through the Rose Law Firm and ADFA (Arkansas Development Finance Authority). Reed goes into detail regarding the money laundering that allegedly connects Rose Law Firm to ADFA, Felix Rodriguez, James and Susan McDougal (Whitewater Development Corporation), Stephens Incorporated (Jackson Stephens of Little Rock), Bert Lance of BCCI,

First American Trust, National Bank of Georgia (Lance), Madison Guaranty S&L, Worthan Bank, and several branches of BCCI. During the Iran/Contra years the FBI, IRS and DEA were investigating the CIA drug running through Mena and other locations. Thousands of pages of investigatory reports were written and kept in Arkansas at the above offices and the U.S. Attorney's office.

1995 Developments

According to information of unknown reliability that has surfaced since the bombing regarding the Mena drug running and money laundering, there is more to the affair than Reed understood when he exposed the Iran/Contra operation to writer John Cummings. Sources have offered bits and pieces of the puzzle that appear to form the following picture:

The key player in the Rose Law Firm money laundering was allegedly Vince Foster. Working as a cut-out under Hillary Clinton and Webster Hubbell, Foster worked through an off-shoot company called Systematics, Inc., allegedly to wire transfer deposits to various small banks around the country, then to a larger bank in Chicago. The funds were then transferred to offshore accounts in the Cayman Islands and Switzerland. At this time Foster allegedly set up a personal numbered Swiss account to handle his "cut."

The proceeds from the drug payoffs allegedly exceeded $50 million, and were supposedly hidden in accounts that if cross-checked, would check to a "Chelsea Jefferson."

When Bill Clinton went to Washington as President, he took Foster and several other associates with him. Foster was named liaison to NSA—a remarkable feat since few of Clinton's staff members could reportedly pass a security background check and therefore receive a security clearance.

According to various sources the Israeli intelligence organization, the Mossad, had been monitoring Foster's activities and had a file on him. Foster, once he became an insider at NSC with access to secrets including codes, was allegedly approached by the Mossad and "made an offer he could not refuse." The Mossad knew of the drug running through Arkansas, having been in on the ground floor during the arms-for-hostages phase of the NSC operation, and even having an agent on hand in Panama during drug transfers and other projects, and providing a design for a replacement weapon for the Contras to be manufactured in Guadalajara by Terry Reed's "machine tool company."

The deal, according to insiders, was simple: Foster was to leak codes and secrets to the Israelis in exchange for their promise to not expose him, his connections with drug running and money laundering for Clinton, and in addition, the Israelis would add to his Swiss bank account—which they had already discovered by means of their very special computer software given them by "someone" in the U.S. government.

Foster, Inslaw, PROMIS, and Michael Riconosciuto

By "following the players," a new individual enters the picture at this point. But to understand his significance, one must backtrack on the time-line to the 1970s.

Stanford graduate physicist and mathematician Michael Riconosciuto, son of a former OSS man (Marshall Riconosciuto), became involved with a project under the Wackenhut Corporation, through a cut-out known as Meridian Arms Company, to develop new weapons and high explosive devices. These experiments were taking place on the small Cabazon Indian Reservation in the middle of the California desert, considered a separate nation by the U.S. government and therefore not directly controlled by federal regulations or firearms laws. It should be noted at this point that among the officials who composed the board of directors for Wackenhut Corporation was William Casey, who eventually became Director, Central Intelligence under President Reagan—and a player in the Iran/Contra affair.[217]

Riconosiuto developed an extremely powerful bomb of small dimensions, one which used a two-phase detonation. The first version, according to former FBI SAC Ted Gunderson, was tested at Nellis Air Force Base at a location near Groom Lake, Nevada. It was so powerful that, according to Riconosciuto, it killed one technician and injured several others. It was after this, and several other unpleasant events centering around Wackenhut, Meridian Arms, FMC Corporation, and various individuals within these organizations, that Riconosciuto left California and attempted his own venture in Washington state dealing with extracting platinum from mine tailings. Before this venture could take off, Riconosciuto was offered a job from a computer software company named Inslaw, Inc. Inslaw had developed a new software program called PROMIS (for Procecutors Management Information System), which could track data in mainframe computers such as court cases, bank accounts and so on. In actual fact, PROMIS could track virtually anything, but the intended use, by Justice Department contract, was to track drug money laundering and traffic between banks.

Riconosciuto was contracted to develop a "backdoor" in the program, wherein investigators could actually move funds from an illicit account to another depository—like the U.S. Treasury. It could also be used, once installed on someone else's computer system, to explore *their* data from the outside. The CIA was particularly interested in this aspect. By selling this product to other countries—especially their intelligence services—the CIA data ferrets could remotely enter their computer systems, look around and see what was going on, and leave undetected.

A problem developed when the Department of Justice refused to pay the $2.5 million contract fee for the software. Inslaw sued, but went bankrupt with legal fees, even after being granted the sum by one federal magistrate (who was not reappointed after this decision). Justice never paid, but did distribute the software to "clients" far and wide. One such client was the CIA—who sold it to the Mossad, among others.[218]

It was after this that a small, compartmentalized group within CIA allegedly discovered something very interesting during use of the PROMIS software. According to message traffic on the Internet, they had routinely entered the Mossad computer system to check on who was being paid as agents when they discovered several payments going to a previously untraced Swiss bank account—under the name Vincent Foster. They followed up on this and discovered the balance of the account to be in excess of $2.5 million. If this is true, it is obvious that Foster did not accumulate this wealth under normal/legal means.[219]

The story at this point indicates that the "word on Foster spying for the Israelis" was leaked to the White House on purpose to see Foster's and the administration's reaction. If this was the case, it is probable that the following scenario may have occurred: Foster is called by a member of the upper echelon of the White House and advised that "The CIA is on to you—something about spying for Israel." Foster panics.

He cannot turn to the White House as they now want to divorce themselves from his activities, which would be disastrous if known by the public—especially in relation to the Clinton staff having such difficulty with security clearances in the beginning, and he can't turn to other federal agencies for help. It would only be a matter of time before he was "visited" by the FBI for questioning, and he had no idea how much information they had on him, supplied by this cell of CIA which has no part in Iran/Contra or drug smuggling and money laundering through Arkansas.

Foster decides to "resign" and hope the Clintons can work out the details to keep him out of harm's way. He decides to leave the country, pick up his money in Switzerland, then disappear for an undetermined amount of time until things "blow over."

The problem, according to these reports, is that the CIA team had used Riconosciuto's "back door" to empty Foster's bank account, transferring the money to the U.S. Treasury. When Foster calls Switzerland to prepare the bank for his arrival and withdrawal of a large amount of cash, the bank explains he now has a zero balance.

Broke and with no place to turn, Foster calls the only people he can turn to: the Mossad.

Speculation at this point would probably follow the line that Foster's Mossad contact asks who has talked to him, then if he has been interviewed by the FBI or CIA, and when he reports to the negative, he is told to "meet us tonight in the parking lot (or the "apartment") and we'll take care of everything."

At this point the story becomes convoluted. Foster was found dead in his car in the White House parking lot, then laying on the ground in Fort Marcy Park. He had a gun in his right hand (even though he was left handed); he didn't have a gun when found; the gun was found in his car. The case, a "suicide scene," was not investigated by the FBI, but instead by the Park Department Police. No ballistics evidence was reported, other than a gunshot to the mouth, and very little blood was found at the scene. It was obvious that Foster's body had been placed there after death. And the autopsy showed the powder burns to be on Foster's hands in a pattern that would show a double hand grip over the top of a barrel and cylinder—not the pistol's grip. It was more in line with someone who was trying desperately to pull a gun out of one's mouth, not jam it in. And there was no way he could have pulled the

357

trigger with that particular hand position. The most likely scenario was that he was in his car when two or more people joined him. They either killed him there and left his body in the car, or they drove to an apartment in the D.C. area (possibly "The" apartment where clandestine rendevous' were alleged to occur) then held him while one jammed a gun in his mouth and pulled the trigger—probably with a silencer. In the latter scenario Foster's body was then rolled up in a carpet and taken to the trunk of his car (carpet fibers were found on his suit coat and trousers). He was then taken to Fort Marcy Park and dumped.

No bullet was recovered, so the murder weapon was not the antique .45 caliber revolver that had been sanitized which was found at the scene.

Shortly after Foster's death, his office was raided by White House personnel who carried off boxes of files and documents to upstairs bedrooms for examination. Several credible witnesses have reported this, even though it has been denied by White House staff personnel. It appears that if this occurred, it would be any drug running and money laundering documents that would be of most concern. Even though most of these documents were burned and shredded at the Rose Law Firm during an all-night "house cleaning," certain players would be uncertain exactly what Foster kept out as personal "insurance." It has been speculated that Foster's body was left at the White House by his killers, but was moved after discovery by White House personnel to change the area of the "crime scene." If Foster was discovered in his car in the parking lot, the crime scene would encompass his office—and the files—which would be searched by police or federal investigators.

Oklahoma City Connection?

Besides the "coincidence" of Michael Riconosciuto's appearance in explosives work for Wackenhut/Meridian Arms, and his software development for Inslaw that may have been Vince Foster's undoing, it is possible that his two-phase explosive invention (identified as an Electro-Hydrodynamic Gaseous Fuel Device by former FBI SAC Gunderson) may have been used at the Murrah building.

However, there is another set of circumstances that must be explored that may enter into the investigation. Sources have reported that during the Mena drug smuggling and Iran/Contra affair, the IRS, DEA and FBI investigated the affair and kept records and reports until Clinton moved to Washington. These investigative documents (or copies thereof) were consolidated at the U.S. Attorney's office in Little Rock. But fearing for their safety during the next four years, they were moved out of state. It has been said that they were moved to the Murrah building. If this is true, it sheds a new light on the investigation and the motive. All that would be needed by someone desiring to destroy these documents would be destruction of the building that housed them. According to Israeli sources (not Mossad), this is a typical operation for Islamic Jihad, Hamas, and Hizbollah. Cases in point are the bombings of the embassy building in Beirut, the subsequent bombing of the Marine barracks at the Beirut airport, and the Trade Center bombing in New York. All were truck bombs—with exception in deference to the explosives. The Beirut bombings were Semtex—a Warsaw Pact plastic explosive similar to C-4—and were entirely successful with a simple truck bomb. The Trade Center was ammonium nitrate and did relatively little damage in comparison.

The Iraqi Connection

Three items should be mentioned at this point that have not been approached by the media, nor by investigators.

At the end of the Gulf War, over 5,000 former Iraqi soldiers (mainly consisting of officers) were transported (illegally) to this country by the Administration for "humanitarian purposes," and resettled at taxpayers expense. This created a massive stir in the veterans organizations, who remembered how may American POWs had been abandoned by our government in past wars, but was only publicized in their magazines. One of the largest groupings of resettled former Iraqi soldiers, coincidentally, became Oklahoma City. This places the Iraqis who were experts in demolition (re: Kuwaiti oil field destruction) in the same vicinity as the bombing.[220]

According to Israeli intelligence, many of these former soldiers joined 28 cells of the Hamas terrorist group and the Islamic Jihad group here in the United States. One of these groups is located in the

Oklahoma City/Norman area, and is closely linked to other cells in Dallas/Fort Worth, Houston, Miami, and New York.

The Hussein/Barbouti Connection

An Iraqi national named Ihsan Barbouti, who worked covert operations (mainly logistical) for Saddam Hussein, was an "architect" involved in very "interesting things." He owned an engineering company in Frankfort that had a $552 million contract to build airfields in Iraq, and also designed Moammar Khadaffi's German-built chemical weapons plant in Rabta, Libya. He owns (or owned) $100 million of real estate and oil drilling equipment in Texas and Oklahoma.

In 1969, after the Ba'ath takeover in Iraq which brought Saddam Hussein to power as the second-in-command, Barbouti "escaped" Iraq, resurfacing later in Lebanon and Libya.

Barbouti later invested in two companies in the U.S.: Pipeline Recovery Systems of Dallas, which makes an anti-corrosive chemical that coats and preserves pipes, and Product Ingredient Technology of Boca Raton, which makes food flavorings. He attempted to invest in a third company, TK-7, which is located in Oklahoma City and makes a fuel additive, but the deal fell through when the Gulf War started and Iraqi assets were frozen.

These are important because TK-7 had formulas that could extend the range of jet aircraft and liquid-fueled missiles (such as the SCUD), and Pipeline Recovery who knew how to make pipe coatings that were useful in nuclear reactors and chemical weapons plants. Product Ingredient Technology made cherry flavoring, which uses ferric ferrocyanide, a chemical that's used to manufacture hydrogen cyanide (which can penetrate gas masks, and was use to kill the Kurds in Northern Iraq).

Barbouti had the companies ship their products to corporations he owned in Germany, which in turn shipped them to Libya and Iraq—all of which was illegal.

In 1989, Barbouti met in London with Ibrahim Sabawai, Saddam Hussein's half brother and European head of Iraqi intelligence. Sabawai made sure the products and production technology was rushed to Iraq to be in place by 1990. According to the former owner of Oklahoma City's TK-7, Iraq was developing an atomic device for Khadaffi that would be used against the United States in retaliation for the 1986 U.S. air strike against Libya.

According to a Nightline broadcast, a New Orleans exporter named Don Seaton—a business associate of Richard Secord—assisted Barbouti with the "exporting" of the products. Secord allegedly connected Barbouti with Wackenhut. Barbouti met with Secord in Florida (headquarters state of Wackenhut) on several occasions, and phone records show that several calls were placed from Barbouti's office to Secord's private number in McLean, Virginia. Secord has since acknowledged knowing Barbouti. During the Bush administration, Secord was business partner with James Tully and Jack Brennan (former aide to Nixon), who were involved in a $181 million business deal to supply uniforms to the Iraqi army which they contracted through Nicolae Ceaucescu's Romania prior to his execution. The partners in this particular deal were former U.S. attorney general John Mitchell and Sarkis Soghanalian—a Turkish-born citizen who had been Saddam Hussein's leading arms procurer who introduced Super Cannon builder Gerald Bull to the Iraqis. Soghanalian later sold 103 military helicopters to Iraq illegally, was caught, and served six years in prison in Miami.

In 1990, 2,000 gallons of ferrocyanide were stolen from the Boca Raton plant—right under the noses of the security guards. The security was provided by Wackenhut.

It should be noted that Wackenhut only had one guard on duty at the plant during the times of the theft, a ten day period in 1990. For this one guard, Wackenhut was paid by Barbouti four checks: $168.89 on March 27th, $24,828.07 on March 28th, $756.00 on April 5th, and $40,116.25 on April 6th! Quite a sum for one minimum wage security guard.

According to research, two former CIA operatives stated Wackenhut helped Barbouti ship chemicals to Iraq, and that Barbouti "was placed in the hands of Secord and the CIA, and Secord called in Wackenhut to handle security and travel and protection for Barbouti and his export plans." Wackenhut was doing a contract for the CIA and allegedly helped ship chemical and nuclear weapons-making material first to Texas, then Chicago, then Baltimore where it was shipped overseas. (This shipment was investigated by Customs and USDA).

Remember that Wackenhut formed a front company called the "Meridian Arms Corporation" and set it up on the Cabazon Indian Reservation at Indio, California, to build explosive devices, chemical and biological weapons, and other items. Former FBI agent Ted Gunderson believes the explosive device used at the Murrah Building may have been developed by Meridian on a design invented by Michael Riconosciuto (who Gunderson knows and says programmed the back door into Inslaw's PROMIS software for Department of Justice)—who is now in prison. Also note that Wackenhut has been involved with other strange deals involving explosives and weapons. In the 1980s Wackenhut tried to buy a weapons propellant manufacturer in Quebec, but was turned down by Prime Minister Trudeau who stated "We just got rid of the CIA—we don't want them back." Then we have this: William Corbett, a terrorism expert who was in the CIA for 18 years (and now works for ABC News in Europe) said "For years Wackenhut has been involved with the CIA and other intelligence organizations, including the DEA. Wackenhut would allow the CIA to occupy positions within the company in order to carry out clandestine operations."

Wackenhut also became involved in Iran/Contra arms deals. In 1981, Wackenhut formed the "Special Projects Division," which in turn linked up with ex-CIA agent John Phillip Nichols to set up Meridian Arms on the Cabazon reservation—out of view of Congress, and henceforth the Boland Amendment (non-interference in Central America). Representatives of the Contras came to the reservation to see weapons being demonstrated, then gave recommendations on what to send to Honduras for use in El Salvador.

One of the men hired to provide security analysis for the Florida chemical plant owned by Barbouti was Peter Kawaja, a former federal agent. Kawaja, who has become a Gulf War Disease activist, has stated that both chemical and biological warfare weapons were shipped to Iraq prior to the Gulf War, and that many of these weapons were used on U.S. and allied troops by Hussein. He further states that thousands of documents that detail the Gulf War Syndrome cases and government involvement with both production and shipment, and the disease aftermath, were removed from Houston, Texas, and sent to the Murrah building for "safe keeping." If this is true, could it be possible that the Mena drug smuggling investigation records and the Gulf War Disease records were deposited in the Murrah building together for a reason other than safe keeping? According to federal sources, the records were "destroyed" in the blast.

The Question of ATF Foreknowledge

Several questions have been posed by various individuals concerning whether or not the Oklahoma City office of the ATF had a warning or foreknowledge of the bombing. Some local media sources have reported several items of interest, including:

(1) McVeigh was supposedly seen eating dinner three nights before the bombing with John Doe #2 (an Iraqi), a paid ATF informant, and an ATF agent. It was speculated that McVeigh might have also been a paid informant for the ATF, hence his wanderings at gunshows and visitations to militia meetings.

(2) An eyewitness reported seeing strange activities in front of the Murrah building in the early morning hours of April 19th. He reported driving down the street, arriving to the street in front of the Murrah building, then being directed by someone "directing traffic" to move to one lane as he passed the building. This individual was not a police officer, but was standing next to a marked unit of some type with a "stripe around it, kind of like an Military Police car." As this witness passed, he noted several people on the sidewalk in front of the building with "hoop-like devices, like small 'hula hoops', held over their heads, turning in different directions." His discription matches that of ADF direction finding equipment antennas that are used to home in on an electronic emission source, or search for a given emitter of a certain frequency within range of the receiving unit.

As this individual passed, a roadblock was set up behind him and the street was shut off from approaching traffic, which was then diverted. No explanation for this activity was given.

(3) John Doe #2, according to KFOR TV, Oklahoma City, is an Iraqi officer and former member of the Hammurabi Division of the Republican Guard, who was brought in to the U.S. from the POW resettlement program, who lived in north Oklahoma City, and drove a brown pickup truck with a smoked glass bug shield—matching the description of one of McVeigh's reported getaway vehicles. Several eye witnesses saw this individual (later identified by Channel 9 in

Oklahoma City, and the *Daily Oklahoman* as Iraqi ex-POW Alhussaini Hussain) with McVeigh previous to the bombing, with McVeigh in the truck when they asked directions to the Murrah Building at Johnny's Tire Store, and standing by the Ryder truck across the street from the post office one block from the Murrah building as they waited for a parking place in front of the building. Other witnesses saw this individual exit the Ryder truck with McVeigh in front of the building, then speed away with him in the yellow Marquis with the license tag (described as a *white* tag—not a brown Arizona tag) dangling from the back of the car. The sketches of John Doe #2 closely resemble this individual. Later interviews conducted with this person discovered that he now required an interpreter, even though witnesses state he spoke English on earlier occasions. The interpreter he provided coincidentally is the Jordanian, Abraham Ahmad, who was apprehended on Day Two in London at Heathrow airport as a bombing suspect that had flown to England that day and was returned to the U.S. for questioning—then released. It was this individual who, after being questioned, mysteriously prompted Clinton to announce "there is no middle eastern connection, period." (paraphrased)[221]

(4) A Ryder truck, according to media sources, was seen after the blast two blocks away in an alley. The reporters were being escorted by Oklahoma City firemen around the perimeter, which had been cordoned off, when a Ryder truck was discovered. As they passed the truck, men in black fatigues with no markings came out of a building, got into the truck and drove away. Information that surfaced in January 1996, however, indicates that there were two Ryder trucks rented in Kansas. One was rented by McVeigh, and another was rented by John Doe #2, accompanied by a heavy-set white male with a beard. This second truck was seen at a motel one mile from the motel McVeigh stayed in in Junction City, Kansas, during the same days McVeigh was there. A heavy-set white male with a beard was also seen with McVeigh, working around the Ryder truck, in the parking lot of the motel where he stayed.

(5) KFOR reported that a still photo leaked to their station from the seized video tape showed a UPS truck, not a Ryder truck, parked in the spot at 9:00.04. It is probable that this UPS truck was in the parking place where the Ryder truck eventually parked. As McVeigh and John

Doe #2 waited across the street from the post office, one block west of the Murrah building, two "dark complected middle-eastern males in blue jumpsuits or coveralls" reported by several eye witnesses, stood near the front door of the Murrah building. It is probable that when the UPS truck left the curb, one of these two individuals signaled McVeigh while the other kept the parking place open until the Ryder truck was repositioned. Once this was done, McVeigh and John Doe #2 left the cab of the truck and hurriedly crossed the street to the pre-positioned Mercury Marquis. They then hastily left the parking lot, almost striking another witness who closely observed McVeigh and JD-2, then noted the white license tag dangling on the back of the car by one bolt. At the same time the two dark complected males left the area in the brown GM pickup truck which had been parked by the curb a few spaces east (in front of) of the Ryder truck.

(6) Several stations reported that on Day One the rescue operation was shut down for an extended period of time, and all rescuers were moved outside of the perimeter while "federal agents" came in and removed boxes of records/files for "national security reasons." When questioned, considering rescue efforts were still underway and people were still trapped under rubble, the FBI spokesman, Gene Pogue, stated "It's unfortunate." (Question: Could these be the missing Mena and Whitewater records moved from Little Rock?)

(7) In late August it was released that an "extra leg" had been found and could not be tied to any of the victims. The leg, complete with combat boot and camouflage trouser material, embedded with blue plastic fragments matching the "explosives barrels" allegedly used by McVeigh in the truck, supposedly was that of a black female. This does not match any of the known victims.

(8) A KPOC television, Ponca City, Oklahoma, investigative team interviewed the truck rental in Kansas and discovered that McVeigh and another person—possibly John Doe #2—had rented the truck while a third person waited in the car outside. The third person was described as dark complected, and may have been a female. They also discovered that McVeigh and two other people stopped at a coffee shop after visiting the truck rental and were all seen there by patrons.

(9) According to some media sources, the Oklahoma City office of the ATF was on an all-night stakeout the night before the bombing. What was the stakeout location? Was it possibly the Murrah building?

If so, did the ATF have foreknowledge of the planned bombing and decide to make the "big arrest" when the bomber showed up? Was McVeigh actually the informant, working on the inside of the group?

(10) If the above (9) has any substance, something apparently went wrong. It has been speculated that the truck was supposed to arrive at 3:30 a.m., when the building was vacant. But McVeigh—or the driver, whoever it may have been—got lost and did not arrive until just before 9:00 a.m. The ATF, realizing by 6:30 a.m. that it was a "no show," had gone home. This would explain the lack of ATF agents in the office at the time of the blast.

(11) To add credence to the "foreknowledge" aspect concerning federal agencies, the Tulsa Police Department received a request to "watch" a Ryder rental truck identical to the one alleged to contain a bomb at the Murrah building. This request came the afternoon after the bombing. When a field lieutenant queried the dispatcher regarding the assignment, asking what tie-in the truck had, and where the information came from, he was told: "The information came from the same source that warned the Feds about the Murrah building—which they didn't take seriously at the time." This means that someone (John Doe #2?) did, in fact, warn some federal agency of the bombing in advance.

(12)   Later reports from a McVeigh Grand Jury member were published that stated that a second Ryder truck had cropped up, in Kansas, being driven by John Doe #2, who stayed in a motel one block away from McVeigh during the same time frame McVeigh was in Kansas. This may have been the truck suspected to be in Tulsa at an east Tulsa apartment complex, or possibly the one seen by witnesses a few blocks away from the Murrah building at the same time as the McVeigh truck was pulling up out front. In this second sighting witnesses saw two males in the cab of the truck, one white and one hispanic or "Arabian."

Militia Ties?

Within 48 hours of the blast, just after Abraham Ahmad was hastily released after a brief period of "questioning" by the FBI, the media shifted its attention from the middle-eastern terrorist scenario to so-called Right Wing militias—described in the same sentence as "fringe radical hate groups." Extreme efforts were made by mainstream "reporters" to connect McVeigh with the militia movement, in particular the Michigan Militia. Though McVeigh may have attended one of their meetings, no one could remember him being there, and he later stated that he was never at one of their meetings and was not a member. Backtracking this series of events leads back to the Anti-Defamation League of the B'nai B'rith and the Southern Poverty Law Center—both of which have been designated "experts" on right wing and "hate groups" by the New York City-based mainstream media.

Anyone who has researched the militia movement and other non-paramilitary groups considered part of the "Patriot" movement, will quickly realize the ADL assertions are not only flawed, but appear to be highly slanted, inflated propaganda. The profile of those in these movements would match people who would *guard* the Federal buildings—not attack them. Instead of forming to overthrow the government, as the ADL and SPLC suggests, they appear to form to be a local home-guard to resist unconstitutional moves by government officials and agencies. Such moves may be real or imagined, but the fear exists, thus the formation and growth of the movements.

What is highly unusual about this investigation is the fact that the first information available concerning suspects seen by eye witnesses reflected a definite middle-eastern terrorist connection. This aspect *should* have brought the ADL to the forefront proclaiming the fact that now the "Arab Terrorists" that Israel had had to face for so long, were now initiating terrorist attrocities inside the United States. To the ADL, which has been termed a political arm of the Mossad by former Israeli intelligence sources, this should have been a supreme opportunity to make a point: "Our enemy is now your enemy." What is highly suspect is that this did not happen. Instead, the ADL and SPLC, ignoring all actual evidence and witness statements, shifted the public attention totally away from the actual suspect groups. In most criminal investigations this would indicate intimate knowledge of the act, or complicity in the act itself. Even though McVeigh was the only so-called "Right Wing Radical" involved, according to eye witnesses and all investigators in the field, the ADL and SPLC-advised media shifted the focus completely away from the obvious suspects. The question, of course, is why?

The "Elohim City" Connection

During the course of the investigation information surfaced regarding records indicating McVeigh made at least two telephone calls to a covenant community on the Arkansas/Oklahoma border known as "Elohim City." Investigation into this matter produced the following information:

McVeigh met a member of the Elohim City group at a gunshow, possibly in Tulsa. This member was a German national named Andreas Strassmeir. "Andy" Strassmeir is an interesting character, as he managed to enter the U.S. without a place to stay, and succeeded in living in this country, with no means of support, for four years on a six month visa unmolested by the INS. It has been determined that the federal agencies knew of Strassmeir's presence, however were not interested in apprehending or deporting him.

Strassmeir was the "security officer" for Elohim City, a covenant community founded by a Robert Millar (WM-66). Millar's small group accepts offshoot Christian separatists and others indicating a desire to join their community whose beliefs do not conflict with their own. In the past those who would not conform to their doctrine were evicted from their community. It appears, however, that the group became subject to close scrutiny in the following manner.

Strassmeir lived on a credit card for four years, without having to make payments. He is the son of Gunther Strassmeir, the assistant secretary of state under Helmut Kohl for Germany. He is also reportedly a member of the Mossad-trained GSG-9, the German anti-terrorist police formed after the Munich massacre, and had served in the German army as a lieutenant that worked in military intelligence. It has been reported that Strassmeir was sent into this country to infiltrate neo-Nazi and White Supremacist groups (including the KKK, which is also an ADL/Mossad objective). He did this by using neo-Nazi contacts in Germany to "introduce" him to leaders in the White Aryan Resistance (WAR) movement. It is unknown how the connection was made with the Elohim City separatists, but he eventually ended up infiltrating their organization and establishing himself as a military and weapons expert. In this capacity he convinced the residents that they had to form a "militia" for self defense, had to trade their hunting firearms for military-style weapons, then proceeded to teach them martial arts, military tactics and marksmanship. It should be noted at this time that the actual leader of the community was a former Covenant, Sword and Arm of the Lord (CSA) leader named James Ellison. Ellison served as state's witness against the main CSA leader, Richard Wayne Snell, and thirteen other "White Supremacists" who went to trial for sedition and the killing of an Arkansas state trooper in 1988. Note that Richard Snell was executed on April 19th, 1995—the same day the Murrah building was bombed. Ellison married Millar's 14 year-old daughter and effectively took control of the community, using Strassmeir as "security chief." It should also be noted at this point that Ellison and Snell had made statements as early as 1984 that they "planned to blow up the Murrah building."[222]

Strassmeir left the country about eight weeks after the bombing, just after a connection was made through telephone record searches of McVeigh's activities showed that he called Elohim City looking for Andy Strassmeir. According to information received on 27 January, 1996, McVeigh was making contact with Strassmeir. The connection between McVeigh, Strassmeir, and GSG-9 now becomes apparent. The questions at this point are: (1) Was Strassmeir more than an intelligence gatherer, and was he an "agent provocateur"? (2) Was Strassmeir McViegh's "control"? (3) Was the GSG-9 or German intelligence working, as in the past, with the Mossad (and subsequently the ADL) to gather intelligence on neo-Nazis, WAR, KKK and etc.? and (4) Was the information developed by Strassmeir relayed to federal agencies to conduct a sting operation that ended up going bad when a surveillance effort failed to stop the bombing?

It should be kept in mind that there are several Arkansas connections. Among these are: (1) Elohim City is near the Arkansas/Oklahoma border, not far from Mena; (2) WAR has a large following in western and northwestern Arkansas; (3) CSA had its "compound" in the area and its federal trial in Fort Smith; (4) A license tag found one mile from the point McVeigh was stopped on the same highway (95 Arkansas PTA-811—a *white* tag) had been stolen from Fort Smith a few days before the bombing (and soon after being reported as found disappeared from the computer records in Arkansas and NCIC); (5) McVeigh allegedly stole guns from a person in the Fort Smith area. It should also be remembered that Mena is in the region, and was selected as a gun and drug running airhead because of its remoteness and the "leave us alone" attitude of the local residents.

The Mexican Connection

Shortly after the Murrah bombing, information was received (May 8, 1995) from sources in Texas that a subject named "Arbego Garcia or Garcia Arbego" (spelling unknown at the time) was involved in the bombing as a "cash provider" for the event. The source said that "Arbego" sent two Mexican nationals to Oklahoma City with a satchel full of cash to finance the bombing. "Arbego" was allegedly a Mexican Mafia chieftan involved in the cocaine and heroin trafficking through Mexico from Guadalajara to Texas. He allegedly was the ground transportation link during the Iran/Contra Mena affair.

I forwarded this information to both the FBI (Tulsa) and the DEA (Oklahoma—Tulsa office) and asked for each to check their files and/or computers, using various spellings, to see if they had heard of such an individual. Neither replied back that they had knowledge of this individual and no further action was taken. [Author's note: In actual fact, the FBI's response was that as far as they knew, no such person existed because "we don't know him. Never heard of him."]

On May 9th, 1995, I followed up the original information with a memo containing all information I received from my source, who was relaying it from a former Texas law enforcement officer who had investigated "Arbego" and several high ranking Texas government officials, and who subsequently testified against them. These officials included a high ranking Texas national guard officer on state staff, and two relations—all of which had extensive special ops training, which allegedly included service in the PHOENIX assassination program conducted in the later years of the Vietnam war.

Later information arrived, with the source now using proper spelling, that (quoting): "Abrego's contact in Texas was a former Colonel...There are three brothers in this particular family. All three had special ops training, were involved in Project Phoenix...one or more involved with the 'Company.' One or more were on a Wet Team...One is or was a professor at Rice University. Two are, or were, fugitives. These boys are the link to Abrego and Texas. Very bad. Abrego probably set up to silence him like Noriega. He was part of same drug importation ring during Iran/Contra and after. Clinton's boys and committee followers have got to get rid of the main contacts to the Mena mess and anyone so associated."

On Tuesday, January 17th, 1996, Juan Garcia Abrego, 51, was extradited from Mexico, where he was arrested in Monterrey on Sunday, January 15th, to Houston to face federal charges of smuggling billions of dollars worth of cocaine into the U.S. Facing a a 20 count indictment, he was arraigned on February 2nd. During the arraignment testimony indicated that Abrego's network smuggled $20 billion worth of cocaine into the U.S. every year, and budgeted $50 million to bribe U.S. officials. The source indicated that even the Texas governor's office was involved in taking bribe money.

Abrego was involved in the Iran/Contra drug smuggling operation that had entry points in Los Angeles (via CIA-sponsored Contra officers to LA street gangs for further dispersal); Mena, Arkansas; Omaha, Nebraska; and other cities in the midwest (via the Abrego land route) such as Houston, Dallas, Oklahoma City, etc.

Abrego is a member of the Columbian Cali cartel, which shipped 30% of the cocaine used in the U.S.

Abrego was number three on the FBI's "Ten Most Wanted" list since March of 1995—a month before the Murrah bombing and almost two months previous to my original enquiry to the DEA and FBI in which I was told that Abrego did not exist!

It has now been alleged that the records in the Murrah building that were salvaged for reasons of "national security" on Day One may have tied Abrego in with the Mena drug smuggling—along with "other" players up to, and including, the highest levels of government.

It should be noted that former CIA Chief of Station Theodore Shackley, who (with his assistant Thomas Clines) set up the Laotian heroin smuggling operation in Laos during the war in Southeast Asia, now lives in Bogota, Columbia, and is rumored in intelligence circles to be responsible for forming the Cali and Medillin cartels for the purposes of smuggling cocaine and marijuana into the U.S. to support certain compartmentalized CIA covert operations with a source for black funding. The route of smuggling cocaine and marijuana by the "Enterprise" as it was called at the time, was from Bogota, to Panama (where Manual Noriega and Mossad agent Amiram Nir and Israeli colonel Michael Harare took their respective cuts), to Illopango Air

Base in El Salvador, where it was divided into three routings. These routings took the drugs via air to the Los Angeles area, Mena, and to Guadalajara. The drugs at Guadalajara were then transported by truck in crates stenciled "machine tools" to Matamoros, Mexico, then across the border to Brownsville, Texas. Abrego handled this route.

The Cebu City Connection and Nichols' Expenditures

It has been reported that in the two years leading up to the bombing, suspect Nichols expended in excess of $60,000 in expenses traveling to the Philippines. His destination was Cebu City, on the island of Cebu. Cebu is the home of international terrorism in the western Pacific, and includes cells of communist, anti-communist, and Islamic terrorists.

After Nichols' arrest, he left a note to his Filipino wife to look behind a false back of a dresser drawer for an envelope. The contents were hers to keep. The contents proved to be $20,000 in cash.

Nichols had no consistent means of income during that period, and allegedly received this money from McVeigh—who had no job. McVeigh was obviously receiving funding from an outside source, which appears to be a typical "black bag" operation. $80,000 is far more than the duo would have received in trafficking in stolen guns from a single burglary, even if the burglary had occurred.

Anti-Terrorist Legislation and "Cui Bono"

Following close in the aftermath of the bombing was a rapid resurgence of the Foreign and Domestic Terrorism Prevention Act, which had lain dormant previous to the event. The major proponents of the act, which increases federal agency capabilities to conduct surveillance, monitor paramilitary groups, and arrest for a myriad of crimes the same, are organizations that can use the act (such as the ADL and SPLC), once it becomes law, to monitor, harass or attack any rival group that they can cast media attention on as terrorists. It also creates a system of national police by giving added powers to federal authorities, thereby increasing their number of personnel and annual budget.

RIDING THE TIGER

Synopsis of this Report

As stated at the beginning, several questions had to be answered in an effort to further, if not complete, this investigation. One of the main questions was "Who Benefitted?"

First, it becomes obvious that under close scrutiny, especially in light of the events that followed the bombing and the reactions of so-called Right Wing Radicals and militia types, that such an act was the worst thing that could have happened to them and their various "causes." Almost all that were interviewed were both shocked and enraged that anyone would perpetrate such an activity. Still, they became the focus of negative media attention for an extended period, and even investigated by a Congressional sub-committee concerning whether or not they were a "threat to national security."

In the end, not one "right wing" group benefitted from the Oklahoma City bombing. Nor could any such group be connected in any way to the event, despite the efforts of the media and select special interest organizations.

However, when the investigation into motives shifts to other possible benefactors, three main groupings seem to become apparent: (1) Drug traffickers and money launderers; (2) Radical Left Wing political organizations, and (3) Certain government bureaucracies currently under investigation. This last is added because it is one of the main focuses of attention by the various citizen's groups and organizations that consider such agencies as the BATF an out-of-control oppressive entity.

The question is in what way to these various entities benefit?

Drug Traffickers and Money Launderers:

(1) If the records from the Mena drug smuggling operation were moved to the Murrah building from Little Rock (or duplicates kept there after originals were previously destroyed or disappeared), then it would prove very beneficial to those about to come under congressional investigation in the following months (May-June '95) to have those records destroyed, or seized and moved for later destruction.

(2) If records implicated Arkansas and international companies that hold ties to covert paramilitary operations (such as Iran/Contra and international drug smuggling), both past and present, then a covert action activity to destroy or "capture" the records is not out of the question.

(3) Two weeks after the bombing, a fireman videotaping the relief efforts accidently stumbled upon a very suspicious activity behind the Oklahoma City post office, located cater-corner to the Murrah building. Having visited the post office on Day One to tape the relief supplies located in the rear of the building, he had noted a temporary wall and locked door that separated the supply area from another part of the large room. He asked his federal agent "guide" what was behind the wall, and was told that it was mail "that had not been checked" that was being held until it could be screened. The agent did not say what the mail was being "checked" for. On Day Ten the fireman returned to the post office as he video taped subsequent relief efforts and discovered that two all-white unmarked trucks, similar to Ryder box trucks, were backed up to the post office loading area on the west side of the building, and several men in black fatigues appeared to be guarding them. He was told immediately by his FBI "guide" to "put the camera on the ground and do not film this." He complied and stood by to observe the activity. As he watched, he could see that each truck had many SWAT-types dressed in black, wearing black ski masks, carrying submachine guns, standing guard in cordons that ran between the back of the trucks and the post office building. Outside of these shoulder-to-shoulder lines were agents in plain clothes who wore unmarked blue nylon jackets and carried hand-held radios. Several of the blue-jacketed agents were busy loading the trucks with boxes that they were carrying from the post office back room that the fireman had previously noted. He described the boxes as "cardboard file boxes full of documents." Once loaded, the trucks departed the area under guard. Before he was allowed to leave the disaster scene at the end of the day the personnel at the FBI command post watched his entire videotape to make sure the above scene was not recorded. It is possible that the mystery documents were those which were removed on Day One, and then were held at the post office until they could be safely removed to another holding area—or destroyed, depending upon who moved them.

RIDING THE TIGER

Left Wing Political Action Groups/Entities

(1) Such an event (the bombing) would provide a great boost to sagging liberal policy, considering what has happened since November, 1994. When the power shifted in Congress from the Left to the Right, many things began to happen. One of these was the second look at portions of the Omnibus Crime Bill (such as the ban on so-called assault weapons), the Brady Law, and other previous liberal victories. With the exception of a handful of liberal congressmen and senators, the attack on the NRA, the Christian Coalition, and other conservative groups slowed in intensity to virtually a trickle of what had previously been on the agenda. But immediately after the bombing, this attack renewed its strength.

(2) The dormant Anti-Terrorism bill was revived, inflated, and put on the fast track to passage—a mainstream liberal (and Clinton) objective.

(3) Focus of attention shifted from investigations into Whitewater, Waco, Ruby Ridge, Mena, ATF conduct, and the death of Vincent Foster—all originally scheduled to begin congressional investigations four weeks after the bombing—to "more pressing issues."

(4) Media preparation of the "mind of the public" to accept laws that infringe on the Constitution and Bill of Rights. Shortly after the bombing several polls were conducted asking the question: "How many of your rights would you be willing to give up to be secure from terrorism?" A great number of people responded with "some."

(5) A new "Barbarian at the Gate" in the form of "militias" was created in the media, giving citizens a "domestic threat" to worry about. This follows the typical Hegelian Principle of creating a problem to force a solution not readily accepted by the subject previous to creation of the problem. As an example, one can observe the media and politicians connect guns and drugs. Drugs, according to them, are the problem—but the solution is to take away the guns. This obviously has little, if any, correlation, but the end objective is to use the government-induced "drug problem" as a means of reducing the number of firearms in the hands of the citizenry. Massive amounts of data is available that links various government entities and agencies to drug smuggling. In fact, it was President Clinton that, besides being

linked to Iran/Contra drug smuggling, dismantled the drug intervention program shortly after his inaugaration.

(6) The Anti-Defamation League and Southern Poverty Law Center benefitted by utilizing the media to draw attention to their causes, attack their perceived "enemies"—the ADL-identified "hate groups"—and bolster their liberal following (and subsequently their financial contributions). Also, the ADL's actions after the bombing created a diversion away from further Iran/Contra exposure to Israel's participation in cocaine smuggling (into the U.S.) and drug profiteering. This issue might, if exposed to the American people, effect American foreign aid to Israel (estimated at $3.5 million per day). This might explain why the ADL and SPLC attempted to use the media to divert attention away from the actual perpetrators.

Government Bureaucracies Under Investigation

(It would be remiss to not mention those government bureaucracies and sub-organizations suspected by many citizens as benefactors of the bombing)

(1) Bureau of Alcohol, Tobacco and Firearms: The BATF, after the failed raid at Waco, the Ruby Ridge debacle (which cost the government/taxpayers $3.5 million in the subsequent wrongful death suit), and other reported "abuses of power," was to come under government/congressional investigation in the summer months. It was rumored that steps were being considered to disband the BATF. Also to occur in May were the scheduled Waco hearings. It has been reported that the Waco investigative documents and all documents seized from the Mount Carmel site were kept in files at the Murrah building. Also, *if* the story of the stake-out on the Murrah building to "catch the bomber" has substance, and due to timing such did not occur and the bomb *did* explode after the ATF went off duty, it would be extremely awkward for ATF personnel to come forward in the aftermath and explain why they issued no warning to other agencies and building occupants. At this point the question on "which Federal agency received advance warning from the source that provided the information to Tulsa PD?" must be asked. It has been reported that the BATF in Oklahoma City received advance warning that there was a bomb threat

on the building. Could this be the same source? If so, it must be asked if the BATF might be guilty of inaction.

(2) FBI: The FBI would not have benefitted. FBI did not have an office in the building, and other than possible references to activities in Waco in the Waco reports/documents, had no connection. FBI investigated the Mena affair, and destruction or loss of such documents would have been detrimental.

(3) DEA: DEA would not have benefitted. DEA investigated the Mena affair, and went to great lengths to protect their sources and documents for later use. Destruction or loss of these documents would have been detrimental.

CONCLUSION

It should be apparent to the investigator that McVeigh and Nichols, virtually unassisted, could not have planned, provided for, financed, and executed the bombing by themselves. Much has been written by explosives experts and professional investigators concerning the lack of capability of the single truck bomb, containing only 4600 pounds of ammonium nitrate explosive mixture, to do the damage that was accomplished.

Little is known about McVeigh's activities since he left the Army in 1992. It is possible that he was identified by a "recruiter" during his military service during the Gulf War or shortly thereafter, and was subsequently recruited into the covert intelligence community.

If this is the case, then it becomes apparent that many "theories" concerning the Oklahoma City bombing appear more valid. Examples: There were military high-explosive devices inside the building; McVeigh was working with the BATF to help apprehend the actual "bombers"; a contract "wet-team" organized and executed the bombing to destroy records, inflame public sentiment for political expediency, and embarrass the conservative politicians in power in Congress; drug trafficking and money laundering by the covert intelligence organizations would not be exposed by hard evidence; and other theories and items of suspicion.

Still, one cannot disregard the initial thrust of the investigation linking a middle-eastern connection to the bombing. It has been determined since the event that a "holy Jihad" has been declared against the United States, and that orders have been given to various Hamas, Hizbollah and Islamic Jihad cells in this country to "bring down towers, buildings of finance, buildings with women and children, and other targets" to show the "infidels" that no one is safe from the Jihad. This Jihad can be traced to three countries: Iran, Iraq, and Libya—all supported by clandestine Russian advisors. In fact, an interview with the daughter of a PLO officer exposed the fact that a PLO office exists in Mexico City, and that many PLO and middle eastern males passed through the office on their way to America to participate in the Jihad. She stated that they were taught by the Russians, equipped by Islamic Jihad organizations, then sent to destroy buildings and other targets. She also said that the Russians told them to "use American neo-fascists to do the jobs, so they get the blame." When questioned, she explained that the Russians called American neo-Nazis neo-Fascists.[223]

The end result, whether it was a covert operation to destroy records and inflame the public, or an attack by Islamic Jihad terrorists, or a combination of both, is that it appears that other, much higher entities than McVeigh and Nichols are involved.

The investigation should not stop, or even slow down, with the apprehension of McVeigh and Nichols as the only suspects. With leads into the Right Wing, Christian, Constitutionalist, Militia, Patriot, NRA, Conservative, and other groups—with the exception of WAR and the Elohim City/Strassmeir connection—not developing anything of substance, it is now time to explore the other side of the political spectrum.

It is the opinion of this writer that the investigation is far from over.

END OF REPORT

I submitted this report shortly before I retired. My investigation, however, was far from complete. Since then I, along with a team of other investigators, have discovered even more frightening information linking possible covert operations to the Oklahoma City bombing. But one item should be kept in mind above all else—what ever happened to the search for John Doe #2?

In actual fact, there are at least eight "John Does" linked to this case: McVeigh (John Doe #1), JD-2 in the Ryder truck with him, the dark complected person in the car in Junction City Kansas, the heavy-set white male "biker-type" with the beard in Junction City, another "McVeigh" and passenger in a second Ryder truck seen in the Brick Town section of Oklahoma City at the same time the first Ryder truck was pulling to the curb in front of the Murrah Buidling, the two "Middle-Eastern types" in blue jogging suits at the Murrah building, and a swarthy male who drove the yellow Marquis get-away car from the parking lot north of the Murrah building.

I cannot go into a great deal of information regarding this case in this book. It would take an entire book in its own right to do the case justice. But I can close this chapter with a set of interesting facts for the reader to peruse.

I offer the parallels between Timothy McVeigh and Lee Harvey Oswald, and the Murrah Building crime scene and Dealey Plaza. I wrote and published the following article in *Assassination Chronicles* magazine (JFK-Lancer):

The Parallels
Oswald and Dealey Plaza vs. McVeigh and the OKC Bombing

This writer has been personally involved in the investigation of the Oklahoma City bombing since the third day after the tragedy, and the scenario that has developed is chillingly close to that which transpired after 11:30 a.m. on November 22nd, 1963. Following are many of the items to be noted:

Around 9:00 a.m. Oklahoma time on 19 April, 1995, a huge explosion rocked the downtown area of Oklahoma City. Within minutes, during the evacuation of what remained of the building, searching for casualties, arrival of police, fire and rescue personnel, and mass confusion, two more "devices" were found inside the building. Bomb squad personnel had to deactivate at least one of the devices and remove them from the area for safety. Within the hour the media stated that they were "ATF training devices, not actual bombs." If this were so, why were they placed in strategic locations inside the building, on floors away from the ATF offices?

In Dealey Plaza, a scenario quickly developed wherein a lone shooter, from the 6th floor of the TSBD, allegedly fired three shots which amazingly created over a half dozen wounds (including one missed shot) and escaped the scene undetected. Later investigation showed that only two empty 6.5mm shell casings were found on the 6th Floor and turned in, along with a rifle and one live round. Yet these documents were altered during the Warren hearings to reflect *three* empty cartridges to fit the "Magic Bullet" theory.

Oklahoma City: Two seismic events transpired according to the University of Oklahoma Seismic Center. The tape, which actually shows three equal events, is quickly debunked by the government as being "the initial explosion, followed by the building collapsing" (ignoring the first event entirely). Yet, when the entire remaining building was demolished by controlled demolition, the event recorded on tape was barely noticeable. Still, the investigators insist that only one bomb was used: the Ryder truck bomb allegedly delivered by McVeigh.

Within twenty-four hours the Ryder truck grows from a small van to the largest box-truck in Ryder inventory to contain the ever growing amount of ammonium-nitrate explosives required to create the damage done to the building. Yet, according to sources outside the government, very little indication of nitrate deposits at the scene are found—indicating a different type of explosive.

In Dallas, following the ambush of JFK, damage control seemed to begin immediately with the focus of attention being directed away from the Grassy Knoll to the Book Depository building—and a shooter on the sixth floor. In OKC, the first two leads indicate that two "middle-eastern males" were seen hanging around the scene and were probably involved; and an all points bulletin was broadcast by OKC Police Department to search for a brown pickup truck with a smoked-plastic bug shield. Within a few hours, the FBI cancelled both leads—and told the police that they had not issued an "attempt to locate" on the pickup truck. But the OKC PD had the original release from the FBI asking for the APB, and it had been duly noted in their radio logs.

McVeigh is picked up for speeding, in a car with no license tag, for doing 85 mph, by the Oklahoma Highway Patrol. Oswald was picked up, for allegedly shooting Dallas officer J.D. Tippit, after entering the Texas Theater without buying a ticket. In each case, the FBI was notified within a short period of time that a "suspect" was in custody.

In Oswald's case, items "linking" him to the Kennedy assassination were "found" in various locations: photos of him with a Carcano, a Mannlicher-Carcano found on the 6th floor, etc. For McVeigh, his license plate was allegedly "found" within two blocks of the bombing scene, having been supposedly ripped from the rear of the car by the concussion of the explosion—yet cars in the parking lot where the explosion occurred still had their license tags, and most had not even been blown out of their parking places!

For Oswald, the Carcano was traced to him by the FBI, who, before the advent of computers and data bases, managed to track the weapon from its entrance into the U.S., to an importer, to Klein's Sporting Goods, to a sale to "A.J. Hidell," to Lee Harvey Oswald. All in two days. Over a weekend!

For McVeigh, the rear axle (differential?) of the Ryder truck was discovered, wherein an ID number was allegedly discovered, which was supposedly traced from the manufacturer, to Ryder, to a truck rental in Kansas—all within hours. Interviews with the rental agent produced two sketches: McVeigh and John Doe #2. The media did not report that a third person was present, who waited outside in a car, and who appeared to be dark complected. And John Doe #2, as a lead, evaporated when the FBI stated that there was a mistake, and that he was a soldier from Fort Riley who rented a truck the previous day, and was not involved with McVeigh. But media outside of Oklahoma did not report that *another* John Doe #2 was discovered by KFOR TV in Oklahoma City, and that he matched the suspect sketch; was seen by six eye witnesses in a bar with McVeigh and Nichols only days before the bombing; drove a brown Chevrolet pickup with smoked plastic bug screen; and was an Iraqi officer who had fought against us in the Gulf War! It also was not reported that over 5,000 Iraqi POWs had been brought into this country for "humanitarian reasons," and a large segment ended up being settled in Oklahoma City.

In Oswald's case, it is interesting to note that he had connections to the White Russian community of Dallas-Fort Worth, and that these people had been settled here by the OSS when Allen Dulles brought the SS Galizien Division out of Europe at the end of World War II, to Greece, then Canada, then New York City and Dallas/Fort Worth. The teenage children of the Galiziens were later utilized as CIA assets for infiltration into Russia—they spoke Russian and had relatives inside who might provide support after infiltration. (This makes one wonder about the Oswald who, during his time in the Marine Corps in Japan, "taught himself" Russian within a few weeks).

The investigation of the Kennedy assassination rapidly focused on the "lone nut" scenario. Witnesses who did not support this rapidly-building case against Oswald as the lone participant were intimidated, debunked or misquoted in reports. Most who saw something other than a man in the 6th floor window were not subpoenaed to testify before the Warren Commission. In McVeigh's case, anyone who brings forward information that there had to be more than one bomb, or that there were higher powers involved in the bombing, or more than just McVeigh and Nichols involved, is quickly debunked, discredited or ignored. On at least three occasions this has already occurred: Brigadier General Partin (USAF ret.), an explosives expert that said that the ammonium nitrate truck bomb could not have done the damage inflicted on the building by itself; and former FBI SAC Ted Gunderson, who stated other devices exist in inventory that are much smaller and more powerful that could have caused the damage; and Debra von Trapp, a former high level government contractor who brought forth information linking members of the Clinton administration to the bombing, have been ignored or discredited with the full weight of the mainstream media.

Instead, within twenty-four hours of the event the mainstream media, *en total*, slanted the dagger of suspicion to "far right radicals," such as the burgeoning militia movement. In particular, the Michigan Militia was targeted as being "tied" to McVeigh. In actual fact, though two members of the Michigan Militia stated that they think they saw McVeigh at one of their open-to-the-public meetings, McVeigh himself says he never attended. Still, even if he was seen at a meeting, it could easily have been part of a setup to develop manufactured connections to a group already under scrutiny by certain bureaucrats.

For Oswald, a radical background (this time Left Wing) was built in the press long before Dallas. He was filmed handing out "Fair Play for Cuba" pamphlets on a New Orleans street corner, and was interviewed on television wherein he declared himself a "Marxist" for public consumption. The media has maintained ever since that Oswald was a Marxist by his own admission, and killed Kennedy for radical political reasons.

The media's attack on the militia—who had absolutely nothing to gain and everything to lose in the aftermath of the bombing—resulted in new "anti-terrorism" laws being ram-rodded through Congress in the wake of media-generated public emotion. These laws had been laying stagnant for months, having been written following the New York City Twin Towers bombing but delayed due to their conflict with Constitutional rights. Interestingly, one major result of the Kennedy assassination was the "Firearms Control Act of 1968," which was the first major legislation regarding governmental control of citizens firearms since the 1930s where private ownership of automatic weapons had to be licensed by the federal government—another restriction on Constitutional rights.

Then there are the "Wild Goose Chases" of the national investigation. During the Kennedy investigation, hundreds of FBI agents were sent hither and yon to interview, question, and report on even the most obscure leads and "witnesses." The agents, all trying to do as sterling a job as possible, then sent their reports to FBI headquarters for screening and absorption. Few agents ever saw the "big picture," could compare notes, or even knew just why they were following up on a given lead. The same is happening with the OKC bombing investigation. Hundreds of agents have "followed up" on even the most obscure leads, but, like their predecessors who investigated the Kennedy assassination, they are left out of the grand scheme of things and are only privy to certain pieces of the puzzle. It is also interesting to note that the main question is not being answered concerning the motivation behind any crime: Who Benefits?

FBI agents who attempted to follow the money, and the powers, behind the murder of JFK were quickly redirected by Washington to other activities. The agents who smell a large rodent with the Oklahoma City bombing (as in Who Benefits) are finding themselves subject to the same circumstances. It appears to once again be a system of directed investigation, ignoring or debunking of anything that does not fit the mold of a predetermined outcome ("A Patsy Gets The Blame"), and disassociation with the idea that higher powers are involved.

The television coverage of the transfer of McVeigh from jail to the holding facility at Tinker Air Force Base, outside of Oklahoma City, was quite reminiscent of Oswald's transfer attempt from the Dallas PD jail to the county jail. The only difference was that there was no Jack Ruby to intervene. However, it should be noted that McVeigh was dressed in bright orange, and wore *no bullet proof vest*! It makes one wonder if an opportunity was not being presented by design.

Until the investigation begins to follow leads concerning "Who Benefits?" it is unlikely the Oklahoma City bombing investigation will progress to a full, believable, conclusion. If the case against McVeigh and Nichols, who the government maintains acted by themselves, was so iron clad, then we must ask ourselves why the government prosecutors had to ask for a ninety day extension on their investigation before attempting to present McVeigh for indictment before a federal Grand Jury.

There's one more element to consider: the video tape. In 1963, Abraham Zapruder's film recorded the events that transpired in Dealey Plaza. It was seized by the FBI, obtained by *Life* magazine (who employed former OSS and CIA personnel such as senior editor Charles D. Jackson), and not released until much later. When it was released it had been altered. In Oklahoma City, the media reported that the camera on an automatic teller machine (*or* the Southwestern Bell building security camera, *or* a camera on an apartment building a block west) recorded McVeigh parking the Ryder truck, then walking away from it to get into a vehicle to speed away. The federal authorities seized the tape for evidence.

Why have we not seen this tape? If it is being kept secret until trial, then it should be released after it has been exhibited in a court room. The question is: will we ever see it?

Many other questions remain to be answered, as in the Kennedy investigation, but will probably never be breached. Questions such as: Was there an Iraqi connection? Were there actually two (or more) explosions? Were there two or more other bombs inside the building? Why did McVeigh's license tag "fall off" his car? Why was the APB on the brown pickup not followed up on, then later cancelled altogether and denied to exist by the FBI? Exactly what number was found on the truck axle that would identify the vehicle? Why have we not seen photographs of this number plate? Why was not John Doe #2, the Iraqi Republican Guard Division officer, not followed up in detail by the FBI? And why, after it was shown there was no connection, did the media continue to shift public attention to right wing groups ranging from the NRA to various militia organizations when those entities had the most to lose from such a tragic event? And most of all, what exactly were the documents taken out of the Murrah building's ruins that were so important that rescue operations had to be curtailed?

And one cannot help but wonder if Timothy McVeigh will utter, at some point in time, "So I'm the patsy!"

One last note to consider: The June 25, 1996 bombing of the Khobar Towers apartment building in Dhahran, Saudi Arabia, which killed 23 Americans was briefly referred to by the media as "proof" that a truck bomb could do the damage to a building that the ammonium-nitrate packed Ryder truck supposedly did. But the claims quickly died when it was determined that 1) the building was built with poor grade materials and was not reinforced to American standards; 2) that only the front wall fell and little damage occurred past that point; 3) the Murrah building was built to strict modern codes using the strongest materials; and 4) the explosives used were in excess of 5,000 pounds of RDX and Semtex *high* explosive. A bomb twenty-five times as powerful as the "Ryder bomb" did only one-tenth the damage.[224]

Chapter 33

Incident at Gila Bend

It was only five months after the bombing of the Murrah Building when the next target on the category list was hit. On Monday, October 9th, 1995, the only "Mass Transportation—Land" target available in the United States was attacked.

The news broke first on television, monopolizing the airwaves on the news channels first, then spewing forth from the mouths of the talking heads of the main networks: Domestic terrorists, calling themselves "Sons of Gestapo," have derailed a passenger train near Hyder, Arizona. According to the news blurbs, sometime around 1:00 a.m. that morning the Amtrack "Sunset Limited" passenger train, enroute from Phoenix to San Diego, jumped the tracks in a remote mountain wilderness area northwest of Gila Bend, Arizona. This placed the location in Maricopa County, outside of Phoenix. Two investigative agencies would come into play: the Maricopa County Sheriff's Office (under Sheriff Joe Arpaio) and the FBI (since the incident concerned interstate commerce).

Three points were made by the news media: 1) the rails had been sabotaged by someone who knew what they were doing, as they had effectively disabled the electronic warning system by using some type of jumper cables to bypass the disconnected rail, 2) the area was extremely remote, almost inaccessible, and occurred on a downhill curve that S-turned onto a bridge over an arroyo, and 3) there was a note found at the scene that pointed directly toward what the media was labeling an anti-government or right wing extremist group. The note was signed "Sons of Gestapo—SOG."

The next morning I studied an aerial view of the scene depicted in an AP wire photo. Four passenger cars, still coupled together, were off the tracks laying on their side to one side of a small bridge, with two angled down into a dry wash. The caption explained that of the 268 people that were aboard one was killed and 100 injured. The article mentioned that deputies found a message at the scene that mentioned Waco, Ruby Ridge, the FBI and the Bureau of Alcohol Tobacco, and Firearms. It was from this single note that the media derived the idea that some extreme Right-Wing group was responsible. The article went on to mention that "An electronic database search of U.S. newspapers big and small found no mention of "Sons of Gestapo." [And] a search of about six months worth of Internet discussion groups and World Wide Web pages also found nothing."

After reading the rest of the article and watching the news network broadcasts for the remainder of the day, I could see that something was definitely wrong. From my experience investigating the Oklahoma City bombing, and digging into the various political groups that were suspect during that investigation, I felt that what was occurring was a continuation of an agenda. I also knew that the Maricopa County deputies would not have access to what we had discovered during our investigation of the Oklahoma City event, and that if the federal agencies followed the same course as they had in Oklahoma, and if they were directly controlled by the Justice Department in Washington, the Maricopa deputies would find themselves left out of the picture concerning what really might have happened and who should be put on the suspect list. I feared that if I was right in my analysis, and if the perpetrators were more than a pickup truck load of local radical bubbas, then the case might go much higher and eventually be covered up by the shadow powers in Washington.

I knew from 26 years experience as a law enforcement officer that there are hundreds of good, honest federal agents who try their best to do a sterling job in investigating criminal events. But I also knew that when certain crimes have a national or international perspective, and politics regarding higher agendas are involved, then the investigation is taken out of the hands of the local federal authorities. When this happens, they are controlled from a much higher level—normally in the

Washington, D.C. arena. And because of my experience with the investigations of events that form the preceding chapters of this book, I knew that if a high level political agenda was being served in this case, the chance of a coverup was not out of the question.

I also found the note, signed by a group that neither I, nor any of my contacts, had never heard of, most intriguing. I felt that if I could read the full contents of the note, I might be able to determine if it was a legitimate claim or a false flag. If it was indeed a plant to lead the investigators and media astray, it would mean a great deal to the case in determining the proper direction for the investigation to proceed.

I also found it very suspect that the location of the derailment was in such a remote area. If a small group of saboteurs, bent only on derailing the train, were involved, then they would have picked a much more accessible place to vandalize the tracks. By picking such a remote place, the chance of discovery during a getaway was much greater than simply selecting a location only a mile or so from a highway—unless they did not arrive at the scene or leave by ground transportation. In that case, such a location made sense.

I then spread out aerial and ground maps of the area and began studying the terrain. Both my military and aviation backgrounds came into play as I dissected the terrain features surrounding the crash site and noted several things that made me believe that the job had been planned by professionals who knew exactly what they were doing.

First, the railroad tracks ran fairly straight from Phoenix, southwest to the northeast base of the Gila Bend Mountains. There, they made a gentle curve up through a mountain pass, then began a downgrade toward the bridge. Just before the bridge was a well-defined S-turn. It was here that the perpetrators had selected a rail and pulled 29 spikes, then installed the jumper to defeat the warning system.

Beyond the bridge to the west the tracks ran almost in a straight line to Yuma. The target point selected was in the most remote point along the route, at the end of an S-turn, at a bridge over a dry wash, where a derailment would cause the most damage. Beyond that, the surrounding terrain features told an additional story.

The aviation sectional map showed the bridge to cross a wash at the north end of a U-shaped valley. Mountains surrounded the site on the west, north and east. The most logical access route would be from the south, which was fairly flat and open. What I saw as a pilot was that if the perpetrators came in on the ground, they probably approached from the south, possibly from a mining road that ended at the dry Gila Bend River bed only six miles away. Though a dirt service road ran along the tracks, the distance they would have to travel would be a circuitous route approximately 38 miles in length to the nearest highway, Highway 8, which runs from Eloy (30 miles south of Phoenix) to Yuma. The question that needed to be answered at this point concerned physical evidence that was not mentioned by the media. Were there tracks of a vehicle, either four wheel or dirt bike, going to or from the scene of the crime? If not, and the saboteurs had not driven the rough dirt road at nighttime for 38 miles, then I found myself developing another prospective mode of ingress and egress from the scene.

By coupling my knowledge and background as a military officer with my experience as a police helicopter pilot, I began analyzing the map as if I were going to plan such an operation, taking in the terrain, time of night, weather, and obstacles. First, I would want to be inserted and extracted by air. Taking into account what appeared to be a professional job of picking the target site, I surmised that a team would have been formed and that they might have access to a helicopter. I knew I was reaching, but it seemed a theory worth exploring.

If a helicopter was used, then it would be a simple job to fly in from the south, land near the bridge, drop off a team, then leave the area until called back by radio. Then I'd return to the site pick up the team, then egress the area, all below the hill tops. This, however, meant that the pilot would have to fly in and out twice, which would draw attention from any hikers or campers in the area. If the team was well trained, however, the pilot could remain on the ground for the amount of time needed to pull the spikes, then leave with the team. Risky, but possible. The additional benefit to this particular section of desert is the fact that the mountains would block radar from Phoenix, and a helicopter could fly in low and undetected.

I had additional reasons to consider the air-insertion theory. I had heard of covert operations training that had been conducted for some time only 90 minutes flying time away at a highly secret base called Pinal County Airpark, known in the aviation industry as "Marana." This "airport" is a locked-down secure facility run by Evergreen Inc., reputed to be a "contractor" to government agencies, including the

CIA. Rumors had run rampant during the Iran/Contra investigation that the airstrip had been one of several used for drug shipments into the U.S., but little documentation exists indicating this was followed up on during the Congressional investigation into the affair. I knew the facility, which was located near Highway 10 that runs from Phoenix to Tucson, had access to military-type helicopters, and that a great deal of strange "night training" had been reported by passersby. Exactly what went on there behind the front of being a desert aircraft storage facility for the various airlines, no one knew. But very reliable individuals had reported seeing both dark, unmarked helicopters, and skydivers dropping in mass into the nearby desert wearing black uniforms and black square "Paracommander"-style steerable parachutes.

Was some covert paramilitary agency training troops in night commando-style insertions? I couldn't help but wonder if there might be a connection between these strange activities and the nearby train derailment.

I had to know more. And I wanted to see a copy of the actual "Sons of Gestapo" note. On the afternoon of October 10th, I sent the following fax to Sheriff Arpaio.

FAX MESSAGE

To: Sheriff Joe Arpaio, Maricopa Co. AZ
From: MPO Craig Roberts, Tulsa PD, Air Support Unit
Ref: AMTRACK train sabotage case, Hyder, AZ
Date: 10-10-95

Sheriff Arpaio,
I am a Tulsa PD police officer who has worked with our local office of the FBI on the Oklahoma City bombing case. During that investigation, which is still ongoing, I have had occasion to discover many things that may be of interest to you and your investigators regarding your Amtrack case.

First, from the information I have heard on the news and read in the local newspapers, I would suggest you proceed with extreme caution regarding opinions on suspects or suspect groups. The below examination of facts, when evaluated together, paint a very suspicious set of circumstances:

RIDING THE TIGER

1. Anyone who has been in the military and received training on ground combat operations in a guerrilla environment knows that the number one basic target for partisans, guerrillas, and terrorists who have limited resources are open, non-secured remote stretches of railroad tracks. Simply by removing key structural components, such as spikes, couplings and tie-bars, preferably over a bridge or on a bend near a ravine, an entire train can be derailed. This will tie up a section of rail line for an indefinite period of time. In Special Forces Warfare School at Fort Bragg, training manuals discuss teaching guerrillas to do just exactly what was described. Special emphasis is placed on the facts that it is easy to accomplish, and that the planners should pick a remote area to preclude discovery.

2. This attack could have been accomplished by very few people, maybe only one. Not seeing the scene I cannot comment, however, it definitely would not take a large "team" to do this.

3. Question: Were there any four-wheel drive vehicle tracks on the scene when the first outside elements arrived? If not, then whoever came in and performed the sabotage would probably have utilized a helicopter. If this is so, it is unlikely to be any local militia bunch. And if a helicopter was used, please contact me as I may be able to provide more information on where you might look for leads.

4. Question: Is this section of track normally on the Amtrack run for the Sunset Limited? If not, then someone would have had to know that it was a diverted run, and that the Amtrack train would take it.

5. Question: Did anything in the note reflect on this particular train? Or would the saboteurs have settled for any train? Look very hard at the intelligence gathering capabilities of the sabotage "team" concerning the timing of the train, relative to the remote location, the section of tracks, and the fact that a freight train passed unmolested 18 hours previous.

6. Examine the structure/grammar of the note carefully. The biggest flaw I see is that they call themselves "Sons of Gestapo." My experience is that only those who learned English as a second language have a habit of leaving out the word "the" in a sentence. This is most prevalent in the speech of Eastern Europeans, Middle-Easterners, and Russians. Instead of saying "I am going out to *the* car to get *the* book," such an individual would say "I am going to car to get book." These

individuals correlate their own native language to ours by using their sentence structure and replacing the words for those in English. If they normally do not use the word "the," then it will be missing. If the writer of the note was someone who spoke English as a primary language, he or she would probably use such a name as "Sons of *the* Gestapo."

7. The problem here is that *no one* would choose such a hokey name. Not unless they were trying to shift attention to neo-nazis. Even the so-called "extreme right" would not choose such a stupid and incriminating name. Any amateur investigator can see that whoever did this purposefully attempted to leave "evidence" incriminating so-called militias and other paramilitary groups. Especially with the references to Waco and Ruby Ridge. We ran into the same thing with the OKC bombing, but McVeigh has very little, if any, "ties" to any militia. Still, the bomb was detonated on the anniversary of the Waco climax, which launched the media on a huge right-wing witch hunt.

8. During my investigation of militia groups I have never come across any called "Sons of Gestapo," nor anything remotely like it.

9. Ask yourself this question: "Who benefits?" This is the most important question of all. I think you will find that if anything, these types of attacks are totally against everything the militia groups believe in. In fact, if you can find any local members of such organizations, they will probably tell you that they would help *guard* railroad tracks, not destroy them. From my investigation I discovered that the vast majority of the paramilitary militia types are people who do not "hate" the government, nor are they anti-government. They simply fear the government and what has happened in Congress over the past two-three years. They especially fear attacks on their Second Amendment rights. But they do not fit a psychological profile of someone who would hurt innocent people.

10. RE: the Waco and Ruby Ridge "rallying cry" on the notes: Neither has anything to do with trains, Amtrack, or Arizona. Someone who wanted to "attack the government, FBI or BATF" would not do so by simply attacking some passenger train with no government connections. They would go after a government facility or personnel.

11. So back to "who benefits?" If the media plays this up, with stage direction from the Southern Poverty Law Center's "Klan Watch,"

supported by Morris Dees and the ADL, just like what happened on Day Three of the OKC bombing, then the thrust will be pressure to pass the stalled "Anti-Terrorist" bill. If you do not know what is contained in this bill, obtain a copy and read it carefully.

12. Examination of the chronological facts:

1. World Trade Center bombing occurs in NYC. Little national impact outside of the Northeast.

2. Oklahoma City bombing. Massive news coverage, nationwide manhunt, focus shifts from "Middle Easterners" to "Militia" under preplanned manipulation of certain left wing organizations in just over 24 hours. Anti-terrorism bill rejuvenated. Investigation stalls with capture of only McVeigh and Nichols (who obviously are not in this alone). Despite $2 million reward and hundreds of agents no other arrests are made and the search for "John Doe #2" ends.

3. Hyder train derailment. Note(s) left in feeble attempt to point fingers at "right wing extremists," or neo-nazis, or militia groups. Local law enforcement is not so quick to jump on the bait this time. Even the media is being more cautious.

4. What's next? Upon examination of the events, we have these targets that have been subject to terrorism:

A. World Trade Center: Downtown NYC, home of ABC, NBC, CBS. Lots of media coverage.
B. Government building in Oklahoma City—right in the heartland in "good ol' boy" patriotic America. More deaths of innocent civilians, lots of blood, more massive media coverage.
C. Largest mass-transportation vehicle in inventory, a train. Not only a train, it's Amtrack, and it was hit in Conservative Arizona—which also just happens to be an area reportedly inhabited by numerous militia groups. It is also the state where McViegh visited Fortier (Kingman).

If you follow this pattern you find: The world's largest civilian corporate building, a middle-America Federal Building (with massive loss of lives), and a passenger train. Of the five basic (land-based) terrorist targets, only two remain: An airliner and a large gathering of people (the Black Sunday scenario). If these events are related, (and the same people are involved for

393

whatever motive), it would follow that a civilian airliner or maybe a sports event would be a candidate for a future "domestic terrorism" target. If your investigators would like to visit with me to compare notes, I would be happy to share any ideas, theories, or information that might assist in your case. I think my five months of investigating the Oklahoma City bombing to date might provide a few items of interest that could relate to the Amtrack case.

I would be particularly interested in knowing if the possibility exists that a helicopter may have been used in this event. If so, I may be able to provide further leads.

END OF MESSAGE.

Two days after sending the fax I received a phone call from one of the sheriff's detectives working the case. He told me that he had been given the fax and was going to pass it along to the lieutenant in charge of the Sheriff's investigation team. He also told me that "it's a mad house, and the FBI was pulling agents in from all over. All they have us doing is fetching coffee."

I asked if they were sharing information and he laughed. "They're the big FBI pros. We're just a bunch of hick deputies who don't know anything." I sympathized with him. I had been down this same road myself a few times when dealing with the feds. He promised to have the lieutenant call me.

My next step was to begin calling some of my contacts who have expertise in various fields that would be relevant to this case. The first and most important contact I made was with a federal officer who must remain anonymous to protect him from repercussions. For purposes of this story we will call him "Jack." Jack's expertise was in the area of government and civilian aviation operations, and he had contacts throughout the NTSB, FAA, and other agencies.

I called Jack and we spent over an hour discussing the case. Like me, he pulled out his aviation maps and studied the area. And like me, he was also a pilot with military and civilian experience in both fixed-wing and rotary-wing aircraft. We eventually arrived at four possibilities of what may have occurred if this was indeed a professional team-type insertion. First, a helicopter flew in, dropped the team, left, came back and pulled them out. Second, a helicopter flew in, waited on the ground while the job was done, then flew out with the team. Third, they jumped in, then were recovered by a helicopter either just after the mission was accomplished, or when the huge number of medical, news and emergency helicopters arrived after the derailment. In this scenario, it would be simple for a helicopter to show up as one of many, load up a few of the "victims," then leave the scene without anyone taking particular notice. The last scenario would involve a ground insertion and extraction by vehicle. Proof that this last possibility was the case would depend on what information came back from Maricopa County regarding vehicle tracks.

Jack decided that it would be pertinent to check the weather conditions the night of the incident. As he broke loose to do this, I began making notes and compiling a case file.

Meanwhile, the FBI, who had dubbed the case "Operation Splitrail," continued the investigation in Arizona. Within two days they were exploring the possibility that the note was a plant and that the saboteurs might not be a terrorist group after all, but possibility a disgruntled railroad employee. Such an individual might have a working knowledge of how to derail a train, and also disable the warning device—something so-called "militia types" would probably not even think of. Also at this time the governor of Arizona, Fife Symington, told the press that he had read one version of the note that was left at the scene and said that there were several versions, but most were "comparable in terms of content."

Acting special agent in charge of the Phoenix office for the FBI, Larry McCormick, said he believed the case was the bureau's second-biggest crime scene investigation after the Oklahoma City bombing, encompassing over a square mile of rugged desert. Assistant U.S. Attorney Janet Napolitano stated that "We are going to pursue every bit of evidence and every lead very thoroughly...until we find the person or persons who committed this crime." I remembered Janet Reno saying the same thing about the Oklahoma City case.

An "unnamed source" leaked to the AP that the case had been put under Assistant FBI Director Robert Bryant, who heads the bureau's national security division. According to the source, "Bryant's national security division has the case because it has the potential to become a terrorism case, but we have not reached any conclusions yet whether terrorism is the motive or not."

It appeared that the public, by way of the media, was being mentally prepared for the eventuality that the Amtrack derailment would become another case of "domestic terrorism."

When Jack called me back he was elated at what he had discovered. First, the weather on the night in question was this: A full moon, wind out of the south at 8 knots, and a clear sky. It would be an ideal night for air operations. Next, he was almost choking when he said "guess what else I dug up? I pulled some strings and had the Albuquerque Center run their radar tapes for that night and you won't believe what they found. We've got a target."

"What kind of target? You mean over the site?"

"More than that. We have a VFR target squawking 1200 that left Tri-City airfield in Albuquerque on a southwest course, climbed to 10,500 feet, then, when it was exactly due east of the Amtrack site, turn due west and flew a course line that took it one mile south of the site. But just before arriving over the site, it dropped to 8,500 feet. After crossing the target zone, it turned on a southwesterly course towards California at 8,500 feet. Albuquerque contacted the Los Angeles Center which tracked the aircraft to a landing at Montgomery Field in San Diego."

"What was the time frame?" I asked.

"It crossed the valley south of the bridge at 1940 hours."

7:40 p.m. on a full moon night, with the wind out of the south. The plane was one mile south of the bridge, which would compensate for wind drift. Things were beginning to fall in place.

"You know what we need to do now?" asked Jack. "We need to contact the DEA or Air Force guys down at Tucson or Yuma and have them run their radar tapes for that night from their Aerostat drug balloon radar units."

The DEA and Air Force have several tethered "blimp" type balloons staked out along the border with down-looking radar to watch for low flying drug flights. If a helicopter was involved in the pickup, which may have approached from the south as we speculated, then they might have it on tape.

"Can you get that information?" I asked.

"I'll get on it."

My next contact from Maricopa County came from a detective working the case. He had read my initial fax and called to explain that his people were taking an interest in the possibilities I mentioned. For starters, he said that they had conducted a search and had not located any ground vehicle tracks coming into the scene, other than those that they attributed to rescuers and the media. No tracks extended across the desert, and they were now exploring our suggestion of an air insertion being involved. It still seemed far fetched, but the idea of air assets being used was beginning to carry more weight as the investigation progressed. He asked if I would put my ideas together in a more detailed memo and fax it to them for consideration. That afternoon I sent the following memo:

MEMO
To: Det. Div. Maricopa Co. SO
From: MPO Craig Roberts, Tulsa PD, (Air Support)
Re: Amtrack sabotage, Arizona
Subj: Aircraft ingress/egress possibilities

Considering the nature of the area/terrain at the derailment site, it would appear (from the aviation map) that entering by 4WD vehicle would be very unlikely for anything less than the most dedicated individuals. Without having first-hand knowledge of the site, I can only speculate on how saboteurs could have entered the area, sabotaged the tracks, then exited.

Air Assets
If there is a complete lack of tire tracks entering the area after a systematic circumferential search of the crime scene, accomplished at a distance far enough away to preclude contamination by rescuers, then it would appear that air assets might have been used. Two modes of insertion become apparent: helicopter and parachute.

  1. The most likely insertion and extraction mode would be by helicopter. The same aircraft could fly in at low level, after dark, from the south, and by following the canyon indicated on the aviation sectional map, fly north from Painted Rock Dam until intersecting the railroad tracks or trestle. It would be a simple matter to drop a few people off, exit the area, then return later to pick them up.

A. A second method of egress would be for such individuals to hide nearby, watch the train derailment, then enter the scene when rescuers arrived. They could then blend in to the mass of traffic and be extracted with victims or rescuers.

2. The second most likely method of ingress would be by parachute—probably HALO (High Altitude Low Opening) method. Please do not rule this out, as there is some basis for this observation:

A. Radar track records show a target (aircraft) "squawking" 1200 (Visual Flight Rules—VFR) on its radar transponder at 1940 hrs (7:40 p.m.) on the night of the derailment, flying east to west at an altitude of approximately 8500 feet. This radar track was recorded by FAA air traffic control assets. This target passed 1 mile south of the wreck site—which put it over the relatively flat open area of the canyon north of the horseshoe bend of the Gila River wash. It would be a simple matter to drop HALO sky divers to this DZ (ground level at site approximately 2100 feet MSL), wherein they could hide their chutes and walk north to the trestle site. They could then be extracted later by one of the above described means.

Items to Note:

1. Organized training for HALO night drops by paramilitary teams have reportedly been conducted in the desert for the past two years in a semi-remote location 1.5 hour's flying time from the wreck site. According to sources, these drops have occurred on an almost nightly basis near an airport located approximately 108 nautical miles east-south-east from the wreck site. The individuals are parachutists who jump from twin-engine cargo airplanes. They jump at dusk or after dark utilizing square steerable parachutes that are black in color. According to some of your local sources and newspaper reporters, some of these individuals have been encountered by hikers in the mountains northeast of Phoenix conducting "military exercises."

2. This same organization also has access to numerous helicopters of various sizes and configurations.

Synopsis

There may be no connection between the above organization and the Amtrack incident, however if ground infiltration and egress is ruled out, and air assets are considered a possibility, then the above information may be of value.

Additional Lead

There is a DEA "Aerostat" tethered radar balloon located near Yuma that has the capability of "look down" observation for low- level aircraft. Your office can request a check of the radar photo records to see if any high or low level aircraft (such as helicopters flying at low level) are depicted in the area in a 24-hour time frame prior to the incident. A request would probably be best served if the time frame was narrowed to approximately the time of darkness to the time of the derailment. Of particular interest would be the radar track to determine point of origination and/or termination of flight. If the flight was picked up near a closed former military auxiliary strip, such as Luke 11 which is just south of the site, further investigation of radar records would be required to determine where a target arriving at that location would have originated.

If anyone from your office would like to visit further on this, I can be contacted at my office number.

The next day Jack called. I could tell the satisfaction in his voice as he said "Bingo!"

"What do you have?" I asked.

"I talked to a master sergeant at Yuma. He said his people would be more than happy to help out with the Aerostat radar search. Seems they get bored and this would give them something interesting to do. Said he'd get back to me as soon as he could."

"Great! If they come up with a low target going into the site from the south, say at 80 or so knots, then I have my helicopter. So with your high level target that came out of Albuquerque..."

"Dumbo."

"What?"

"That's what we'll call the airplane. I love code words."

"Yeah, well, all we need now is 'hummingbird' and we'll have this thing nailed. The biggest question, though, is who are these guys?"

"Maybe Yuma can tell us that if we can follow a radar target back to its base."

"Check."

The next call from Maricopa County was from the lieutenant in charge of the investigation for the Sheriff's Department (Jack codenamed him "Ringmaster"). I gave him a brief oral resume of my background, a short rundown on my experiences investigating the Oklahoma City bombing, and cut to his case.

"So, how's the FBI treating you guys, Lieutenant?"

"Let me put it this way. They are chasing ghosts out here and pissing a lot of people off, and as far as they're concerned, we're just baggage. The Sheriff told me that we have a homicide involved that is our jurisdiction, and that we are going to work this thing until we either make a bust or run out of leads. It doesn't matter what the feds do, we're going to work this case our way, with or without them."

I was always gratified to find other law enforcement officers at the local level who searched for the truth no matter what politics were involved at the national level. We chatted for a few moments then I broke a question I was dying to ask.

"Any chance on seeing a copy of the Sons of Gestapo note?"

"Sure. We've got a copy and I can fax it to you. It doesn't really say much of anything, though."

"No matter. I just want to eyeball it and see if anything stands out that might be of interest."

"Sure. No problem. Here it comes..."

Five minutes later I was reading a copy of the only piece of physical evidence found at the scene (verbatim from original version, including errors):

Indictment of the ATF and the FBI

Before dawn the women awoke to say their morning prayers. The women slept upstairs. They lit their kerosene lamps because the electricity had been turned off by the FBI. After observing lights in all the upstairs windows, the FBI ordered the teargas bombardment. Afterwards only two upstairs windows were lit. The location of each was recorded. Over the next few hours, ventilation holes were poked into the walls. These holes made the fire burn very much faster. Otherwise the fire department would have had time to put out the fire before the women and children died in the flames. At noon the light from the two kerosene lamps was obscured by bright sunlight. Everyone had forgotten about them except the man who carried their locations written on a scrap of paper in his pocket. He ordered the tank drivers where to crash through. Guess under which two windows. He ordered them to raise their guns. As they backed out, the guns were lowered. The video tape shows clearly the floor being raised by the tank a foot and a half. Guess what happened to the kerosene lamps in the rooms above the tanks. A minute afterwards black smoke started to pour out of the windows where the lamps had burned. This is the normal time needed for a kerosene fire to build up.

Who is policing the ATF, FBI, state troopers, county sheriffs and local police? What federal law enforcement agency investigates each and every choke hold killing committed by a police officer? each and every beating of a drunk whether or not a passerby videotapes it? each and every shooting of a police officer's wife who knows too much about drug kickbacks? each and every killing at Ruby Ridge? The Gestapo accounts to no one. This is not Nazi Germany. All these people had rights. It is time for an independent Federal agency to police the law enforcement agencies and other government employees.

Sons of the Gestapo

SOG

To me, the note seemed to contradict itself in several areas. I especially noted that there was no explanation of the reason behind the derailment. I also noted that in the last paragraph the writer condemns Nazi Germany and Gestapo tactics, then signs the note: "Sons of the Gestapo." I also saw for the first time that there was the word "the."

But what I saw that really raised my eyebrows were the letters "SOG."

Maybe it was nothing. But as an old Southeast Asia hand, I remember that one of the terms used by Phoenix Program assassins working under MACV-SOG (Military Advisory Command, Studies and Observations Group) was a twisted bar-room version of the last

401

acronym. "Yeah," a drunk trooper would mention. "I'm SOG...a son of the Gestapo."

Was this some type of message being sent to others who would know the meaning? Or was it just a coincidence? Without an arrest or more clues, we would never know.

I typed up a memo regarding my analysis of the SOG note and faxed it to the lieutenant:

Maricopa Co. S.O.
Homicide Division
REF: Amtrack case

Lt. ["Ringmaster"]
Good to talk to you yesterday. I have a large packet of information on the topics we discussed that I will drop in the mail in the morning.

I received the SOG note and have been giving it some study. Considering my research into the various political groups and the mentalities of the various factions we discussed, I have a few observations that may prove useful in your investigation.

1. Was this note given to you by the FBI, and did you have a chance to see the actual original note to make sure they are identical?

2. Is it possible that someone could take the original note, retype it in a computer, and issue the retyped version to you or the media?

I ask these two questions because I wonder why, since they are computer generated notes, the FBI confiscated the suspect's typewriters? Were there other notes sent to the railroad that we do not know about? Also, I can't help but wonder why all the press releases referenced "Sons of Gestapo" on Day One, and the note that we have here says "Sons of *the* Gestapo." Note the word "the" added.

3. I can't help but note the acronym "SOG" with a line over it, not under it. Is there some significance to this?

4. Regarding the note itself, it appears to be a feeble attempt to hook this thing up with the right wing extremist groups, especially the militias (without specifically naming them). This might be because by the time the wreck occurred, the militias had already fought their public relations battle in the media and Washington to the point where anyone

behind this was hesitant to point a direct finger at them for fear of raising the public's eyebrows.

5. It could be that there is absolutely no connection to any right wing political or paramilitary group. The reason is that there is no one on the conservative side that wants *bigger* government—and especially a super-watchdog or superior federal law enforcement bureau or administration as the note demands.

6. I also find suspect the fact that the writer(s) state "The Gestapo Accounts to no one. This is not Nazi Germany" then goes on to call themselves "Sons of the Gestapo." What in the world is *that* supposed to mean? I think it's all smoke and mirrors. It appears to me that the whole thing is an attempted diversion away from the real perpetrators.

7. Whoever did the derailment was very dedicated to doing it in that particular spot, as there are so many more accessible locations that would serve the purpose—except for the bridge over the dry wash. Still, they would have to have a topographical map, a railroad map, or an aerial map to see that the tracks made those turns and hit the bridge at that point. The S-turn and bridge area are not visible from any road and would not be known by the average person.

Let's examine the last paragraph and try to get inside this guy's head:

"Who is policing the ATF, FBI, state troopers, county sheriffs and local police?"

This statement is basically "who watches the watchers, and who guards the guardians?" It lumps federal and local law enforcement together in the same boat—which the militias and right wingers do not do. They simply suspect the federal guys, and sometimes distrust the local sheriffs if they feel they are corrupt politicians.

"What *federal* law enforcement agency investigates each and every choke hold killing committed by a police officer?"

No one on the right wing wants a federal bureau to interfere in local affairs. They do not trust the FBI, nor the federal courts, to be oversight committees.

"each [sic] and every beating of a drunk whether or not a passerby videotapes it?"

Note the non-capitalized "each." Also, this statement obviously refers to the Rodney King affair.

"each and every shooting of a police officer's wife who knows too much about drug kickbacks?"

This might refer to the Arkansas State Trooper's wife who "committed suicide" because she knew too much about the drug smuggling in Arkansas during the Clinton governorship. But now we have a guy who damns and accuses law enforcement, then wants to stick up for us?

"each and every killing at Ruby Ridge?"

This reference, plus the first "Waco" paragraph, are definite finger pointing to groups on the Right (or anyone who questions government).

"The Gestapo accounts to no one. This is not Nazi Germany. All these people had rights. It is time for an independent federal agency to police the law enforcement agencies and other government employees."

Again, no one on the Right would have suggested such a thing. They would have demanded "states rights" and "10th Amendment restrictions on 'federal gestapo agencies.'" They definitely would *not* have demanded a new or superior *federal agency* to do be an oversight or watch dog outfit.

A last thought: The heading is "Indictment of the ATF and the FBI." What does the railroad, or Amtrack, have to do with the ATF or FBI, or Waco or Ruby Ridge?

This was what I would call a "publicity hit." It was done for media effect, not for revenge or to make a political statement. That's why I can't help but wonder *Cui Bono*—Who Benefits? I keep coming up with the anti-terrorist bill in Congress.

I would suggest that you do not make the same mistake that the Dallas Homicide Bureau made in November, 1963. I would work this case as a local homicide case and keep the investigation separate from the FBI. The FBI in '63 was more concerned with political damage control than they were with catching the bad guys.

Let me know if there's anything else I can do between now and January when I come out to pick up our new helicopter. Jack will be flying in as well and we can go over what we have at that time.

The investigation dragged on through December with little headway. By then the FBI had raided a suspect's house in California and confiscated his typewriter and some large railroad tools. He allegedly fit the profile of "disgruntled railroad employee." Eventually they let him go and returned to Arizona.

On the same day the California suspect's house was searched I received a fax from a contact that contained an extract the FBI Behavioral Science Unit's psychological report on the "Actor" responsible for the derailment. According to my source, the unit analyzed the "Sons of the Gestapo" note and discounted the "right wing" theory. They then began concentrating on the disgruntled employee theory, which accounted for the raid on the California house. They also had been working on the "local yokel" theory, and that such a person or persons may have intended to "loot the train."

My source wrote: "Another possibility (which brings us back to the Right Winger) may be an attempt to embarrass the FBI so as to allude to their incompetence by not solving this case or possibly suggest the FBI (Feds in general) need to be *strengthened* to 'prevent' such occurrences in the future—back to "Anti-Terrorist Bill." *Cui Bono*?

The FBI analysis of the note mentioned that the "possible actor had a working blue collar knowledge, not just familiarity with railroads. Had specific knowledge of the area of the derailment, had a lot of anger directed against the railroad," then went on to ask: "Disgruntled employee/former employee? Local resident affected by the rail road? Railroad customer?"

The end paragraph of the analysis is most telling. In it the writer states that "[It] Appears the note that was left may have been left to distract the investigators away from the actor, as the actor feels that the crime scene would point to him quickly."

In the interim, Jack and I had been eagerly waiting for a response from the Aerostat radar unit in Arizona. Finally, Jack called and reached the master sergeant whom he had first made contact with and was so eager to help.

"Sorry," he said. "We can't help you out."

"What? Why?" asked Jack.

"The plug's been pulled."

"What does that mean?"

The sergeant sounded very uncomfortable when he replied "We really wanted to check this out, but all I can say is the balloons were down that night."

"Why?" asked Jack.

"Maintenance."

"All of them?" asked Jack, incredulously.

"Yes, sir." The sergeant sounded very nervous.

"Why?"

"All I can tell you is that they were ordered down for maintenance. It came from above my pay grade."

That ended it. There would be no cooperation from DEA or the Air Force. We couldn't help but wonder who "above the sergeant's pay grade" had ordered the only radar assets available in the region "down for maintenance." We reasoned the order had to come from Washington. But why would Washington be concerned with routine maintenance, and why *all* the balloons? It was obvious to us that the balloons had been up and they were ordered not to release the radar information, or someone did not want any "look down" capabilities available that night. No right wing bunch of Gestapo/militia types had the capabilities of pulling that off. It was obvious that this investigation was, like Oklahoma City, being steered away from the truth.

Jack and I decided to get together and compare notes. Both he and I were scheduled to be in Phoenix in January and planned on meeting with some of the Maricopa County investigators. We saw little more that we could do to help out, other than make them aware of the possibilities of where this investigation could go and why we felt there was a higher agenda involved. Beyond that it would be in their hands.

To protect those involved in the investigation who met with us in Phoenix, I can only provide the reader with this: the meeting lasted almost three hours, wherein we went over maps, reports, and the various plausible scenarios regarding the aerial aspects of the case. The Maricopa County element was very receptive, though somewhat skeptical about the possibility of shady commandos parachuting in to sabotage the tracks. We wargamed each scenario, but kept arriving back to the same elements that we could not ignore: the radar track of the unidentified airplane, the time frame it occurred, the fact that *all* of the radar balloons were mysteriously down that night with an inadequate explanation from the military, the lack of ingress and egress tracks to the site overland, and the evident non-existence of any group before or since who called themselves "Sons of the Gestapo."

There was one other odd element. One of the Maricopa sources advised us that they were chasing down a "rumor" that two campers had reported seeing men in parachutes dropping into the vicinity that night!

At the same time our unofficial meeting occurred, the FBI was busy in the local communities that bordered the wilderness area. According to the *Arizona Republic*, residents of the vicinity "complained that the FBI is harassing them. But Callahan [FBI] said a majority of those questioned have willingly cooperated. 'I understand that there are some desert rats out there who naturally don't like authority...But we have to follow up.'" Interestingly, the FBI asked the local residents questions about knowledge of any local militia unit. One local replied, "Buddy, you can't get three people out here to get together on what kind of pickup to drive, and you think we're going to form a militia?"

The article mentioned "Of new interest to authorities is the note's reference to an unnamed police officer's wife who was shot because she knew 'too much' about drug-related activities...Officials have failed to connect the reference to an actual law enforcement incident." I couldn't help but wonder if this "incident" was that concerning an Arkansas police officer who was "suicided" on June 12, 1994 in Arkansas. On that date, the body of an Arkansas officer, Bill Shelton, was found dead on his girl friend's grave with a bullet behind his right ear. His girlfriend, Kathy Ferguson, was the former wife of an Arkansas state trooper who was being sued along with President Clinton in the Paula Jones sexual harassment lawsuit. Ferguson had been killed exactly a month earlier, on May 12th, and her death was being investigated as a suicide. Cause of death was a gunshot wound to the right temple. According to *The Economist*, Ferguson had been collaborating with Ms. Jones and "may have been aware of details" of other activities at the time. Whether these "other activities" included Iran/Contra drug running through Mena was not mentioned. But if the motives behind her death did involve knowledge of cocaine smuggling, it would correlate with the mention in the Gestapo note about a police officer's "wife" being shot for knowing too much about drug activities.

When we left the meeting with our Maricopa contacts, one asked "what do you think we could do next? We're about out of leads."

"If there's more to this than a couple of renegade malcontents deciding to derail a train then leaving a note as a false trail, then I'd say it would be interesting to just fire a shot down range and see who sticks their head up."

"How's that?"

"You might consider leaking the word that your agency was interested in a possible connection between the activities at Marana and what happened at Hyder. You might even mention that you are following up on the idea that someone may have used air assets to attack the railroad—that you've heard rumors of helicopters and guys in parachutes, and that you plan to get together with the Pinal County folks and see about paying a visit to Marana. Then just sit back and see what happens. If you are told to stay away from Marana, or are obstructed from looking in this direction, then that should tell you something."

Whether or not this "bait" was leaked I do not know. But within a week after our visit to Phoenix, the investigation seemed to trickle to a halt and no further mention was made in the media about the event.

The last contact we had with the Maricopa County Sheriff's deputies came in the form of a telephone call from one of our contacts soon after the meeting. "You know the five types of terrorist targets you listed?"

"Yes."

"Well," he said in a very concerned tone, "We've got the Super Bowl coming up in a few days. That would sure fit your 'large gathering of people' scenario."

"Yes, it definitely would. I don't know if they, whoever 'they' are, would try something so close to the last event or not. If my theory holds water, these attacks—if they are related and part of someone's agenda—seem to be geographically spaced across the country. The World Trade Center bombing was in New York, then the Murrah Building was further west, then the Amtrack incident almost to the West Coast. I would suspect that the next incident, if there is one, would be either on the coast or in the northern Mid-West, or possibly back on the East Coast again. But it wouldn't hurt to lay on some extra security."

"We're planning on that."

"One last thing that has been bothering me that you should give some consideration to. If the perpetrators of these crimes have Middle-Eastern connections and are really professional terrorists, don't discount the possibility of a chemical or biological weapon being used. Saddam Hussein and Iran both have access to both. And if they can get them, so can Islamic terrorists. Also—and this sounds like something out of a Hollywood thriller—someone inside this country who wants to blame the Jihad-types might try the same thing. Watch the water and food supplies."

"I don't know how we'll do that, but I'll pass it along."

"One more thing to watch," I warned. "There's *two* types of targets left: besides a large gathering of people you have mass transportation—air. They just might try for an airliner next."

Six months later, on a major Iraqi holiday, TWA 800 fell from the sky in a massive fireball into the Atlantic ocean.

And then there was one.

Chapter 34

Behold a Pale Horse

A few days after the TWA 800 tragedy, a small pipe bomb detonated at the Summer Olympic games in Atlanta. Following the tried-and-true law enforcement axioms regarding arsons and bombings, the FBI and BATF began looking for the "face in the crowd that enjoys the action the most" and "the 'hero' who helps out the most during and after the event." Within two days the FBI attention focused on a lone security guard as the possible perpetrator. This particular individual was the person who "found" the backpack containing the pipe bomb, then issued the initial warning to the crowd. After questioning him and searching his apartment and conducting follow-up surveillance, adequate proof of his involvement was not obtained. As of this writing the investigation continues.

Whether a small pipe bomb could qualify as the terrorist attack on the fifth category target, "a large gathering of people," is doubtful. Though the Olympics would have made a prime target for this category, the massive amount of security involved may have precluded such a strike.

What few people realize is the fact that those agencies responsible for security were concerned with more than a repeat of the hostage situation exhibited by Black September (El Fatah) in the Munich Olympics or the threat of a bombing. One of the prime threats that security forces were concerned with involved the possibility of an attack by either chemical or biological agents. Military units that specialize in chemical and biological weapons detection and neutralization had been deployed to Atlanta in advance and were constantly on standby. Precautions were obviously taken by monitoring teams, which may have precluded any such attack. Still, the threat was real and precautionary actions were taken.

Indeed, the possibility of a large scale biological or chemical attack on the American population is more probable now than in any time in our history. Because of events in the Middle East, the American population could feasibly be the next target of such madmen as Saddam Hussein, Moammar Khadaffi, or radical Iranian fundamentalists who consider the United States as the "Great Satan."

During the Gulf War, Allied forces nearly annihilated the Iraqi war machine. Thousands of Iraqis were killed by coalition forces not only in Kuwait, but in Iraq itself. Saddam Hussein did not hesitate to use these attacks and their resultant damage to his political advantage. Massive propaganda was generated and broadcast throughout the region vividly showing the aftermath of Allied bombings in Baghdad and other areas, and whenever possible it attempted to convince the populations of neighboring Islamic countries that the Allied targets were buildings inhabited by civilians—especially women, children and babies. In one infamous circumstance, an Iraqi chemical weapons facility was exhibited as actually being a "baby milk factory."

The fact that Hussein had used nerve gas on entire villages of Iraqi Kurds, or on thousands of Iranian troops during the border war with Iran, had little bearing on the anti-American mindset of the Arab population of the region. Nor was the fact that Iraq had built numerous sites where massive quantities of chemical and biological weapons were being created and stored a relevant factor in the propaganda issuing from Baghdad. The point that Hussein was attempting to make was that the Americans were evil and cruel, and had little or no regard for life. These graphic images of "attacks on the innocent civilian population" were reinforced by video footage of burned vehicles and bodies throughout Kuwait, including those of hundreds of vehicles and troops burned and stacked up on the highway west of Kuwait City during the Iraqi retreat.

Instead of pursuing the attack against Iraq by taking Baghdad and unseating the corrupt and sadistic Saddam Hussein, the coalition forces stopped short of what should have been an actual and legitimate military objective and allowed Hussein to remain in power. The excuses made by the senior commanders and politicians at the time were that the U.N. "mandate" only addressed ejecting Hussein's troops from Kuwait, and that if Hussein was removed from power, a "power vacuum" would exist in the Middle East which would be worse than leaving him in power.

Both of these excuses are weak at best. First, 90% of "U.N." forces in the conflict were American, and had the U.S. government pressed the issue, a thrust to Baghdad to unseat a corrupt and dictatorial government that based its power on intimidation, torture, assassination and other violations of human rights, and who threatened the stability of every surrounding country, would have been approved. Second, the Iraqi government was stockpiling tons of chemical and biological weapons, building long range delivery systems, financing and controlling huge terrorist organizations, and was on the verge of completing development of nuclear weapons. These activities alone threatened the stability of not only the Middle East, but the entire world. Third, taking Baghdad and eliminating the Hussein regime would not have created the so-called "power vacuum" that the politicians used as an excuse to not finish the war in a military manner.

The U.S. Army and other coalition forces, such as Britain and France, all have units known as Civil Affairs battalions or their equivalent. The specialty of these units is to follow closely behind the combat forces and establish and stabilize governments and government services for the civilian population was quickly as possible after an area has been secured. As an example, during World War II these civil affairs units, working with attached engineer units, set up new governments and reestablished such things as food and water distribution, electrical power, sanitation, mail, and other needful services in virtually every city and town that was liberated. Saying that the elimination of the Hussein government would create a power vacuum is tantamount to saying the elimination of Hitler would have done the same thing. Had the U.S./U.N. taken Baghdad and ousted the Tyrant from Tikrit, many of the terrorist organizations and capabilities that exist now would never have been born.

Today, the U.S. is faced with the infiltration of terrorist cells from virtually every hostile fundamentalist Islamic country in existence. Reports indicate that over a hundred cells exist that have ties to, or are a subcell of, the Hamas, Hizbollah, PLO, Islamic Jihad, Egyptian Jihad and others. And for all intents and purposes, the most capable and threatening of the lot are those staffed with former and current Iraqi soldiers. For it is Iraq that has repeatedly threatened to kill more Americans than the number of Iraqis lost during the Gulf War.

The question now is this: does the capability exist for such an event to occur? According to several knowledgeable sources, it not only exists, a plan is in motion. In the scenario that follows, the "large gathering of people" that would more than qualify as the fifth category target could entail every living person in the United States.

During the week of October 10th, 1996, a microbiologist knowledgeable in the Iraqi intent and capabilities went public on shortwave radio and AM radio talk shows with the allegation that he had acquired information concerning a possible Iraqi plan to distribute massive quantities of deadly disease microorganisms across the U.S. His name was Larry Harris, and he introduced himself as a former CIA microbiological lab technician. According to his story, he received a very personal warning from a female Iraqi terrorist cell member shortly after the bombing of the World Trade Center.

Another event added credibility to what he was saying. Approximately two months before he went public, the military decided to inoculate all American service personnel against Anthrax, a disease normally found in sheep and goats and not considered a threat under normal circumstances. Only two times in recent history has the American military shown concern over Anthrax: World War II and the Gulf War. In World War II, it was General Ishii's experiments with Anthrax, Botulin and Plague that frightened the military hierarchy, and in the Gulf War it was the knowledge of Iraqi experiments with these same bioweapons that initiated the defensive measures for our troops. But why would the Pentagon decide it was necessary in 1996?

By the 18th of October, I had received numerous telephone calls from various individuals asking if I had heard of an impending "attack" by Iraqi terrorists utilizing disease organisms—specifically Anthrax and Plague. Realizing that such an event would fit the fifth and final category of land-based terrorist targets, I began to investigate the rumors. I could not discount them out of hand by simply considering that if there was anything to them, the government would be doing something about it and the media would carry the stories, because I knew by this time that the "government" could not be trusted to be honest with the American people, and the mainstream media was controlled by powers who have their own agendas.

After making enquiries, I received a portion of a long document written by Mr. Harris. In it, he describes his encounter with the Iraqi female, Mariam Arif, and relates her story regarding Iraqi intentions to employ biological weapons against unsuspecting American citizens. This, coupled with other bits and pieces of information and rumors that were circulating, instigated me to write an "executive summary" type report for submission to key personnel in various agencies that would be effective in investigating the accuracy of the data and replying with some type of action to counter the threat, if such a threat actually existed.

The following is my memo:

MEMORANDUM FOR RECORD

To: [Agency's name]
From: Craig Roberts, Tulsa PD (Ret.)
Notes re: Biological Weapons Threat (Anthrax, Plague, and
          Botulin)
Date: 22 Oct 96
Ref: Iraqi Terrorism and Terrorist Cells in U.S.

SYNOPSIS

1. We have received information that there is a distinct possibility that a planned terrorist attack involving biological warfare agents may occur inside the U.S. The information has come from various sources, but most specifically appears to have originated from a microbiologist named Larry Carrol Harris whose resume includes duty with the CIA Biowar section at Aberdeen Proving Grounds (1969-72), A CIA Biowar lab in Coshocton, Ohio (1985-91), and now is employed as a Epidemiologist and Microbiologist. (See end of report for contact numbers)

2. In February 1993, Mr. Harris interviewed a female Iraqi bio/med student named Mariam Arif at Ohio State University. Arif was a relative of a former president of Iraq,

General Arif, who was killed in a helicopter crash in 1966. Ms. Arif told Mr. Harris that Iraq was planning a large scale terrorist operation against the U.S. population inside CONUS utilizing biological warfare weapons. She explained that these weapons would consist of Anthrax and Bubonic Plague. [NOTE: The Iraqis are also reported to possess other bio weapons which include Pneumonic Plague and Hemorrhagic Fever].

4. Arif explained that there are at least a hundred "cells" of Iraqi terrorists inside the country, and that each consists often men and one woman (who serves as a "carrier"). She stated that since the Gulf War, Iraqi females have been smuggling various cultures of Anthrax and Plague into this country by secreting sealed vials in their vaginas. Each vial, upon delivery, is used as a base culture to manufacture large quantities of the end product.

5. NOTE: Other confirmed sources have reported a minimum of 28 Hamas and/or Hizbollah cells operating inside the U.S., and that they coordinate with both the PLO and the Egyptian Jihad (who was involved in the World Trade Center bombing). We also discovered that over 5,000 former Iraqi soldiers, who were captured during our advance into Kuwait, were resettled in the U.S. in various cities. Many of these ex-POWs are "former" members of the Republican Guard Division who participated in the demolition of the Kuwaiti oil fields. Specifically, many are/were members of the Hammurabi Division--one of the most blood thirsty units Saddam Hussein has. Further, there is a definite link between Pakistan terrorist activities and those that have occurred in the U.S.

After the Afghan war, the Mujihadeen training camps used by the CIA to train the Afghans were turned over to the Pakistani ISI (Internal Security Service--secret police). The ISI turned the 100-plus camps into Islamic terrorist training camps specifically to train and export Islamic terrorists to non-Islamic countries for the world-wide Jihad. U.S. military intelligence sources estimate they produce 3,700 trained terrorists at one time. The information I have read does not reflect duration of the training cycles, whether one month, six months, or somewhere in between. However, it is known that some of the countries that have been targeted for infiltration for terrorist operations include the U.S., the Philippines, Saudi Arabia (anti-US and anti-monarchy operations), Israel, Jordan and Egypt. What must be understood is that Pakistan (which has the world's fifth largest army—the U.S. is now seventh) trains guerrilla/terrorist personnel for both Iran and Iraq whether they are Shiite or Sunni Moslem. Many of the instructors are Pakistani Baluch, which have no preference between the two sects. [World Trade Center bomber Ramzi Yousef, AKA Abdel Basit Mahmoud Abdul Karim, is a Baluch Pakistani who worked for and was funded by Iraq].

6. According to Harris, immediately after the World Trade Center bombing Mariam Arif considered her arrest imminent. As a friend, she confided in Harris that something terrible was in the works and that he needed to take precautions to protect himself. She stated that she had personally worked in a germ warfare laboratory in Iraq, and they had taken mycoplasma fermentans (incognitus) and genetically manipulated a relatively benign mycoplasma to be much more invasive and pathogenic and capable of attacking many organ and tissue systems in the body. She also stated that they also had isolated and used a form of Ebola Zaire virus that took over 3-7 years to prove fatal (which she claims was used on the Gulf War veterans).

7. Arif said that "when the time comes Iraq would demand at least one American life for every Iraqi killed during the Gulf War." She explained exactly how the cultures of Anthrax, Plague and Botulin were being brought into the country, and how they were being cultured and produced into an effective bioweapon in various "safe house" laboratories across the nation.

8. Arif explained that many of the Iraqis that have come into the country are pilots, and their mission is to locate for later rental, or steal light aircraft, such as Cessna 152s, which could be used to aerial spray population centers with biological agents. She stated that the targets would be "many hundreds

simultaneously across the country. The prime targets would be large metropolitan centers. The subway systems would make a good selective target; who would notice another maintenance man down there spraying for bugs?" Other inviting targets would be the air ducts of large office buildings, or *a large gathering of people like at a stadium.*" [Author's emphasis] She said that they also had ordered external aircraft venturis which are designed to be mounted on the side of airplanes to provide suction for the vacuum instruments, which they have modified to extract the bioweapon product from stainless steel tanks (such as pump-up pest sprayers), for aerial application over cities. [This could explain the "test" flights we've had in the early morning hours over various U.S. cities by low-flying, blacked out unknown aircraft who have been reported flying "grid" patterns between 0200-0400 hrs.—some spraying chemicals that to witnesses taste and smell like "insecticides."].

9. Arif also said a plan existed to mount spray apparatus under cars, fed from pressure tanks, which could drive down freeways and deliver the mist from a venturi by simply opening a valve.

10. She stated that Plague and Anthrax are the "bacterias of choice" because they are easy to manufacture and have an extremely high kill ratio. Medical records show that both Bubonic Plague and Anthrax, once in the human population, are approximately 95% fatal in all cases. Prophylactic measures can be taken in advance to preclude infection in the individual provided enough antibiotic compounds are available for mass distribution over a sustained period of time (in excess of 30 days which would include distribution at least 16 hours before the attack to up to thirty days after the attack).

11. Harris, after research, also wrote that four microorganisms would be the most likely candidates for use in a biological attack by a terrorist organization or nation. They are, in order of preference: Yersinia Pestis (plague), Bacillus Anthracis (anthrax), Vibrio Cholera (cholera), and Salmonella

Typhi (typhoid fever). Countermeasures include Panmycin, Tetracycline, Terramycin, Tetramycin, and Penicillin.

12. Iraqi Motivation Indicators: In 1994, Saddam Hussein, through the state press, indicated that his remaining unconventional warfare weapons (biological) would be used when Iraqi patience wore thin regarding economic sanctions. On September 29, 1994, the government newspaper *Babil*, warned: "Does the United States realize the meaning of every Iraqi becoming a missile that can cross to countries and cities?"

Other quotes that followed over a period of time:

"When peoples reach the verge of collective death, they will be able to spread death to all."

"When one realizes that death is one's inexorable fate, there remains nothing to deter one from taking the most risky steps to influence the course of events."

"We seek to tell the United States and its agents that the Iraqi patience has run out and that the perpetration of the crime of annihilating the Iraqis will trigger crises whose nature and consequence are known only to God."

13. ITEM: The U.N. Special Commission (UNSCOM) assured the United Nations that the Iraqi chemical and nuclear weapons manufacturing facilities were accounted for and destroyed. But they admit that the biological weapons manufacturing facilities could not be found and no evidence of their destruction exists.

14. ITEM: According to General Wafiq Samarrai, former head of Iraqi military intelligence, "Tell the allies that they have to destroy Iraq's biological agents before Saddam can use them...Iraq could attack its neighbors by missile, *or America through terrorism*." Samarrai said that the U.S. might retaliate

through nuclear weapons, but by then "the disaster would already have happened."

15. ITEM: The military is now, for the first time since WWII, decided to inoculate U.S. service personnel against anthrax, both overseas and in CONUS.

16. ITEM: We have received unconfirmed information that an Iraqi/Hamas cell may exist in [blacked out], and that such a cell is linked with a cell in the [blacked out] area, which in turn reports to a major cell in Dallas. [blacked out] also has had a large number of Middle-eastern students taking flight training at [blacked out], and the city has experienced nighttime low-level aircraft "grid pattern" flights by aircraft displaying no navigational lights.

This report, plus other documentation that I could gather, was passed on to people I trusted in various government agencies. Most of these people would, like a bomb threat, take the matter very seriously until it could be proved or disproved. The ball was now in their court.

The question then became: if there indeed existed such a threat, what would the Washington level bureaucrats and politicians do about it? The choices they would have would be thus:

1. Ignore the threat and hope it goes away;

2. Diffuse the threat through negotiations with Hussein and lift the embargo;

3. Clandestinely neutralize the threat by locating and arresting or eliminating the "cells" of suspected or known terrorists;

4. Handle the threat by taking public health precautions in advance;

5. Take all necessary precautions and make everyone aware of the threat by use of the media;

6. Say nothing, then deal with the aftermath with disinformation and coverup, using scenarios that provide for later political advantage by blame shifting and spin doctoring. In this scenario a "national emergency" could be declared which could result in the need for "foreign assistance" by foreign troops and medical personnel. This scenario would fill the "UN Takeover" nightmare feared by various politically aware anti-globalist organizations.[225]

As of this writing the situation is still unfolding. The final result will depend upon how the government decides to deal with it should this threat actually exist. The problem now, considering the cases of criminal coverup by government entities presented to the reader in this book as "case files" from what I have dubbed *The Medusa File* (after the many-headed evil Gorgon of Greek Mythology), is whether or not this issue, or a future one like it, will also be covered up or ignored until it is too late.

The bottom line is this: when we weigh the evidence, using only the samples exhibited in this book, what we have is this:

By the patterns established, it is not beyond certain bureaucratic and political entities in Washington, who infest government offices like cancerous tissue, to use past experiences and the knowledge base gained by those who have gone before to conceal or cover up the truth, and use unfortunate incidents to their personal advantage. In this book, I have endeavored to present a credible set of case files that show how far a government that is no longer controlled by, or answerable to the people can and will go to cover its own political backside, or worse, force the American people to become subject to the Hegelian effect by using fear tactics to achieve a purpose. In the cases presented we have seen people in power violate the trust of the nation by:

A. Breaking their moral contract with our fighting forces and our individual soldiers, sailors, Marines and airmen by abandoning them in foreign lands as prisoners of wars that no longer exist;

B. Use innocent civilian men, women and children, along with unsuspecting servicemen as human guinea pigs in secret, despicable experiments that range from drug experimentation, to mind control, to nuclear aftereffects;

C. Use children in government-controlled international pedophilia rings to gain favors of pedophilic politicians and bureaucrats, both at home and abroad, or in some cases as a means to blackmail or extort high officials;

D. Recruit, hide, and smuggle into the U.S. known war criminals from both Japan and Germany for use by the military in the "arms race," with little regard for what they have done to this nation or our soldiers in the past;

E. Cover up the events, then lie to the American people and our own armed forces about the personal effects of Agent Orange, experiments at Fort Detrick and Edgewood Arsenal, nerve gas and biological weapons releases in Iraq, and the recognition of the causes and effects of the Gulf War diseases;

F. Participate in international drug smuggling and money laundering involving heroin and cocaine in the most massive operation in history, beginning with OSS operations in World War II and carrying through the war in Southeast Asia, the Iran/Contra affair, all the way to our present situation with the White House stopping all drug interdiction and refusing to close off our borders;

G. Lying about or covering up the true circumstances behind the World Trade Center bombing, the Oklahoma City bombing, the bombing of Pan Am 103, the Gander Newfoundland crash of Arrow Air, the derailment of Amtrack in Arizona, the downing of TWA 800, and using these tragedies to pass, then reinforce an Orwellian silver bullet known as the "anti-Terrorism Law" that basically shreds the Constitution and shoves us into the so-called New World Order of the 21st Century—the exact objective of the global-socialist elitists.

Is this the world and the government we will pass on to our children and our children's children? Our shall we educate ourselves and our progeny to be able to understand the basic facts of mankind, that there are only two entities in the world—good and evil—and that we must choose the correct side? Will we eventually learn and pass on to others the fact that each and every person is accountable to not only themselves and the rest of mankind for their actions, but to God himself? And finally, is it too late for this country to make government—and the individuals within the government—accountable for their actions?

These are the questions each and every American must ask themselves at this moment.

Before it's too late.

My people are destroyed for lack of knowledge.
Hosea 4:6

421

Postscript

In *The Medusa File* I have endeavored to present to the reader a sampling of events that have been hidden from the public by a government that has shunned its responsibilities and violated its trust. Many other examples exist, however not every story can be told in one book. The object of *The Medusa File* is to provide the reader with a foundation of knowledge from which to build.

Knowledge is in itself power, and power is best controlled and used when it rests in the hands of the people. It is the people who must control government, not the government which would, if not kept in check, control the people.

George Washington put it well when he warned, "Government is not reason; it is not eloquence; it is force! Like fire, it is a dangerous servant and a fearful master."

"The only thing necessary for evil to triumph is for good men to do nothing."

Edmund Burke (1729-1797)

"And I saw, and behold a white horse; and he that sat on him had a bow,; and a crown was given unto him; and he went forth conquering and to conquer...And there went out another horse that was red; and power was given to him that sat thereon to take peace from the earth, and that they should kill one another; and there was given unto him a great sword...And I beheld and lo a black horse; and he that sat on him had a pair of balances in his hand. And I heard a voice in the midst of the four beasts say, A measure of wheat for a penny, and three measures of barley for a penny; and see thou hurt not the wine...And I looked, and behold a pale horse; and his name that sat on him was Death, and Hell followed with him. And power was given unto them over the fourth part of the earth, to kill with sword, and with hunger, and with death, and with the beasts of the earth." Rev. 6:2-8

"And the rest of the men who were not killed by the plagues yet repented not of the works of their hands, that they should not worship devils, and idols of gold, and silver, and brass, and stone and of wood; which neither can see, nor hear, nor walk; Neither repented they of their murders nor of their sorceries nor of their fornication, nor of their thefts." Rev. 9:20-21

"He that overcometh shall inherit all things; and I will be his God, and he shall be my son...He that is unjust, let him be unjust still; and he which is filthy, let him be filthy still; and he that is righteous, let him be righteous still; and he that is holy, let him be holy still...And, behold, I come quickly; and my reward is with me, to give every man according as his work shall be...I am the Alpha and the Omega, the beginning and the end, the first and the last...Blessed are they that do his commandments, that they may have right to the tree of life, and may enter in through the gates into the city [of Heaven]...For without are dogs, and sorcerers, and whoremongers, and murderers, and idolaters, **and whosoever loveth and maketh a lie.***"* Rev 21:7, 11-15

Endnotes

1. *The Bulletin of Atomic Scientists*, Oct 1991, "A Hidden Chapter in History," by John W. Powell.

2. The squadron attached to Pingfan was the Heibo 8372 Field Aviation Unit.

3. Williams, Peter, and Wallace, David, *Unit 731; Japan's Secret Biological Warfare in World War II*, The Free Press, NY, 1989.

4. *Hearing before the subcommittee on oversight and investigations of the Committee of Veteran's Affairs, House of Representatives*, June 19th, 1982.

5. Ishii used the name in veneration of the famous Japanese admiral who fought the Russians in the Russo-Japanese War of 1905. When Ishii travelled incognito, he called himself Captain Hajime Togo.

6. Ishiwara was later replaced by Saburo Endo, former assistant to the chief Japanese Army representative at the 1925 Geneva talks.

7. Testimony given at Khabarovsk war trials.

8. Testifying at the Soviet War Crimes trials at Khabarovsk.

9. In the facility at Pingfan alone, over 3,000 people were sacrificed in the name of science.

10. The Montgomery Committee on Veteran's Administrations Programs in Montana--hearing before the House Subcommittee on Oversight and Investigations, June 19th, 1982.

11. By this time U.S. intelligence units already knew of Ishii in that he had received awards in Tokyo for his efforts in perfecting water

purification equipment and special water filters that were considered some of the best in the world for field use.

12. *Unit 731*, pgs 124-125.

13. The Naito Document did not mention using humans as guinea pigs. When Sanders asked Naito about this, Naito replied that such a thing never occurred. Sanders noted it at the bottom of the document in his own handwriting and let the matter drop.

14. *Unit 731*, pg 133.

15. SWNCC was the American State-War-Navy Coordinating Committee. Though General MacArthur's powers were sweeping in the Far East, his orders came from the SWNCC in Washington. The SWNCC delegated MacArthur to conduct war crimes trials on one hand, and secretly recommended protection for the Ishii unit on the other.

16. *Unit 731*

17. In the Potsdam Declaration, the Allies announced publicly that they intended to prosecute Japanese war criminals and that "...stern justice shall be meted out to all war criminals, including those who have visited cruelties upon our prisoners..."

18. Warren "Pappy" Whelchel died in September 1983, just months after testifying before the congressional committee. He never received government benefits for his war-connected medical problems.

19. The V-1 flying bomb was known as the "Doodle Bug," and the "Buzz Bomb." These names were derived from the strange buzzing sound made by the pulse-jet engine. The engine fired by means of a set of shutter doors on the intake that alternately opened to let ram air into the combustion chamber, then closed to seal the chamber for ignition. This process created a burping sound as the missile flew. The stubby-winged pilotless craft carried a 1,870 pound warhead filled with Trialen, an explosive with almost twice the power of the conventional RDX types. Unlike the later V-2s, which cost over $24,000 per missile, the V-1 cost the Germans only $250.00 per copy.

However the range and accuracy left a lot to be desired. Of the 8,000 V-1s that were launched at London, only half ever reached the city.

20. The V-2 was designated A-4 by the German rocket teams. The V-1 "buzzbomb" carried the German designation FZG-76.

21. The first organized project, codenamed OVERCAST, was a JCS approved project whose stated purpose was to bring German and Austrian scientists to the U.S. to aid in developing weapons that might shorten the war with Japan. It was originally limited to "those chosen, rare minds" whose skills could not be utilized in Europe. The caveat to Overcast was the fact that the scientists, once the war with Japan was concluded, would be returned to Germany.

22. The Henschel Hs-293 was the first guided missile of World War II. It's chief designer was Herbert Wagner, who became the first German scientist to be brought to the U.S. Wagner, along with his two assistants, arrived just prior to the inception of Project Paperclip.

23. Hermann Becker-Freysing was convicted at Nuremburg for force-feeding sea water to prisoners and sentenced to 20 years. Strughold's cohort, Siegfried Ruff, who had been charged with killing over 80 Dachau inmates in a low pressure chamber designed to simulate altitudes in excess of 60,000 feet, was acquitted. But of note is the fact that both of these men were on the Army Air Force payroll before their trials to write extensive reports of their experiments and findings.

24. During the same period, the British were secretly exploiting several groups of German scientists under their Operation Matchbox.

25. *Covert Action*, Fall 1990.

26. *Covert Action,* Winter 1986.

27. *Blowback; America's Recruitment of Nazis and Its Effect on the Cold War*, by Christopher Simpson, (Weidenfeld & Nicolson), 1988.

28. Like Warren Whelchel in his dealings with the Veterans Administration after his return from Mukden, Gamble found that there were no records of his service connected disability. Despite his own

documentation of depressive and suicidal moods and their link to LSD, his compensation claim was denied by the VA, who cited no sign of permanent disability. Gamble also found that the Feres Doctrine, a U.S. Supreme Court ruling, states that the government is immune from civil suits by servicemen in cases "where injury arises out of...activity incident to service."

29. Author and investigator Jon Rappaport writes regarding CIA mind control experiments on children: "Children were trained as sex agents, for example, with the job of blackmailing prominent Americans—primarily politicians, businessmen and educators. A great deal of filming was done for this purpose. Eventually, people from the inner core of the CIA program filmed each other, and some of the centers where children were used as sex agents got out of control and turned into CIA-operated sex rings...Some children were considered expendable and simply murdered." See Rappaport's book *U.S. Government Mind-Control Experiments on Children*.

30. Chaitkin, Anton; "Franklin Witnesses Implicate FBI and U.S. Elites in Torture and Murder of Children." Dec. 13, 1993.

31. Paul Bonacci has described in detail being taken to Washington for use as a sex slave for "clients" of Larry King. On several occasions, Bonacci and others were taken on White House "tours" for male prostitutes by lobbyist Craig Spence, an associate of King in the Iran/Contra money laundering affair. Spence was found dead in a Boston hotel in 1989, soon after the Franklin affair blew up in Omaha and the story was picked up by the *Washington Times* in a June 29th, 1989 article titled: "Homosexual Prostitution Inquiry Ensnares VIPs with Reagan, Bush".

32. Chaitkin

33. Many of the bodies that were discovered after the mass "suicide" at Jonestown actually died from gunshots to the skull or back. Though it was made to look as if everyone took cyanide poisoning from a vat filled with grape drink, it is now thought that most, if not all victims were forced to drink or get shot. Also, according to the Guyana medical examiner, many victims had unexplained hypodermic puncture wounds to their necks and backs. These facts were not reported in the

American press. It should be noted that the first U.S. personnel to arrive on the scene were Special Forces personnel who took control of the camp and did a "lock down" to the media. The next arrivals were from the 82nd Airborne Divison's Rapid Deployment Force, who "bagged and tagged" the remains and shipped them to Dover Air Force Base. No autopsy's were done and the bodies were disposed of before any medical evidence could be obtained by relatives. During the events in Guyana, squads of 82nd Airborne troopers engaged Jones' former "security guards" in firefights in the jungle. Most, however, escaped. Some later turned up as mercenaries in Angola.

34. Chris De Nicola, a patient of New Orleans therapist, Dr. Valerie Wolf (who testified before the President's Committee on Radiation on March 15, 1995), said that her (Nicola's) CIA controller was a "Dr. Greene," a name which had been reported by other mind-control victims. According to author Jon Rappaport in an article titled "CIA Experiments with Mind Control on Children" (*Perceptions*, Sep/Oct 1995), Nicola testified to the Committee that "[Dr. Green] used me in radiation experiments both for the purpose of determining the effects of radiation on various parts of my body and to terrorize me as an additional trauma in mind control experiments." Nicola was eight years old at the time. Nicola continued: "The rest of the experiments took place in Tucson, Arizona, out in the desert. I was taught how to pick locks, be secretive, use my photographic memory to remember things and a technique to withhold information by repeating numbers to myself...Dr. Greene moved on to wanting me to kill dolls that looked like real children. I stabbed a doll with a spear once after being severely tortured, but the next time I refused. He used many torture techniques but as I got older I resisted more and more...[later on] I snuck into his office and found files with reports and memos addressed to CIA and military personnel. Included in these files were project, subproject, subject and experiment names, with some code numbers for radiation and mind-contrl experiments which I have submitted in my written documentation. I was caught twice and Dr. Greene tortured me ruthlessly with electric shock, drugs, spinning me on a table, putting shots in my stomach, in my back, dislocating my joints and hypnotic techniques to make me feel crazy and suicidal." [Rappaport]

35. The nerve gas experiments conducted at Auschwitz were used to determine how fast the compounds would kill Allied soldiers. The helpless victims at first died very painfully. But as the gas was perfected, it was reported that they began to die instantly. According to British intelligence, the experiments were justified--by Ambros--on the grounds that "...the inmates of the concentration camps would have been killed anyway by the Nazis, [and] the experiments had a humanitarian aspect in that the lives of countless German workers were saved."

36. Though Ambros was finally tried at Nuremberg, and found guilty of slavery and mass murder, his sentence was a mere eight years. Chief Prosecutor Josiah DuBois exclaimed that the sentence was "light enough to please a chicken thief."

37. The number of service members exposed to radiation is derived from both those that were intentionally exposed during atom and hydrogen bomb tests and those who were prisoners of Japan near Hiroshima and Nagasaki and those who later occupied the same areas.

38. In testimony to the lack of understanding and training on behalf of the troops, Harry Hall, a B-25 crewman who participated in a flight over Hiroshima to take photographs shortly after the bombing, stated: "As we neared Hiroshima, the clouds thickened and smoke swirled in through the open waist windows...The putrid, sickening smoke wafting up from the destruction below became thicker inside the plane as we dropped down to 50 feet or so above the remaining rooftops. At the time we had no idea we might be exposing ourselves to deadly radiation. Captain Piazzo [the pilot] lowered the landing gear and flaps to drop our airspeed as low as he dared, giving us photographers the best conditions possible."

39. The author's grandfather, who worked at Oak Ridge during the war, died of leukemia in 1969. There are no other reported cases of cancer of any type in the family.

40. "Veterans as Government Guinea Pigs: Are They Receiving Care and Compensation?, pgs 8-9, *DAV* magazine, October 1991.

41. The CIA destroyed almost all of its files on the MK/ULTRA operation in 1973. It was only when some of the files leaked to the U.S. Senate that hearings were held that exposed the significance and scope of the human drug testing conducted by the CIA.

42. *DAV*, Oct 91, pg 10.

43. *Is Military Research Hazardous to Veterans' Health?* A Staff Report Prepared For The Committee On Veterans' Affairs, December 8, 1994.

44. "DAV Seeks Justice, Equity for 'Atomic Vets'," *DAV* Magazine, July/August 1996.

45. Because of the mishandling of numerous claims, there is now a Court of Veteran's Appeals.

46. According to *U.S. News and World Report.*

47. Petrochemical poisoning can be ruled out since none of the firefighters that entered Kuwait to put out the oil fires have complained of any sickness, and they were there for three months. Neither have the minefield demo disposal technicians who were there for almost a year.

48. Clark, Ramsey, *The Fire This Time*, pg 97.

49. Ibid.

50. Iraqi medical student Mariam Arif told microbiologist Larry Harris that the Iraqis used a "coctail" mix of biological agents during the Gulf War that would not take effect for months and even years. She claims that this is the real "Gulf War Disease" that surfaced later in U.S. troops after they returned home.

51. Experimental vaccine inoculation programs can be a surreptitious way of introducing harmful infectious agents into an unsuspecting population. Some investigators believe that the polio vaccine programs of the 1950s by the World Health Organization in Africa may have introduced the AIDS virus (HIV) into the black population. The African green monkey is theorized as the source of AIDS virus, and the polio

vaccine was manufactured using the kidney cells of the green monkey. Others think the World Health Organization's smallpox vaccine program is connected to the AIDS outbreak in Africa. One report suggested that a dormant HIV infection was awakened in the African population by the inoculation of millions of doses of smallpox vaccine by the WHO during the 1970s. This story was suppressed in the U.S. and never appeared in any major publication. It is interesting to note that the introduction of HIV into the homosexual population occurred the same year the hepatitis B vaccine experiment began in 1978 in New York City. And it was in New York City that AIDS broke out among homosexuals the following year.

52. In a letter to the newspaper, VA doctor Basil Clyman admitted that "many Gulf War personnel were exposed inadvertently or otherwise to a variety of potentially toxic agents, some of which were administered in hopes of protecting them from still worse toxicities, namely those posed by biological or chemical warfare."

53. Under pressure from activist groups, the physician was released from prison after serving eight months.

54. This follows suit for government concerns regarding both military personnel and civilians. Dozens of secret, planned bioattacks were perpetrated on American cities during the 1950s and 1960s, the most notorious being a six-day bioattack on San Francisco in which the military sprayed massive clouds of potentially harmful bacteria over the entire city.

55. *Tulsa World*, August 29, 1996.

56. There is one other area to be considered regarding GWS. Never in the history of the military have we had the huge number of microwave communications towers, known as "tower farms," located in such concentrated areas close to humans. Most of the soldiers who lived around these commo sites were reservists and lived in canvas tents. Most were rear echelon, such as the Indiana reservists, and were constantly bombarded with microwave radiation for six months, 24 hours a day. It is entirely possible that many of the soft tissue damage and cancers Desert Shield/Storm vets are experiencing actually were initiated by being microwaved.

57. Fall, Bernard; *Hell in a Very Small Place*, pg 481. Though most sources state that only 6,500 troops were captured at Dien Bien Phu, there was an additional 4,500 support troops and civilians.

58. *An Examination of U.S. Policy Toward POW/MIAs*, by the U.S. Senate Committee of Foreign Relations, pg 9-1. Further references to this document will refer to The Senate Report.

59. ibid, pg 9-3.

60. ibid, pg 9-4.

61. Memorandum written to the United States Political Advisor for Germany, by Mr. Parker W. Buhrman on January 28, 1946.

62. Message A-4152, AFHQ, dated 25 May 45.

63. Nikolai Tolstoy, *Secret Betrayel*, London, 1975.

64. *Soldiers of Misfortune*, pgs 81-82.

65. Message S-94080, SHAEF, excerpt.

66. Senate Report, pg 3-18.

67. ibid.

68. Memorandum to General Kenner, Eisenhower's Surgeon General at SHAEF Headquarters, concerning Displaced Persons, Allied ex-PW and German PW. Message dated 30 May 1945, No. S-383.6-2.

69. Senate Report, pg 3-19.

70. Letter dated 31 May 1945, numbered No. 1009.

71. "10,000 Ex-Captives Coming by Week-End; Army Sees All in Europe Accounted For," *The New York Times*, June 1, 1945.

72. *Unit 731*, pg 226.

73. *Soldiers of Misfortune*, pgs 104-105.

74. Department of State confidential memo 611.61241/12-1655.

75. This was a direct violation of the Yalta Agreement. According to the Agreement, which was signed by the United States, Great Britain, France, and the Soviet Union, *all* German war criminals would be accounted for and tried as such. Keeping Gehlen and his organization intact and hidden from the Russians was considered treachery by the Soviets.

76. Prouty, L. Fletcher, *JFK; The CIA, Vietnam And The Plot To Kill Kennedy*, Birch Lane Press, NY, 1992, pgs 17-20.

77. No one has ever satisfactorily explained why brand new military equipment, purchased with tax payers money, was destroyed wholesale simply because the war was over. However, by 1950 war stocks and supplies were suddenly found sadly lacking and massive new contracts for not only new equipment were let, but multi-million dollar contracts in "research and development" for aircraft, arms and weapons systems were handed out to the various manufacturers. It is also interesting to wonder how such items as howitzers, tanks and fighter aircraft could "flood the civilian martketplace" with such surplus "consumer goods."

78. The force consisted of 20,000 men. They managed to fight their way through innumerable Chinese roadblocks until they reached Hungnam. In the process, 13 Chinese Communist (Chicom) divisions were decimated to the point that they were never reconstituted.

79. "8,000 Missing, Van Fleet Says," *New York Times*, August 8, 1953.

80. Report, UN, CCRAK Specific Request No. 66-53.

81. These 21 are obviously the 21 defectors who signed statements that they did not want to return to the U.S.

82. Kelleher Report No. CPOW/3 D-1, dated 8 June 1955.

83. "Freed Flier Says Peiping Is Holding More U.S. Airmen, Canadian Now in Hong Kong Brings News of Americans Other Than 11 Jailed," *The New York Times*, December 6, 1954.

84. Foreign Service Dispatch "From: AMCONGEN, Hong Kong, To: The Department of State, Washington, No. 1716, dated March 23, 1954.

85. Memorandum, National Security Council, January 21, 1980.

86. The Senate Report, pg 4-13.

87. *Soldiers of Misfortune*, pgs 263-264.

88. Ibid.

89. Ibid.

90. A few months after Rastvorov's report, a U.S. senator asked Assistant Secretary of State Thurston Morton about the Korean POWs. Thurston's reply was: "To the Department's knowledge there are no United States soldiers in the category of prisoners-of-war being held in the Soviet Union." This was a play on words. The Soviets did not categorize foreign POWs as "prisoners of war," especially since in Korea, the USSR was not a belligerant. Instead, they were found "guilty" of "war crimes" and sentenced accordingly. Therefore, in the Soviet mind--and the Department of State--the USSR did not hold POWs.

91. Eisenhower-era information concerning POWs being held inside Communist countries has been hidden from the American people since 1955. Many records from this period are still classified *by order of President Bush and the Pentagon. (Soldiers of Misfortune*, pg 265).

92. Memo dated September 16, 1955.

93. It should be mentioned at this point that during Powers' interrogation by the KGB he was asked if he had ever been stationed at Atsugi, Japan. He was also asked if he knew that U-2s flew out of Atsugi. Though Lee Harvey Oswald's name was not mentioned,

Oswald had 90 days earlier "defected" to Russia and had brought with him, being an air traffic controller and radar operator, top secret knowledge concerning the U-2's operational ceiling. This altitude data was vital to the Soviets, who previously did not have information on what altitude to set their SAM proximity fuse. Powers was shot down just before the Eisenhower/Kruschev Summit Conference that was to have taken place in Switzerland to discuss nuclear disarmament and arms control. The conference, because of the shootdown, was canceled. It appears, when weighing the evidence and sequence of events, to have been effectively saboutaged. Eisenhower had given orders to cease overflights of the Soviet Union, the CIA ignored the orders. Allen Dulles was DCI (Director of Central Intelligence).

94. The CIA has never admitted that the SR-71 has flown *over* the Soviet Union, but Soviet MiG-25 pilot Viktor Belenko stated after his defection that he had often attempted to intercept SR-71s but could not catch them. He stated that even if he could reach their altitude, a head-on shot was impossible due to the aspect ratio, and after the Blackbird passed, he could not catch up with it. Neither could his missiles.

95. Operation 40 and Operation MONGOOSE were both anti-Castro operations conducted out of the Miami station, codenamed JM/WAVE, which was located on the south campus of the University of Miami. Chief of Station was Theodore Shackley, and his assistant was Thomas Clines. Both later moved to Laos to conduct drug smuggling operations, among other things.

96. *Inside The Shadow Government*, pgs 12-14.

97. The author landed in Vietnam on China Beach, east of Da Nang, with BLT 2/9 (2nd Battalion, 9th Marines) three months later on July 7, 1965.

98. The Peace Accords were signed on January 27th. Though the February 5th date is not publicly documented, it is nine days after the Accords were signed.

99. The intercepted message stated that "there had been some difficulties in transporting the fliers and the Pathet Lao commander asked if these problems had been resolved so movement could

continue." From an interview conducted during the filming of *We Can Keep You Forever.*

100. *Kiss The Boys Goodbye*, pgs 50-51, 160-161.

101. *Soldiers of Misfortune*, pg 247.

102. Senate Report, pg 5-4.

103. *Soldiers of Misfortune*, pg 249.

104. According to a still-classified CIA report that was filed in 1982, between 200-300 U.S. POWs were transported to the Soviet Union from Southeast Asia during the Vietnam War.

105. Senate Report, pgs 5-10, 5-11.

106. *We Can Keep You Forever*, BBC/Lionheart video production.

107. *Soldiers of Misfortune*, pg 290.

108. Ibid, pg 292.

109. Ibid, pg 293.

110. Senate Report, pgs 7-2 to 7-5.

111. The Pathet Lao did not even attend the conference. The French ceasefire documents were actually signed by a Vietminh general on behalf of the PL. (*The Ravens*, pg 122)

112. *Air America* pg 95.

113. *War In The Shadows*, Time-Life Books, "The Vietnam Experience" series, pgs 22-31.

114. *Crossfire*, pgs 270-271.

115. It was from this distribution network that a rogue member of the Corsican Mafia attempted to encroach on Trafficante's territory. The load of heroin this particular drug runner brought to New York culminated in the famous "French Connection" drug case.

116. Civil Case No. 86-1146-CIV-KING, U.S. District Court for the Southern District of Florida, pgs 14-15, as reproduced in *Inside The Shadow Government.*

117. According to *Inside the Shadow Government*, Shackley brought Rafael "Chi Chi" Quintero and Rafael Villaverde—both reputed members of the original ZR/RIFLE team—and Felix Rodriguez to Laos to form and train an assassination team for Vang Pao. This team's mission was to assassinate various civilian functionaries, Pathet Lao supporters, and rival opium warlords.

118. Ibid, pgs 12-14.

119. Kwitney, Jonathan, *The Crimes of Patriots: A True Tale of Dope, Dirty Money, and the CIA*, W.W. Norton & Company, 1987.

120. *Inside The Shadow Government*, pg 22.

121. From interview presented on "Guns, Drugs and the CIA," from *Frontline* with Judy Woodruff and Leslie Coburn.

122. The Tic-Toc drug scandal in Miami.

123. Hougan, Jim, "The Australian Heroin Connection," *Covert Action Information Bulletin,*" Summer 1987; No. 28.

124. *Inside The Shadow Government*, pg 18.

125. According to *Inside The Shadow Government*, the bagman for much of the illicit money was a former CIA clandestine operative named Jerry Barker Daniels. His senior contact was Daniel C. Arnold, who operated under Clines and Shackley. Daniels, known as "Hog" to his associates, was found dead in Bangkok in the late 1980s. His head had been stuffed into the oven in his apartment and the gas had been turned on. His death was ruled suicide and he was shipped back to the

U.S. and buried *in a sealed lead coffin* near his hometown in Montana. Other players in the drugs/money/guns network would later be found, having "committed suicide" in the same manner in other countries around the world. They obviously knew too much and had become threats to someone.

126. According to Jonathan Kwitny in his book *The Crimes of Patriots: A true Tale of Dope, Dirty Money, and the CIA*, pg 51, and *Inside The Shadow Government*, pg 22, the high ranking people involved included:

Admiral Earl P. Yates, (ret) former chief of staff for Asian and Pacific strategic planning. Served as bank's president or a period.

General LeRoy J. Manor, (ret) former chief of staff for the U.S. Pacific Command. Co-director of Nugan Hand's Manila office.

General Edwin F. Black, (ret) president of Nugan Hand's Hawaii office.

General Eric Cocke, Jr., (ret) headed Washington office of bank.

William Colby, former Director of Central Intelligence, performed legal services.

Walter MacDonald, former Deputy Director of the CIA for economic research served as consultant to Nugan Hand.

Dale Holmgren, former employee of Civil Air Transport, one of the CIA's propietary airlines, ran Taipei branch.

127. Colby had been involved in the operations in Southeast Asia since 1962. He not only was involved in the Laos operations, but became the CIA liaison to the super-secret Phoenix assassination program. Phoenix ended in 1973 when Colby was promoted to DCI.

128. *Kiss The Boys Goodbye*, pgs 197-200.

129. Barnes, Scott, and Libb, Melva, *Bohica*, pgs 127-138.

130. Gritz, Lt. Col. James "Bo", *U.S. Officials in the Heroin Trade*, audio tape, Center for Action, 1989.

131. Ben Jarrell, assistant White House press secretary.

132. Major Randy Morger, Defense Department spokesman.

133. Speech given by Bo Gritz to the Arizona Breakfast Club in Phoenix, Arizona, in 1989.

134. Within 60 days of this statement, the government reluctantly confessed that there *had* been POWs who had been left behind. At least 100 men, who were known to have been kept by the Vietnamese, were written off as soon as Nixon announced that all the Americans had been returned and the Vietnam war was finally over.

135. The Black Budget consisted of millions of dollars of funds that did not have to be accounted for to any outside agency due to their programmed use for "National Security." Anyone who did not have a need to know, did not know.

136. Joint Hearings on the Iran-Contra Investigations. Testimony of Richard V. Secord on May 5-8, 1987, pg 137.

137. Wilson's testimony, pgs 39-46.

138. *Inside The Shadow Government*, pg 30.

139. Ibid, pg 31.

140. *CIA—The Secret Files*, Part 4, "Moving Targets," video tape documentaries, BBC, 1992.

141. This time span occurred due to Iranian demands and the U.S. refusals concerning the forced return of the Shah. The Shah was never forced to return by the U.S. government and soon died of cancer before terrorist activities could be perpetrated to reinforce the Iranian demands.

142. Simon Bolivar (1783-1830) brought revolution to Venezuela, Equador, and Peru. This statement, written in his memoirs in 1823, was in reference to his belief that he was involved in a master plan to fulfill the destiny of South America. Interestingly, this was shortly after his return from Europe where he had joined the order of Freemasonry—whose inner circle, the Illuminati, pursued a course that they hoped would eventually lead to a one-world government, known as the New World Order, which they, and the Rothschilds, would head.

143. Among the "business assets" were the Mafia-run hotels and gambling casinos that had, under the Batista regime, turned a huge profit for the mob.

144. Prouty, L. Fletcher, *JFK, The CIA, Vietnam and the Plot to Assassinate John F. Kennedy*, Birch Lane Press, 1992, pg 172.

145. Ranelagh, John, *The Agency: The Rise and Decline of the CIA*, Simon & Schuster, NY, 1987, pgs 337, 356.

146. The lawsuits, filed on behalf of Tony Avirgan and Martha Honey against John Hull and Felipe Vidal (and several *et al* others), were in reference to CIA activities and the activities of other elements within the covert intelligence community and the "shadow government" in regards to the plaintiffs being wounded by a bomb planted at a press conference by guerrilla elements allegedly under the control of the defendants. The brief, filed in the United States District Court, Southern District of Florida, (civil cases No. 86-1146-CIV-KING, and No. 87-1545-CIV-KING), is quite verbose in its historical lead-ins to the case, which occured during the Sandinista/Contra affair in Nicaragua.

147. E. Howard Hunt served on an OSS team in Asia during World War II with Paul Helliwell, Lucien Conein (Corsican Mafia contact), and Mitchell WerBell (inventor of the Sionics "sound suppressor" silencer). As with the later Laotian situation, opium was used to finance their operations.

148. This attack was never carried out. Before the plan could be put into effect the Brigade at the "Bayo de Cochinos" found itself under heavy air, artillery and land attack. The *ersatz* Cuban troops were

ordered to withdraw as the situation at the Bay of Pigs deteriorated beyond salvation.

149. Sasser, Charles W., "Invasion Abandoned", *Modern Warfare* magazine, November 1989.

150. Some researchers believe this operation was named after Zapata Offshore Oil company of Houston. Chairman of the Board of Zapata at the time was George Bush. It is interesting to note that two of the ships procurred to ferry the invasion force to Cuba were renamed "Houston" and "Barbara" for the operation.

151. *CIA, The Secret Files*, BBC documentary, 1992.

152. Wyden, Peter, *Bay of Pigs*, Simon & Schuster, 1979.

153. Ibid.

154. Ibid.

155. *CIA/KGB; Intelligence and Counter-Intelligence Operations*, pg 83.

156. QJ/WIN and WI/ROGUE have been implicated in the Kennedy assassination by several investigators. QJ/WIN is believed to be French assassin Christian David, and WI/ROGUE is thought to be former a French army captain named Jean Soutre who turned political assassin for the OAS.

157. Middle names are often used in reference in Latin countries. Often they are conjunctions of such names as: Don Pedro Guiterez de Colon. By dropping the "de"—Spanish for "of" which denotes where his family is from (Colon)—we have a subject whose last name is actually Guiterez and is referred to accordingly.

158. *KGB/CIA* pg 135.

159. Many of the Chilean army instructors were, as those of other Latin American countries, German Nazis that had been spirited out of

Europe after the war in Dulles's "Rat Lines" and the SS's Omega network.

160. *KGB/CIA*, pg 172.

161. Singlaub was also chairman of the World Anti-Communist League (WACL), an association that includes Latin American Dictators, death squad leaders, neo-fascists, and former German Nazis that had escaped prosecution in Germany. Singlaub helped Oliver North raise $1 million per month between 1984 and 1985 after Congress cut off aid to the Contras. Singlaub's specialties included unconventional warfare, psychological warfare, economic sabotage, disinformation, terrorism and assassination.

162. Further hostility toward the CIA operation appeared when a CIA manual for subversion and assassination was leaked to the press by Edgar Chamorro, a Contra leader. Chamorro, who was opposed to the more extreme ex-National Guard officers of the FDN, revealed the existence of an 89-page booklet titled *Psychological Operations in Guerrilla Warfare*. The techniques described in the book included assassination, kidnapping, blackmail and murder. The Reagan administration denied that the manual was provided by the CIA, however it was later learned that top White House planners were involved in the production of the book—including, according to *Newsweek*, UN delegate Jeanne Kirkpatrick. The manual recommended "hiring professional criminals" and neutralizing carefully selected targets such as court judges and security officials. After the exposure, Chamorro was conveniently blackballed by the Agency.

163. *The Iran Contra Connection*, pgs 68-69.

164. Entire books have been written about the Illuminati, or "Illuminated Ones." The secret society is basically a small group of international bankers and financiers, many of which are reputed to be Masons, who control the world banking organizations. The history of the Illuminati can be traced back to the Crusades when the Knights Templars returned to France and Italy from the Middle East with fortunes in plundered treasure. To protect their booty, they employed the Freemasons of Europe to build large, well-fortified castles. The treasures were stored, or "banked," in vaults in the fortresses, guarded

by "Banquers." The Knights Templars also developed the use of the "Cheque" to obtain funds from other members of the order while traveling. In 1307, Philip IV of France grew fearful of the Templars and sought to destroy them (hoping also to confiscate their treasures). He had them investigated by the Vatican's inquisitors, who found them guilty of heresy, witchcraft and practicing Satanism. On Friday, the 13th of October, 1307, Philip had all of the Knights Templars in France—save thirteen—arrested. Those taken into custody, led by Jacques de DeMolay, were tied to stakes in Paris and burned as heretics. The remaining thirteen fled into the underground and disappeared into the order of Freemasonry where, as members, they were protected. These became the original "Illuminati." In 1776, a German lawyer named Adam Weishaupt, who was intimate with the House of Rothschild, gave the Illuminati re-birth. It has since become a very powerful and secret international organization of powerbrokers who are intent on the creation of a one world government known as "The New World Order." Because of this, there is a certain degree of commonality with what has been said to be the American counterpart—or branch of--the Illuminati, the Council on Foreign Relations.

165. Penny Lernoux, *In Banks We Trust*, pg 179, Anchor/Doubleday, Garden City, N.Y., 1984.

166. Involved in the air operations for cocaine smuggling was Jorge Ochoa, co-leader of Colombia's giant drug cartel. When Ochoa was indicted for drug smuggling, the chief witness against him, Bobby Seal, was murdered by Colombian hit men who were supplied with assassination weapons by Miami-based Contras who were involved with heroin-for-guns dealings with anti-Castro exiles. Prior to his murder, Seal helped federal drug agents indict the three major kingpins in the Columbian cocaine cartel: Pablo Escobar, Jorge Ochoa, and Carlos Lehder.

167. *The Iran Contra Connection*, pg 152.

168. Ibid, pg 152-153.

169. *San Francisco Examiner*, Dec. 9, 1986.

170. These events would result in the takeover of the U.S. Embassy in Teheran which was then held for 444 days.

171. Of the seven CIA people killed in the Beirut embassy bombing, one was Station Chief Robert Ames.

172. In March of 1982, the *New York Times* cited documents indicating that Israel had supplied half or more of all arms reaching Teheran in the previous 18 months--sales amounting to $100 million. Israeli sources revealed later that they had sold over $100 million in arms, jet engines, spare parts for American M-48 tanks, and other equipment in 1983. By 1984, Israel shipped, by way of a broker in Sweden, hundreds of tons of TNT and other explosives to Iran by way of Argentina. In 1985, Israel sold Iran 45,000 Uzi submachineguns, howitzers, missiles and missile launchers, and other spare military parts. Over the four years of "Irangate" the deals were covered by end-user certificates provided by Ferdinand Marcos in the Philippines—showing that the receiver for all of the above equipment was the Philippine government, and not Iran. (*The Iran-Contra Connection*, pgs 174-175)

173. Shooting down unarmed aircraft was not something unusual to the Soviets. National Security Council member Kenneth deGraffenreid stated in 1983: "KAL 007 was not an aberration; it was part of a murderous pattern. Not only have the Soviets shot down many innocent foreign planes; we know they have also shot down many of their own aircraft, including civilian airliners." Both the American intelligence community and the military knew exactly what would happen to any luckless airplane that strayed within the Soviet boundaries.

174. Some sources say that the interceptors were the later version Su-21 "Flagon-G," or "Flagon-F." However most accounts state that the aircraft flown by Lt. Col Gennadiy Nikolayevich Osipovich was, in fact, the older Su-15 version which is almost identical in appearance.

175. The Sukhoi Su-15 is fitted with two afterburning Rumansky R-11F2-300 turbojet engines rated at 13,668 pounds of thrust with afterburners lit. This mode of operation consumes a considerable amount of fuel. Maximum level speed of the aircraft is Mach 2.3-2.5 (2 1/2 times the speed of sound). Its combat radius—the distance it can

fly to, engage a target, and fly back to base—is only 450 miles. However, from Sakhalin island, the home islands of Japan, depending on where one starts on Sakhalin, are only 100 miles away. It is reasonable to assume that only the most trustworthy pilots are allowed to man international boundary interceptors.

176. It has been theorized that the Russians were overly zealous in their activities on this night due to the fact that they were going to violate an arms agreement and test-fire an SS-25 ICBM, hence the reason for the RC-135's presence. The Russians later stated that they originally mistook the Korean 747 for an RC-135, then even after shooting it down and later determining it to be a civilian 747, still considered it to be on a spy mission for the U.S.

177. *Aim Report*, (Accuracy in Media), May-B 1991.

178. A later *Isvestiya* report put Osipovich to the right rear of the 747 at approximately five kilometers. According to the Soviet newspaper series on the incident, Osipovich reported at 1809:00, about 17 minutes prior to the missile launch, that "target is 80 [degrees] to my left," then three minutes before launch, "located 70 to the left."

179. Even if KAL 007 had seen the Su-15s, they would not have known what to do. There was no way for the Soviet fighters to communicate with the 747 on the radio because Russian military aircraft are not on the same frequency bands as either civilian or Western military aircraft.

180. Osipovich finally admitted in the *Isvestiya* series that he did not fire cannon rounds, though he did not mention why he said so in the first place when it was easily determined his fighter-intercepter could not carry both rockets and cannons.

181. The Ilyushin IL-76 is a transport. The TU-16 is a bomber. Neither is as large as a 747.

182. Moneron Island (Ostrov Moneron) is located approximately 50 statute miles west of the southern tip of Sakhalin Island (Ostrov Sakhalin), and approximately 100 statute miles north of the northern tip of Hokkaido in the Sea of Japan.

183. Later reports by Soviet press indicated that divers recovered pieces of the airplane two weeks after the shootdown, however no records were kept and no pictures taken to prove it. Also, American, Japanese and Korean search vessels were not allowed into the impact area by the Russians, even though it was in international waters.

184. *The Review Of The News*, October, 1983.

185. Lee, Robert W., "KAL 007: The Questions Remain Unanswered," *The New American*, Sept 10, 1991.

186. From the documentary film, *The Maltese Doublecross*.

187. Ibid.

188. Ibid.

189. One story is that an unnamed searcher found this tiny particle of plastic in a wooded area, another in a field, and another that it was found in an item of clothing.

190. The tags supposedly made it possible for an unaccompanied bag to be put aboard an Air Malta flight, then travel to Europe, change planes at Frankfort, then rest quietly in the baggage hold to London, then take off again to blow up over Lockerbie. An item of interest is that Granada TV reported this scenario, then was sued by Air Malta because such a scenario could not occur in the rigid security measures of Air Malta. Air Malta won the judgement.

191. Ibid.

192. Operation *Herbslaub*—Autumn Leaves—selected sixteen targets in six cities across Germany for surveillance squads. It was one of the most extensive operations ever mounted in West Germany.

193. A BKA observation log noted: "Marwan Abdel Razzak Khreesat has been staying with Dalkomoni and Abassi since October 13. It is also officially known about him that he is a member of the PFLP-GC and an explosives expert. It's further known that Dalkomoni, who is directly subordinate to the Palestinian group leader, Ahmed Jibril,

recruits new members for the organization and prepares operations against Israel and/or American targets."

194. "Abu Nidal" is a cover name for Sabry El Bana.

195. The problem with the story of a bomb in a suitcase in Malta being sent all the way to London is two-fold. First, Denis Phipps, former head of security, British Airways, stated "There was no evidence of unaccompanied baggage on that flight [Air Malta flight 100]. [It] had to be checked in by a passenger who actually traveled on that flight." Second, an FBI TELEX sent to Washington on October 23, 1989, stated: "...there is no concrete indication that any piece of luggage was unloaded from Air Malta 100, sent through the luggage routing, was at Frankfort airport then loaded on board Pan Am 103."

196. From an interview conducted in the British documentary, *The Maltese Double Cross*.

197. Ibid.

198. Ibid.

199. An offshoot of the Iran/Contra affair concerned one Monzer Al-Kassar, a Syrian drugs and arms smuggler. Al-Kassar reportedly received $1.2 million from a Swiss company allegedly controlled by Albert A. Hakim and retired Air Force Major General Richard V. Secord. A deal was reportedly struck with Al-Kassar in which he could continue to smuggle heroin into the United States if he would use his influence to assist in the release of the American hostages. It should be noted that Al-Kassar used his drug and arms smuggling underground to smuggle arms to the Contras, the secret army supported by "The Enterprise" and Lt. Col. Oliver North.

200. Khalid Jafaar appears to have been an expendable asset to the PFLP-GC. His job was to "courier" the suitcase full of drugs as business as usual—a job he may or may not have known about, and to also to serve as the conduit to get the bomb concealed inside the Toshiba radio aboard the airplane—a job he obviously did *not* know about.

447

201. *The Maltese Double Cross.*

202. Ibid.

203. Ibid.

204. Filotas, Les., *Improbable Cause*, Seal, Canada, 1991.

205. Ibid

206. Arrow Air was not the only enterprise that took advantage of government contracts in the Middle East. One entrepreneur was none other than Edwin Wilson, former member of Navy intelligence detailed to Teheran during the reign of the Shah, who later hooked up with Theodore Shackley and Thomas Clines, former CIA chief of station and assistant chief of station for Laos. Wilson advanced $500,000 to Clines to help set up Egyptian-American Transport Services, Inc. (EATSCO), who used insider contacts to obtain exclusive rights to ship military equipment to Egypt (and other places). Wilson eventually was found guilty of illegally supplying M-16s and other arms to Libya and was sentenced to fifty-two years in the Federal penitentiary system. Wilson's partner in EATSCO was Albert Hakim, whose name surfaced during the Congressional hearings into Iran/Contra.

207. An article in the August, 1996 issue of the British *Defence & Foreign Affairs Strategic Policy* explained that a "newly structured Hizbollah group under the aegis of senior Iranian leaders held a summit conference in Teheran in June 1996. Hizbollah delegates from over thirty nations attended including the United States, Canada, Italy, France, Germany and Britain." A "joint working committee" of three top individuals (Imad Mughaniyah of the Lebanese Hizbollah Special Operations Command, Usama bin Ladin (a Saudi fundamentalist leader), and Ahmad Salah Salim (an Egyptian Jihad representative) was formed and began working under the chairman, Mehadi Chamran. The principle operations given the "green light" by this council were three terrorist acts that were already beyond planning stages:
1. The bombing of the U.S. barracks in Dharan, Saudi Arabia, assigned to Usama bin Ladin;
2. The fatal stabbing of a U.S. female diplomat, assigned to Ahman Salah Salim, and;

3. The downing of TWA flight 800, assigned to Imad Mughaniyah.

208. *The Guardian*, August 21, 1996, pgs 2-3.

209. According to *Aerospace Daily* of August 20th, 1996, The TWA flight was vectored to within 15 miles of the northwest end of the "hot zone" exercise box. If this is so, the AP diagram assigning Long/Lat coordinates 45 miles further northwest as the crash site is incorrect or disinformation. The article said that a Coast Guard spokesman stated that the patrol boat *Adak* was in the immediate area at the time, but referred the magazine to Coast Guard HQ for more information on what it was doing there. Spokesmen at CG HQ failed to return repeated phone calls to the reporter. TWA 800 was on "Betty Track," one of the two tracks used by commercial flights when areas are set aside for military use off Long Island. A Navy spokesman admitted that Warning Area W-105 was activated at the time of the incident, but refused to discuss what the purpose was. The article stated that the flight reached 13,700 feet before something "went wrong." This is a discrepancy in that the original FAA report from radar put the airplane at 10,300 feet. Some press reports of that night reported the 747 to be at 8,000 feet at the time of the explosion.

210. Of note regarding the Naval vessel aspect of this theory is an unconfirmed story that was reported to William Jasper, the editor of the *New American* magazine. In this story a sailor came home on leave to Norman, Oklahoma, and said that he was very upset because his ship had fired a missile which accidently knocked down the TWA flight and the whole thing was a coverup.

211. One SS agent told the author when flying air cover over a Clinton motorcade that if they flew too close to the motorcade they would be shot down by an agent with a Stinger. He said they always carry them in the back of their escort vehicles along with other weapons.

212. Other weapons systems were mentioned by theorists:
   1. One was the HAARP project in Gakona, Alaska, which is supposed to be a global weapons system capable of bringing down an aircraft as large as a 747 anywhere in the world by using high altitude auroral directed energy to focus on the target. This project is allegedly

449

an offshoot of Nicolai Tesla's electromagnetic weapons designs that disappeared around the turn of the century after Tesla died. It is also supposed to be related to what retired Air Force lieutenant colonel Tom Bearden describes as "Scaler Wave" weapons which use similar technology.

2. Another system is a directed-energy microwave beam weapon that has been accused of knocking down two aircraft in the vicinity of Woodbridge, Virginia (built by Harry Diamond Laboratories on a black budget government contract). One of the aircraft that allegedly flew into the invisible microwave beam and was "shredded" was a Marine VH-60 Blackhawk assigned to HMX-1 at Andrews AFB. This was a presidential transport aircraft and all four crew members were killed prior to impact. All showed massive internal burns, rupturing of the skin, and skin burns. The aircraft did not burn and the fuel did not ignite. The whole thing was covered up by the Marine investigators, blaming the cause of the crash on a defective part in the drive train. They also reported that the bodies were blistered because of contact with spilled fuel at the accident site. However, dead bodies do not blister, and the crew was dead before the helicopter hit the ground as there was no blood at the crash scene! Harry Diamond Labs moved their project to Oregon shortly thereafter. The other aircraft knocked down as a Cessna carrying four passengers, one supposedly a KGB defector or other Russian embassy official (two versions of story). Little is know of this second incident.

3. Another weapons system is a flying laser energy beam that has been developed to destroy missiles. In a test conducted in the 1980s, such a weapon succeeded in destroying five Sidewinder missiles and one cruise missile, according to Colonel Lanny Larfson, director of lasers and imaging at the Air Force's Phillips Laboratory at Kirtland Air Force Base in Albuquerque, which is pioneering work on the systems. Other players in the development of laser and directed energy beam "Star Wars" weapons systems are: TRW, Hughes Aircraft, Lockheed Martin, and Boeing. The platform for such a "flying laser beam" would be a large aircraft, such as a 747, according to Air Force sources involved in the testing of COIL, or Chemical Oxygen Iodine laser system.

213. On September 23, 1996, an article appeared in *USA Today* titled "TWA Crash May Forever Be A Mystery, Reno Says." In the article, Attorney General Janet Reno laid the ground work for an eventual

finding that there would be no finding. Because of the apparent official Clinton Administration denial of the missile evidence, a finding that the airplane was shot down by a SAM apparently would not be released under any circumstances. This appeared to fall in line with what some FBI agents say is an ever-developing unwritten Justice Department directive titled "never let the facts stand in the way of a politically correct investigation."

214. *New York Terror Trial Witness Tells What a Liar He Was*, San Francisco *Chronicle*, March 8, 1995.

215. The Administration initially refused to offer a reward in the case of the World Trade Center bombing, arguing that it was *an act of domestic terrorism* and therefore not eligible for the International Terrorist Information Reward program.

216. Abraham Ahmad, a Jordanian, had actually been spotted acting very nervously at the American Airlines gate in Oklahoma City one hour after the bombing. As he flew to Chicago to make a connecting flight for Rome, American Airlines personnel notified the FBI that he was acting suspicious. He was detained briefly in Chicago, then released. It was British security at Heathrow that not only refused him entry into the U.K., but put him on a plane back to the U.S. as his luggage was intercepted by the Italian police in Rome. His luggage proved to contain wire, tools, and photographs of surface-to-air missiles. When he returned to the U.S. he was not arrested, and only briefly detained. Almost immediately, Clinton and Janet Reno announced there was no middle-eastern connection. Period.

217. Affidavit of Michael J. Rinonosciuto, United States Bankruptcy Court for the District of Columbia, in Re: INSLAW, INC., Plaintiff v. UNITED STATES OF AMERICA and the UNITED STATES DEPARTMENT OF JUSTICE, Defendents. Case # 85-00070 (Chapter 11), Adversary Proceeding No. 86-0069.

218. Ben-Menashe, Ari, *Profits of War*.

219. This data has not been confirmed. It is being shown here because it was part of the original report submitted to the FBI as areas to be

investigated. To the author's knowledge, the FBI never followed up on the information or accomplished the investigation.

220. Israeli military intelligence sources report the figure as 30,000 former Iraqi soldiers, many from the Republican Guards Division.

221. A report by a private investigator hired by KFOR TV reveals that Alhussaini Hussain was in the Hammurabi Division of the Republican Guard, captured by the 24th Infantry Division during a fight on Highway 8, west of Basra. He came to the U.S. in November of 1991, and attempted to settle in Boston. When he discovered he was under surveillance, he moved to Oklahoma City. It should be noted that World Trade Center bomber Ramzi Yousef was also in the Hammurabi Division of the Republican Guard Division during the Gulf War, and was in a Islamic Jihad-type cell in New York City.

222. Intelligence reports indicate that when Terry Reed of Iran/Contra fame moved to Guadalajara, Mexico, he discovered that his neighbor was one James Ellison--the same James Ellison that later surfaced in the Covenant, Sword and Arm of the Lord in Arkansas, then later Elohim City (not far from Mena).

223. Interview with Michelle Tor, conducted 7/23/96 in Dallas, Texas, by David Hoffman and Rep. Charles Key (Okla).

224. In comparison, the crater in front of the Murrah Building was 20 feet deep and 30 feet wide, while the crater in front of the Khobar Towers was 35 feet deep and 85 feet wide.

225. In this scenario, the President declares a national emergency, invokes Executive Order 11490, declares martial law, suspends the Constitution, converts all state governments to be subservient to the "regional" system, orders FEMA to take over local government functions, then calls for assistance from the U.N., which in turn brings in foreign troops to help police this country. These "foreign assets" are then used to disarm the American people, move elements of the population to "relocation centers" (closed down military bases), quarantine sections of the population, restrict or prohibit travel and communications, then initiate a national identification system that would require every man, woman and child to receive a national ID card to

get health care, make purchases, etc. The United States would then become a client state of the World Government, i.e. the "New World Order." This scenario also provides for the various biological weapons to take their toll before being brought under control to help reduce the world's population, which would meet the objectives of the various global foundations who have stated that the world population must be reduced by 80% by the year 2000.

Bibliography

Books

Asprey, Robert B. *War in the Shadows*, New York: Doubleday, 1975.

Bamford, James, *The Puzzle Palace; A Report on America's Most Secret Agency*, New York: Penguin Books, 1985.

Bank, Colonel Aaron, USA (Ret), *From OSS to Green Berets*, San Francisco: Presidio Press, 1986.

Barnes, Scott, with Libb, Melva, *Bohica*, Canton, OH,: Bohica Corp., 1987.

Barron, John, *KGB Today; The Hidden Hand*, New York: Reader's Digest Press, 1983.

Beaty, Johathan, and Gwynne, S.C., *The Outlaw Bank: A Wild Ride Into the Secret Heart of BCCI*, New York, Random House, 1993.

Ben-Menashe, Ari, *Profits of War: Inside the Secret U.S.-Israeli Arms Network*, Sheriden Square Press, 1992.

Barron, John, *KGB; The Secret Work of Soviet Agents*, New York: Bantam, 1974.

Bower, Tom, *The Paperclip Conspiracy; The Hunt for the Nazi Scientists*, Boston: Little, Brown and Company, 1987.

Brown, Anthony Cave, *Bodyguard of Lies*, New York: Harper & Row, 1975.

Chasey, William C., *Foreign Agent 4221: The Lockerbie Cover-Up*, San Diego, ProMotion, 1995.

Clark, Ramsey, *The Fire This Time: U.S. War Crimes in the Gulf*, New York, Thunder's Mouth Press, 1992.

Corn, David, *The Blond Ghost: Ted Shackley and the CIA's Crusades*, New York, Simon & Schuster, 1994.

Dobson, Christopher, and Payne, Ronald, *The Terrorists; Their Weapons, Leaders and Tactics*, New York: Facts On File, 1979.

Dunnigan, James F. and Nofi, Albert A., *Dirty Little Secrets; Military Information You're Not Supposed to Know*, New York: William Morrow, 1990.

Fall, Bernard B., *Hell In A Very Small Place; The Siege of Dien Bien Phu*, New York: J.B. Lippincott, 1967.

Goddard, Donald, and Coleman, Lester K., *Trail of the Octopus: From Beirut to Lockerbie—Inside the DEA*, London: Bloomsbury, 1993.

Gritz, Col. James "Bo", *Called to Serve*, Sandy Valley, NV,: Lazarus Publishing, 1991.

Honegger, Barbary, *October Surprise*, New York, Tudor, 1989.

Hunt, Linda, *Secret Agenda; The United States Government, Nazi Scientists, and Project Paperclip, 1945 to 1990*, New York: St. Martin's Press, 1991.

Johnson, Loch K., *America's Secret Power; The CIA in a Democratic Society*, New York: Oxford University Press, 1989.

Marchetti, Victor, and Marks, John D., *The CIA and the Cult of Intelligence*, New York: Dell, 1980.

Marks, John, *The Search for the Manchurian Candidate*, New York: W.W. Norton & Co., 1979.

Marshall, Jonathan, and Scott, Peter Dale and Hunter, Jane, *The Iran-Contra Connection; Secret Teams and Covert Operations in the Reagan Era*, Boston: South End Press, 1987.

Morin, Relman, *Dwight D. Eisenhower; A Gauge of Greatness*, New York: Simon & Schuster, 1969.

North, Mark, *Act of Treason*, New York: Carroll & Graf, 1991.

Ostrovsky, Victor, and Hoy, Claire, *By Way of Deception*, New York: St. Martin's Press. 1990.

Ostrovsky, Victor, *The Other Side of Deception*, Harper Collins, 1995.

O'Toole, G.J.A., *Honorable Treachery; A History of U.S. Intelligence, Espionage, and Covert Action from the American Revolution to the CIA*, New York: Atlantic Monthly Press, 1991.

Potts, Mark; Kochan, Nicholas, and Whittington, Robert, *Dirty Money: BCCI—The Inside Story of the World's Sleaziest Bank*, Washington: National Press Books, 1992.

Prados, John, *Keepers of The Keys: A History of the National Security Council from Truman to Bush*, New York: William & Morrow Co., 1991

Prouty, L. Fletcher, *JFK: The CIA, Vietnam, and the plot to assassinate John F. Kennedy*, New York: Birch Lane Press, 1992.

Robbins, Christopher, *Air America*, New York: Avon, 1990.

Robbins, Christopher, *The Ravens*, New York: Pocket Books, 1989.

Sanders, Jim, and Sauter, Mark, and Kirkwood, R. Cort, *Soldiers of Misfortune*, Washington, D.C.,: National Press Books, 1992.

Simpson, Charles M. III, *Inside the Green Berets; The First Thirty Years*, San Francisco: Presidio Press, 1983.

Stevenson, Monika Jenson-, and Stevenson, William, *Kiss The Boys Goodbye; How the United States Betrayed Its Own POWs in Vietnam*, New York: Plume, 1991.

Stich, Rodney, *Defrauding America: Dirty Secrets of the CIA and Other Government Operations*, Alamo, CA: Diablo Western Press, 1994.

Vankin, Jonathan, *Conspiracies, Cover-ups, and Crimes; Political Manipulation and Mind Control in America*, New York: Paragon House, 1992.

Volkman, Ernest, and Baggett, Blaine, *Secret Intelligence*, New York: Doubleday, 1989.

Welsh, Douglas, *The History of the Vietnam War*, New York: Galahad Books, 1981.

Williams, Peter, and Wallace, David, *Unit 731; Japan's Secret Biological Warfare in World War II*, New York: The Free Press, 1989.

Woodward, Bob, *Veil; The Secret Wars of the CIA, 1981-1987*, New York: Pocket Books, 1988.

Miss. Publications

The Vietnam War, New York: Crown Publishers, 1983.

An Examination of U.S. Policy Toward POW/MIAs, U.S. Senate Committee on Foreign Relations, May 1991 report.

Hearing Before The Subcommittee On Oversight and Investigation of the Committee On Veterans' Affairs, House of Representatives, Washington D.C., 1982.

Inside the Shadow Government, Delcaration of Plaintiffs' Counsel filed by the Christic Institute, U.S. District Court, Miami FL., March 31, 1988.

The Vietnam Experince: War in the Shadows, Boston: Boston Publishing Co., 1988.

ORDER FORM

To: Consolidated Press International
       3171-A South 129th East Ave., Ste 338
       Tulsa, OK 74134

Please ship to me at the address shown below the following books. Enclosed is my check or money order for $_____ which includes $2.50 (each) for shipping and handling. (Oklahoma residents add .65 @ book for *Kill Zone* or $1.09 @ book for *The Medusa File* for state sales tax).

Kill Zone: A Sniper Looks at Dealey Plaza ($11.95) $ _____

The Medusa File ($19.95)   _____

    Shipping and Handling @ $2.50 ea.   _____

    Oklahoma Sales Tax (OK only)   _____

    TOTAL AMOUNT ENCLOSED   _____

Ship to:

Name _____

Address_____

City _____

State _____ Zip _____

Telephone: (   ) _____